AF333309

Many Believed Because of her Testimony

Many Believed Because of her Testimony

Essays Celebrating the Scholarship and
Service of Dorothy Lee

Edited by
ROBERT A. DERRENBACKER JR.,
CHRISTOPHER A. PORTER,
and MURIEL PORTER

Foreword by Philip Freier

WIPF & STOCK · Eugene, Oregon

MANY BELIEVED BECAUSE OF HER TESTIMONY
Essays Celebrating the Scholarship and Service of Dorothy Lee

Wipf & Stock
An Imprint of Wipf and Stock Publishers
199 W. 8th Ave., Suite 3
Eugene, OR 97401

www.wipfandstock.com

PAPERBACK ISBN: 978-1-6667-3874-2
HARDCOVER ISBN: 978-1-6667-9980-4
EBOOK ISBN: 978-1-6667-9981-1

08/18/23

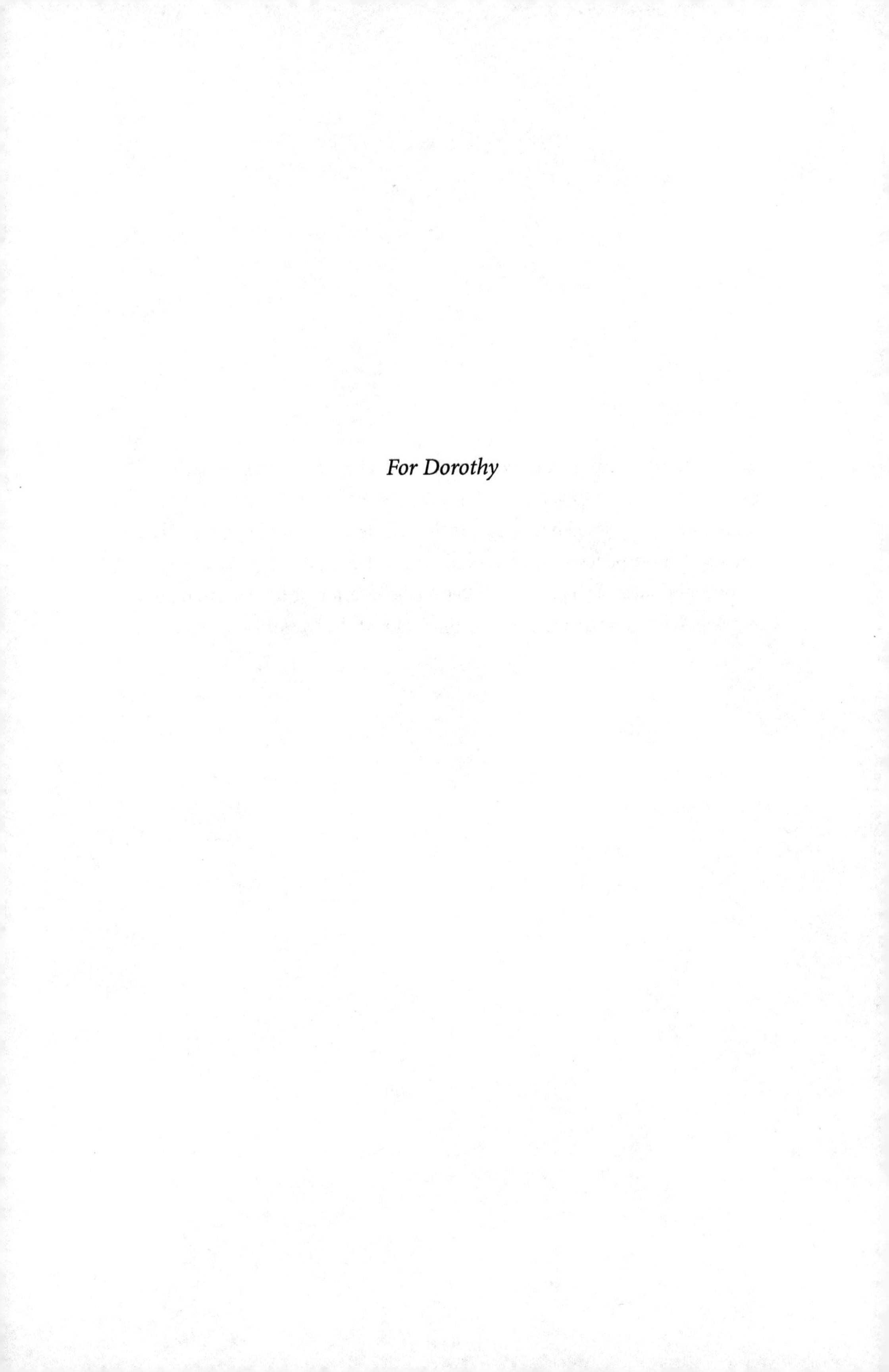

For Dorothy

Many Samaritans from that city believed in him because of the woman's testimony, "He told me everything I have ever done." So when the Samaritans came to him, they asked him to stay with them; and he stayed there two days. And many more believed because of his word. They said to the woman, "It is no longer because of what you said that we believe, for we have heard for ourselves, and we know that this is truly the Savior of the world." (John 4:39–42)

Contents

Women, and Ecclesiology

Interdisciplinary Approaches

Illustrations and Tables

Abbreviations

AAA&S	*American Academy of the Arts & Sciences*
AB	Anchor Bible
ABC	Australian Broadcasting Commission
ABR	*Australian Biblical Review*
AJP	*The American Journal of Philology*
AM&B	*Applied Microbiology and Biotechnology*
AP	Ancient Philosophies
ArgPhil	Arguments of the Philosophers
ASMS	American Society of Missiology Series
ATDC	Inter-Anglican Theological and Doctrinal Commission
BBC	Blackwell Bible Commentaries
B&CT	The Bible & Critical Theory
BCP	Book of Common Prayer
BETL	Bibliotheca Ephemeridum Theologicarum Lovaniensium
BINS	Biblical Interpretation Series
BIS	Biblical Interpretation Series
BJSP	*British Journal of Social Psychology*
BNT	Black's New Testament Commentaries
BTB	*Biblical Theology Bulletin*
BWV	Bach-Werke-Verzeichnis (Bach Works Catalogue)
BZNW	Beihefte zur Zeitschrift für die neutestamentliche Wissenschaft
CE	*Cronache Ercolanesi*

CIL	*Corpus Inscriptionum Latinarum*
CNT2	Commentaire du Nouveau Testament, deuzième série
C&L	*Christianity and Literature*
CRFSFS	*Comprehensive Reviews in Food and Science Safety*
CSR	*Christian Scholar's Review*
CTHPT	Cambridge Texts in the History of Political Thought
EB	Earth Bible
EBC	Earth Bible Commentary
ECL	Early Christianity & Its Literature
EBot	*Economic Botany*
EJPCA	*European Journal of Post-Classical Archaeologies*
EJSP	*European Journal of Social Psychology*
EPPET	Explorations in Practical, Pastoral, and Empirical Theology
ETL	*Ephemerides Theologicae Lovanienses*
F&F	Foundations & Facets
FBS	Fellowship for Biblical Studies
FRP	Fortress Resources for Preaching
FT	*Feminist Theology*
G&R	*Greece and Rome*
HTCNT	Herder's Theological Commentary on the New Testament
HCS	Hellenistic Culture and Society
Hermen	Hermeneia
HNT	Hebrew New Testament
HSCP	*Harvard Studies in Classical Philology*
HSNS	*Historical Studies in the Natural Sciences*
IATDC	Inter-Anglican Theological and Doctrinal Commission
IICM	Intercultural Institute for Contextual Ministry
Int	*Interpretation*
IVBS	International Voices in Biblical Studies
IVP	Inter-Varsity Press
JBCE	Joint Board of Christian Education
JBL	*Journal of Biblical Literature*
JRA	*Journal of Roman Archaeology*

JRMA	*Journal of the Royal Musical Association*
JSP	*Journal for the Study of the Pseudepigrapha*
JSNT	*Journal for the Study of the New Testament*
JSNTSup	Supplements to the Journal for the Study of the New Testament
JSJ	*Journal for the Study of Judaism*
JSJPHRP	*Journal for the Study of Judaism in the Persian, Hellenistic and Roman Period*
JSJSup	Supplements to the Journal for the Study of Judaism
JTI	*Journal of Theological Interpretation*
JTSA	*Journal of Theology for Southern Africa*
KJV	King James Version of Bible
KRS	*Kirchanblatt für die reformierte Schweiz*
LCL	Loeb Classical Library
LQ	*Lutheran Quarterly*
LNTS	Library of New Testament Studies
MCD	Melbourne College of Divinity
MCL	Martin Classical Lectures
MOW	Movement for the Ordination of Women
NB	*New Blackfriars*
NBC	New Bible Commentary: 21st Century Edition
NIB	New Interpreter's Bible in 12 volumes
NICNT	New International Commentary on the New Testament
NIV	New International Version of Bible
NRSV	New Revised Standard Version of Bible
NTTS&D	New Testament Tools, Studies and Documents
NTS	*New Testament Studies*
OECS	Oxford Early Christian Studies
OTL	Old Testament Library
OTR	Old Testament Readings
Pac	*Pacifica*
Paideia	Paideia Commentaries on the New Testament
PCA	*Post-Classical Archaeologies*
PEQ	*Palestine Exploration Quarterly*
Phil	*Philosophia*

PNTC	The Pillar New Testament Commentaries
PPS	*Perspective on Political Science*
RBPH	*Revue Belge de Philologie et d'Histoire*
RCL	Revised Common Lectionary
RM	*Review of Metaphysics*
RUSCH	Rutgers University Studies in the Classical Humanities
SBL	Society of Biblical Literature
SBLDS	Society of Biblical Literature Dissertation Series
SGRR	Studies in Greek and Roman Religion
SHCT	Studies in the History of Christian Traditions
SJT	*Scottish Journal of Theology*
SNTS	Studiorum Novi Testamenti Societas
SNTSMS	Society for New Testament Studies Monograph Series
SVTQ	*St Vladimir's Theological Quarterly*
TCPS	Transactions of the Cambridge Philological Society
TNTC	Tyndale New Testament Commentaries
T&S	*Theory and Society*
TS	*Theological Studies*
UBS	United Bible Society
UBSHS	United Bible Society Handbook Series
UD	University of Divinity
WBC	World Biblical Commentary
WC	Wisdom Commentary
WUNT	Wissenschaftliche Untersuchungen zum Neuen Testament
ZS	Zaccheus Studies

Foreword

I am delighted to write this foreword to a Festschrift for Dorothy Lee, whose contribution to the Diocese of Melbourne, to the Australian Anglican Church and further afield, is nothing short of remarkable.

Dorothy is internationally renowned as a Biblical scholar, specializing in the New Testament, and particularly St John's Gospel; her scholarly publications are wide-ranging and prolific. She has contributed much, much more to Church and society, however.

For almost four decades, Dorothy has been a significant Australian theological educator, as well as a pioneering female clergy leader at local, diocesan, national, and ecumenical levels. As well, she is much sought after as an engaging religious communicator in mainstream press, radio, and television.

She is a significant promoter of the ministry of women within the Church, not only because of her academic leadership, research, and publications, but also through her personal example as a priest, preacher, and church leader.

A Canon of St Paul's Cathedral, Melbourne, she is also Canon Theologian of the Diocese of Wangaratta. She preaches regularly, and often leads spiritual retreats for clergy. Nationally, she serves on the General Synod of the Anglican Church of Australia, where she is a member of the Doctrine Commission, contributing significant essays to the Doctrine Commission's publications.

As she celebrates a significant birthday, 22 of her colleagues and friends have honoured Dorothy with this Festschrift. The list of contributors—from the broader Anglican Church, colleagues at Trinity College Theological School, and theological educators and researchers in the Roman Catholic and Uniting Churches—demonstrates the reach of Dorothy's influence and the high regard in which she is held.

Congratulations, Dorothy, and thank you for your outstanding ministry.

The Most Revd Dr Philip Freier,
Archbishop of Melbourne

Editors Preface

It has been a wonderful privilege and honour for us to solicit, compile, and edit this series of essays to commemorate the scholarship and service of Professor Dorothy Lee, on the occasion of her 70th birthday. Dorothy has been a colleague, friend, and mentor to the three of us as editors; and, indeed, to all who have contributed essays to this volume.

Dorothy is a renowned scholar in Johannine studies and has made significant contributions to the study of the Fourth Gospel and the place of women in the Bible through her writing and research. She is widely known for her interpretations of the Gospel in engagement with a broad range of conversation partners. This Festschrift includes a wide range of contributions that reflect the breadth of Professor Lee's interests. We have essays on a variety of topics, including biblical studies, women in the Bible and the church, contemporary reception history, and ecclesiology. Many pieces also examine and interact with Dorothy's own work, including her approach to Johannine literature, and her contribution to recovering the role of women in the early church. We hope that this Festschrift is an inspiring tribute to the scholarship and service of Professor Dorothy Lee.

After two biographical essays from Muriel Porter and Richard Treloar focusing on Dorothy's life and service, the following chapters are divided into three sections, broadly in line with her focus of scholarship and service. The first section, focusing on New Testament studies opens with *The Jesus, Mary, and Martha Chain* from Christopher Porter on the Fourth Gospel's depiction of Mary and Martha in contrast with the Lukan depiction, picking up on Dorothy's dual interests in women in the Bible and the Fourth Gospel. John Capper follows this with *Joy, Abiding, and Human Flourishing*, examining the joy motif in the Fourth Gospel, and Christian community. Continuing the Johannine theme, Mary Coloe's essay *Salvation as Liberation* probes the liberative nature of salvation in the Gospel of John. Mark Lindsay's essay seeks to *Read[ing] John's Prologue Through Contemporary Kenoticism*, drawing together the conversations on Karl Barth from Richard Bauckham and Bruce McCormack through the site of the Johannine prologue. Launching from Christology, Brendan Byrne's *Christology from Paul to John* assesses the links from Paul's Christological declarations in the expansions of Fourth Gospel thinking. Similarly, Sean Winter draws connections between the Pauline and Johannine sending formulae within the broader model of historical Jesus studies in *The "Sending of the Son" Formula in Paul, John, and the Historical Jesus*. Fergus King's *Live and Let Live* continues with Paul and considers the ethical impact of the "Weak" and "Strong" in Romans, and how this passage in Romans may be contextualized for the modern church. Finally, Francis Moloney rounds out this section by exploring the difficult portrayal of *The Jews, Israel, and Jerusalem in the Book of Revelation*, reading these challenging passages in an alternative paradigm of worship after the Jerusalem temple destruction.

The second set of essays turns towards Dorothy's passionate advocacy for the work of women, and her love of the church. Opening with Rachelle Gilmour studies *Daughter-in-law of Eli, Wife of Phinehas and Mother of Ichabod* as a political pivot within the narrative of 1 Samuel. Michael Bird turns to the New Testament and questions whether the interaction of *Jesus and the Syro-Phoenician Woman* may be read as a story of inclusion, and the overcoming of prejudice. Along with these essays are three essays on the place of the church, starting with Colleen O'Reilly and Muriel Porter investigating whether *The Queen's funeral service [really is] from the* Book of Common Prayer, concluding that while the trappings of the service emulated the BCP services, the service itself instead reflects much more modern funeral practices. Stephen Pickard takes on *The Precarious Church* by questioning the links between kenosis and healing and whether an appropriate ecclesial framework can utilize this precarity to enliven its purpose. Finally, Christiaan Mostert exhorts the reader to *Keep Awake* in an exploration of how to live eschatologically in "the overlap of the ages," and the implications of this for the Church. Finally, Peter Campbell considers the historical and theological environment of Dorothy's scholar-ship with a historical retrospective on theological education in Australia: *"This teaching is difficult; who can accept it?": Theology in Australian Tertiary Institutions*.

The final tranche of chapters explores the horizons of biblical scholarship, entertaining a variety of new media and foci—as Dorothy is often wont to study. Three of these essays examine biblical engagements in new media. Bob Derrenbacker asks the question *Why Didn't the Transfiguration Make the Cut?* probing the omission of the transfiguration within the Jesus-film genre, tying this to its larger neglect in the Western Christian tradition.

Christy Capper follows with *Ecce homo—Jesus and the call to authenticity,* questioning the place of "authenticity" in Jesus' teachings and in the life of the church. Robyn Whitaker inspects Albrecht *Dürer's Apocalypse Woodcuts as a New Form of (Visual) Commentary* distributed alongside, and then separately from, biblical material as a form of reception of the book of Revelation, with an eye to their impact on biblical interpretation in the reformation period. Kathrine Firth and Andreas Loewe examine the reception of the Johannine passion narrative in *"It is accomplished!"—Perfection and Accomplishment in J. S. Bach's John Passion,* arguing that Bach's passion musically portrays the perfect work of Christ. Scott Kirkland finishes the volume in completion and eschatology, contemplating the place of history and immortality with Kojève and Agamben in *On Entry into Paradise.*

Finally, we thank a host of individuals whose support has been essential in the editing of this Festschrift: Hugh McGinlay for his copyediting of each essay; the Warden of Trinity College—Professor Ken Hinchcliff—for his unceasing support of this project and his long appreciation of Dorothy Lee's contribution to theological education; and, to the team at Wipf & Stock for their professionalism and excellent editorial support.

The Editors: Robert Derrenbacker, Christopher Porter, and Muriel Porter
Ash Wednesday 2023

Introduction/Biographical

1.

Dorothy A. Lee
from Scottish Presbyterian to Australian Anglican priest, scholar and church leader

MURIEL PORTER

Beginnings

How appropriate that Barbara and Edwin Lee should name their first-born child Dorothy. "Dorothy," meaning "Gift of God," is derived from the Greek and so is a highly appropriate name for Dorothy Lee as a Greek scholar. More importantly though, many people both in Australia and across the academic world regard Dorothy in so many respects as truly a "Gift of God"— as scholar, writer, teacher, pastor, priest, church leader, colleague, and friend.[1]

Dorothy was born in Dunfermline, Scotland, in 1953, followed by a sister Ruth, and brother Edwin. When she was six, the family moved to Melbourne. It was there that her father was ordained a minister in the Free

---

1. As a close friend and colleague who has benefited greatly from Dorothy's giftedness over more than three decades, I am inevitably a biased compiler of her story. I have drawn on my personal knowledge as a close friend. Also, as a professional journalist, I have on several occasions interviewed her for the Melbourne Diocesan monthly newspaper, *The Melbourne Anglican* (*TMA*). I have drawn extensively on one of those interviews for this essay.

Presbyterian Church of Eastern Australia, an off shoot of the Free Presbyterian Church of Scotland, popularly known as the "Wee Frees." He had already completed theological studies in Edinburgh and came to Melbourne to take on a tiny church in East Kilda, developing it into a growing, lively center of prayer, discussion— and cricket!

The family returned to Scotland in 1966, where Edwin became the minister of a Dundee parish. A small, dispirited church, it was soon built up by Edwin's boundless energy. The stipend was so low, however, that he had to work as a teacher as well, which adversely affected his health. So, in 1970 the family decided to return to Australia, this time to Taree, a town on the mid north coast of New South Wales. Edwin Lee's ministry prospered in the thriving Taree congregation; he stayed there until his retirement eighteen years later. He died in 2016, six years after his wife, having in his retirement graduated with a PhD in history from the University of Melbourne at the noteworthy age of 88. Dorothy, who was deeply attached to her kindly, erudite father, has described Edwin as a "moderate man of faith."

In her teenage years, arguing strenuously about theology with her father, Dorothy drifted away from the Wee Frees, although she continued to admire that church's strong intellectual tradition. In her last year at high school in Taree, she began worshipping with a schoolfriend in the local Anglican church. Although she found it very different from her childhood worship, she loved it.

Having completed her rather disrupted schooling, Dorothy began her university education at the University of Newcastle, New South Wales, graduating Bachelor of Arts with first class honors in classics in 1975. In her honors year, she taught Greek at the now-closed St John's Theological College, an Anglican seminary in Morpeth, an historic port town north-west of Newcastle. It was for her a valuable introduction to the world of Anglican theological enquiry.

Having completed a Diploma of Education, on her marriage she relocated to Sydney, where she undertook a Bachelor of Divinity degree at the University of Sydney. Majoring in New Testament with first class honors in 1982, she was awarded the University Medal—believed to be the first woman to receive the University Medal in Divinity. While at the University of Sydney, she worshipped regularly at the Anglican parish of St Luke's, Enmore, and loved it.

The Call to Ordination

At this time, she began to feel a strong call to ordained ministry. That certainly would not have been an option in the Wee Frees; they have no role at all for women, not even reading the Scriptures in worship. But nor was it an option then in the Anglican Church, which had become her spiritual home. From the early 1980s, the Anglican Church of Australia was convulsed by a prolonged and bitter debate about women in the ministry, with some at the time despairing it would ever be possible for women to be ordained. So, with that church sadly unable to respond to her call, she turned to the recently formed Uniting Church in Australia, undertaking ministerial studies at that church's United Theological College, Sydney. She has commented that she joined the Uniting Church "with ambivalent feelings" but did so "precisely over the issue of ordination." She added: "I wanted to study theology and I needed to be in a church that would take seriously my call to ordained ministry."[2]

She was soon appointed Lecturer in New Testament at the college, an appointment she was able to continue to hold when she was ordained a Minister of the Word in 1984. At the time, ordination in the Uniting Church was always to a parish placement, but thanks to the persuasive powers of the theological college's principal, the Rev. Dr. Graeme Ferguson, that hurdle was overcome. The college became her placement, and so Dorothy was able to continue bringing her rare giftedness to the college. Dr. Ferguson remembers that Dorothy was part of an "outstanding cohort" of women at the college, "who transformed the basic ethos of the community to become more inclusive and welcoming of the distinctive contribution women were making to ministry in the church." Her teaching at the College was, he said, "brilliant."[3]

Meanwhile, her doctoral studies were proceeding at the University of Sydney under the supervision of Jesuit Scripture scholar, Brendan Byrne, and the late Rev. Dr. Bill Jobling, archaeologist, Scripture scholar and Anglican priest. In 1990, she completed her thesis on "The symbolic narratives of the fourth gospel: the interplay of form and meaning," the beginning of her deep academic engagement with the Gospel according to John. Her research findings were published in book form four years later,[4] and numerous other books, book chapters and refereed articles on various aspects of

2. Lee, "An Anglo-Uniting Perspective," 253–54.

3. Graeme Ferguson, author communication, 24 November 2021.

4. Lee, *Symbolic Narratives of the Fourth Gospel.*

John's Gospel have followed. She has an international reputation as a specialist on that Gospel.

Her scholarship and publications have since expanded into the other canonical gospels, feminist theology, and the place of women in the church. As said in the biographical notes on her election as a Fellow of the Australian Academy of the Humanities in 2015, "She is renowned for developing new insights from her interdisciplinary approach to her research, bringing perspectives from contemporary literary criticism, the study of the visual arts and gender studies to her analysis of canonical texts."[5]

In 1990, Dorothy and her family, which then included two daughters, Miriam and Irene, relocated to Melbourne, where she lectured in New Testament at the Uniting Church's Theological Hall. She enjoyed the ecumenical perspective the new role gave her, as the Theological Hall was part of the interdenominational United Faculty of Theology, later absorbed into the University of Divinity.

Four years later, she was appointed Professor of New Testament at the Hall, celebrated at the time as a highly significant appointment. Women theological educators, particularly at professorial level, were rare, even though the number of women among theological students was beginning to increase. At just 40, with flame-red curls and a warm, engaging personality, she brought a fresh, youthful dynamic to the Melbourne theological world.

She became increasingly well-known there for her prolific theological writing, frequent addresses at seminars and conferences, and sermons across a range of churches. Her ecumenical reach was extensive as well, including close involvement with various areas of the Roman Catholic Church. With her daughters brought up as Catholics and attending a Catholic school (Dorothy's then husband was Catholic), Dorothy often worshipped with them in Catholic churches. She was sometimes introduced at conferences as a "Protestant pastor and Catholic mother"!

The Call to the Anglican Church

The siren call of Anglicanism had not disappeared, however. Twenty-three years after her ordination in the Uniting Church, she could resist no longer. By 2007, she had been worshipping regularly at the Anglican parish of Christ Church, South Yarra, where she sang in the parish choir. She was also frequently invited to preach and teach in other Anglican churches as well, and found her theology becoming much more sacramental, much more

5. Australian Academy of the Humanities, "Fellow Reverend Canon Professor Dorothy Lee"

"small-c" catholic. She appreciated Anglican sacramental ministry, and the characteristic formality and warmth of Anglican worship. She was also glad that she did not have to turn her back on Charles Wesley's hymns, which she loves.[6] So on All Saints' Day 2007, in her parish, Dorothy was formally received into the Anglican Church.

While she was delighted about the move, there was a deep sense of loss as well. "The Uniting Church has been very good to me," she told *TMA*, the Diocese of Melbourne's monthly newspaper, at the time. "They have given me a great deal of support, particularly in the beginning when they encouraged me to become a scholar. I will really miss those colleagues who have travelled this journey with me and understand why I am leaving. There is a lot that is wonderful about the Uniting Church, but it is no longer home."[7]

She honors the Uniting Church for its role as the ground breaker in Australia for women's ordination; its constituent churches had been the first to ordain women in Australia, and the newly-formed church honored that history.[8] The Uniting Church, she said, gave a home, "not only to women but also to ideas that other traditions would not permit to be named, let alone discussed." She continues to respect its "adventurous and prophetic" stance, and its preparedness "to take risks in embracing the ministry of all God's people, women and men alike."[9]

It was however her concern with the Uniting Church's growing theologically liberal wing that she found concerning. In its commitment to feminism — a commitment Dorothy shares— some in the Uniting Church had become increasingly hostile to traditional Trinitarian language, coming to a point where, she said, "it seemed sometimes as if God had become almost an irrelevance in Uniting Church discourse, particularly its worship." Core metaphors within the Christian tradition cannot, in her view, be easily altered.[10] She has explained her view in the following terms:

> My own research on religious symbolism in the Fourth Gospel convinced me that certain metaphors lie at the heart of the Christian tradition and are not negotiable without serious loss of content. To dispense with the imagery of Father-Son, for example, would mean the loss of key conceptions, core symbols that conveyed truth in themselves. Feminism . . . had to take the core metaphors of the Christian tradition seriously,

6. Porter, "Coming Home."

7. Porter, "Coming Home."

8. Porter, *Women in the Church*, 25–32.

9. Lee, "An Anglo-Uniting Perspective," 265.

10. Lee, "An Anglo-Uniting Perspective," 263–64.

re-interpreting them to show where their truth actually lay and where it did not.[11]

Dorothy was also troubled by "the steady diminution in the role and status of ordained ministry" in that church, as it began practicing lay presidency at Holy Communion. These were the concerns, she said, that finally caused her to leave.[12]

She was warmly welcomed by the Anglican hierarchy, and began the journey towards Anglican ordination the following year, reading up on Anglican history, polity, theology and spirituality. Before becoming an Anglican, when she would necessarily become a layperson and then deacon for a year, she imposed on herself a "fast at the altar," refraining from presiding at the Eucharist in her last little while as a Uniting Church minister. She realized she would need to observe this fast until she was ordained priest.

She told *TMA* at the time that she was not perturbed about being re-ordained. "I really appreciate the three-fold order of ministry," she said. "I believe that my role as a Uniting Church minister has been entirely valid, but I see Anglican episcopal ordination as a re-ordering, a re-affirmation, and I am really looking forward to that."[13]

She was ordained as an Anglican priest in St Paul's Cathedral, Melbourne, on 29 November 2008. She presided at the Eucharist for the first time as an Anglican priest the following day in her parish, Christ Church, South Yarra, wearing a chasuble that had once belonged to one of her doctoral supervisors, the late Bill Jobling. She served as an associate priest in the parish for a number of years.

Church leader

As an Anglican, Dorothy was appointed lecturer in theological studies at Trinity College Theological School, a seminary for the Victorian Anglican dioceses. Because the theological school was part of the United Faculty of Theology, she was able to continue teaching students from the other constituent bodies, the Uniting Church Theological Hall and the Jesuit Theological College. From 2011 to 2017, Dorothy was Dean ("head") of Trinity's Theological School, one of very few women to head an Anglican theological seminary in Australia. Since 2017, she has been Stewart Research Professor of New Testament at Trinity.

11. Lee, "An Anglo-Uniting Perspective," 264.

12. Lee, "An Anglo-Uniting Perspective," 262–65.

13. Porter, "Coming Home."

In 2012, she had been appointed one of ten senior scholars appointed an inaugural professor of the new University of Divinity. All ten were "recognized for their outstanding scholarship, teaching excellence, and leadership within and beyond the academy." Her citation reads that she is "internationally recognized for her research on symbolism in the Gospel of John, displaying pastoral sensitivity and cultural awareness in exegesis and interpretation. Her focus is on a literary and theological approach to the Gospels and she is widely published in books and journals. Her esteem is evident in the high demand for her scholarship as a lecturer, supervisor, preacher and writer."[14]

Since becoming an Anglican, she has become deeply involved in the Australian Anglican Church at many levels. She is a significant leader in the Synod of the Diocese of Melbourne, and in the General Synod of the Anglican Church of Australia, where she has been a member of the General Synod's Standing Committee. Her extraordinary knowledge of the Christian Scriptures often enabled her to offer fresh and insightful biblical input into the Standing Committee's deliberations, sometimes confounding conservative male clergy members of that body used to considering themselves the sole biblical experts. That she offered her views gently, generously (and often while knitting!), marked the distinct contribution she made there.

Doctrinal views

Dorothy's doctrinal views are clear. She loves St John's Gospel because, she says, "it is so centered in the Incarnation, which is really the most radical aspect of our faith — that God became human. And the Incarnation leads to the Cross." She describes herself as an orthodox theologian in terms of the Nicene Creed. "The Creed is not so much a series of propositions, but rather defines the core symbols of Christian faith. The teachings of the Nicene Creed are core, central and non-negotiable."[15]

She continued: "I get upset when people want to define matters such as sexuality or the role of women as core. They are not; they are secondary. I would be far more concerned if clergy were denying the Trinity or the Incarnation or the Resurrection than I would be if they were promoting particular views on sexuality, for instance. We need to be absolutely united on the core matters contained in the Nicene Creed, and allow the flexibility

14. Melbourne College of Divinity, "MCD University of Divinity Appoints its First Professors."

15. Porter, "Coming Home."

to explore and discuss secondary matters openly until we come to a common mind."[16]

While holding firm to her doctrinal beliefs, she has a rare gift of engaging people of different doctrinal positions in respectful and often life-giving dialogue, as has been apparent from time to time in Synod debates. She is highly respected across the board in a church currently bitterly divided by issues such as the role of women, and the recognition and blessing of same-sex marriage.

Since 2008, she has been a member of the General Synod Doctrine Commission, where her profound Scriptural knowledge and theological expertise have greatly added to the Commission's work. She has particularly offered valuable fresh insights into pressing current discussions concerning gender, equality, sexuality and marriage, and has contributed significant articles to its various publications.[17]

In 2014, Melbourne Synod elected her a canon of St Paul's Cathedral, and she has also been appointed Canon Theologian of the Victorian rural diocese of Wangaratta. Associate priest in the parish of St Mary's, North Melbourne, she continues to preach widely both there and across a range of parishes, and is in wide demand to conduct spiritual retreats in numerous Australian dioceses.

She is a regular contributor of articles for church press, as well as for secular media, including *The Age* and *The Conversation*, and is also a frequent commentator on radio programs such as the ABC's *God Forbid*. Her engaging, highly accessible style of both writing and speaking is rare among academics of her standing.

Dorothy is a pioneering female leader among Anglican clergy at local, diocesan, and national levels, as well as at the ecumenical level. She is a significant promoter of the ministry of women within the church, not only because of her academic leadership, research, and publications,[18] but also for her inspiring personal example as priest, preacher and church leader.

Family

Family is extremely important to Dorothy. While her father, whom she loved dearly, was always very proud of her academic achievements, and of her as a person, the conservative Wee Free minister was uncomfortable with women leading worship. In his final years, however, their biblical bond was a source

16. Porter, "Coming Home."

17. For example, Lee, "Marriage, Headship and the New Testament."

18. For example, Lee, *Ministry of Women in the New Testament.*

of great consolation to him, and he gradually became more comfortable with her role as he drifted back towards the Anglicanism of his childhood. In his last days, Dorothy was continually by his bedside, reading Scripture to him and praying with him. She presided at his dignified Anglican prayer book funeral in 2016.

She is close to her extended family, particularly to her sister Ruth and her family. As a mother and grandmother, she is adored by her daughters, their husbands and her three grandchildren—Jemima, Theodore and Harriet—on whom she dotes. An animal lover, she is besotted with her cats, Daphne and D'Arcy.

Dorothy is very highly valued as a dear friend and colleague by many, some of whom are privileged to contribute to this recognition of her significant achievements.

Bibliography

Australian Academy of the Humanities, "Fellow Reverend Canon Professor Dorothy Lee," accessed 14 January 2022. https://humanities.org.au/fellows/fellow/?contact_id=3133

Lee, Dorothy A. "An Anglo-Uniting Perspective: The Journey Taken," in Elaine Lindsay & Janet Scarfe. Editors, *Preachers, Prophets & Heretics*, Sydney: University of New South Wales Press, 2012, 253–267.

———. "Marriage, Headship and the New Testament." In The Anglican Church of Australia. *Same-Sex Marriage and the Anglican Church of Australia: Essays from the Doctrine Commission*, Mulgrave, VIC: Broughton Publishing, 2019, 123–138.

———. *The Ministry of Women in the New Testament: Reclaiming the Biblical Vision for Church Leadership*. Grand Rapids, MI: Baker Academic, 2021.

———. *The Symbolic Narratives of the Fourth Gospel*. Sheffield: Sheffield Academic Press, 1994.

Melbourne College of Divinity, "MCD University of Divinity Appoints its First Professors," 17 October 2012. Accessed 22 April 2023 https://web.archive.org/web/20131111215705/http://www.mcd.edu.au/professorial-appointment

Porter, Muriel. "Coming Home," *The Melbourne Anglican*, October 2007.

———. *Women in the Church: The Great Ordination Debate in Australia*. Ringwood, Vic: Penguin Books, 1989.

2.

Dorothy's (and our) Great Commission

RICHARD TRELOAR

When I came to Christ Church South Yarra in 2007, Dorothy Lee was a member of the faith community there. She was received as a member of the Anglican Church on All Saints' Day 2007 by Bishop Philip Huggins, at the same service as was my partner, Leanne Habeeb. The preacher on that occasion was Dorothy's friend and Uniting Church colleague, the Rev. Prof Christiaan Mostert.

Both as Dorothy's Vicar, and with my own connections to Trinity College Theological School where she was newly appointed, I was delighted to be invited to preach at a service for her commissioning as Frank Woods Distinguished Lecturer in Biblical Studies on Trinity Sunday 2008. The gospel text for the Choral Eucharist in the Chapel of Trinity College and Janet Clarke Hall was Matt 28:16–20, and the title of the sermon was "Dorothy's (and our) great commission." The sermon is reproduced in large part here, for it speaks to the significance of Dorothy's experience of the order of deacons as she transitioned from the Uniting Church in Australia (UCA) into the Anglican Church of Australia:

"Too intellectual to lead?"[1] This question was raised in the British press during the furor over remarks that Rowan Williams (then Archbishop of

---

1. Rice-Oxley, "Anglican Archbishop: too intellectual to lead?"

Canterbury) had made about *sharia* law in a lecture at the Royal Courts of Justice. That someone can be deemed "too intellectual" to lead presents a challenge to an institution such as this, which seeks to prepare women and men for service and leadership in the world and in the church — not least by providing academic programs, and staff, of the highest quality. Has that part of what we celebrate and give thanks for on this feast of title become a devalued currency? Not for Anglican layman Justice Michael Kirby, who has lamented that the church is losing rational adherents because of what he sees as the selective and uninformed interpretation of Scripture being practiced by some of its leaders;[2] precisely the situation Bishop Moorhouse was concerned to address when establishing the Trinity College Theological School. In the 1960s, Frank Woods likewise sought to educate and equip a whole generation of laity and clergy through the *Forward in Depth* movement.

In the sense of the ancient Chinese proverb, we might say that Dorothy has stumbled upon "interesting times" in which to be received into the Anglican Church, to take up authority as a deacon in Anglican orders, and to join the faculty of an Anglican college. Dorothy came to this position from distinguished service as a presbyter in the Uniting Church: a tradition she continues to engage with and to draw upon in this richly ecumenical setting, and to value personally and professionally. It seems fitting, then, that she be commissioned not only on one of the principal feasts of the church universal, but also a day on which we hear the apostolic commission at the end of Matthew's Gospel, including the charge to encourage and shape baptismal vocation, and to teach. And if exercising leadership in these respects is a difficult calling, Dorothy is in good company.

Moses, returning from forty days on Mt Sinai, text of the covenant in hand, surprises the Israelite camp. Impatient for some (preferably less wordy) token of divine presence, they had made a golden calf, and were having a terrific time worshipping it, until Moses — like a college Dean in days of old breaking up an Orientation Week party — reads them the riot act, smashing the tablets of the law in the process. So much for things being written in stone! He then, of course, has to trudge back up the hill to get a replacement, where, in Exod 34:1–8, he sees the Lord's glory in terms of covenant faithfulness: keeping steadfast love.

So too in Corinth, not unlike a certain Anglican Primate, Paul's apostolic authority has been under attack. As with the question of *sharia* law, he is addressing tensions between wider societal norms and more sub-cultural — in Paul's case, gospel — imperatives.[3] He knows what the talk is; he reads

2. Morris, "Admit your sins to the Lord," para 12.

3. Wright, "Conflict and Covenant," §2.iii.

the papers. Earlier in the letter from which our second reading comes, Paul writes of himself, "For they say, 'His letters are weighty . . . but his bodily presence is weak, and his speech contemptible'" (2 Cor 10:10). "Too intellectual to lead?" might well have been the headline the *Corinthian Tribune* was running with at the time. Other so-called "super" apostles were better at the snappy sound bite, less vulnerable or prone to nuance, more attune to the prevailing indices of success. Paul, it seems, is far too preoccupied with the cross: that most ambiguous and irreducible of signs, which leads him — tongue firmly in cheek — to boast of all the "wrong" things in the latter part of his correspondence.

In making his final appeal, as we see in 2 Cor 13:11–13, Paul too invokes God's covenant faithfulness and steadfast love. Here, as for Moses, God's nature is God's glory; and, for Paul, God's gracious, loving, and faithful being in and for the world is to be known by the churches in Christ crucified. Unfolding from this starting point, the doctrine of the Trinity has been described as "nothing other than a . . . version of the Passion narrative of Christ."[4] A trinitarian version of the Passion narrative is recounted at the Eucharist table in bread and wine, as this panel from the tenth chapter of the Revelation to St John, in a fourteenth-century illustrated manuscript attests.[5]

Revelation 10:10 as depicted in The Cloisters Apocalypse

4. Moltmann *Crucified God*, 246.

5. Metropolitan Museum of Art, The Cloisters Collection, 1968, 68.174.

Gerard Loughlin responds to this image as follows:

> As John lifts the book to his mouth, the angel gently supports John's . . . elbow while steadying the book . . . as if . . . assisting with the chalice. 'It is the familiar gesture of taking the Eucharist' . . . As the angel assists John in eating the book, their forearms constitute a symbol of trinitarian life, a triangular shape at the center of the picture . . . It is a symbol hardly visible, yet secretly present in this scene of God's infinite compassion: the giving of the story for the nurturing of the world.[6]

It's a story told also tonight in music. In 2008, the 50th anniversary year of Ralph Vaughan Williams' death, his *Mass in G Minor* recalls for us the revival of English polyphony.[7] Polyphony: the painstaking making room for, and creative holding together of, different but mutually attentive voices — a trinitarian sound bite, perhaps, and surely the necessary form of that "note" of the church, its catholicity, from which comes a vision of Anglicanism we would hold dear. The Passion narrative of Christ, in all of its simplicity and complexity, its wisdom and its foolishness, is what Dorothy is commissioned to continue telling — yes, through her superb scholarship and long experience in ordained ministry, but also by her discipleship. For, in its many versions and with many voices, this is the story that baptism commissions each of us to tell and to give for the nourishment of the world. May the sharing of this fleshy text form and re-form us into a living symbol of the infinitely compassionate One for whom Trinity College is named: Father, Son, and Holy Spirit. Amen.

For Dorothy, who joined the Ministry Team at Christ Church South Yarra in an honorary capacity around this time, the journey into Anglican orders meant formally inhabiting the diaconate for the first time. In the polity of the UCA, the diaconate is a distinct order of ministry; there is no "transitional" diaconate as is customary in Anglican ecclesiology. Having been ordained a UCA Minister of the Word in 1984, when in 2008, as an Anglican, Dorothy was made deacon, this meant stepping back from presiding at the Eucharist for a season.

Coming from a different direction as a cradle Anglican, and with only a fraction of Dorothy's experience in ministry when ordained deacon myself, I had reason to ask my bishop at the time if I could remain in deacon's orders for a further twelve months before being ordained priest, resulting in a similar abstention from eucharistic presidency. This intentionally elongated

6. Loughlin *Telling God's Story*, 245, citing Jesse M. Gellrich in quotation marks.

7. Creasy, "Mass in G Minor," para 2.

transitional diaconate gave me an opportunity to reflect on the centrality of this order of ministry in a "concentric" (as distinct from a "consecutive" or "sequential") understanding of ordination.

Sometimes the analogy of the Russian *Matryoshka* dolls is used to explain this concentricity (i.e., inside every priest there is a deacon, and inside every bishop there is a priest and a deacon). The limitation of this trope comes with the (necessarily) decreasing size of inward manifestations so that the inner dolls can be contained within the outer ones. Symbolically, this reinforces a hierarchy of orders that is quite contrary to Anglican understandings. It also suggests that diaconal ministry is somehow hidden, whereas the argument here is that it is the touchstone of all priestly and episcopal ministry, and an embodiment of baptismal ministry. When I'm asked what I "do" and how long I've been "doing" that for, I always use my ordination to the diaconate as the index. Since 1990, I have been in the orders on which all priestly and episcopal ministry is predicated. The diaconal impetus of priesthood was not jettisoned two years hence in 1992 so that the priestly bit of the clerical apparatus could orbit gently on, unencumbered by the centrifugal character of that earlier dispensation. Nor indeed since 2018 has the heuristic lens of the diaconate been any less vital in learning what the servant leadership of a bishop entails; quite the contrary.

Perhaps, as may have been the case for Dorothy in exercising diaconal ministry for the first time after decades of presbyteral ministry, during an extended transitional diaconate I became more conscious — and enduringly so — of the emblematic nature of the diaconate in the life and work of the church. If the bishop's role is to an extent metonymical — where the bishop is, there is the church, to paraphrase Ignatius of Antioch — can we think of the deacon's in a similar sense: where the deacon is, there is the gospel? In attempting to translate some of these personal recollections to a broader ecclesial plane — and doing so within a *lex orandi, lex credendi* tradition — let me offer a liturgical framework for further reflection.

This is a lens that Dorothy brings to her own reading of Johannine literature. In the Fourth Gospel, a series of characters come to worship at the divinely ordained temple of the incarnate Word, with Jesus himself at once an object of worship and true worshipper, hallowing the community of faith as it is gathered into his communion with the One he calls Father, signified in the cross: "his worshipful exaltation to the Father's side, the ultimate prayer of his human life."[8] Worship is intrinsic to Johannine spirituality as an ecclesial, corporate, and corporeal response to being drawn into this trinitarian circle of love. In speaking to our deepest identity, worship

8. Lee, *Hallowed in Truth and Love*, 251.

may be profoundly personal. In no sense, however, can it be private. With its source in the Spirit of truth, worship is concerned with truth-telling — about God and humanity — truthfulness that includes a properly hermeneutical dimension, as the gospel is constantly interpreted under the Spirit's emboldening guidance.

Which is not to say worship ought not be beautiful, as Dorothy's reading of Revelation makes clear. Indeed, its attractiveness is part of the prophetic, counter-cultural critique that the imagery of worship delivers in the Apocalypse, where the Spirit represents the church's mission as gatekeeper of the heavenly city: not to keep its gates closed, but to keep them open; to offer welcome and hospitality to those outside. This is not some anodyne, self-indulgent piety:

> Sacred ritual is not a delicacy to be enjoyed by aesthetes in the Book of Revelation . . . True worship indicates where the heart lies; it becomes the foundation for radical action . . . [Conversely] the essence of sin in Revelation is idolatry, worship of the imperial powers . . . which seek material gain and are ready to bow the knee to whatever will guarantee prosperity and comfort.[9]

For a little over eleven years at Christ Church South Yarra, I was privileged to work in a ministry team context, including with a colleague whose vocation is specifically diaconal. Having a permanent deacon in a parish or other ministry setting is an all too rare and very great blessing. The Parish Deacon's (honorary) role at Christ Church in those years was first and foremost a liturgical one. That is, the ministries in health care and the academy outside of the Parish were — for us and for her — an extension of the liturgical ministry undertaken on Sundays and at other times.

In each of these respects, the liturgical action impelled her diaconal work beyond the liturgy, which in turn informed the liturgical action: each an outworking and expression of the other in a ceaseless, mutually interpreting hermeneutical circle. The liturgical function is primary, however. In a larger Anglican instinct writ small, that Parish's self-understanding as an intentional community called to participate in God's mission to the world in Christ has for decades been explicitly grounded in worship. As Anglicans, liturgy serves as both mirror and lamp to our common life and work: reflecting back to us all that we are and do and shedding light on all that we are called to be and become. It is in worship that we are gathered and formed by God's gracious invitation; and it is our worship that sends us out into the world God loves to exercise baptismal (and in some cases also ordained) ministry. Everything we undertake as a household of faith and fellowship is

9. Lee, *Hallowed in Truth and Love*, 227.

resourced and critiqued by our eucharistic practice as we live into and out of word and sacrament.

Within this, the ministry of the liturgical deacon — which ideally would always be exercised by someone in deacon's orders when present — is especially instructive. What I have long since understood about the diaconal quality of Christ's own ministry, and hence the church's mission, is quite properly ritualized for us Sunday by Sunday, so as to help us connect our Sundays with our Mondays. There is much for the liturgical deacon to do in our tradition — more, perhaps, than is sometimes obvious from the pews. Dorothy experienced and expressed this ministry at Christ Church, where there's a very real sense in which the deacon leads the worship: carrying the Gospel book in procession; initiating most of the liturgical movement; calling the people to prayer and confession; proclaiming the Gospel; preaching when rostered; preparing and ministering at the altar-table during the Great Thanksgiving; prompting the acclamations; overseeing the ablutions and the reservation and distribution of the sacrament for pastoral ministry during the week; and dismissing the people for their Christian discipleship in the world. I recall from times when I fulfilled this liturgical role that it demands a different kind of attentiveness than does presiding. It is an active ministry, yet one that requires a certain stillness, or centeredness in that activity, and all it represents, if it is not to devolve into liturgical "busy-ness": the deacon's Martha to the priest's Mary, as it were.

Perhaps the most significant action the deacon performs in the liturgy is to carry the Gospel book out of church in procession at the end of the Eucharist. As the people watch the Gospel book held aloft (liturgically crowd-surfed, as it were) and going before us into the community in which we are set and to which we are sent, our baptismal calling is symbolically enacted. We follow the deacon, pied-piper-like, out of church and into our jobs, our classes, our families, our social circles, our discourses, our consuming, our voting, our philanthropy, our conflict, our carbon footprints and whatever else the week holds for each of us, carrying the Gospel. The place of liturgy in Christian discipleship and ecclesial mission is not incidental; nor is it a gloss. Nicholas Wolterstorff, Emeritus Professor of Philosophical Theology at Yale University, has been arguing for over fifty years that, when we gather for liturgy, we no more shut the world out than we forget the liturgy when it (specifically, the deacon) disperses us.[10] As one reader of Wolterstorff, puts it:

> we bring the world with us to the liturgy, giving thanks for it as
> an epiphany of God, but also bearing before him all its injus-
> tices; and when we return to the world we remember that the

10. Macleod, Review of *Hearing the Call*, 87.

God we worship is the one who loves justice, and that therefore "liturgical actions lose their authenticity when those who participate in the liturgy do not practice and struggle for justice."[11]

The liturgical action of the liturgical deacon is central in reminding us that, whenever we invoke God in worship, we hold ourselves accountable to God's call on our lives. The servant leadership of the deacon in the liturgy incarnates the servant leadership into which all the baptized are drawn by virtue of our being in Christ, "our great Archdeacon" ("arch" as in archetypal), whose ambassadors by grace we are. As Christ's own ministry was essentially diaconal, so is that of his body, the church. If we can speak meaningfully of the priesthood of all believers, then we may speak with no less integrity of the diaconate of all the baptized, including, of course, the clergy.

My own elongated transition from lay person to deacon to priest was the result of many factors, and I am not simply advocating that those accepted as ordination candidates for the priesthood might benefit (as I believe I did) from spending more time as transitional deacons. Yet my experience — both in those early years of ordained ministry, as one variously involved in ministry formation, and more recently charged with the privilege and responsibility of ordaining — has highlighted that the intention of this intentional period of transition, however long it may be, tends to lean towards the "transition" component of being a transitional deacon.

As those whose model of ordained ministry holds to the concentric rather than sequential pattern, how can we better enable our transitional deacons — and thereby the churches and ministry settings in which they serve — to experience and express, liturgically and thus in other ways, the full dignity and paradigmatic vocation of this office, such that the re-ordering of deacons as priests is without erasure? In the gift of our polity, clergy are not palimpsests whose baptismal identity is simply "written over" by a diaconal one, and then (for most) by a priestly one.

Just as being marked as Christ's in the waters of baptism is integral to any capacity to be his ambassador as a deacon, so too in Anglicanism ordained priestly ministry is utterly contingent upon the prior identity and calling of the diaconate, on which it continues to draw, as it surely does on the grace of our most fundamental re-ordering in baptism. If that is so, how might our processes better reflect the same? How might our liturgies form and re-form us as God's priestly people: called by baptism to bear Christ to the world? And how as a church might we give due authority to this full and equal order,[12] and to the individual men and woman who serve and lead

---

11. Macleod, Review of *Hearing the Call*, 87, citing Wolterstorff in quotation marks.

12. Barnett, *Diaconate.*

in it, both transitionally and permanently, in whose ministries the church's singular apostolicity is variously taken up?

These questions go to our capacity to tell the story we are commissioned in baptism to tell for the life of the world, in worship and in service, which are profoundly integrated in the paradigmatic ministry of the diaconate. Dorothy's ministry as a theological educator of the highest caliber and a distinguished New Testament scholar makes her uniquely well placed to help us answer them. Whether as a lay person, a UCA Minister of the Word, or as a Canon Professor in Anglican orders, Dorothy's life of service to the church and leadership in the Christian Academy has always been distinctly diaconal. *Laus Deo.*

Bibliography

Barnett, James M. *The Diaconate: A Full and Equal Order.* Minneapolis: Winston, 1981.

Creasy, Barry. "Mass in G Minor, Ralph Vaughan Williams (1872–1958)." http://www.choirs.org.uk/prognotes/Vaughan%20Williams%20Mass%20in%20G%20Minor.htm.

Lee, Dorothy A. *Hallowed in Truth and Love: Spirituality in the Johannine Literature.* Melbourne: Mosaic, 2011.

Loughlin, Gerard. *Telling God's Story: Bible, Church, and Narrative Theology.* Cambridge: Cambridge University Press, 1996.

MacLeod, Donald. Review of *Hearing the Call: Liturgy, Justice, Church and World* by Nicholas Wolterstorff. *The Expository Times* 123.2 (2011) 87.

Moltmann, Jürgen. *The Crucified God: The Cross of Christ as the Foundation and Criticism of Christian Theology.* London: SCM, 1974.

Morris, Linda. "Admit your sins to the Lord, priest tells gay judge." https://www.smh.com.au/national/admit-your-sins-to-the-lord-priest-tells-gay-judge-20080410-gds8vp.html.

Rice-Oxley, Mark. "Anglican Archbishop: too intellectual to lead?" https://www.csmonitor.com/2008/0220/p07s01-woeu.html.

Wright, Tom. "Conflict and Covenant in the Bible." https://www.fulcrum-anglican.org.uk/articles/conflict-and-covenant-in-the-bible-by-tom-wright/.

New Testament Scholarship

3.

The Jesus, Mary, and Martha Chain

CHRISTOPHER A. PORTER

Introduction

The paired characters of Mary and Martha are often read as two parts of the same character, albeit usually with contrasting and conflicting characterization. Indeed, commentaries on the Gospel of Luke often draw a strong contrast between the "work" of Martha and the "discipleship" displayed by Mary. When this contrast is drawn in the narrative, the contrasting characterization drives an internal dissonance for the reader, one which has been well recognized. These models of contest inevitably elevate the actions of one sister above the other—usually in line with the exegete's theological or ecclesiological tradition—with the corollary denigration of the other sister. In contrast to the terse Lukan pericope, the two-chapter long interaction with Mary and Martha in the Fourth Gospel presents a different pattern of interaction between the sisters. However, even in the Johannine reading, many exegetes import the conflict of the Lukan account into the text, generating a denigration of one sister or the other. This chapter seeks to read these characters within the Johannine discipleship theme, rather than as thin characters—*ficelles*—ancillary to the narrative.

Mary and Martha as Characters in Luke

Mary and Martha's appearance in the Gospel according to Luke takes up a rather brief five verse pericope: Luke 10:38–42. Yet, despite the brevity, the Evangelist imbues both women with a rich characterization—which many exegetes have extrapolated upon. However, the vast majority of these interpretations characterize both women in a contrasting relationship, with the characteristics of one inextricably influencing the interpretation of the other.

The Lukan pericope opens with Jesus approaching a "certain village" (10:38), continuing the journey theme that links together this section of the Gospel. In this context, Jesus—presumably along with his travelling companions—is welcomed into the house of Martha. As John Nolland sagely observes, the hospitality inherent within this welcome "cannot be separated from 'hospitality' to the message," picking up on the theme of responses to faith within the gospel: "salvation has come to the house of Martha and Mary."[1] On this basis, we may read the characterization of Martha—and subsequently Mary—as falling within the scope of exemplified faith for an audience with which to engage.

Subsequently, Martha is introduced into the story as the one who welcomes Jesus, although it is unclear as to whether she is acting as the matron of the house, or simply as the one present for receiving.[2] For the audience, this act of receiving—combined with a broader understanding of household patronage codes—primes an understanding of Martha in the domestic setting, with its associated paradigms and strictures. From this basis, questions abound as to the status and structure of Martha's household, as she appears to perform the welcoming function of the *paterfamilias*. As Margaret MacDonald observes "very often women who are presented as offering services . . . have been understood to be widows [or] her husband might frequently have been away, leaving her to manage the house."[3] By categorizing Martha in this role, the audience is led to conceive of her as holding a position of power within the household structure, coloring any further relations in the pericope.

Immediately after this welcome, Mary is introduced in sisterly relation to Martha "τῇδε ἦν ἀδελφὴ καλουμένη Μαριάμ" (Luke 10:39), rather than as a sudden introduction in her own right. The introductory formula emphasizes the relationship between the two sisters and, given the prior

1. Nolland, *Luke 9:21–18:34*, 35b:603.

2. "Some manuscripts read 'received him into her house' and others 'received him.'" Vinson, *Luke*, 345.

3. MacDonald, "Women Householders of Acts," 173.

introduction of Martha as the paterfamilial stand-in, places Mary in a subordinate position within the family. In this context, Mary is depicted as one "who sat at the Lord's feet" in the same posture typical of a pupil at a teacher's feet, highlighting her "zeal to learn."[4] Mary's pupil status confronts a typical Rabbinic position on the place of women in discipleship, which shows opposition to such relationships.[5] Even outside the context of Rabbinic instruction, such a position would be considered less than typical engagement. Nevertheless, Jesus' engagement in teaching with Mary at his feet—in the same position as the healed demoniac of 8:35—displays the discipleship associated with the coming of salvation into the house (see too Luke 19:9).

However, the narrative progresses rapidly from Mary's silence at Jesus' feet, returning the focus back to Martha who is "pulled away with much serving" ("περιεσπᾶτο περὶ πολλὴν διακονίαν" [10:40]). Before Martha can even open her mouth, the evangelist's narrative contrasts Mary's stillness with Martha's busyness. Busyness that prompts the only speaking part from either woman in the narrative: "Do you not care that my sister has left me to do all the work by myself?" (10:40). The implicit tension between the two sisters is suddenly made explicit within the narrative, on the lips of Martha as the paterfamilial stand-in, and accompanied by a strong request: "Tell her to help me!" In response it appears that Jesus offers a mild rebuke of Martha's distraction, uttering the (in)famous words "There is need of only one thing, Mary has chosen the better part" (10:42).[6]

The tension between the two women in Luke 10 has led to a plethora of interpretations, almost all focusing on the contrast generated between Martha and Mary, with some portraying this as a stereotypical "type scene" in line with Sarah and Hagar or Leah and Rachel.[7] Martha's role in the narrative is often portrayed as representing the "action" of a disciple, while Mary engages with the "contemplation" side of the coin.[8] The construal of Martha and Mary in a form of perpetual conflict mirroring the "internal" conflict of a disciple leads to problematic outcomes. As Reid observes: "Why, if the Christian ideal is to integrate contemplation and action, are the two cast dualistically in this text, with the one choice approved, and the

4. Marshall, *Gospel of Luke*, 452.

5. "'May the words of the Torah be burned, they should not be handed over to women' (j Sota, 10a, 8). 'The man who teaches his daughter the Torah teaches her extravagance' (Sofa, 3, 4; cf. b. Sota, 21b)." Oepke, "Γυνή," 781–82.

6. While textual variants draw into question what this one thing is, and what the better part may be, we will focus on the contrast between Martha and Mary here.

7. Spencer, *Salty Wives, Spirited Mothers, and Savvy Widows*, 145.

8. Reid, *Choosing the Better Part?* 144.

other denigrated?"[9] One possible approach is to view the sisterly dichotomy through the lens of discipleship and faith. As Chris Seglenieks observes of πίστις language in Luke, propositional belief leads to faithful action,[10] which we see in two forms in this pericope. This complexifies the relationship between the two sisters, their two responses, and generates a creative tension to address this engagement.

Mary and Martha as Characters in John

While Luke presents Mary and Martha in a terse five verse encounter, the Fourth Gospel expands their interaction out across multiple chapters and extends their interaction with Jesus and a range of supporting characters. As Dorothy Lee highlights

> Mary and Martha are among Jesus' friends and disciples; and, throughout the illness and death of their brother, they come to understand and reveal Jesus' identity and the significance of his mission. While they are technically minor characters, their key roles in the central narrative of John's Gospel give them greater force as Johannine characters.[11]

Unlike the Lukan narrative, in the Fourth Gospel, Mary is the first to be introduced (John 11:1). Initially introduced with primacy of order over her sister Martha, they are both brought into the narrative in relationship with "Lazarus of Bethany." Furthermore, the narrator immediately foreshadows Mary's anointing in chapter 12, which may be taken as evidence of Mary's presence within the memory of the audience, the shifting of the Lazarus scene earlier in the narrative, or as a thematic foreshadowing of the anointing significance.[12] Whichever option is taken, the narrative clearly opts for the narrated primacy of Mary over Martha in this instance.

Martha

It is only after the request, and Jesus' deliberation over whether to travel to Judea, that Martha is finally introduced in her own right. Upon the arrival of Jesus' party in Bethany, Martha is again referred to in relation to Mary by referring to the host of Ἰουδαῖοι who have come to comfort them (11:19),

9. Reid, *Choosing the Better Part?* 144–145.

10. Seglenieks, "Faith and Faithfulness in Luke," 62.

11. Lee, *Flesh and Glory*, 115.

12. Keener, *John*, 838.

before she steps forward to head out of the house to greet Jesus (11:20).[13] Similar to her depiction in Luke, this presents Martha with a significant degree of agency within the household. Furthermore, this initial characterization of Martha both signifies her great respect for Jesus, and also something of a transgressive nature by leaving the house during a period of mourning.[14] This is reinforced by the nature of her dialogical challenge, lamenting Jesus' delay in arrival—"if you had been here, my brother would not have died" (11:21)—known to the audience, even if not to Martha. But here the lament directly leads to an "implied, oblique request" in 11:22, as she indirectly suggests that even at this point the present situation may have a new end.[15] But in response to Martha's knowledge that "God will give you whatever you ask," she receives a similarly oblique answer—a theological prompt—related to a relatively uncontroversial aspect of Jewish belief.

While some have suggested that Martha's initial response here represents a lack of faith, hinted at by the use of οἶδα rather than πίστις language,[16] this more likely highlights the Johannine misunderstanding trope for character development as previously displayed by Nicodemus or the Samaritan woman. Jesus' style of circuitous discourse in the Fourth Gospel gives ample opportunity for character development. Martha's response to Jesus' assertion that Lazarus "will rise again" is not an inadequate faith—for her response is accurate—but rather a misunderstanding of the immediacy of Jesus' words. Yet, the Evangelist does not pass up an opportunity to highlight a theological opportunity, emphasizing Jesus' words as the "resurrection and the life" (11:25–26), this time couched in a challenge of belief. This high Christological confession outstrips the Petrine confession a few chapters earlier (6:69) and ascribes Jesus the status of "the Messiah, the Son of God" ("ὁ χριστὸς ὁ υἱὸς τοῦ θεοῦ" [11:27]). If there was any doubt earlier (11:22) of the sincerity of Martha's faith, then what is expressed here should clear any lingering questions away. In the Johannine narrative, Martha is given the prime place in confessing faith in the messiah.[17]

Mary

Following Martha's confession and return to the village, the narrative finally turns to Mary's encounter with Jesus outside the village. While Mary's

13. Beirne, *Women and Men in the Fourth Gospel*, 121.

14. Keener, *John*, 843.

15. Keener, *John*, 844.

16. Haenchen, *John*, 2:61.

17. O'Day, "Martha: Seeing the Glory of God," 496.

challenge to Jesus (11:32) is effectively identical to that of Martha (11:21), differences in their characterization are soon apparent.[18] Where Martha appears to focus on the cognitive and dialogical, Mary pairs the discursive with physical and emotive responses: falling at Jesus' feet (11:32) and weeping (11:33).[19] Some commentators have criticized Mary at this juncture for failing to realize the high Christology present in the Fourth Gospel, especially given Martha's strong proclamation only a few verses earlier.[20] Thus, these critics assert Mary to be the secondary character in this narrative, dominated by Martha's declaration. But, as Keener observes, it is likely that "Mary's role in the narrative is second not because it is secondary, but because it is climactic,"[21] and as we have already seen she is given primacy in the earlier narrative engagement (11:1). Mary's emotions are contagious. In reaction to Mary's emotive engagement, Jesus is similarly "troubled" (ἐτάραξεν) and "grieved" (ἐνεβριμήσατο) and appears to be emotionally moved by Mary's weeping rather than Martha's confession, eventually culminating with his own weeping in 11:35. The ideal reader too would also be caught up with the intense emotions on display from Mary, Jesus, and the mourners. Thus, Mary's shorter initial engagement in the Fourth Gospel echoes her silence in the Lukan narrative, eliciting a cognitive narrative response without requiring significant narrated engagement. In comparison, Martha's longer discourse conveys a significant theological point, but does not drive the action within the narrative.

Rather, despite Martha's christological declaration, the evangelist returns to her misunderstanding with a brief note at the tomb entrance. In an encounter reminiscent of her practicality in the Lukan narrative, Martha objects that Lazarus will smell rather unpleasant after four days in the grave (11:39). Even here, Martha is given a mild rebuke, as Jesus asks a rhetorical question of her—and the Gospel audience—in 11:40. In many ways, this rhetorical question makes more sense for the Gospel audience, who have already been primed by Jesus' words to the disciples in 11:4, which "makes clear that Martha serves here as representative of the reader, who is also being addressed by Jesus' question."[22] At this point, the sisters recede into the background, as Lazarus comes out of the grave to the foreground of the narrative.

18. Miller, "Mary (of Bethany)," 477.

19. Carson, *Gospel According to John*, 415.

20. Lincoln, *Gospel According to Saint John*, 325.

21. Keener, *John*, 846.

22. Lincoln, *Gospel According to Saint John*, 328.

The Anointing

Yet, the sister's subsequent entrance into the narrative—in the prefigured anointing with perfume (11:1)—is inextricably linked to the graveside scene by the characters mentioned and the contrasting olfactory description. In this scene, Lazarus is initially keyed to unlock the memorialization of the raising scene from the previous chapter, before Martha is introduced in a serving role similar to that of the Lukan account (11:2). Mary's silent interaction here is similarly congruent with her approach in the previous chapter: an emotive expression of faith.[23] The anointing of Jesus' feet with perfume and using her hair to wipe them serves as a practical expression of her devotion, and contrasts strongly with the scheming of the previous passage.[24] Instead, it is Judas here who provides the narrative engagement, explicating one course of narrative cognition. Notably no agency is given here for Mary's own explanation for her motivation in the act; rather, the Evangelist uses the opportunity to examine Judas' motives in the engagement. Rather than the Lukan rebuke directed at Martha's interjection, the Johannine engagement utilizes Judas as the narrative foil for the audience. As such, one could question whether this scene is a Mary scene at all, or whether she merely acts as a *ficelles* for external plot advancement.

Comparing the Sisters

However, before we turn to the outcome of Mary and Martha's characterization in the Fourth Gospel, it is instructive to return to the challenges inherent within their comparison, and indeed the broader harmonization exercise inherent in such a project.

The Mary and Martha narrative appears in various forms throughout the fourfold gospel canon and is well attested in variety throughout our manuscripts. However, it is by no means clear as to the origins of the narrative. Certainly, the association of Mary and Martha together is displayed in their introduction in John 11:2, as the audience already has a connection of Martha with Mary's anointing in the following chapter. As Keener notes, this "suggests that John's audience already knows a form of the tradition in which the person who anointed Jesus was Mary."[25] But, as we have already noted, Mary's interaction in the anointing scene is exceedingly brief and in the Johannine context serves as a foil to Judas. Rather, in the Fourth Gospel,

23. Miller, "Mary (of Bethany)," 481.
24. Keener, *John*, 859.
25. Keener, *John*, 861.

there appears to be two interactions at hand, which we can examine separately: Lazarus' revivification narrative—which has no other parallel in the canon—and the anointing scene, which we shall focus on here.

The Johannine anointing scene finds significant parallels throughout the fourfold gospel canon, although a significant proportion of the details vary between accounts. The shared context narrates Jesus' physical anointing by a woman with precious perfume in a house. But, from this base the narratives diverge. While Matthew (26:6–13), Mark (14:3–9), and John (12:1–8) all situate the event in Bethany, Luke (7:36–50) gives no location. Each of the Synoptics situate the scene in the house of a character named Simon—who is either a leper (Matthew and Mark) or a Pharisee (Luke)—in comparison to the Johannine house of Lazarus, Mary, and Martha. Of course, perhaps the biggest difference is the naming of Mary in the Johannine account, in comparison to the Lukan "sinful woman" (7:37), and an unnamed woman in the other Synoptics. These differences did not go unnoticed in the early church, as we may see that Eusebius struggled to determine the relationship of the Johannine account with that of the Synoptics.[26]

Eusebius, in his apparatus, allocated the bulk of the Johannine anointing narrative within §98, which he categorizes to Canon 1, along with the Matthean (§276), Marcan (§158), and Lukan (§74) versions; this indicates that he believes the majority of the narratives deal with the same identifiable memory. However, the picture becomes more complex with Eusebius also allocating a subset of these to Canon 4: John §98, Matthew §277, and Mark §159. This presents some challenges, with apparent chronological discrepancies between the events, and changes in location between the narratives. Nevertheless Eusebius' canon apparatus pushes towards harmony, as O'Loughlin suggests "one crucial implication of the complex of four sections indicating a single event (§246//§158//§74//§98) being linked to a single purpose by the second set of parallels to John (§277//§159//§98) was that the event had to occur according to the single most precise time signature found in the four accounts."[27] Yet, one must still account for the discrepancies, and therefore "Eusebius clearly intends his users (by his choosing to place John 12:1 in section §97) to consider these diverging statements as simply errors of memory on the part of Matthew (and consequently affecting his abbreviator Mark) and Luke."[28]

Indeed, this attempt to harmonize the gospel narratives has flowed on to modern commentators, such as E.P. Sanders' assertion that the anointing

<hr>

26. O'Loughlin, "Harmonising the Anointings of the Christ," 9.

27. O'Loughlin, "Harmonising," 12.

28. O'Loughlin, "Harmonising," 12.

narratives rely on shared memories, or Craig Keener's approach to the events as "accurate preservation of tradition."[29] In contrast, other commentators have read the Johannine account as contradicting that of the Synoptics, as J.F. Coakley catalogues: "scholars seem to be able to rest in the judgment that the sequence of events in John is 'clearly secondary,' 'totally anomalous,' 'unintelligible,' 'absurd,' and even 'utter nonsense.'"[30] It is this same harmonization that is also applied to the Mary and Martha narrative in Luke 10:38–42, with corresponding attempts to relate it to John 11.

However, as John A. T. Robinson argued, the Synoptics need not be prioritized over the Johannine accounts, as is especially the case with attempts to harmonize their various narratives. Rather, as Jeremiah Coogan writes of Eusebius' canon tables, we can use these overlapping and parallel narratives to produce "new itineraries through the fourfold canonical gospel."[31] Therefore rather than reading the Johannine Mary and Martha as conflicting foils, as they are set up for in the Lukan narrative, we may ask what we find by reading them as separate but related characters. Instead of importing the contrast from the Lukan narrative, we may also find a differently nuanced reading of the Synoptic accounts of these characters. It is to this approach of reading the characters separately and then reading them back into Luke which we shall now turn.

Interpretive Characterization Options

We have already considered the basics of characterization for Mary and Martha in an earlier section; therefore, we will now turn to other interpretive options at hand.

Conflation

Working outside a dichotomous paradigm, one interesting suggestion has come from Elizabeth Schrader, who argues from a text critical approach that Martha's characterization in the Johannine account is a second-century interpolation, and that the original narrative only contained Mary's character. Drawing upon the text form in P^{66}, she argues that scribal errors and corrections to the manuscript suggest that a familiarity with a memorial form

29. Keener, *John*, 860.

30. Schnackenburg, Cribbs, Barrett, Goodenough, and Holst; cited in Coakley, "Anointing at Bethany and the Priority of John."

31. Coogan, "Mapping the Fourfold Gospel," 346.

that simply identified Mary as the sister of Lazarus, without any mention of Martha, could account for a certain scribal tradition that was inclined to omit Martha from the manuscript.[32] From this position, she posits "Perhaps the Mary of Luke 10 was somehow confused in second-century oral tradition with the Mary of John 11, and scribes began harmonizing their text of John 11 to Luke 10—possibly even going so far as to expand the actual content of the Lazarus story to include Martha."[33] While the text critical argument is outside the bounds of this chapter, in some ways conflating the two characters together assists in reducing the tension between the sisters, and goes some way to allowing for a reading that does not portray each sister as a one dimensional character—akin to the traditional reading of the Lukan dichotomy.

Indeed—as Schrader also notes—Boismard and Lamouille have suggested that the imported reading of the Lukan dichotomy stemmed from second-century disputes over whether service or contemplation should take priority in the church.[34] Rather, this allows for a single character—Mary—to portray a model of discipleship that incorporates both active service and contemplative devotion. However, while this presents a helpful interpretation for the characterization of the sisters, it relies upon a reconstruction of—admittedly significant—variant readings within the manuscript tradition and minimizes the benefits of the sisterly tension on display.

Paradox

In this vein, another option is to consider these characters outside of the dualistic paradigm that is writ large in interpreting the Fourth Gospel. Recently, Douglas Estes has suggested that dualistic paradigms should be repealed in favor of an understanding of these polar constructs in a framework of paradox.[35] A framework of paradox maintains a portrayal of polar constructs as dichotomous opposites but refuses the cognitive minimization in their reconciliation or resolution. Rather than seeking resolution via polarity, a paradoxical understanding suggests that attempting to hold both polarities together creates a synergy that is helpful for complexifying the dichotomy and reveals new insights or approaches. As Lewis et al. opine: "Managing paradox seeks 'both/and' alternatives that may foster novelty,

32. Schrader, "Was Martha of Bethany Added to the Fourth Gospel in the Second Century?," 365.

33. Schrader, "Was Martha of Bethany Added," 387.

34. Boismard and Lamouille, *La Vie Des Évangiles*, 83, 85, and 87–90.

35. Estes, "Dualism or Paradox?"

creativity, and long-term sustainability."[36] A similar reading is possible here for our two sisters. By characterizing Mary and Martha separately, a paradoxical tension is generated for the audience—including the broader conflict if they are familiar with the Lukan narrative. This paradoxical tension gives full agency to both sisters but asks the audience themselves to resolve the tension between their approaches to faith. A paradoxical interpretation here is asking whether faith that prioritizes discursive confession and service is compatible with faith that emphasizes emotional engagement and physical acts of devotion.

A paradoxical reading of the Mary and Martha characterization also presents a strong impetus for an audience to receive both aspects of characterization for their own identity formation. Psychologically, it is well recognized that identity is formed through narrative, and the continual construction of these narratives.[37] Significantly, even literary narratives provide this opportunity as it allows an audience to explore possible identity constructions as they walk alongside the characters in the narrative. Marco Cinnirella describes these identity constructions as "possible future social identities" that allow the assessment of an identity structure and processing of their consequence for the individual.[38] This is especially the case where characters—or in this case the confluence of two characters and their gender—presents an ambiguous or liminal characterization, presenting here the challenges and complexity of discipleship.[39] The apparent paradoxical dissonance between the characters forces a cognitive assessment of the importance for the differing possible future social identities on offer, but also allows for a creative engagement with a variegated hybridization of the paradox. As with other characters that are liminal in their own right, the duality of Mary and Martha allows for a deeper engagement with the identity outcomes than a simple *ficelles* would suggest.

Indeed, this is the intent of the Fourth Gospel. While the purpose statement of 20:31 indicates that the Gospel is recorded such that the audience may "believe . . . and have life in his name," this belief has secondary consequences. Throughout the discourse of the Gospel, we find that belief in Jesus contains ethical ramifications, many linked to frameworks of discipleship. As Chris Seglenieks observes, "the concept of belief is not made up of wholly discreet elements but rather it is a complex concept with numerous

---

36. Lewis, Andriopoulos, and Smith, "Paradoxical Leadership to Enable Strategic Agility.," 59.

37. McAdams and McLean, "Narrative Identity."

38. Cinnirella, "Exploring Temporal Aspects of Social Identity," 235.

39. Conway, "John, Gender, and Genre," 82.

facets . . . [namely] a cognitive aspect, a relational aspect, an ethical aspect, an ongoing aspect, and a public aspect."[40] In this context, the characters presented in the Fourth Gospel represent opportunities for the Evangelist to demonstrate what belief entails in all of its complexities. Therefore "the characters function to model parts of the ideal response, in order to evoke a response of genuine belief in the audience."[41] Here the audience's response is likely further reinforced by their prior knowledge of Mary within the community (John 11:2) and their prototypical status for the group.[42]

Evidence for initial responses to these presentations can be seen in the Johannine epistles, and especially 3 John. There the link between belief and action is writ large in the Elder's rebuke of Diotrephes' failing to welcome the brothers to the community (3 John 10). Here the belief in the command to love one another (John 13:34–35) is linked to the actions of hospitality within the believing community.

Reading Mary and Martha as Twinned Characters

Therefore, the apparent Lukan tension between Mary and Martha over service or devotion is clearly not presented in the same fashion in the Fourth Gospel. Both Martha and Mary show aspects of belief in Jesus which cannot be extricated from one another, nor does the Evangelist present them as contrasting *ficelles*. Rather, their characterization in the Fourth Gospel highlights their "twinned" nature, with each displaying complementary patterns of discipleship to the other. In this case, correct belief requires discursive confession, and service-based hospitality, along with emotive responses and acts of fidelity. Placing Mary and Martha in a paradoxical characterization forces the audience to reckon with their complex characterization in ways that treating them as completely separate, or completely conflated characters cannot. Furthermore, the dual Johannine characterization suggests a method of reading the Lukan narrative that defuses the sisters' stark contrast engendered by Martha's exasperated interjection. For a Johannine reader, the Lukan narrative need not generate a dualistic dissonance, but rather—to echo Matthew Crawford's observation of the Eusebian canon tables—can create "the conditions for a reader to construct new meaning from the textual juxtaposition."[43]

---

40. Seglenieks, *Johannine Belief and Graeco-Roman Devotion*, 106.

41. Seglenieks, *Johannine Belief*, 206.

42. Esler and Piper, *Lazarus, Mary and Martha*, 88.

43. Crawford, *Eusebian Canon Tables*, 104.

Bibliography

Beirne, Margaret Mary. *Women and Men in the Fourth Gospel: A Genuine Discipleship of Equals*. London: T & T Clark international, 2004.

Boismard, M. E., and A. Lamouille. *La Vie Des Évangiles: Initation à La Critique Des Textes*. Initiations. Paris: Editions du Cerf, 1980.

Carson, D. A. *The Gospel According to John*. Leicester, England: Grand Rapids, MI: Eerdmans, 1991.

Cinnirella, Marco. "Exploring Temporal Aspects of Social Identity: The Concept of Possible Social Identities." *European Journal of Social Psychology* 28:2 (March 1998) 227–48. https://doi.org/10.1002/(SICI)1099-0992(199803/04)28:2<227::AID-EJSP866>3.0.CO;2-X.

Coakley, J. F. "The Anointing at Bethany and the Priority of John." *Journal of Biblical Literature* 107, 2 (1988) 241–56. https://doi.org/10.2307/3267698.

Conway, Colleen M. "John, Gender, and Genre: Revisiting the Woman Question after Masculinity Studies." In *The Gospel of John as Genre Mosaic*, edited by Kasper Bro Larsen, 1st ed., 69–84. Göttingen: V&R, 2015. https://doi.org/10.13109/9783666536199.69.

Coogan, Jeremiah. "Mapping the Fourfold Gospel: Textual Geography in the Eusebian Apparatus." *Journal of Early Christian Studies* 25:3 (2017) 337–57. https://doi.org/10.1353/earl.2017.0032.

Crawford, Matthew R. *The Eusebian Canon Tables: Ordering Textual Knowledge in Late Antiquity*. First edition. Oxford Early Christian Studies. Oxford: Oxford University Press, 2019.

Esler, Philip F., and Ronald Piper. *Lazarus, Mary and Martha: Social-Scientific Approaches to the Gospel of John*. Minneapolis, MN: Fortress Press, 2006.

Estes, Douglas. "Dualism or Paradox? A New 'Light' on the Gospel of John." *The Journal of Theological Studies* 71:1 (April 1, 2020) 90–118. https://doi.org/10.1093/jts/flz168.

Haenchen, Ernst. *John: A Commentary on the Gospel of John*. 2 vols. Hermeneia. Philadelphia: Fortress Press, 1984.

Keener, Craig S. *The Gospel of John: A Commentary*. Grand Rapids, MI: Baker Academic, 2003.

Kittel, Gerhard & Gerhard Friedrich (editors). *Theological Dictionary of the New Testament: Volumes I—X. 10 Vols. Translated & Edited by Geoffrey W. Bromiley. Index (Vol. X) Compiled by Ronald Pitkin*. Grand Rapids, Michigan: William B. Eerdmans, n.d.

Lee, Dorothy A. *Flesh and Glory: Symbol, Gender, and Theology in the Gospel of John*. New York: Crossroad, 2002.

Lewis, Marianne W., Constantine Andriopoulos, and Wendy K. Smith. "Paradoxical Leadership to Enable Strategic Agility." *California Management Review* 56:3 (2014) 58–77.

Lincoln, Andrew. *The Gospel According to Saint John*. Grand Rapids, MI: Baker Academic, 2013.

MacDonald, Margaret Y. "The Women Householders of Acts in Light of Recent Research on Families." In *Finding A Woman's Place: Essays in Honor of Carolyn Osiek*, edited by David L. Balch and Jason T. Lamoreaux, 171–90. Eugene, OR: Wipf & Stock Pub, 2011.

Marshall, I. Howard. *Gospel of Luke: A Commentary on the Greek Text*. Grand Rapids, MI: Eerdmans, 1978.

McAdams, Dan P., and Kate C. McLean. "Narrative Identity." *Current Directions in Psychological Science* 22:3 (June 1, 2013) 233–38. https://doi.org/10.1177/0963721413475622.

Miller, Susan. "Mary (of Bethany): The Anointer of the Suffering Messiah." In *Character Studies in the Fourth Gospel: Narrative Approaches to Seventy Figures in John*, edited by Steven A. Hunt, D. F. Tolmie, and Ruben Zimmermann, 473–86. WUNT 314. Tübingen, Germany: Mohr Siebeck, 2013.

Nolland, John. *Luke 9:21–18:34*. Edited by Bruce M Metzger, David Allan Hubbard, and Glenn W Barker. Vol. 35b. WBC. Dallas, TX: Word Books, 1993.

Oepke, Albrecht. "Γυνή," Theological Dictionary of the New Testament (Grand Rapids, MI: Eerdmans, 1964) 776–789.

O'Day, Gail R. "Martha: Seeing the Glory of God." In *Character Studies in the Fourth Gospel: Narrative Approaches to Seventy Figures in John*, edited by Steven A. Hunt, D. F. Tolmie, and Ruben Zimmermann, 487–503. WUNT 314. Tübingen, Germany: Mohr Siebeck, 2013.

O'Loughlin, Thomas. "Harmonising the Anointings of the Christ—Eusebius and the Four-Gospel Problem." *Milltown Studies* 73: Summer (2014) 1–17.

Reid, Barbara E. *Choosing the Better Part? Women in the Gospel of Luke*. Collegeville, MN: Liturgical Press, 1996.

Schrader, Elizabeth. "Was Martha of Bethany Added to the Fourth Gospel in the Second Century?" *Harvard Theological Review* 110:3 (July 2017) 360–92. https://doi.org/10.1017/S0017816016000213.

Seglenieks, Chris. "Faith and Faithfulness in Luke." *Australian Biblical Review* 70 (2022) 48–64.

———. *Johannine Belief and Graeco-Roman Devotion: Reshaping Devotion for John's Graeco-Roman Audience*. WUNT 2 528. Tübingen: Mohr Siebeck, 2020.

Spencer, F. Scott. *Salty Wives, Spirited Mothers, and Savvy Widows: Capable Women of Purpose and Persistence in Luke's Gospel*. Grand Rapids, MI: Eerdmans, 2012.

Vinson, Richard. *Luke*. The Smyth & Helwys Bible Commentary. Macon, GA: Smyth & Helwys, 2008.

4.

Joy, Abiding, and Human Flourishing

JOHN MARK CAPPER

Abiding

"Who may abide the day of his coming?" So Handel's *Messiah* asks (Mal 3:2 [KJV])[1]. Abiding may not be off to a great start for Messiah-listening New Testament readers. Its vernacular usage has shifted in recent times as well. It has come to portray a sense of survival and toleration, often expressed negatively: "I can't abide so-and-so or such-and-such." Yet the term is–ahem–an abiding reality in biblical translation.

In John 15:4–6, the verb *menō* appears five times. It is translated "abide" in NRSV, following the KJV-RSV tradition, "remain" in NIV and NASB—although NASB 1995 reverts to "abide," "(be) joined" in CEV, "make your home" and be "joined" are used in The Message, "share the life" and "growing in" in J.B. Phillips, and so the list could continue. Its positivity—evoking trust, rest, hope, and faith—is not captured as well in alternative terms, such as stay, remain or, archaically, tarry. There is something about the use of *abiding*, used positively, that infers mutuality, security, and hope. It is a foundation for greater things.

---

1. Note that NRSV gives us "who can endure the day of his coming, and who can stand when he appears?"

Leon Morris sees the many uses of *menō* in John 15:4ff as a pointer to the mutuality of the two abidings: followers abiding in Christ, and Christ abiding in followers. These are inseparable.[2] Morris notes the term's usage amongst the Rabbis, such as "Where ten sit together and occupy themselves with the Torah, the Shekinah abides among them."[3]

The term is common, almost ubiquitous, in the text of John's Gospel. As Dorothy Lee points out:

> The verb *menō* ("abide") occurs about forty times throughout the narrative. Sometimes its usage is mundane, as in the English "stay" or "remain," but more often John conveys a deeper meaning, sometimes concealed in translation.[4]

The spiritual meanings are often operating at a metaphorical level. The clarity of this is explicated in a number of places in John's Gospel. The verb is first encountered in association with the Spirit's descent on Jesus (John 1:32) where John the baptizer says that he "saw the Spirit descending from heaven like a dove, and it remained (*menō*) on him."[5] No recital of other usages is needed here, since the verb's usage is concentrated in the Farewell Discourse (normally considered John 14–17)—our chapters of interest.

Lee notes that "the image of abiding is a unique term for discipleship in the Fourth Gospel."[6] This paper extends this to affirm the dual abiding— Christ in the disciples and the disciples in Christ—as the basis for Christian communities of discipleship, joy, and flourishing. It also notes abiding as exemplified in the image of the vine as drawing together the images of abiding in the Spirit, in truth, in light, in eternity, in love, and in God, further developed in 1 John 2:10; 17 and 4:15.

Karl Barth, to whom attention will be given, also notes the importance of the theme of abiding in the scriptures, noting the Johannine and Pauline writings particularly.[7] Abiding, for Barth, is the basis for standing firm. It is not "merely passive" but "demands obedience and is therefore a command."[8] It is the basis for the new identity of the followers of Jesus Christ. It is the foundation for their growth, in faith and in witness.

2. Morris, *John*, 670.

3. Morris, *John*, 670, n 13, quoting from E. M. Sidebottom, *Christ of the Fourth Gospel*, 1961, 37.

4. Lee, *Hallowed*, 143.

5. Biblical quotations are from NRSVA, unless otherwise noted.

6. Lee, *Hallowed*, 143. Note that the term is used twelve times in the three synoptic gospels combined.

7. Barth, CD II/2:600 explores the theme of abiding broadly.

8. CD II/2:601.

Flourishing

The Vine: It is one of many agricultural images used by Jesus, though in John's gospel it is one of two key ones. The shepherd of John 10 is the other. The significance of these two extended images should not be lost. The true shepherd was promised in many places to replace those who took too little care of God's flock (Isaiah 56; Jeremiah 23; Ezekiel 34, famously). Just as God as shepherd took delight in the flock, so God as vinedresser took delight in the vine and the fruit of the vine. Thus, the image of John 15, "I am the true vine," draws upon a significant tradition. It is immediately a word of promise and hope (See Ezekiel 17:1–8, Psalm 80:14, and Isaiah 5:1–7). Its place in this focal point in John's Gospel should come as no surprise. At this fulcrum in leveraging both images and insight, it invites deep exploration and reflection.

The vine has been a longstanding image in the church, from iconography to the name of church movements. I note warmly my colleague Dorothy Lee's consistent use of visual imagery in supporting her teaching and communication. I was unsurprised to find the Icon of Christ the Vine reproduced in *Hallowed in Truth and Love*.[9] It shows the image of Christ the vine and, through the branches, the connection to the twelve apostles, representing the church, all of them looking towards Jesus. The vine is conspicuously the source of life for all. The vine is the connection for all to Christ and from each to each other.

The imagery of the vine is the foundation for Jesus referring subsequently to his disciples as "friends," the ones for whom life is given (John 15:13)[10]. It is not only with Jesus that the disciples become friends. The preceding verse calls them to "love one another" as Jesus has loved them. To be a friend of Jesus is to be a friend of the friends of Jesus. Little wonder that Christian groups through the ages have taken the name "friends." The call to friendship makes animosity between disciples yet more debilitating, disappointing, and discomforting. It also points to the tragedy of animosity between people, or distrust, racism, sexism, and all that the denies the possibility of friendship and trust between those who, whilst perhaps not describing themselves as disciples, are still those whom Jesus has or may call into friendship.

9. Lee, *Hallowed*, 147.

10. Lee, *Hallowed*, 151–52.

Icon of the Vine

The liberty and yet demand of friendship requires a recognition of the other as equally worthy of the attention of God and the friendship of Jesus. Not only each is called "friend." Each is to be friend to the other. What a tragically withered vine it would be where there was competition or disdain between the branches! There is a code of conduct to be found in recognizing that one has the same roots and draws on the same means of sustenance as others.

Libby Byrne's Number 27 in her series *Resurrection: A Daily Navigation 2016*[11] evokes the struggle of abiding and flourishing in difficult times, where abiding is weak, and the soil appears bereft of nourishment. The picture is inspired by the Baobab Prison Tree, an ancient hollow *Adansonia gregorii* in Western Australia with a girth of 14.7 meters, reputedly used to imprison indigenous prisoners as part of the imposition of imported "justice." In this case, that evocation is the lack of trust between settler/invaders and the traditional (thousands of generations) of those with intimate connection with the land.

---

11. https://libbybyrne.com.au/gallery/resurrection-a-daily-navigation/#resurrection -27 accessed 13 June 2022, used with the artist's permission.

Number 27, *Resurrection: A Daily Navigation 2016*, by Libby Byrne

Joy

The image of the vine conjures delight: protection (if limited) from the sun, sweetness in the promise of the grape harvest, and for the patient, the dangerous pleasure of the gift of wine. The promise is significant. The vine is, perhaps, the most eschatological of the agricultural images of Jesus. Grounded in nature, shaped through human care, and refined through careful technology, the grape vine, possibly more than the olive tree, holds out future promise. It symbolizes hope.

In the vine is the promise and hope of celebration. The vine gives hope of the harvest. Harvest is its own work and pleasure. It brings the hope of further blessing. In the true vine this is not just personal pleasure. It is hospitality and the shared table. And it is not simply a joy of this world. It is a joy of celebration to come. It is a joy that may in fact be a transformed sorrow (John 16:20).

Jesus' statement rings loud: amid the call to love one another and to love God, "these things I have spoken to you, that my joy may be in you, and that your joy may be full" (John 15:11). This is not a passive love that is called forth. It is an ebullient love that overflows in joy. It is the triune joy of the Father, Son, and Holy Spirit. As Karl Barth puts it:

> God's glory is the indwelling joy of His divine being which as
> such shines out from Him, which overflows in its richness,
> which in its super-abundance is not satisfied with itself but com-
> municates itself.[12]

This shining out is seen in the person of Jesus. It is he who shares this joy, on behalf of God, in the world at its creation and through the disciples, in particular at its redemption. The active engagement of God with the world is an expression of love and an invitation to joy. Its present and its future dimensions are intrinsic to the incarnation and to the life of disciples of Christ.

For Barth, this goes beyond mere understanding of one's place in the divine purpose. It is the foundation for understanding God and God's world.

> All God's works must be understood also and decisively from
> this point of view. All together and without exception they take
> part in the movement of God's self-glorification and the com-
> munication of His joy.[13]

This then is the basis, in Barth, for understanding the love of God for the world (*kosmos*) and the ground of understanding the gift of love, for all who believe in Jesus (John 3:16). In speaking of all of God's works, including humankind, Barth says that

> God wills them and loves them because, far from having their
> existence of themselves and their meaning in themselves, they
> have their being and existence in the movement of the divine
> self-glorification, in the transition to them of His immanent
> joyfulness.[14]

To a brief exploration of how the immediacy of God's being, in glory and joy, are engaged with human joy and life, we now turn.

The Di-vine nature

The basis of Barth's engagement with joy as part of the divine nature is the nature of glory as presented in the Scriptures and the sense that God is not sedentary but dynamic, not quiescent but engaged. In this, says Barth, God's glory is fundamentally joyful.[15]

12. Barth, CD II/1:647.

13. Barth, CD II/1:647.

14. Barth, CD II/1:648.

15. Barth, CD II/1:655.

Whichever technical terms are used (if any)—coinherence, circumincession, perichoresis—the truth communicated by a relational view of the triune nature of God is of an abiding through mutuality. In John 14, we see Philip reminded that to see the Son is to see the Father. "As the Gospel narrative progresses, the meaning of abiding unfolds."[16]

Just as the Trinity is historically considered the logical precondition for the incarnation of the eternal Son, so "the imagery of abiding and homecoming, in this Gospel, is one way of outlining the incarnation."[17] It is also a prefiguration of the eternal reality of the relationship of mutual abiding, wherein the one grafted into the vine is the one who inherits the fullness of the benefits of that ingrafting, tasted in this world and fully transformed in the world to come.Bartolomé Esteban Murillo's *The Heavenly and Earthly Trinities* (c.1681) shows the connection that the Christ child brings between the triune eternal nature and human nature, fully human and fully divine, linking the eternal relationality of heaven to the temporal human experience of relationality. What is interesting about the picture is that it is not a static image of relational rigidity. Rather, the movement in the painting is both of the Father actively sending the Son and the son being received by human parents. It seems also to be an invitation through the child to come, to enter, and—dare we say—to abide in the place of eternal belonging.

"The Spirit is the one who enables this (trinitarian) love, who channels it, both within the divine being and between the world and God."[18] Whether we begin our reflection with the eternal love which is the trinity or with the love of God seen in the incarnation, the source lies in the love of God. The love of God for the world and the mutuality of love within the life of God are mutually affirming. The fullness of God is seen in Jesus ("If you have seen me, you have seen the Father" [John 14:9]). Thus it is that Lee can claim: "The inner relationship between Father and Son, through the agency of the Spirit, is archetypal also for discipleship. God's love comes first and human love is given in response."[19]

16. Lee, *Abiding*, 127.

17. Lee, *Hallowed*, 148.

18. Lee, *Hallowed*, 150.

19. Lee, *Hallowed*, 150.

The Heavenly and Earthly Trinities, by Bartolomé Esteban Murillo

Abiding Community[20]

The first disciples, witnesses to John the baptizer's observation of the Spirit abiding on Jesus (John 1:32–33), ask where he is staying (*menō*) (1:38) and they remained (yes, *menō*) with Jesus. From the outset, John has described being with and following Jesus in terms of deep engagement, in terms of abiding. That the pinnacle of teaching in the farewell discourse should engage and further build on the concept of abiding should come as no surprise to us.

The call to follow Jesus is a call to community. There are, as the saying goes, no solitary disciples, since all are called into the fellowship of Christ—a

20. Further on this, see John Capper, "Divine Joy and Human Gladness in Life in Christ," in *Wesleyan Perspectives on Human Flourishing,* ed. Dean Smith and Rob Fringer, Wipf & Stock, 2021, 44–62.

fellowship with God and with each other. The call is to abiding, engagement, participation. We find it expressed clearly in Calvin:

> For we await salvation from him not because he appears to us afar off, but because he makes us, engrafted into his body, participants not only in all his benefits but also in himself.[21]

The abiding is not simply for one's own identity, salvation, or ministry. It is for the benefit of others. It is pointed to by Morris, who notes that "abiding is the necessary prerequisite for fruitfulness."[22] It is picked up by Lee, who points to the foundational aspect of abiding for Christian life and learning. "In this Gospel, believing and learning are set in the context of disciples' abiding on Jesus."[23]

The mutuality and communality is seen in an earlier part of the Gospel (John 6:51–59) where feeding on the flesh and blood of Jesus is a means of abiding in and with Jesus and the community of Jesus, in language "unambiguously symbolic."[24] The mutuality of this abiding—"they abide in me and I in them" (John 6:56)—should be noted. It points to and derives from the mutual abiding of the Father and the Son (John 6:57; See also 17:11; 17:22–24).[25]

Thus "in John's Gospel, disciples find their true home in God and God finds a true home in them."[26] The connections between abiding, love[27], trust, and hope cannot be ignored. They are often, in John's Gospel, found explored through the metaphor of friendship, also an image of mutual self-giving. The purpose of this is both temporal and eternal: "so that they may be one, as we are one" (John 17:11).

Kathryn Tanner suggests that

> Participating in God is just what it means to be a creature. God is (for example) life itself, life through itself, while everything else receives its life from God, without simply being it, in and of itself. Any creature therefore has life in some degree or fashion and can lose it. Expressing much the same thing in a Thomistic way, one could say God does not participate in being but is it: to

---

21. Calvin, *Institutes*, III.2.24.

22. Morris, *John*, 670.

23. Lee, *Hallowed*, 143.

24. Lee, *Hallowed*, 145.

25. See also Lee, *Hallowed*, 145.

26. Lee, *Hallowed*, 148.

27. Lee, *Hallowed*, 149.

be God just is to be; in God there is no distinction between what God is (essence) and the fact that God is (existence).[28]

This analogy of being takes us only so far. It is in self-giving love that abiding becomes possible, thus flourishing and joy are enabled in some form of relationality. In the gift of self-giving lies the possibility of the response of self-giving. In love sustained is the possibility of life transformed and love renewed.

Abiding means participation. Abiding calls to the fullness of performance of life in the world. It is a performance informed and empowered by participation in the divine life through abiding in Christ. Abiding in Jesus, and thus participating in the life of the eternally living being of the triune God, is a call to action. As Barth puts it

> It is their destiny to offer a true if inadequate response in the temporal sphere to the jubilation with which the Godhead is filled from eternity to eternity.[29]

This belonging and participating in the life of God brings transformation in the temporal sphere. It is transformation through light (another favorite Johannine image). Barth describes it as "light from the darkness of the cross of Jesus Christ into the darkness of our existence" which brings about "a definite illumination. And in so doing, even in all the sadness which may otherwise engulf us, it effects a clear and invincible joyfulness. . . . To live in this light is always to have joy."[30]

A useful summary of the centrality of community is found in Dietrich Bonhoeffer.

> Alone you stood before God when God called you: alone you had to answer that call; alone you had to struggle and pray, and alone you will die and give an account to God. . . . But the reverse is also true. Let those who are not in community beware of being alone. Into the community you were called. In the community of the called you bear the cross, you struggle, you pray. You are not alone, even in death, and on the Last Day you will be only one member of the great congregation of Jesus Christ.[31]

28. Kathryn Tanner, In the Image, 130.

29. Barth, CD II/1:648.

30. Barth, CD IV/2:311.

31. Bonhoeffer, *Life Together*, 77.

A spirituality of joyful Johannine abiding

To conclude this study, I turn to three aspects of community: meals, ministry, and reconciliation.

Meals

As the festivals of the old covenant included eating and drinking, and were in many cases family meals writ large, so the new covenant, to be founded through the body of Jesus, is encapsulated in the giving of bread and wine at the table of friends. The Passover remembrance of the exodus meant remembering with joy the deliverance brought through the death of a lamb. The new deliverance is through the death of "Christ our Passover, sacrificed for us"[32] and is to be recalled with joy and gratitude. The recollection takes the shape of a meal.

In fact, not only is the "abiding lesson" of the Farewell Discourse taught in Jerusalem, it is also enunciated at a meal table. Jesus gathered with all "sorts and conditions" of people around food. It is a context for spoken and seen lessons, relating to hospitality and generosity, and underlining the fact that God loves all and looks into the heart of each person. But the fact that Jesus taught so often at table—and that the gospel writers chose so to record the locations—is important.[33] At the point of acknowledging one's createdness in eating, at the location of recognizing one's own dependence on God's created order, Jesus reveals the need for something more, and shows himself to be the answer. With Jesus at the table, the confluence of createdness with redemption is to be found. The meeting of physical need is symbolic of the feeding of hunger in its deepest, spiritual form. The kingdom of heaven is revealed as a banquet (Rev 19) and Jesus tells his disciples that he will not eat or drink until he does so anew in the kingdom of heaven (Matt 26:29; Mark 14:25), where he promises them that he goes "so you may eat and drink at my table in my kingdom" (Luke 22:30).

The journey of meals and mission, led until now by Jesus, was in future to be led by the Spirit to ensure the ongoing witness of the community of those in Christ (John 14:16–17; Acts 1:8). To be in mission is to know joy (Luke 10:17 tells us that the seventy returned to Jesus *with joy*). Mission is sent from a community of joy with an eye on the eternal banquet, to invite others to share in the feast—and the joy.

32. A biblical theme picked up and amplified, typically in liturgy, through such devices as the "Easter Anthems."

33. See, for instance, Kelley, "Meals with Jesus in Luke's Gospel"

Bernard of Clairvaux invited his monks to engage in a life of discerning spiritual joy, warning them of false joys and pointing them to the shared joy of community which prefigures the kingdom of God. Its joy, notes Bernard, is ultimately joy in the Holy Spirit.[34] Thus "Joy found. . . in God frees the heart and expresses itself in praise uniting human joy with angelic joy."[35] Joy ultimately "is about relationship with God."[36]

The glorification of the Son of Man was to be in death and the resultant bearing of much fruit (John 12:23). The fourth gospel places its teaching on "abiding in God," in the midst of Jerusalem, the place of both joy and misery. To be in God is to live in love, to keep the commandments and thus to have Jesus' joy and with it completeness of the disciples' own joy (John 15:4, 5, 8–11).

Ministry

In John, the call to the first disciples is a call to "come and see" where Jesus is staying (*menō*) (John 1:39). They saw where he was staying (*menō*) and stayed (*menō*) with him (John 1:40). Their call to being sent and being filled with the Holy Spirit is focused in John 14–17, where the call to receive and to abide reinforces and strengthens the empowerment for ministry when Jesus will no longer be physically present with them. The Father, who abides (*menō*)) in Jesus (John 14:10), is the one who will give the Spirit who will be with (*menō*)! them forever (John 14:16)[37]. They will know the truth through the Spirit of Truth abiding (*menō*) in them (John 14:17).

This raises a question for contemporary formal ministry selection which often has, to my mind, an unhealthy concern with hearing of the "call to ministry." What matters in empowerment for ministry according to the Farewell Discourse is the openness to abide, to receive the Spirit, and from that to exercise hospitality with joy. It is this spiritual fruit that abides and is evidence of the powerful equipping work of the Holy Spirit, allowing the disciple to abide in Christ and Christ in them. This is about suitability for ministry. It is the basis for being chosen to serve.

It is the ones who abide and in whom Jesus' words abide who will see prayer answered (John 15:7) and who are called to keep the commandments (John 15:9). And, significantly, it is those in whom love will abide who will also find themselves having God's joy abiding and being made full

---

34. Div 18.1; SBOp 6/1:157, cited in Supper, 358.

35. Supper, "Spiritual Joy in Saint Bernard," 359.

36. Supper, "Spiritual Joy in Saint Bernard," 370.

37. Morris, *John*, 644 notes that "'abiding' points to a permanent relation."

(John 15:10, 11) both within them and amongst them. This is the call for disciples. Those who are chosen by Jesus are called to bear fruit that will remain (*menō*), again)—that is, that will last—and who have and know joy. Barth stated that "the whole meaning and purpose of the mission of Jesus is to bring joy."[38] The disciples are invited to share in this joy, not as servants, but as friends (John 15:15). As Brian McLaren notes, "The early Christians elevated the equality of friendship rather than the supremacy of hierarchy."[39] It is these called, abiding, and joyful ones who will receive what they ask of the Father (John 15:16). These, surely, are those who, chosen by God, should also be chosen by Christ's church to bring the good, glad, and joyful news of the gospel invitation to abide in Christ.

Reconciliation

Our focus so far has been on abiding as a basis for joy and flourishing and has concentrated on the first half of the Farewell Discourse. Whilst *menō* does not appear in chapters 16 and 17, they build on this foundation. Jesus has spoken these words "to keep you from stumbling" (John 16:1). They now have the basis of truth and the Spirit (who abides in them) and who will lead them into all truth (John 16:13). Jesus' abiding in the Father means that he will return to the Father (John 16:16–19) with the result that the disciples will have pain, but it will be pain that will turn into joy (John 16:20).

The tragic imperfection of the community of faith neither denies faith nor eliminates witness, though both may be tarnished. The with-ness of Jesus and the Father, and of God with the community in their mutual abiding, means that growth may come from what seems dormant. That life comes from death, is, of course, the climax message of John's Gospel. In the worst of times, that God is with us and that we are in Christ, provides hope. This is illustrated vividly in Libby Byrne's etching, showing the vine flourishing behind, or perhaps from, barbed wire.[40]

38. Barth, CD IV/2:182.

39. McLaren, "Christianity's Violence Problem."

40. Libby Byrne, (2017). Hope, Dry point etching on rag paper, 297 x 420 mm, Melbourne. A version of this work is also available on https://libbybyrne.com.au/gallery/an-ordinary-gift used with permission of the artist.

Hope, by Libby Byrne

It is this transformative power of abiding and of joy that will allow the disciples themselves to flourish, even as they are left alone (John 16:32). They have had the truth made known to them by Jesus (John 17:6) and now Jesus will be glorified in them (John 17:10; 22–24). The return of Jesus to the Father is the basis that they, the disciples, "may be one, even as we are one" (John 17:11), and that they may have their joy "made complete in themselves" (John 17:13).

In this completeness of joy and friendship, abiding is the ground by which they may be one, so that the mission of Jesus may continue. The end is, as Jesus declared to the Father, "that the world may know that you have sent me and have loved them even as you have loved me." (John 17:23).

The final curious dual usage of *menō* is in John 21:22, 23 where Jesus is asked by Peter about the disciple Jesus loved. There Jesus speaks of the possibility that the disciple remains (*menō*) until Jesus returns. It is an interesting pointer to the eternal value, the permanency, and power of abiding.

The oneness of the abiding (and joy) of the eternal trinity, brought to the earth in the incarnation of the Son, is the basis for the life of shared joy and witness of the disciples and the subsequent Christian community, so that all may abide the day of God's coming.

AND THANK YOU

I have not touched on the important aspects of abiding as a motif to open up feminist discourse, as began Dorothy Lee's published work in this important area[41] in 1977, nor have I explored the liturgical or sensory aspects (save some artworks) evoked by joy and abiding.[42] What I have enjoyed doing is engaging texts which have inspired and sustained Dorothy as scholar and teacher. And friend.

Bibliography

Barth, Karl. *Church Dogmatics*. Translated by G. T. Thomson et al. Edinburgh: T. & T. Clark, 1936–77.

Bonhoeffer, Dietrich. *Life Together*, New York: Harper & Row, 1954.

Calvin, John. *The Institutes of the Christian Religion*. Translated by Henry Beveridge, 1559.

Kelley, Robert L Jr. "Meals with Jesus in Luke's Gospel," *Horizons in Biblical Theology: An International Dialogue*, 17, 2, (1995) 123–131.

Lee, Dorothy. "Abiding in the Fourth Gospel: A Case-Study in Feminist Biblical Theology." *Pacifica*, 10. (1997) 123–136.

———. "Friendship, Love and Abiding in the Gospel of John." *Transcending boundaries: contemporary readings of the New Testament*. Libreria Ateneo Salesiano, Rome, 2005.

———. "The Gospel of John and the Five Senses." *JBL* 129, (2010) 115–127.

———. *Hallowed in truth and love: spirituality in the Johannine literature*. Preston, Vic: Mosaic, 2011.

———. 'Spirituality and the Gospel of John'. *The Bible in Transmission*, (Spring 2015) 14–16.

McLaren, Brian in conversation with Richard Rohr, Center for Action and Contemplation, "Christianity's Violence Problem" https://cac.org/daily-meditations/christianitys-violence-problem-2022-05-23/.

Morris, Leon Lamb. *The Gospel According to John*. NICNT, Eerdmans, 1971.

Sidebottom, E. M. *The Christ of the Fourth Gospel; in Light of First-Century Thought*. London: SPCK, 1961.

41. Lee, *Abiding*.

42. Lee, "Gospel of John and the Five Senses."

Smith, Dean G. and Fringer, Rob A., *Wesleyan Perspectives on Human Flourishing.* USA-OR: Eugene. Wipf and Stock, 2021.

Supper, Sylvie. "Spiritual Joy in the Works of Saint Bernard," *Cistercian Studies Quarterly* 39.4 (2004) 357–370.

Tanner, Kathryn, "In the Image of the Invisible." In *Apophatic Bodies: Negative Theology, Incarnation, and Relationality*, ed. Chris Boesel and Catherine Keller. Fordham University Press, 2010, 117–134.

5.

Salvation as Liberation

MARY L. COLOE

Preface

I am delighted to contribute to this celebration of Dorothy Lee's life and ministry as she reaches this milestone. Dorothy has been my teacher, advisor, mentor, inspiration and, of course, my friend within the Melbournian Johannine "Schule."[1] Dorothy's work on symbolic narratives,[2] and her award-winning book on the ramifications of the incarnation,[3] have been very influential in my research and writing. In particular, I am indebted to her careful analysis of the symbolism of divine fatherhood. She writes,

> The Johannine understanding of divine fatherhood thus involves a two-way movement. On the one hand, God's fatherhood, symbolically portrayed in the Father-Son relationship, is an outward movement of giving away power, surrendering selfhood as autonomous and self-sufficient. Such vulnerability places God on the side of the vulnerable, the outcast, and the

1. The "Schule" consists of Dorothy Lee, Frank Moloney, Brendan Byrne and myself; we have all written on the Gospel of John and companioned each other in our research.

2. Lee, *Symbolic Narratives.*

3. Lee, *Flesh and Glory.*

powerless. On the other hand, divine fatherhood draws others into the filial relationship between God and Jesus, so that the Father-Son relationship becomes the fundamental icon of God's relations with the world.[4]

Becoming children of God is a statement of Jesus' mission (1:13) and provides an essential metaphor for understanding the nature of "salvation" in this Gospel. As always in John, metaphors coalesce, as will become clearer in this essay.

In the Johannine narrative, the first title ascribed to Jesus comes from the lips of John, the one who bears witness to Jesus: "Behold, the Lamb of God who takes away the sin of the world!" (John 1:29). Since John has been introduced with high credentials as one coming from God to bear witness (1:6), his words, and therefore this first title, must shape our reading of the following narrative, and our understanding of Jesus' mission. In what follows, I will examine the two key phrases in John's title—"lamb of God" and "sin of the world"—and then what it might mean to "take away" the sin of the world. I believe that this examination will reveal John's particular understanding of salvation as an act of liberation.

Lamb of God

As a title, this phrase is ambiguous, since within Israel's tradition and rituals there are many possible references, with three common suggestions: the paschal lamb (Exod 12:1–14), the Suffering Servant who is compared to a lamb that is silent at its slaughter (Isa 53:7–8) and the lamb that God provides for Abraham, to replace the sacrifice of Isaac (Gen 22:1–20).[5] In addition, there is the apocalyptic lamb (Rev 7:17) favored by Dodd,[6] and also the twice-daily holocaust sacrifice of the Tamid Lamb.[7] The meaning of the title remains suspended until the narrative has unfolded, only then will this first title of Jesus be clarified.

---

4. Lee, "Iconic 'Father' of Jesus."

5. In her 2010 Presidential Address to the Catholic Biblical Association of America, Sandra Schneiders summarized these three suggestions. See, Schneiders, "Lamb of God and the Forgiveness of Sin(s)," 1–29.

6. Dodd, *Interpretation*, 230–238.

7. I proposed this Tamid lamb in 2013, but have since changed my view, as this essay will show. See, Coloe, "'Behold the Lamb of God,'" 337–50.

There are clues in John's passion narrative that Jesus dies as "the Passover lamb." John follows a different time sequence to the Synoptic Gospels and portrays Jesus' death occurring on the eve of Passover. The Jewish authorities do not enter the Praetorium to avoid ritual defilement that would prevent them eating the Passover (19:28). Several times, it is noted that his death occurs on "the day of preparation" (19:14, 31, 42). The time detail when Pilate hands Jesus over to death, at the sixth hour (19:14), coincides with the time the first lambs are taken into the Temple for ritual killing (m. Pesah 5.3). In response to Jesus' thirst, a soldier dips a sponge into a jar of sour wine and passes this up to Jesus on a "branch of hyssop" (19:29). When the people of Israel were preparing for the escape from Egypt, they used a bunch of hyssop to brush the blood of the lamb on the lintels of their doors (Exod 12:22). John uses hyssop in this scene, not for its practical use, but as an allusion to the Exodus event, and the slaying of the Passover lamb. Following Jesus' death, the soldiers break the legs of the two crucified with Jesus, but note that he is already dead. They confirm his death by piercing his side followed by a scripture reference: "none of his bones shall be broken" (19:36). Given the constellation of Passover imagery, the most like reference is to the Passover lamb (Exod 12:46).

In these many ways, Jesus is imaged as the Passover lamb. The Passover lamb, therefore, is the most likely referent to John's statement "Behold the lamb of God" (1:29).[8] But this raises a serious difficulty, since the Passover Lamb was not associated with "taking away sin." More will be said on "taking away" following the analysis of the second part of John's title—"sin of the world."

The Sin of the World

When reading John's Gospel, Adele Reinhartz proposes that we read the narrative as telling three different "tales." At one level, the Gospel narrates the story of the historical Jesus in the early part of the first-century CE. At another level, it provides insight into the experience of the later Johannine community in their struggle with Judaism after the destruction of the temple in 70 CE. But beyond these "tales" lies a larger "meta-tale" that has "the cosmos as its setting and eternity as its time-frame."[9]

---

8. Zumstein notes that the evangelist creates a significant *inclusio* between the beginning and end of the narrative through the "Passover lamb" imagery. Zumstein, *L'Évangile*, 79.

9. Reinhartz, *Word in the World*, 4.

John's title "lamb of God," then speaks of the "sin of the world." He is not referring to the personal sins of individuals, but cosmic sin as a world power of evil. The view that the current age was held captive by a power of evil developed in "segments of early Judaism from ca. 200 B.C.E to ca. 200 C.E."[10] David Aune describes this way of thinking as narrative theology:

> " . . . centering in the belief that (1) the present world order, regarded as both evil and oppressive, is under the temporary control of Satan and his human accomplices, and (2) that this present evil world order will shortly be destroyed by God and replaced by a new and perfect order corresponding to Eden before the fall. During the present evil age, the people of God are an oppressed minority who fervently expect God, or his specially chosen agent the Messiah, to rescue them."[11]

This apocalyptic view pervades the Gospel, and colors what is meant by "the world," which has various meanings in the Fourth Gospel; both the world as the arena of God's creation (1:1) and love (3:16), but also the world as an "inimical force" in opposition to God's purposes (15:18).[12] The cosmic force opposed to God is termed sin and it has power to enslave: "everyone who commits sin is a slave to sin" (8:34). To take away this world-sin requires more than atonement, or forgiveness, it is a power-struggle between Jesus and the "Ruler of this world," and Jesus is victorious: "Now is the judgment of this world; now the ruler of this world will be driven out" (12:31; also 16:18, 33). The human drama is penetrated by cosmic powers and depicted through the characters in the narrative in their response to Jesus.

In the trial before Pilate, Jesus testifies/witnesses to the truth (18:37), but Pilate and the Jewish authorities refuse to believe him. When the chief priests and police demand that he be crucified (19:6) and Pilate surrenders Jesus to them, these characters enact the desires of their "father, the devil" (8:44). On this human stage, the power of God, incarnate in Jesus, confronts the cosmic power of Evil, embodied in Pilate, the chief priests and police who call for his crucifixion (19:6).

Furthermore, while Pilate appears to be the judge, it is unclear who is seated on the judgment bench (19:13)—Pilate or Jesus[13]—the narrative

---

10. Aune, "Understanding Jewish and Christian Apocalyptic," 236.

11. Aune, "Jewish and Christian Apocalyptic," 256.

12. Stuckenbruck, "Evil in Johannine and Apocalyptic Perspective," 200–201.

13. If it is Pilate, it means reading the verb ἐκάθισεν in an intransitive sense—Pilate sat himself. But it could also be read in a transitive sense with Jesus as the object—Pilate sat Jesus on the judgment seat (βῆμα). Grammatically, either sense is possible. The question is, what might the evangelist have intended—to be historically plausible— in

calls for the readers to decide. I think Jesus is seated on the judgment seat.[14] While Jesus sits in silence on the judgment seat, his judgment has already been proleptically given, "Now is the judgment of this world; now the ruler of this world will be driven out" (12:31). As Judith Kovacs states, "[T]he cross is not merely the metaphorical jumping off point for Jesus's reascent to his heavenly Father. It is the locus of a cosmic battle, in which Jesus achieves a decisive victory over Satan."[15] Jesus had assured his disciples: "In the world you face persecution. But take courage; I have conquered the world" (16:33).

The final words in Jesus' public ministry are on judgment—"The one who rejects me and does not receive my word has a judge; on the last day the word that I have spoken will serve as judge, for I have not spoken on my own, but the Father who sent me has himself given me a commandment about what to say and what to speak" (12:48–49). In the "hour" of Jesus, the last day has come and so the "ruler of this world" now sits under the judgment of Jesus' word. Haenchen observes that it is not Pilate who is the judge but Jesus, and "he speaks in silence, by sitting on the seat of judgment with his mock crown, and purple mantle."[16]

Jesus was sent to bring salvation and eternity life to all who believe (3:16). Opposed to him is a power of evil called Satan (13:27), the devil (13:2), the evil one (17:15) and the ruler of this world (12:31; 14:30; 16:11).[17] Jesus is in the world, but does not belong to this world as he says to "the Jews" opposed to him, "You are from below, I am from above; you are of this world, I am not of this world" (8:23). This power of evil influences the actions of the characters such as Judas, entering into him when he had received the morsel of bread (13:21).

---

which case Pilate would sit in judgment; or ironically to stress that it is Jesus who is making the judgment? For more detail on this extensive debate among interpreters see Brown, *Death of the Messiah*, vol. 2: 1388–93.

14. This position is well argued by Lincoln, *Gospel according to Saint John*, 469. Here, Lincoln refers to Justin's *Apology* (1.35) where it is understood that Jesus sat on the judgment seat: "And as the prophet spoke, they tormented Him, and set Him on the judgment-seat, and said, Judge us."

15. Kovacs, "'Now shall the ruler of this world be driven out,'" 246.

16. Haenchen, *John 2*, 188. Haenchen also refers to Justin, Apology 1.35.6, and *Gospel of Peter* 1:7 to show that this tradition of Jesus sitting on the judgment seat was known in the early centuries (187).

17. On the power of Evil operating in the crucifixion see Kovacs, "'Now shall the ruler of this world be driven out,'" 227–47; Koester, "Why was the Messiah Crucified?," 163–80. Dennis, "The 'Lifting up of the Son of Man,'" 678–91.

Taking away World Sin

Having established that Jesus dies as the Passover lamb and that in his ministry and death he conquers the cosmic power of evil called "the ruler of the world," what is the relationship between the Passover lamb and "taking away" world sin?

First, some clarification about the function of the Passover lamb. This was not considered a sacrifice for atonement or forgiveness of sin, "bulls and goats were the more common offering for these purposes (Lev 4:1–31)."[18] While the Passover lamb was not considered a sin-offering, Hylen writes, that "at Jesus death, John evokes the story of Israel's salvation from slavery in Egypt."[19] Liberation from slavery is explicitly raised in John's Gospel in Jesus' heated dialogue with his former followers and this dialogue sheds light on the significance of the Passover lamb imagery in the Johannine passion.

> Then Jesus said to the Jews *who had believed in him*,[20] "If you continue in my word, you are truly my disciples; and you will know the truth, and the truth will make you free (ἐλευθερώσει)." They answered him, "We are descendants of Abraham and have never been slaves to anyone (οὐδενὶ δεδουλεύκαμεν πώποτε). What do you mean by saying, 'You will be made free'?" (8:31–33).

In answering this question, Jesus speaks of those who sin as being "slaves" and then draws a contrast between the slave whose place in a household is not guaranteed, but reliant on the will of the master, whereas the son, because of his filial relationship, has a permanent place in the household.

> Jesus answered them, "Very truly, I tell you, everyone who commits sin is a slave to sin. The slave does not have a permanent place in the household; the son has a place there forever" (8:34–35)

This brief parable is then applied to himself as the son able to liberate a slave. "So if the Son makes you free, you will be free indeed (John 8:36)."

Lying behind this discussion about freedom and slavery lies an apocalyptic understanding that the current world, is ensnared by a power of Evil, leading individuals to sin.

---

18. Hylen, "Lamb," *NIDB* 3 (2008) 563. Similarly, Menken writes, "the blood of the Passover sacrifice has an apotropaic, not an expiatory function." See, Menken, "'Lamb of God'," 4–7.

19. Hylen, "Lamb," 563.

20. Emphasis added.

"... let not the spirit of Belial rule over them to accuse them before Thee, and to ensnare them from all the paths of righteousness, so that they may perish from before Thy face. But they are Thy people and Thy inheritance, which thou hast delivered with thy great power from the hands of the Egyptians: create in them a clean heart and a holy spirit, and let them not be ensnared in their sins from henceforth until eternity"(Jubilees 1:19–20).[21]

Who is your father?[22]

The comparison between the freedom of the son/daughter, and the bondage of slavery within the household, leads into the issue of one's paternity. Jesus' former followers claim to have the freedom of being children of Abraham (8:33, 39), but Jesus' challenges this claim by pointing to their behavior.

In an earlier confrontation regarding the Sabbath, Jesus had argued from a principle, that sons do what their father does—"whatever the father does, the son does likewise" (5:19). This same principle is now restated—"If you were Abraham's children, you would be doing what Abraham did" (8:39). In trying to kill Jesus, these opponents show that "you are from your father the devil, and you choose to do your father's desires. He was a murderer from the beginning" (8:44).[23] Rather than being children in the household of God, these opponents show by their behavior that they are children of Satan, in bondage to the "ruler of this world."

Taking away world sin is, therefore, not a matter of forgiveness, or expiation for personal sins, but an act of liberation from the cosmic power of evil. Only such liberation will enable individuals to live with the freedom of

21. Similarly, the Dead Sea Scrolls describes Israel living under the "dominion of Belial" 1QS Col. i:18; 4Q256 Col. ii:3; 4Q390 Frag. 2 i:4. The Qumran documents clearly show a first century belief that the world was under the rule of demonic powers and needed the protection of God to be free from these powers. See the discussion of Jesus's prayer (John 17) in Warren, "What do Angels Have against the Blind and the Deaf?," 115–29.

22. I have discussed the function of Abraham and the issue of sonship in an earlier article, Coloe, "Like Father, Like Son," 1–11.

23. It is important when reading these harsh words of Jesus, that the narrative context is recognized, namely, that he is not speaking to "the Jews" in general, but to a group of his former followers "who had believed in him" (8:31). In their response to him, they accuse him of having a demon (8:52). The charge and counter-charge of demonic possession seems to have been part of the rhetoric in disputes. Jesus even accuses Peter of being "Satan" (Mark 8:33), and Jesus is accused of being Beelzebul (Mark 3:22). See Setzer, *Jewish Responses to Early Christians*. And for an alternative view Reinhartz, "'Children of the Devil,'" 43–54.

the son/daughter in the household. And this liberation requires Jesus, the son, to act. "If the son makes you free, you will be free indeed" (8:36).

Children in the Household of God[24]

Among the many unique aspects of the crucifixion in John's Gospel is the change of relationship Jesus establishes with his mother and the beloved disciple.

> When Jesus saw his mother and the disciple whom he loved standing beside her, he said to his mother, "Woman, behold your son." Then he said to the disciple, "Behold your mother." And from that hour the disciple took her as his own (εἰς τὰ ἴδια)" (19:26–27).

This declaration establishes the woman as the mother of the disciple, and in so doing establishes the disciple as Jesus' brother, and in a filial relationship with the God Jesus calls "father." The nature of discipleship is changed to one of siblings within the Father's house. Jesus confirms this reality in his words to Mary following his resurrection:

> Jesus said to her, "Do not touch me, because I have not yet ascended to the Father. But go to my brothers and sisters (τοὺς ἀδελφούς) and say to them, 'I am ascending to my Father and your Father, to my God and your God'" (20:17)

Jesus' followers now have the freedom of being children in the household of God, and are no longer living under the dominion of Satan.

Conclusion

The Johannine model of salvation is, in the light of the Exodus, an act of liberation from the dominion of slavery under the Ruler of this world,[25] to the freedom of children within the household of God. In this model, there is a liberation from sin, where sin is perceived as a power which enslaves

---

24. Over many years I have written on the Johannine Crucifixion as the establishing of the "Father's House." See for example Coloe, "Raising the Johannine Temple (Jn 19:19–37)"; *God Dwells with Us; Dwelling in the Household of God.* For the most recent expression of this, see Coloe, *John 10–11.*

25. "By strength of hand the LORD brought us out of Egypt, from the house of bondage" (Exod 13:14).

humanity, just as Israel was once held captive within the house of slavery.[26] To bring humanity from the status of "slave" to the status of "children" is liberative and the quintessential image of such liberation for Israel is the Passover lamb. John, the witness, is correct in identifying Jesus as "the Lamb of God who takes away the sin of the world" (1:29).

Bibliography

Aune, David E. "Understanding Jewish and Christian Apocalyptic." *Word & World* 25:3 (2005) 233–45.

Brown, Raymond. *The Death of the Messiah: From Gethsemane to the Grave.* 2 vols. New York: Doubleday, 1994.

Coloe, Mary L. "'Behold the Lamb of God': John 1:29 and the Tamid Service." In *Rediscovering John: Essays on the Fourth Gospel in Honour of Frédéric Manns,* edited by L. Daniel Chrupcala. Studium Biblicum Franciscanum 80, 337–50. Milan: Edizioni Terra Santa, 2013.

———. *Dwelling in the Household of God: Johannine Ecclesiology and Spirituality.* Collegeville, MN: Liturgical Press, 2007.

———. *God Dwells with Us: Temple Symbolism in the Fourth Gospel.* Collegeville: Liturgical Press, 2001.

———. *John 10–11.* WCS 44B. Collegeville, MN: Liturgical Press, 2021.

———. "Like Father, Like Son: The Role of Abraham in Tabernacles—John 8:31–59." *Pacifica* 12 (1999) 1–11.

———. "Raising the Johannine Temple (Jn 19:19–37)." *ABR* 48 (2000) 47–58.

Dennis, John. "The 'Lifting up of the Son of Man' and the Dethroning of the 'Ruler of this World': Jesus' Death as the Defeat of the Devil in John 12:31–32." In *The Death of Jesus in the Fourth Gospel,* edited by Gilbert van Belle. BETL 200, 678–91 Louvain: KUL 2007.

Dodd, Charles H. *The Interpretation of the Fourth Gospel.* Cambridge: Cambridge University Press, 1970.

Haenchen, Ernst. *John 2: A Commentary on the Gospel of John Chapters 7–21.* Translated by R. W. Funk. Hermeneia. 2 vols. Philadelphia, PN: Fortress, 1984.

Hylen, Susan E. "Lamb." *NIDB* 3 (2008) 563.

Koester, Craig R. "Why was the Messiah Crucified? A Study of God, Jesus, Satan and Human Agency in Johannine Theology." In *The Death of Jesus in the Fourth Gospel,* edited by Gilbert van Belle. BETL 200, 163–80. Louvain: KUL 2007.

Kovacs, Judith. "'Now shall the ruler of this world be driven out': Jesus' Death as Cosmic Battle in John 12:20–36." *JBL* 114 (1995) 227–47.

Lee, Dorothy A. *Flesh and Glory: Symbolism, Gender and Theology in the Gospel of John.* New York: Crossroad, 2002.

———. *The Symbolic Narratives of the Fourth Gospel: The Interplay of Form and Meaning.* JSNTSup 95. Sheffield: JSOT Press, 1994.

26. "Take care that you do not forget the LORD, who brought you out of the Land of Egypt, out of the house of slavery. The LORD your God you shall fear; him you shall serve and by his name alone shall you swear. Do not follow other gods . . . " (Deut 6:12–14a. cf. 5:6; 13:10).

————. "The Iconic 'Father' of Jesus." In Mary L. Coloe, *John 1–10*, WCS, 156–59. vol. 44a. Collegeville: Liturgical Press, 2022.

Lincoln, Andrew T. *The Gospel according to Saint John*. BNTC. London: Continuum, 2005.

Menken, Maarten J. J. "'The Lamb of God' (John 1, 29) in the Light of 1 John 3, 4–7." In *The Death of Jesus in the Fourth Gospel*, edited by Gilbert van Belle. BETL 200, 581–90. Louvain: KUL 2007.

Schneiders, Sandra M. "The Lamb of God and the Forgiveness of Sin(s) in the Fourth Gospel." *CBQ* 73 (2011) 1–29.

Stuckenbruck, Loren T. "Evil in Johannine and Apocalyptic Perspective: Petition for Protection in John 17." In *John's Gospel and Intimations of Apocalyptic*, edited by Catrin H. Williams and Christopher Rowland, 200–32. London: Bloomsbury T & T Clark, 2013.

Reinhartz, Adele. "'Children of the Devil': John 8:44 and its Early Reception." In *Confronting Antisemitism from the Perspectives of Christianity, Islam, and Judaism*, edited by Kerstin Mayerhofer Armin Lange, Dina Porat and Lawrence H. Schiffman, 43–54. Berlin: De Gruyter, 2020.

————. *The Word in the World: The Cosmological Tale in the Fourth Gospel*. SBLMS 45. Atlanta, GA: Scholars Press, 1992.

Setzer, Claudia. *Jewish Responses to Early Christians: History and Polemic, 30–150 C.E.* Minneapolis, MN: Fortress, 1994.

Warren, Cecelia. "What do Angels Have against the Blind and the Deaf? Rules of Exclusion in the Dead Sea Scrolls." In *Common Judaism: Explorations in Second-Temple Judaism*, edited by Wayne O. McGready and Adele Reinhartz, 115–29. Minneapolis, MN: Fortress, 2008.

Zumstein, Jean. *L'Évangile selon Saint Jean (1–12)*. CNT IVa 2nd Series. Genève: Labor et Fides, 2014.

6.

Reading John's Prologue Through Contemporary Kenoticism

A Parting of the Scriptural and Theological Ways?

MARK R. LINDSAY

Introduction

In August 1932, Karl Barth affirmed, at the head of his monumental *Church Dogmatics,* that "the Church accepts from Scripture, *and with divine authority from Scripture alone,* the attestation of its own being as the measure of its utterance. . ."[1] This foregrounding of Scripture in the task of theology was not new to Barth. As early as 1916, he had boldly claimed— against, it must be said, the anthropocentric hermeneutical trajectory of much of the nineteenth-century liberal Protestantism in which he had been trained— that the world of the Bible was "the world of God" (*die Welt Gottes*).[2] As Donald Wood has recently put it, "scriptural exegesis was not a peripheral . . . concern for Barth"; on the contrary, his entire theological endeavor was characterized by a "scriptural orientation."[3] Mary Kathleen Cunningham has emphasized even more firmly the centrality of the Bible for Barth's

1. Barth, *Church Dogmatics* I/1, 16 (emphasis added).

2. Barth, "Die neue Welt in der Bibel" 345.

3. Wood, "Exegesis," 263.

life's work: "Few contemporary theologians have been as self-consciously concerned to do theology in accord with Scripture as Barth."[4] Indeed, it is frequently forgotten—or perhaps willfully ignored—that Barth's second academic appointment, to Münster in 1925, was as Professor of Dogmatics and New Testament Exegesis.

And yet, it must be said that the academy of biblical scholars—perhaps especially those who work, or have worked, in the field of New Testament studies—has, for a century now, been scathingly critical of Barth's engagement with Scripture. From Jülicher's and Vischer's derisive dismissal of Barth's 1919 *Römerbrief* as the ham-fisted attempt of "a *theologian*" (*ein Theologe*),[5] to Van Til's anathema that Barth "reject[ed] the orthodox doctrine of Scripture in its entirety,"[6] to Stephen Williams's conviction that we "must part company with [Barth] in the way he relates Scriptures to dogmatics,"[7] there has been no shortage of scholars for whom Barth's exegetical endeavors undermine at least his scholarly credentials, and perhaps even his Christian commitment.

Nevertheless, despite these criticisms, it is the contention of this chapter that Barth's exegesis provides a fertile ground for rich and fruitful theological conversation that advances the cause of the gospel. In particular, this chapter will explore the manner in which Barth's understanding of John 1 has influenced two quite different readings of the relationship between Jesus and the eternal identity of God. I will be considering, on the one hand, the British Anglican scholar, Richard Bauckham and, on the other, the American Presbyterian theologian, Bruce McCormack.

Bauckham on Barth and the Johannine Logos

In 2015, at the Center for Barth Studies' annual conference in Princeton, Richard Bauckham addressed the way in which Barth's exegesis of the Johannine Prologue evolved, from his earliest lectures on the topic in 1925–26 in Münster (and which were repeated in Bonn in 1933), to his later employment of this passage throughout the *Church Dogmatics*. In his concluding comments, Bauckham noted that he found himself "in broad agreement" with Barth's "general approach to exegesis"—not just methodologically, but also in relation to this particular portion of Scripture. By refusing to speculate on *Urtexts* on which the Prologue might conceivably have been

---

4. Cunningham, *What is Theological Exegesis?*, 11.

5. Barth, *Der Römerbrief (Zweite Fassung) 1922*, xiv.

6. Van Til, *Has Karl Barth Become Orthodox?*, 143.

7. Williams, *Election of Grace*, 198.

based, and by dismissing as essentially unhelpful the various attempts to find parallel *Logos*-concepts in broader religio-philosophical traditions of the ancient world, Barth was "far ahead of his time."[8] Only insofar as he omitted any discussion of the Prologue's literary structure—a structure that, for Bauckham, helps shape the text's meaning—was Barth's approach methodologically deficient.[9] Nevertheless, Bauckham's final assessment was negative. "Barth," he complains, "seems to have missed much of what the Prologue is actually saying. . ."[10] So what, then, does Bauckham think Barth was doing (and doing wrong)?

Quite rightly, Bauckham demonstrates that, according to Barth's consistent exegesis of this passage—in both the Münster/Bonn lectures and then later through the *Church Dogmatics* —the *Logos* is understood, not as a principle or thing in and of itself, but rather more modestly as a *locum tenens*. It acts as a placeholder, or substitute, for something else to which it more properly refers.[11] As Barth himself puts it, the *Logos* is analogous to the incomprehensible inscription on the diadem of the white rider of Revelation 19, or to "the x in an equation whose value will appear only when the equation is solved."[12] And what is that thing to which the *Logos* refers? It is none other than Jesus Christ. Theologically, of course, this conclusion is hardly remarkable. In saying that the Prologue is about Jesus, Barth is simply reaffirming that "on which all exegetes agree . . ."[13]

Yet he comes to this view by way of what Bauckham refers to as a "rather eccentric exegetical choice."[14] Citing Adolf Schlatter for support, Barth claims that the *houtos* of John 1:2 refers not only (or even primarily) backwards to the *Logos* of John 1:1, but principally forwards to the one named by the Baptist, much later in the Prologue, as Jesus.[15] Thus, contends Bauckham, Barth's argument rests on drawing an identity of relation between the one of whom John 1:1 speaks, and the final disclosure of who that one in fact is in John 1:15–17. But this, stresses Bauckham, is Barth's fatal

---

8. Bauckham, "Revelatory Word or Beloved Son?" 28.

9. Bauckham, "Revelatory Word or Beloved Son?" 28–29.

10. Bauckham, "Revelatory Word or Beloved Son?" 31.

11. Bauckham, "Revelatory Word or Beloved Son?" 18.

12. Barth, *Witness to the Word*, 27.

13. Bauckham, "Revelatory Word or Beloved Son?" 19.

14. Bauckham, "Revelatory Word or Beloved Son?" 19.

15. Barth, *Witness to the Word*, 28. Bauckham is able to cite only one other New Testament scholar who makes the same exegetical move—the Australian Salesian scholar, Francis Moloney. See F. Moloney, *Gospel of John*, 35; also F. Moloney, *Belief in the Word*, where Moloney says that the forwards-backwards reference is "grammatically possible" (30).

exegetical mistake. While there are reasons (which we shall come to shortly) for suspecting that Bauckham might be sympathetic to the *theological* move that Barth makes here, it is nonetheless an *interpretive* move that "cannot be maintained." Why? Largely, it seems, because John's literary style does not permit the type of gap between signifiers (*ho Logos, houtos*) and signified (Jesus Christ) that Barth's reading requires. "When *houtos* is used [by John] to refer forward," contends Bauckham, "what it refers to follows immediately." On the basis of this stylistic analysis, claims Bauckham, Barth's interpretation is "linguistically impossible."[16]

We will return to Bauckham's criticism—and other counter-critiques—later. In any event, according to Bauckham, Barth—at least in the context of his lectures on John—made little constructive use of this exegetically-grounded conclusion, beyond its utility in establishing the doctrine of the Trinity, and thus a triune-shaped revelation. That is, the identification of the *Logos* with Jesus renders the Word of God much more than an impersonal principle, but—conversely—*no more* than "a verbal placeholder for Jesus Christ." "[W]hat is said of the Word before incarnation is said only and for the sake of the light it throws on the incarnation itself."[17] In the commentary, says Bauckham, Barth does not employ the continuity of the eternal Word and the Word made flesh to argue for an eternal divine decision to become human. Thus, at this point, it would seem that Barth was advancing a Christology of the Prologue that can rightly be understood "in no stronger terms than the traditional understanding of the hypostatic union . . ."[18] Despite the alleged linguistic impossibility of its grounding, Bauckham is positively disposed towards Barth's christological conclusion.

However, the situation is markedly different when Barth incorporates his exegesis of the Prologue into the *Church Dogmatics*. There, says Bauckham, despite his exegesis "pass[ing] unchanged" into the *CD*, Barth puts it "to a different theological use" entirely. In particular, the non-controversial identification of Jesus and the Word serves Barth's (much more controversial) "distinctive doctrine of election," as it is proposed in *CD* II/2. As Bauckham says, the Jesus-Word identity now speaks, not merely of the hypostatic union, but of "the election in eternity of the God-human Jesus Christ as God's self-determination to be, in him, the God who creates, loves, and redeems the world."[19] Much of the rest of Bauckham's 2015 paper serves to underscore this point: that according to Barth's rendering, in and after *CD* II/2,

16. Bauckham, "Revelatory Word or Beloved Son?" 30.

17. Bauckham, "Revelatory Word or Beloved Son?" 20.

18. Bauckham, "Revelatory Word or Beloved Son?" 19.

19. Bauckham, "Revelatory Word or Beloved Son?" 20–21.

what John says of the *Logos* can be attributed also to Jesus, because—insofar as Jesus Christ is the one (*houtos*—John 1:2) who is "in the beginning" (John 1:1)— the event of Jesus Christ is an event "in both eternity and time."[20] We have, says Barth, "no need to project anything into eternity, for at this point eternity is time, i.e. the eternal name has become a temporal name, and the divine name a human."[21] According to Mary Cunningham, this constitutes a "spirited exegetical assault on the notion of a *Logos asarkos*."[22] Insofar as the Word is already, in the beginning, identified with Jesus Christ, this means for Barth that "the incarnation was God's eternal purpose," with Jesus Christ being the name that "from all eternity he elected to bear . . ."[23] And, while Bauckham notes that some scholars have rejected the idea that Barth employs his exegesis of the Prologue primarily to ground his doctrine of election, he contends that Barth's doctrine nevertheless consistently and deliberately uses John 1:1–2 as its scriptural justification.[24]

As I have said earlier, Bauckham thinks that here, Barth has missed the Johannine point. His troubling exegesis has led him, not perhaps into theological error, but certainly into a faulty reading of the Fourth Gospel. So, what would Bauckham have had Barth do instead? The issue, he contends, is one of misplaced emphasis. The stress of the Prologue is not, says Bauckham, on the name "Jesus Christ" but on the identification of the Word with the *monogenēs* ("only Son"). "The point of the incarnation is not just that God is revealed in the God-human Jesus Christ, but that Jesus Christ, in his concrete human life and work, is the Son of the Father."[25] Only when Barth adumbrates the message of the Prologue in §69.3— in which he speaks, Origen-like, of the Fourth Gospel as the "Gospel of the Gospel"[26]—does Barth finally express what Bauckham understands to be the basic point of the Prologue; not so much the particularity of Jesus, but

20. Bauckham, "Revelatory Word or Beloved Son?" 21.

21. Barth, *Church Dogmatics* II/2, 98.

22. Cunningham, *What is Theological Exegesis?* 23. Bauckham does not agree that Barth rejects in principle the idea of a *Logos asarkos,* but does accept that the logic of his exegesis renders it a theoretical possibility only.

23. Bauckham, "Revelatory Word or Beloved Son?" 22–23.

24. Bauckham, "Revelatory Word or Beloved Son?" 21 n. 7. See also Gibson, *Reading the Decree,* 53.

25. Bauckham, "Revelatory Word or Beloved Son?" 31.

26. Barth, *Church Dogmatics* IV/3.1, 231. In his commentary on the Fourth Gospel, Origen says that "if the gospels are the first-fruits of the entire Scripture, then the first-fruits of the gospels is the gospel according to John." Origen, "Commentary on John, Book 1," in Trigg, *Origen,* 109.

that the incarnation reveals God as Father and Son in loving relationship.[27] The point here is not whether Bauckham has correctly understood Barth in this section of the *Dogmatics*. I would argue that Barth does not under-emphasize God's particular decision to be in Jesus Christ to the extent that Bauckham perceives—and certainly not in a way that is inconsistent with his earlier prioritization of Jesus as the identification of the *houtos*. Be that as it may, in Bauckham's reading of *CD* IV/3, Barth is seen to be finally, if belatedly, perceiving what John is on about—but this realization, contends Bauckham, is reached theologically, and not exegetically.[28]

McCormack on Barth and the Johannine Logos

An intriguing comparison to Richard Bauckham—on precisely this question of the *houtos*-Jesus Christ identity—comes from someone who works in a different field, and from a different confessional perspective, namely, the American Presbyterian systematician, Bruce McCormack. McCormack is effusive in his praise of Bauckham's work. "I have learned more from Bauckham," says McCormack in his most recent book, "than from any other Pauline scholar."[29] More to the point in our current context, McCormack notes that the claim he wishes to advance—that if the exalted Jesus is given the "name that is above every name," and if that most highly exalted name is the same as *the* divine Name that "Jewish believers ha[ve] long since ceased to take upon their lips," then the human person of Jesus Christ is proper to the identity of the God of Israel—has already been made by Bauckham before him.[30] So, for example, Bauckham has previously had no qualms in insisting that "the form of Christology fundamental to all the New Testa-ment texts is a 'Christology of divine identity' in which Jesus was seen as belonging to the unique identity of the God of Israel."[31] And yet, despite this indebtedness to Bauckham's teachings, McCormack is forced to part company with him. Why might this be, and what might be the relevance to a Barthian-informed reading of the Johannine Prologue?

27. Bauckham, "Revelatory Word or Beloved Son?" 33.

28. Barth's coming to see John's emphasis on the Father-Son relationship appears "*not* as [an] interpretation of the Johannine Prologue . . ." (Bauckham, "Revelatory Word or Beloved Son?" 32 [emphasis added]). It would, of course, be impossible for Barth to reach this conclusion exegetically, because—according to Bauckham—it is Barth's consistent (and consistently problematic) exegesis that is the very barrier to see-ing the emphasis of the Prologue.

29. McCormack, *Humility of the Eternal Son*, 215.

30. McCormack, *Humility of the Eternal Son*, 16.

31. Bauckham, "Incarnation and the Cosmic Christ," 31.

In contrast to Bauckham's critique of Barth's "eccentric exegesis" of John 1:1–2, and despite acknowledging himself that Barth's exegesis is "unusual," McCormack nevertheless wishes to affirm that Barth "was right in all essentials with respect to what he had to say about John's concept of the Logos . . ."[32] Whereas, as we have seen, Bauckham finds Barth's identification of the *houtos* with Jesus Christ exegetically unsustainable on linguistic grounds, thus meaning that Barth misses the whole point of the Prologue, McCormack counter-argues that the identification is both theologically coherent and persuasive, when read in the light of both the Prologue and the rest of the Gospel. Barth, claims McCormack, reads the *houtos* of 1:2 forward "primarily because of what is said of the Word as life and light in 1:4–5 and how it connects with all that is said elsewhere in John's Gospel about Jesus as life and light."[33] That is, suggests McCormack, Barth's argument rests on stronger grounds than Bauckham allows—not least the theology of the Fourth Gospel as a whole—and thus it is in fact Bauckham's linguistically-based rejection of Barth's conclusion that is deficient.

But what, one might ask, is the consequence of Barth's interpretation? According to McCormack, what Barth has done through this exegetical move is render the Word a predicate of Jesus, rather than Jesus being a predicate of the Word. In Barth's reading of John—and in particular John 1:1—there is no abstract Word, and not even an abstract relationship of the Father to the Son, but only ever the closest and most necessary identification of that Word and Son with Jesus Christ. Whereas Bauckham avers that it is indeed possible to speak of "the Word in itself, not yet as Jesus Christ . . ."[34], McCormack's contrary claim is that "there is no eternal Word *as such*, no eternal Word *in himself* that is not already defined by his relation to the Jesus who is still to come. And that means too that the only-begotten Son is already in himself, in pretemporal eternity, Jesus Christ by way of anticipation of the event of incarnation in time."[35] Or, as he puts it elsewhere, "Jesus is the Word both in eternity (by anticipation) and in time (by concrete

32. McCormack, *Humility of the Eternal Son*, 239.

33. McCormack, *Humility of the Eternal Son*, 242.

34. Bauckham, "Revelatory Word or Beloved Son?" 24. There is, says Bauckham, "a moment in which readers [of John] contemplate the divine Word as such *before* immediately recognizing that it is identical with the figure of Jesus Christ" (24 [emphasis added]). Bauckham thus proposes at least a possible temporal space in which the Word might be known independently of the incarnation. He goes on to say that John's intent in the Prologue is to proclaim to a Jewish audience that "'the Word you already know about in Genesis is the Word that has become flesh in Jesus Christ," a summary statement that McCormack interprets as positing a Word already truly known without reference to Jesus (McCormack, *Humility of the Eternal Son*, 243 n 49).

35. McCormack, *Humility of the Eternal Son*, 243.

realization)."[36] To cite Barth himself—in the very volume of the *Church Dogmatics* in which Bauckham thinks Barth finally to have appreciated the proper centrality (as Bauckham sees it) of the Father-Son relationship—"the whole Prologue . . . —although it certainly speaks of the eternal Logos — speaks also of the man Jesus."[37]

McCormack and Bauckham: Why the Parting of the Ways?

Evidently, there is a clear distinction between Richard Bauckham and Bruce McCormack on the proper exegesis of John's Prologue—in particular, the question of whether there is a filial (Bauckham) or Christological (McCormack) priority—and thus also a difference between them with regards to the legitimacy of Barth's own interpretation. But, for reasons I shall attempt to outline, we ought not be surprised by this parting of the ways between two exceptional interpreters of Barth, who have both learned much from the other.

For his part, Bauckham is reading Barth's exegesis of the Prologue through the prism of exegetical history. As we have seen, with the two exceptions of Schlatter and Moloney, he is unable to find any other Johannine scholar who even canvases Barth's primary identification of *houtos* with Jesus Christ as a possibility to consider.[38] We have already noted that Bauckham does not shy away from affirming that the name Jesus Christ is proper to God's own identity as the God of Israel. Nevertheless, and to McCormack's bemusement, he seems to have bracketed out that conviction from what he believes to be exegetically possible. The reference in John 1:1 to the Word, and the backwards reference of *houtos* in 1:2 to that Word, and not forward to Jesus Christ, means that—whatever may be said about the connection of Jesus' name to the eternal identity of God—cannot be said on the basis of an exegesis of the Prologue. This, says McCormack, is where the "real conflict" between Barth and Bauckham lies.[39]

Why might Bauckham be unwilling to integrate his theological affirmation with his exegetical insistence? This question is perhaps answered

36. McCormack, *Humility of the Eternal Son*, 244.

37. Barth, *Church Dogmatics IV/2*, 33. Interestingly, Bauckham cites this very sentence in support of Barth's permission for a theoretical (but necessary) *Logos asarkos*. Bauckham, "Revelatory Word or Beloved Son?" 23.

38. Bauckham, "Revelatory Word or Beloved Son?" 30.

39. As McCormack puts it, "all of this seems very strange coming from the NT scholar who, more than any other, taught me to think that Jesus of Nazareth is *proper* to the identity of the *eternal* God of Israel. Perhaps he has changed his mind; I am not sure." (McCormack, *Humility of the Eternal Son*, 243 n 49).

by a brief consideration of what Bauckham refers to as "divine identity Christology"—his way of referring to early Christian portrayals of the relationship between Jesus and God, that does not employ the later (and arguably more alien) language of "nature," or "being." In Bauckham's view—and *contra*, in particular, Daniel Kirk—Jesus must be understood as more than simply an idealized human who embodies God's eschatological presence.[40] On the contrary, Jesus enjoys a "cosmic sovereignty"—where sovereignty over all things is one of the two unique characteristics of God's identity that Bauckham emphasizes—which is symbolized by "his enthronement on the divine throne in the highest heaven . . ."[41] Thus, Bauckham's most frequent descriptor is that Jesus is "included in the unique identity of God."[42] Moreover, in the earliest Christian reflection, this inclusion was not, Bauckham says, something that was incidental or additional to Jesus' own personhood. On the contrary, "If Jesus was integral to the identity of God, he must have been so eternally . . ." In order to safeguard a Jewish Christian commitment to monotheism, Jesus could not be added "to the unique of the God of Israel" but had to be understood as integrally and eternally part of that identity.[43]

However, there are limits, it seems, to this inclusion. In his book *Jesus and the God of Israel*, Bauckham insists that the exegetical logic of Phil 2:6–11 requires that Christ does not simply *begin* to belong to the divine identity at his exaltation, but that he already had that identity from the beginning. Of the pre-existent Christ, Bauckham says that "the issue is not whether Christ gains equality or whether he retains it . . . He has equality with God and there is no question of losing it; the issue is his attitude to it."[44] However, Bauckham is equivocal on the extent to which this can be said to be true of the human *Jesus*. In a 2017 summary of Philippians 2, he argues that there is a distinction to be made between Jesus' divine and human identities. While the story of Jesus begins with his pre-existence "in the form of God," his earthly life expresses his divine identity "in the form of a human life . . ." Thus, while eternally equal with God, Jesus' exaltation is—while not a "divine promotion"—nevertheless the exaltation of his human identity which had not previously been so exalted. "He is now exalted in his human identity and shares the divine sovereignty as the human Jesus as well as in

---

40. Bauckham, "Is 'High Human Christology' Sufficient?" 504.

41. Bauckham, *Jesus and the God of Israel*, 176.

42. Bauckham, "Is 'High Human Christology' Sufficient?" 514.

43. Bauckham, *Jesus and the God of Israel*, 235.

44. Bauckham, *Jesus and the God of Israel*, 41.

his divine identity."[45] Bauckham puts it bluntly: "God exalts Jesus and gives him the divine name (which he had not previously possessed *as human*)."[46]

I have already alluded to Bruce McCormack's puzzlement at Bauckham's preparedness to separate out a pre-existent Word as such from the human person of Jesus. Either Bauckham is being inconsistent, or (as McCormack suggests), he has changed his mind between 2008 and 2015–17. In 2008, he was speaking freely of Jesus as eternally integral to the identity of God; by the time of the 2015 Barth conference, and then again in his 2017 response to Daniel Kirk, however, he was sharply critical of Barth's Johannine exegesis that made precisely that point and was differentiating between Jesus' divine and human identities. A third option, and one mooted by McCormack himself, is that Bauckham distinguishes between divine identity and divine nature—or, as McCormack puts it, the *who* and the *what*. "The value of the concept of divine identity appears partly if we contrast it with a concept of divine essence or nature. Identity concerns who God is; nature concerns what God is or what divinity is."[47] The difficulty with this, argues McCormack, is that such a distinction seals off the metaphysical question of nature from the more personal question of identity, as if the former is more basic—and thus more ontologically "proper"—than the latter, with metaphysical nature being somehow able to be discerned apart from identity. "This simply won't do," says McCormack. On the contrary, if Jesus—including in his suffering and death—is basic to the eternal identity of God (as Bauckham claims), then the nature of that God must be such that he can be the "experiencing subject" of those human conditions of life, without them needing to be "exalted into" God's presence at a later point in time.[48] In any event, this is the point—a distinction between the *what* and the *who*—at which McCormack finds himself unable to follow his British Anglican colleague.

McCormack's critique of Bauckham is at one level simply the extension of a longer and often vitriolic debate within the Barthian academy, on the relationship between God's triune being and the divine decision for election. In its simplest form, is God's eternal constitution as Trinity the prior ontological ground out of which that triune God then chooses, in freedom, to elect? Or is God's decision to elect itself the eternal constitution of God's triunity? In most previous bouts in this fight, the contested terrain has been Barth's own theological *corpus*, and who reads it most faithfully on

45. Bauckham, "Is 'High Human Christology' Sufficient?" 516.

46. Bauckham, "Is 'High Human Christology' Sufficient?" 516 n 34.

47. Bauckham, *God Crucified*, 8.

48. McCormack, *Humility of the Eternal Son*, 215.

this particular question.[49] Anyone with even passing familiarity with the debate will know that McCormack (who opts for the second alternative, and believes that that is the logic of Barth's theological ontology) has been most consistently and vociferously opposed throughout by George Hunsinger and Paul Molnar (who take the first option, and who decry McCormack as a "revisionist").

More recently, however, McCormack has shifted the ground slightly. Instead of offering yet another reading of Barth *per se*, he has embarked upon a trilogy of works that seeks to construct "a personal ontology of the triune God that takes as its starting point the act of God's self-revelation in Jesus Christ."[50] If this sounds like a modest enough undertaking, the explosive potential of the work becomes clearer when McCormack acknowledges that what he has in view is nothing less than a "repair of Chalcedon." Why is this needed? Because "there exists at the very heart of the Chalcedonian Definition a logical aporia, an unresolved contradiction," that consists in the fact that "Jesus of Nazareth contributes nothing to the constitution of the 'person' [of the hypostatic union]."[51] It is that contradiction that McCormack wishes to address. In fact, though, this latest project is not a new work, but rather the systematic constructive realization of his earlier intra-Barthian contention. That McCormack has retained his commitment to the so-called "Barth's rule"—that statements about God's eternal being cannot be different in content from statements about God's being-in-revelation[52]— is therefore not surprising and helps explain why he applauds Barth's exegesis of the Prologue insofar as it emphasizes the eternal identification of the Word with Jesus Christ. In the context of this wider project, McCormack has simply swapped out Hunsinger and Molnar for Bauckham, as the one who represents the opposite of what he is wanting to claim.

49. The origins of the debate go back to McCormack's 1995 monograph, but the implications of it did not fully emerge until he fleshed out the ramifications of his argument in a collection of essays five years later. See McCormack, *Karl Barth's Critically Realistic Dialectical Theology*; McCormack, "Grace and Being," 92–110. For an excellent summary, see *Trinity and Election in Contemporary Theology*, edited by M.T. Dempsey, (Grand Rapids: Eerdmans, 2011).

50. McCormack, *Humility of the Eternal Son*, 6.

51. McCormack, *Humility of the Eternal Son*, 29, 31, 58.

52. "[D]ASS DIE AUSSAGEN ÜBER DIE WIRKLICHKEIT DER GÖTTLICHEN SEINSWEISEN 'ZUVOR IN SICH SELBER' INHALTLICH KEINE ANDEREN SEIN KÖNNEN ALS DIEJENIGEN, DIE ÜBER IHRE WIRKLICHKEIT EBEN IN DER OFFENBARUNG ZU MACHEN SIND," BARTH, *KIRCHLICHE DOGMATIK I/1*, 503.

At issue for McCormack is the *kenosis* of the Son and Word of God, and, in particular, the subjective agent of that self-emptying. Rather than forcing a choice between the *Logos asarkos* (Athanasius, Augustine) and the *Logos ensarkos* (Erasmus, Luther, Calvin) as the kenotic subject, McCormack proposes an "ontological receptivity on the part of the eternal Son that makes the humility and obedience of Jesus to be his 'own'—not merely in a figurative possessive sense but in a sense that makes it clear that the subject of that human attitude and activity is also the eternal Son."[53] Bauckham, however, would appear to shy away from this conclusion, preferring to say that there is an exaltation of Jesus in his human identity to a status that, in that particular identity, he did not have before. In the same way that Bauckham thus argues for at least a possible gap between the Word as such and the Jesus who is to come—a distinction that he finds missing in Barth's exegesis of the Johannine Prologue—he seems also to tolerate a distinction between the divine and human identities of Jesus, thus creating (in McCormack's view) a confusion between the *what* of God and the *who*.

The intention of this chapter has not been to adjudicate between McCormack or Bauckham. Certainly, McCormack's broader project is, it seems to me, the more provocative—though not necessarily, for that reason, the less persuasive. More modestly, I have sought in this chapter to outline two quite different sets of theological presuppositions, and to show the ways in which they have led to contrasting evaluations of Karl Barth's exegesis of John 1. Let the reader now decide!

Bibliography

Barth, Karl. *Church Dogmatics I/1 The Doctrine of the Word of God*. Edited and translated by Thomas F. Torrance and Geoffrey W. Bromiley. Edinburgh: T&T Clark, 1936.
———. *Church Dogmatics*. Edited by G. W. Bromiley and T. F. Torrance. Translated by A. T. Mackay and T. H. L. Parker. 2nd ed. Hendrickson, 2010.
———. *Church Dogmatics II/2 The Doctrine of God*. Edited and translated by Thomas F. Torrance and Geoffrey W. Bromiley. Edinburgh: T&T Clark, 1957.
———. *Church Dogmatics IV/2 The Doctrine of Reconciliation*. Edited and translated by Thomas
———. *Church Dogmatics*. Edited by G. W. Bromiley and T. F. Torrance. Translated by A. T. Mackay and T. H. L. Parker. 2nd ed. Hendrickson, 2010.F. Torrance and Geoffrey W. Bromiley. Edinburgh: T&T Clark, 1958.
———. *Church Dogmatics IV/3.1 The Doctrine of Reconciliation*. Edited and translated by Thomas F. Torrance and Geoffrey W. Bromiley. Edinburgh: T&T Clark, 1961.
———. *Der Römerbrief (Zweite Fassung) 1922*. Zürich: Theologischer Verlag Zürich, 2015.

53. McCormack, *Humility of the Eternal Son*, 19.

———. "Die neue Welt in der Bibel." In *Vorträge und kleinere Arbeiten, 1914–1921*. Edited by H-A Drewes. Zürich: Theologischer Verlag Zürich, 2012.

———. *Kirchliche Dogmatik I/1 Die Lehre vom Worte Gottes*. Munich: Christian Kaiser, 1932.

———. *Witness to the Word: A Commentary on John 1*. Translated by G.W. Bromiley. Eugene, OR: Wipf & Stock, 2003.

Bauckham, Richard. *God Crucified: Monotheism and Christology in the New Testament*. Grand Rapids: Eerdmans, 1998.

———. "The Incarnation and the Cosmic Christ." In *Incarnation: On the Scope and Depth of Christology*. Edited by N.H. Gregersen. Minneapolis: Fortress, 2015.

———. *Jesus and the God of Israel: God Crucified and Other Studies on the New Testament's Christology of Divine Identity*. Grand Rapids: Eerdmans, 2008.

———. "Revelatory Word or Beloved Son? Barth on the Johannine Prologue." In *Reading the Gospels with Karl Barth*. Edited by D. Migliore. Grand Rapids: Eerdmans, 2017.

———. "Is "High Christology" Sufficient?" Bulletin for Biblical Research, 27:4 (2017), University Park PA: Penn State University Press.

Cunningham, Mary K. *What is Theological Exegesis? Interpretation and Use of Scripture in Barth's Doctrine of Election*. Valley Forge, PA: Trinity Press International, 1995.

Dempsey, Michael T. (ed). *Trinity and Election in Contemporary Theology*. Grand Rapids: Eerdmans, 2011.

Gibson, David. *Reading the Decree: Exegesis, Election and Christology in Calvin and Barth*. London: T&T Clark, 2009.

McCormack, Bruce L. "Grace and Being: The Role of God's Gracious Election in Karl Barth's Theological Ontology." In *The Cambridge Companion to Karl Barth*. Edited by J. Webster. Cambridge: Cambridge University Press, 2000.

———. *The Humility of the Eternal Son: Reformed Kenoticism and the Repair of Chalcedon*. Cambridge: Cambridge University Press, 2021.

———. *Karl Barth's Critically Realistic Dialectical Theology: Its Genesis and Development 1909–1936*. Oxford: Oxford University Press, 1995.

Moloney, Francis. *Belief in the Word: Reading John 1–4*. Minneapolis: Fortress, 1993.

———. *The Gospel of John*. Sacra Pagina 4. Collegeville: Liturgical, 1998.

Trigg, Joseph W. *Origen*. London and New York: Routledge, 1998.

Van Til, Cornelius. *Has Karl Barth Become Orthodox?* Philadelphia: The Presbyterian and Reformed Publishing Co, 1954.

Williams, Stephen N. *The Election of Grace: A Riddle without a Resolution?* Grand Rapids: Eerdmans, 2015.

Wood, Donald. "Exegesis." In *The Oxford Handbook of Karl Barth*. Edited by P.D Jones & P. Nimmo. Oxford: Oxford University Press, 2019.

7.

Christology from Paul to John
Not Evolution but Disclosure

BRENDAN BYRNE, SJ

Introduction

The letters of Paul the Apostle provide the earliest documentary witness to Christian faith. The Fourth Gospel, on the other hand, stands late in the New Testament canon, and, in its final form (John 1–21), is the last of the four Gospels to appear. Moreover, along with the wide chronological gap, letters and gospels represent very different literary genres. One might well ask whether there is much to gain by instituting a comparison between them. The question is a good one and a response, positive or negative, will only emerge at the end of an exploration along these lines.

My choice for embarking on such a project in a volume honoring Dorothy Ann Lee stems from the fact that her field of expertise, while wide-ranging, has focused upon the Gospel of John, while I have specialized in Paul. Our long-standing friendship and collegial collaboration seemed to require a tribute that might draw the two areas together in a fruitful and illuminating way.

While Paul and John appear to go very different ways in theology and Christology, I have long been impressed in this connection by a remark made several decades ago by the Cambridge scholar C. F. D. Moule. In his short, classic work, *The Origin of Christology*, Moule wrote: ". . . development is a better analogy than evolution for the genesis of New Testament Christology. . . . communities and individuals gained new insights into the meaning of *what was there all along*."[1] In many respects, I believe, the Fourth Gospel draws out and makes explicit views of Christ and his redemptive work that Paul presupposes or alludes to simply in passing. In making this claim, I am not suggesting that the Fourth Evangelist wrote in conscious commentary on the letters of Paul. Rather, I am suggesting areas in which a reader of both writings today might find in John a rendering explicit of aspects of an unfolding tradition seen in its early stages in Paul. To this end, I shall address three areas of comparison: God's Word of creation shedding light and glory; the continuity of the Father and the Son in the work of redemption; the Son's soteriological abasement in the service of humanity.

The "Illumination" of Glory on the Face of the Crucified

From the start, the Fourth Gospel does not hesitate to plunge the reader into the Son's pre-existent being with the Father, presenting him as the Word (of God) through whom "all things were made" (John 1:3). Reclaiming the first account of creation, the evangelist portrays the Son as the first word God spoke, "Let there be light" (Gen 1:3),[2] whereupon light shone in the hitherto prevailing darkness. Beginning in this way, the Prologue anticipates the theme of conflict between light and darkness that will continue throughout the narrative of the gospel, which, of course, portrays Jesus as "the Light" of the world (John 8:12; 9:5; 12:46). The consequence of portraying him as God's creative Word is that, wherever he speaks or acts later in the story, it is always God saying: "Let there be light," a light that will shine on in the darkness that the darkness will not overcome (John 1:5). Creation is not over and done with "in the beginning" (John 1:1). Creation continues in the life-giving ministry of the Son.

There is an attractive parallel to this Johannine recapturing of the creation story in the course of Paul's apologia for his apostolic ministry in 2 Corinthians 2:14–7:4. As is so often his way, Paul affirms the credibility of his ministry by setting it over against a contrasting or inferior dispensation, in this case Moses' promulgation of the law. In both cases, what lends divine credibility to the ministry is the glory that attends it, glory being the effect of

---

1. *Origin of Christology*, 135 (emphasis added).

2. The English phrase "Let there be" translates a single word, *yehi*, in Hebrew and in the Greek translation (LXX), *genētheto*, of Gen 1:3.

the presence and power of God.[3] Paul sets up an extended argument on an *a priori* logic: if so bright a glory attended Moses' promulgation of the law, an instrument of condemnation and death (2 Cor 3:7), that the patriarch had to have recourse to a veil to spare the Israelites, how much greater must be the glory that attends the administration of the Spirit, one that brings righteousness and life (2 Cor 3:8–11). If the gospel is "veiled," it is only so for those being lost, whose thoughts Satan has blinded so that they cannot see the gospel's "illumination of the glory of God on the face of Christ, who is the image of God" (2 Cor 4:4). And, Paul continues, "(It is) the God who said, 'Out of darkness let light shine,' who has shone in our hearts to light up knowledge of the glory of God on the face of Christ" (2 Cor 4:6).

The striking allusion to the first creation story here suggests that Paul understands the proclamation of the gospel to be a continuance of the activity of God in creation in a way comparable to the Fourth Gospel. As Paul makes clear, especially in 1 Corinthians and Galatians, his preaching of the gospel involved confronting those who heard it with the crucified Christ. "O you senseless Galatians," he exclaims, "who has bewitched you, before whose eyes Jesus Christ was publicly placarded as crucified" (Gal 3:1). And among the Corinthians, he decided to "know nothing save Jesus Christ and him crucified" (1 Cor 2:2; see 1:22–23). The "face" of Jesus Christ upon which God shone glory in the preaching of the gospel (2 Cor 4:4b) was the face of the Crucified. To see the face of a crucified person as the revelation of God, the very "image" (*eikōn*) of God, required an "illumination" (*phōtismos*) that only the creative power of God could effect (v 6).

The gospel of the Crucified addresses a world, both Jewish and Gentile, universally alienated from God (Rom 1:18–3:20; 3:23; 5:12; Gal 3:22). In Paul's apocalyptic perspective, the revelation of the divine wrath is the background to the proclamation of the gospel and that which gives it urgency (Rom 1:18; 1 Thess 1:10).[4] The gospel confronts its hearers with the judgment upon human sin implicit in God's sending of a Crucified Messiah. At the same time, the gospel offers those who respond in faith a divine remedy and rescue from condemnation at the judgment—in effect "salvation"—in the shape of a divine righteousness embodied in the person of the Son of God. In the self-sacrificial death of the Son, God has graciously dealt with the seriousness of human sin, while at one and the same time, opened up the way to (eternal) life (Rom 1:16–17; 3:21–26).

---

3. Byrne, "'Glory' as Apostolic Credibility," 16–21. On the biblical sense of "glory" in general, see Lee, *Flesh and Glory*, 34–35; *Transfiguration*, 103–104.

4. See Byrne, *Economy*, 34, 44, 76–80, 134–35.

The original audience of the Fourth Gospel were presumably no less aware of the horrors involved in crucifixion than the apostle Paul. The evangelist does not shrink, however, from pointing to the "lifting up" of Jesus (the Son of Man) upon the cross as the moment of the revelation of his glory, the moment when he will be truly "transparent" to the revelation of God: "When you have lifted up the Son of Man, then you will know that I am" (*hoti egō eimi*) (John 8:28; see 3:14; 12:32, 34). The mysterious final expression, lacking predicate, echoes a divine formula of revelation occurring over and over in (Second) Isaiah (see [LXX] 43:10, 25; also 41:4; 45:19, 22; 46:4, 9; 48:12; 51:12).[5] At the final supper, as soon as Judas has departed on his errand of betrayal, thereby setting in motion the process that will immediately lead to the crucifixion, Jesus declares, "Now the Son of Man has been glorified, and God has been glorified in him" (John 13:31). The passion is now so inevitably begun that Jesus can speak of the glorification of God that will take place next day as already under way.[6] The Fourth Evangelist has imbued the narrative of the Passion story with the glorification of the Crucified that Paul attributed to the creative power of God when people respond in faith to the gospel.

The Continuity of the Father and the Son in the Work of Redemption

Some formulations of Christian soteriology, reflected in hymnody as well as doctrine, imply a wedge between the operation of the Father and the Son in the work of human redemption. Such formulations—suggesting an angry Father who only grudgingly agrees to release human beings from the punishment due to sin through the painful expiatory death of Christ—create a fissure in the image of God hardly conformable to the doctrine of the Trinity.[7] Such an understanding does not emerge from accurate readings of Paul and John.

The Pauline passage from which a sense of a wedge between the action of God and that of Christ has traditionally been drawn is Rom 3:21–26. What has given rise to such an interpretation, especially in light of the wider context that places the proclamation of the gospel under the horizon of the revelation of God's wrath (Rom 1:18; see 2:5, 8; 4:15; 5:9), is the description in v 25 of Christ, in the shedding of his blood, as a *hilastērion*. The word

5. See Moloney, *Gospel of John*, 271–72, 274; Coloe, *John 1–10*, 219–21.

6. Moloney, *Gospel of John*, 384–86.

7. For a survey and critique of these tendencies, see O'Collins, *Christology*, 197–212, 279–95.

group *hilas–* does have a propitiatory sense in secular Greek, especially in connection with the appeasing of the wrath of a god or angry person and it would be likely that Paul's use of the term would be understood in this way by the audience of his letter in Rome.[8] Any sense, however, of Christ's placating a reluctant Father is overcome by the plain statement of the divine initiative: ". . . who (Christ) God put forward as a *hilastērion* in the shedding of his blood" (Rom 3:25a). The objection that such an interpretation leads to the unacceptable proposition of God's placating Godself is overcome by the parallel provided, in terms of "reconciliation," in 2 Corinthians 5:18: "God was in Christ *reconciling the world to himself*" (italics mine). God does not simply dismiss human sin. In the sacrificial death of the Son, God shows its seriousness and offense to the divine justice ("righteousness") in a forensic sense (Rom 3:25b), while bearing the cost of the removal of the alienation in the death of the Son.[9]

Paul's sense of the continuity between Father and Son is patent in the "sending of the Son" statements found in Romans and Galatians. In the face of the impotence of the law to bring about the righteousness required for salvation (see Rom 7:7–25), Paul continues,

> (God), sending his own Son in the likeness of sinful flesh and as a sacrifice for sin, condemned sin in the flesh, in order that the righteous requirement of the law might be fulfilled in us, who walk now, not according to the flesh but according to the Spirit (Rom 8:3–4).

The capacity of believers to live righteously and so be set in line for salvation is the creation of the Father, through the redemptive agency of the Son and the consequent release of the empowering Spirit. The complete continuity in this "trinitarian" formulation appears also in the parallel "sending" statement in Gal 4:4–4:

---

8. A much-favored alternative finds here an allusion to the "mercy seat" (*kapporet*) in the Holy of Holies, the cover over the Ark of the Covenant, upon which the high priest sprinkled the blood of a slain animal in the Day of Atonement ritual. As the LXX regularly translates *kapporet* with *hilastērion* in this connection (Exodus 25:17–22; Leviticus 16:15–16), it is argued that in describing Christ in the shedding of his blood as *hilastērion* Paul is alluding to this ritual (as is certainly the case in Hebrews 9:5): the shedding of Christ's blood on Calvary would be the culminating Day of Atonement on which God was wiping away (expiating) all sin, not only that of Israel but of the world as a whole. This explanation lends a more expiatory rather than propitiatory note to the description of the divine action. However, whether Paul could expect that the community of believers in Rome, which he himself had not founded, would pick up so specific a biblical allusion, is a good question. See further Byrne, *Economy*, 97–99.

9. See Cranfield, *Romans* 1:211–12; Byrne, *Economy*, 92–102, 231–33.

> When the fullness of time had come, God sent the Son, born of woman, born under the law, in order to redeem those under the law, in order that we might receive the adoption (as sons and daughters of God).

Even more striking—perhaps because the continuity is related expressly to the divine love—is the sequence in Rom 5:6–10 where Paul alternates between the love of God and that of Christ:

> It was while we were still weak (i.e., trapped in sin), that Christ died for us. . . . God has proved his own love for us in that it was while we were still sinners that Christ died for us. . . . If it was when we were enemies that we were reconciled to God through the death of his Son, how much more now that we have been reconciled (will it be the case) that we shall be saved through his life.

See also 2 Corinthians 5:18–21.

Paul's evocation of the judgment in Romans 8:31–39,[10] begins with the question, "If God is for us, who can be against us?" (v 31b) and continues, "(God), who did not spare his only Son but gave him up for us all, how (could it be) that he will not graciously bestow on us all things?" (v 32). With its echo of Abraham's near-sacrifice of his only son (Gen 22:16), we may find here a sense of the vulnerable love of God in the Christ event: what God did not in the end require of Abraham, God, in love for sinful humanity, did require of Godself.[11] The sequence as a whole begins to draw to a conclusion with the question "Who will separate us from the love of Christ?" (v 35a) and, after listing—and dismissing—any factor (suffering) or agency (spiritual powers) that might be thought able to do so, concludes with the ringing conviction that nothing will "separate us from the love of God (that has come to us) in Christ Jesus, our Lord" (v 39).

When we turn again to the Fourth Gospel, we find that again and again in the Gospel, Jesus stresses the origin of his mission in the Father, who is always with him in that mission (John 3:17; 5:17–23, 36, 37; 6:40, 57; 8:16, 28; 10:15, 36–38; 12:27–28, 49; 13:3; 14:8–13, 24; 16:27–28; 20:21; see also 1 John 4:9–10). Everything Jesus does is an expression, in total obedience, of his love for the Father and the Father's salvific love for the world.

That the Fourth Gospel associates the mission and death of Jesus with the removal of human sin is clear from the start in the Baptist's indication of Jesus as "the Lamb of God who takes away the sin of the world" (John 1:29;

10. See Byrne, *Economy*, 1 68–72.

11. See Byrne, *Economy*, 190–91; *Romans*, 275–76, 279.

see v 36). In the sequel to the account of the visit of Nicodemus by night (John 3:1–10), Jesus applies to himself and his mission the type provided by Moses' lifting up of the bronze serpent in the wilderness following the Israelites' grumbling against God (Num 21:4–9). When the Israelites looked on the raised serpent, they were freed from the death-dealing bites of the serpents that God had sent to punish them. The Israelites were compelled to confront their sinful rebellion by looking at the very image of that which God sent to punish them, a confrontation that led, paradoxically, to their rescue and life. So, Jesus says, "As Moses lifted up the serpent in the wilderness, so must the Son of Man be lifted up that whoever believes in him may have eternal life" (John 3:14–15). The revelation of God to be given at the crucifixion will be, for those who come to faith, at one and the same moment both judgment (associated with the Son of Man title; see 5:27) and release from sin.[12] Jesus goes on,

> God so loved the world that he gave his only Son, so that every-
> one who believes in him may not perish but have eternal life.
> Indeed, God did not send the Son into the world to condemn
> the world but so that the world might be saved through him
> (John 3:16–17).

Belief turns revulsion at an appalling manner of death into a revelation that is both divine judgment upon sin and at the same time loving rescue from sin's consequences. In recalling Moses' erection of the bronze serpent as a type of God's dealing with human sin in the lifting up of the Son on the cross, the Fourth Gospel is making imaginatively explicit Paul's sense of how the gospel of the Crucified, through God's creative illumination (2 Corinthians 4:6), confronts those who respond in faith with both judgment and salvation.[13]

The imparting of the Spirit to the disciples by the risen Jesus empowers them to carry on the ministry of forgiveness and reconciliation that flows from his death (John 20:22–23). As he was sent by the Father on this mission, so he sends them on the same mission of reconciliation (v. 21). Here again both the Pauline and the Johannine traditions cohere in their sense of the absolute continuity between the Father and the mission of the Son,

---

12. The revelation given on the cross in terms of the "I am" (*ego eimi*) formula (8:28) echoes Isaiah 43:25: "I am He, I am He (LXX *ego eimi, ego eimi*) who blots out your transgressions for my own sake and I will not remember your sin."

13. While nothing corresponding to *hilasterion* occurs in the Fourth Gospel, the cognate form *hilasmos* occurs in 1 John 2:2 and the "sending of the Son" statement in 4:9–10. See Raymond E. Brown, *Epistles of John: New Translation with Introduction and Commentary*, 217–22

a continuity that extends to the disciples in their ministry of reconciliation (see 2 Cor 5:17–21).

The Soteriological Abasement of the Son in Philippians 2:6–11 and John 13:1–17

Though outwardly very different, Paul's depiction of the abasement and exaltation of Christ in the hymnic passage Philippians 2:6–11 and the washing of the disciples' feet at the beginning of the supper in John 13:1–17 offer a further instance where the Johannine account makes explicit in narrative form the divine action to reconcile the world. Common to both is the motif of "slavery"—more particularly, the voluntary embrace of the condition and "service" performed by a slave.

Paul cites the Christ hymn in his letter to the Philippians as an example of the "self-emptying" attitude that should characterize relationships and dispositions between members of the community (Phil 2:1–4).[14] The "mind" (*phronein*) of Christ (v 5), however, is not simply an example that they should look to "from outside," as it were. It is a "mind" that should well up within them because of their existence "in Christ Jesus," that is, "in" his person as risen Lord, in whom, through faith and baptism, they communally exist. The hymn then follows, in three stanzas (vv 6–7c; 7d–8; 9–11), outlining the "career" of Christ, in each of which he displayed or displays the self–emptying disposition that the community should emulate in their relations with each other.

It is widely, though not universally, accepted that the first stanza of the hymn refers to Christ in his way of being "prior" to his taking on the human condition from "outside," as it were.[15] Though as such he enjoyed a form of being that was divine (*en morphē theou hyparchōn*) (v 6a), he did not choose to exploit this by grasping at equality with God (*ouch harpagmon hēgēsato to einai isa theou*) (v. 6b) "but emptied himself, taking on the form (*morphēn doulou labōn*), becoming in the likeness of human beings" (v 7a-c).[16] The

---

14. In Philippians 4:2–3, Paul explicitly exhorts two women, Evodia and Syntyche, to reconcile with one another, and goes on to ask another person, simply addressed as "noble yokefellow," to assist in this process, adding that they have labored together with him in the work of the gospel. Dorothy Lee points to these women as significant examples of women's leadership and activity in ministry in the early church; see *Ministry of Women*, 105.

15. For a survey and references to discussion of the question, see Byrne, "Christ's Pre-existence," 309–311.

16. Every phrase in vv. 6–7 has been a matter of controversy for centuries. Here I can only set out my own understanding and refer to fuller discussion elsewhere: see Byrne, "Christ's Pre-existence," 315–20; *Economy*, 185–90

hymn is expressing the prior disposition of Christ that led to what, following the terminology of the Fourth Gospel (John 1:14), has traditionally been described as his incarnation.

The presupposition of the hymn is that the human condition is one of slavery, a slavery to sin consequent upon a universal alienation from God initiated by humanity's patriarch Adam (Rom 5:12; see 7:14). The hymn, especially in its employment of the rare word *harpagmos* (v 6b), is contrasting Christ with Adam. Where Adam, at the instigation of the serpent, snatched (the basic meaning of the *harpag–* stem) at equality to God (Gen 3:1–7, esp. v. 5, in Paul's reading), Christ did the very opposite, he "emptied himself" of his own advantage (see Romans 15:3) taking on the polar opposite of being in the *morphē* of God, namely, being in the *morphē* of a slave, the necessary price of entering into the human condition.

As the second stanza continues, in that condition (*schēmati heuretheis hōs anthrōpos*), he further took on the lot of a slave, becoming obedient until death, even the slave's death on a cross (vv. 7d–8). In contrast to Adam, Christ was "obedient" (see Rom 5:19). "Obedient to what, to whom?" we might ask. The temporal pronoun "until" (*mechri*) suggests an enduring obedience, an obedience that not only encompassed his earthly life but that reached "back" to his pre-existent disposition as well: an obedience to God that led him to become human, as elsewhere expressed in the "sending of the Son" statements (see especially Gal 4:4–5; also Rom 8:3–4; 2 Cor 8:9).

The hymn does not explicitly point to any soteriological purpose in connection with the incarnation and resultant death of Christ. However, such a purpose is surely presupposed in that Christ enters the sinful and death-destined situation of humanity "in Adam" (1 Cor 15:22) in order, as "last Adam" (1 Cor 15:45), to create through his obedience a new liberating possibility of righteousness leading to life (Rom 5:15–19, 21).

The final stanza of the hymn describes the divine response to the obedience of Christ in terms of his "hyper-exaltation" (Phil 2:9): a "promotion" to the status that he did not snatch,[17] the lordship of the universe contained in the bestowal upon him of the "name" ("Lord") that is above all names (vv 9b–11a). Having obediently embraced the lowliest human status, that of a slave, Christ has had graciously bestowed upon him the polar-opposite of that status, namely, that of Lord (*kyrios*). Even here, he does not achieve this status for his own glory. Rather, fulfilling the vision of Isaiah 45:23, he holds the lordship of the universe for the glory of God (Phil 2:11b).

We are obviously in a very different world when we turn from the Pauline hymn to the Johannine foot washing scene at the beginning of the last

---

17. See Holloway, *Philippians*, 125–26; Byrne, *Economy*, 188–89.

supper (John 13:1–17). Nonetheless, though the necessities of English translation mask it, the long sentences in the Greek of the opening verses bring out the total continuity between the origins of Jesus' mission with the Father and the now-imminent expression of that mission in the "taking away" of the sin of the world (John 1:29), symbolized in the lowly service whereby Jesus performs a task normally reserved to slaves.[18] In the context of the opposition—the "darkness" (John 1:5)—noted in the presence of Judas Iscariot as tool of Satan (John 13:2b), the text lingers on the consciousness of Jesus concerning his mission: "knowing that the Father has given all things into his hands and that he had come out from God and was going to God" (v 3). Then, within the same sentence, it proceeds immediately to describe the concrete actions preparatory to washing the disciples' feet: "(he) rose from the supper, laid aside his outer garment, and tied a towel around himself" (v 4). This single prolix sentence in Greek (vv 2–4) portrays the preparedness of Jesus to perform the service of a slave as the expression of obedience to the mission he has received from the Father. The movement into the actual process described in v 5—the taking of water and commencing to perform the slave-like task—corresponds to the transition between stanzas one and two of the Philippians hymn. The service is the expression of a preformed divine determination to address and remedy the sin-laden alienation of the world.

That the washing of the disciples' feet symbolically anticipates the taking away of human sin that Jesus will enact the following day on the cross is shown by the dialogue with Peter that ensues (vv 6–7). The leading disciple understandably protests the enormity of having Jesus, his "teacher and Lord" (see v 13), perform this task. For us readers, who have just been reminded of the origin and full status of Jesus, the enormity is so much greater. Peter is looking down at God at his feet, washing away any dirt that adheres to them, which is exactly what God will achieve in regard to the "dirt" of sin when Jesus fulfills his mission on the cross. If Peter does not allow this cleansing to take place, he can have no part with Jesus (v. 7). In likely allusion to the rite of baptism, the washing is the symbol of the once-and-for all entry into the community of Jesus; it suffices to make one wholly "clean" (vv. 8–10).

The instruction that Jesus proceeds to give when, the washing complete, he has resumed his seat at table turns the symbolic anticipation into an ethical example (*hypodeigma* [v 15]). The liturgical custom of washing feet on Maundy Thursday obviously stems from this instruction (see v 14). However, it is not so much the particular concrete action that Jesus has in

18. For a recent discussion of the social background and symbolic meaning of the foot washing, see Coloe, *John 11–21*, 364–66.

view here but the disposition of lowly—and loving (see v 1bc)—service to which it gives expression. If precisely as teacher and Lord (v 13), Jesus has performed this service, how even more fitting it is that the servant, who is not as great as his or her lord, or the apostle, who is not as great as the one who sends, should act likewise (v 16). We are not at all far from the introduction to the Philippians hymn (Phil 2:1–4) in this indication of the example and precedent set by One whose very nature is divine.

Conclusion

This study has discussed three interrelated areas where the Fourth Gospel draws out and gives narrative expression to what we find in Paul. The discussion points to the unfolding over time of a basic core vision, going back to the earliest days post-Easter, as the disciples began to make sense of what God was doing for them and for the world in the death and resurrection of Christ.

Bibliography

Brown, Raymond E. *The Epistles of John: A New Translation and Commentary*. (Anchor Bible series. Garden City: Doubleday, 1982

Byrne, Brendan. "Christ's Pre-Existence in Pauline Soteriology," *TS* 58 (1997) 308–330.

———. "'Glory' as Apostolic Credibility in 2 Corinthians 2:14–4:18," *ABR* 66 (2018) 13–30.

———. *Paul and the Economy of Salvation: Reading from the Perspective of the Last Judgment*. Grand Rapids: Baker Academic, 2021.

———. *Romans*. Sacra Pagina 6. Collegeville, MN: Glazier, 1996.

Coloe, Mary L., *John 1–10*. Wisdom Commentary 44A. Collegeville, MN: Glazier, 2021.

———. *John 11–21*. Wisdom Commentary 44B. Collegeville, MN: Glazier, 2021.

Cranfield, C. E. B., *A Critical and Exegetical Commentary on the Epistle to the Romans*. 2 vols. ICC. Edinburgh: T&T Clark, 1975, 1979.

Holloway, Paul A., *Philippians: A Commentary*. Edited by Adela Yarbro Collins. Hermeneia. Minneapolis: Fortress, 2017.

Lee, Dorothy A., *Flesh and Glory: Symbolism, Gender and Theology in the Gospel of John*. New York: Crossroad, 2002.

———. *The Ministry of Women in the New Testament: Reclaiming the Biblical Vision for Church Leadership*. Grand Rapids: Baker Academic, 2021.

———. *Transfiguration*. London and New York: Continuum, 2004.

Moloney, Francis J. *The Gospel of John*. Sacra Pagina 4. Collegeville, MN: Glazier, 1998.

Moule, C. F. D., *The Origin of Christology*. Cambridge: Cambridge University Press, 1977.

O'Collins, Gerald, *Christology: A Biblical, Historical, and Systematic Study of Jesus*. Oxford: Oxford University Press, 1995.

8.

The "Sending of the Son" Formula
in Paul, John, and the Historical Jesus

SEAN WINTER

I   Introduction

On two occasions, Paul speaks of the "sending of the Son." In Galatians 4:4, redemption from the law's enslaving power is the consequence of God having "sent his Son, born of woman, born under law."[1] In Romans 8:3, Paul states that God has "dealt with sin" by "sending his own Son in the likeness of sinful flesh." The form of these two statements is similar: ὁ θεὸς + verb of sending + [τὸν] υἱόν. Two additional shared features identify: (a) the relationship between God and the son, by means of a pronoun and (b) between the son and humanity, by means of a prepositional or participial phrase. In both verses, the soteriological consequence of the sending of the Son is conveyed by a ἵνα clause. For a number of scholars, the similarities between the two verses suggests the possibility of a preexisting confessional formula on which Paul is drawing.[2]

1. While Paul's use of the phrase "under the law" (cf. Rom 6:14–15; 1 Cor 9:20–21; Gal 3:23–25) might simply evoke Jesus' participation in "the status, life-setting and condition of Jews generally" (so Dunn, "'Under,'" 58), the reference to redemption from the law's curse suggests Christ's sharing "the human condition of enslavement 'under' the law" (so de Boer, *Galatians*, 263).

2. The classic formulation is Seeberg, *Katechismus*, 59–70. See also Kramer, *Christ*, 111–15.

It is often noted that a similar collocation of theological ideas and syntactical features occurs at one point in the Gospel of John and then, again, in 1 John. In John 3:17, we are told that "God did not send the Son into the world" to condemn it, but in order to save it.[3] First John 4:9 speaks of God's sending of his Son into the world as the revelation of divine love. There are briefer formulations, with appositional phrases rather than purpose clauses, in 1 John 4:10, 14. Together, these verses form a specific component of the broader Johannine witness to the motif of Jesus being sent by God (see John 1:33; 3:34; 4:34; 5:24, 30, 36, 38; 6:29, 38–39; 7:16, 18, 28–29, 33; 8:26, 29, 42; 9:4; 11:42; 12:44–45; 13:20; 15:21; 16:5; 17:3, 8, 18, 21, 23, 25).[4] While Jesus refers to being sent by the Father on a number of occasions (John 5:27; 6:44, 57; 8:16, 18 10:36; 14:24; 20:21), it is those phrases that specifically denote him as the "son" that are most clearly parallel to the examples from Paul discussed above. Thus, there is extensive similarity between the Pauline and Johannine variations:[5]

	God	Verb of Sending	Son	Modifying Pronoun	Modifying Clause	Purpose Clause
Rom 8:3–4	ὁ θεὸς	πέμψας	τὸν υἱὸν	ἑαυτοῦ	ἐν ὁμοιώματι σαρκὸς ἁμαρτίας	ἵνα τὸ δικαίωμα τοῦ νόμου πληρωθῇ ἐν ἡμῖν
Gal 4:4–5	ὁ θεὸς	ἐξαπέστειλεν	τὸν υἱὸν	αὐτοῦ	γενόμενον ἐκ γυναικός. . .ὑπὸ νόμου	ἵνα τὴν υἱοθεσίαν ἀπολάβωμεν
John 3:17	ὁ θεὸς	ἀπέστειλεν	τὸν υἱὸν	[αὐτοῦ]	εἰς τὸν κόσμον	ἵνα σωθῇ ὁ κόσμος
I John 4:9	ὁ θεὸς	ἀπέσταλκεν	τὸν υἱὸν	αὐτοῦ τὸν μονογενῆ	εἰς τὸν κόσμον	ἵνα ζήσωμεν δι' αὐτοῦ.
1 John 4:10	αὐτὸς	ἀπέστειλεν	τὸν υἱὸν	αὐτοῦ		ἱλασμὸν περὶ τῶν ἁμαρτιῶν ἡμῶν
1 John 4:14	ὁ πατὴρ	ἀπέσταλκεν	τὸν υἱὸν			σωτῆρα τοῦ κόσμου

Table 1: Sending Formula in John and Paul

3. The Johannine formula is constructed as an οὐκ. . .ἀλλα sentence. Certain MSS include the modifying pronoun αὐτοῦ which brings the verse even closer to the Pauline texts.

4. The easy variation between the terms πέμπω and ἀποστέλλω in John is exemplified by 20:21: καθὼς ἀπέσταλκέν με ὁ πατήρ, κἀγὼ πέμπω ὑμᾶς.

5. While the purpose of this essay is not to explore the relationship between the Pauline and Johannine traditions at any length, the 'sending of the Son' motif is a specific feature of a wider pattern of connections and similarities. For analysis of those patterns see Harding, "Kyrios Christos"; Kruse, "Paul and John."

Previous scholarship on this cluster of texts has been largely concerned with two key issues: (a) to identify a plausible conceptual background and/or history of religions explanation for the "sending" formula; (b) to consider the relationship between the formula and the development of early Christology, with specific reference to the question of whether it implies the idea of preexistence. In this essay, I will consider both questions, but with a focus on the second. I begin by briefly highlighting the distinctiveness of the formula in relation to antecedent philosophical and biblical traditions. The main section of the essay surveys the key New Testament texts with particular attention paid to the question of whether the idea of preexistence is a necessary category for making sense of the formula in its literary and theological context. The final section of the essay connects these two modes of enquiry, suggesting that the formula belongs to a body of memory tradition relating to the question of Jesus' self-understanding as one commissioned by God. The categories of sending and sonship combine in early Christian tradition, I suggest, less as a prototypical articulation of the idea of preexistence and more as a commemoration of Jesus' sense of divine appointment and vocation.

II   The Sending of the Son: Antecedent Traditions

The most substantive treatment of the history of religions context for understanding the "sending of the Son" formula is Eduard Schweizer's oft-cited 1966 article which surveys a range of potential antecedent traditions that may have informed the "idea of a sending of the Son of God from heaven."[6] Despite its erudition, several features of that analysis are striking. To begin, Schweizer himself is clear that the basic structural features of the formula (God as subject + verb of sending + the son as object) do not in themselves imply notions of preexistence.[7] In the vast majority of cases, the idea of being sent on a mission by God carries with it no sense of heavenly origin or divine identity. The LXX, for example, seems to use the language of divine sending primarily in relation to the commissioning of Moses and other prophets.[8] Notably, it is a motif that occurs in connection with the vocation of Isaiah's servant.[9]

---

6. Schweizer, "Zum religionsgeschichtlichen," 199–210, here p.199. A summary can be found in *TDNT* 8.374–376.

7. *TDNT* 8:375

8. See Judges 6:8; 1 Chronicles 25:5; Jeremiah 35:15; 43:1; Ezekiel 2:4; Haggai 1:2; Zechariah 6:15; Tobit 14:4; Judith 11:16, 22; Baruch 1:21; cf. Josephus, *Jewish War.* 3.400.

9. Isaiah 48:16; 61:1 cf. Jeremiah 43:10.

Texts that seem to refer to a sending "from heaven" almost never specifically identify the one sent as God's "son." The very "Johannine" reference to Raphael in Tob 12:20 ('I am ascending to the one who sent me'/ἀναβαίνω πρὸς τὸν ἀποστείλαντά με) for example, lacks this crucial element. Schweizer himself notes that the combination only really occurs in Jewish texts informed by Egyptian/Alexandrian speculation.[10] It is debatable, however, whether even the Philonic texts to which he appeals offer convincing parallels.[11] Schweizer himself makes much of the reference in Wis 9:10–17 to the sending of Wisdom and the Spirit, but this text again lacks the very specific filial relationship of the early Christian formula.[12] The closest parallels with that mythological scheme are found in Greek and Jewish speculation about the immanence of the *logos* and/or divine wisdom in creation.[13] Crucially, however, and in contrast to the focus of the Pauline and Johannine formulations, these sources are oriented primarily towards cosmological speculation, rather than soteriological reflection.

Perhaps the main lacuna in Schweizer's study is his failure to give adequate attention to the possibility of a more proximate antecedent tradition that, as I will propose below, provides us with a more appropriate context for explaining the appearance of the sending of the Son formula in Paul and John.[14] Stated more precisely, the formula clearly belongs to the body of Jesus traditions that speak of Jesus' own vocational awareness; traditions that, we can hypothesize, are best explained by the proposal that Jesus of Nazareth spoke of himself and his mission in this way. Before exploring that proposal in more detail, however, we should turn to the formula itself as we encounter it in the New Testament and consider the claim that its presence there is the result of early attempts to articulate a Christology of preexistence or doctrine of incarnation.

10. Schweizer, "Zum religionsgeschichtlichen," 204–06.

11. See Lee, *From Messiah*, 298.

12. The connection between Wisdom 9:10–17 and a text like Gal 4:4–6 is not anywhere as obvious as some assume. See the discussion in Lee, *From Messiah*, 303–304.

13. See Wisdom 9:10; Philo Conf. 145–48; Psalm 106:20; 147:4, 7.

14. Schweizer, "Zum religionsgeschichtlichen,," 206–207 offers brief comments, noting that, while Synoptic Jesus traditions might 'have prompted further development', it cannot explain the preexistence aspect of the sending formula. By arguing as we do that the formula contains no such aspect, the way is left open for a reconnection to the Jesus tradition as the main interpretative context for understanding.

III   The Pauline Evidence

As is the case with the traditions that Schweizer surveyed, on the face of
it there is nothing that is inherent in Paul's language of God's "sending his
son" that requires interpretation by reference to the son's heavenly origin.[15]
Nevertheless, there is a dominant line of interpretation that concludes that
preexistence is assumed by Galatians 4:4 and Romans 8:3.[16] In what follows
I indicate why, ultimately, I find those arguments unpersuasive.

Galatians 4:4

As James Dunn shows, Paul's use of the verb ἐξαποστέλλω here "does not tell
us tell us anything about the origin or point of departure of the one sent."
Instead, "it underlies the heavenly origin of his *commissioning* but not of the
one commissioned."[17] To say, as Gathercole does, that the verb sounds like
"a mission from God or from the heavenly counsel" is a real stretch.[18]

Two further exegetical arguments, commonly deployed, support the
claim that Paul's statement about the sending of the Son in Galatians 4:4
probably or necessarily implies the Son's preexistence. First, in Gal 4:6, Paul
uses the same formula to describe the sending of the Spirit into the hearts of
believers, explicitly connecting the Spirit to the Son in the process.[19]

4:4	ἐξαπέστειλεν ὁ θεὸς τὸν υἱὸν αὐτοῦ
4:6	ἐξαπέστειλεν ὁ θεὸς τὸ πνεῦμα τοῦ υἱοῦ αὐτοῦ

This "double sending," it is claimed, presupposes a shared pre-existent identity between the Spirit and the Son and, according to Fee, "makes certain that
. . . Paul is also speaking presuppositionally about Christ's preexistence."[20]

Yet, the two verses quite clearly refer to separate events, and separate
aspects of God's action in "the fullness of time" (4:3), and the repetition of
the verb may simply be stylistic. Crucially, what determines the presence
of preexistence in 4:6 is not the verb but the noun πνεῦμα with its likely
allusion to Psalm 104:30.[21] That the sending of a non-preexistent, prophetic

---

15. So, rightly, Kuschel, *Born*, 275.

16. Kramer, *Christ*, 114–15; George, ""God Sent,"" 65–85

17. Dunn, *Christology*, 39.

18. Gathercole, *Preexistent Son*, 29.

19. Gathercole, *Preexistent*, 29, Fee, *Pauline Christology*, 213–4, 509; Keener, *Galatians*, 337.

20. Fee, *Pauline Christology*, 509.

21. "ἐξαποστελεῖς τὸ πνεῦμά σου, καὶ κτισθήσονται" (Ps 104 (102 LXX):30). Cf. Exod

messenger and the sending of the Spirit can appear in the same breath is established by Isaiah 48:16 (LXX): "and now the Lord has sent me and his spirit" ("καὶ νῦν κύριος ἀπέσταλκέν με καὶ τὸ πνεῦμα αὐτοῦ"). Isaiah 61:1, with its reference to Spirit anointing and commissioning, serves also to illuminate the significance of the connection between the Spirit and the Son in Galatians 4:6. There, the "Lord" bestows the Spirit on the anointed one without any indication that the one so anointed is somehow pre-existent.[22] The existence of a clear purpose clauses in Galatians 4:4 and 4:7 (ὥστε) suggests that this commissioning scenario is in view and that the phrase "spirit of his Son" in 4:6 makes best sense when read as indicating the Son's possession of the Spirit as the consequence of that divine bestowal.[23]

The second argument lies in the claim that the sending of Galatians 4:4 is clearly related to Christ's being "born of woman."[24] A reference to birth is unnecessary, so the argument goes, if it were not making the point that the one "born" had a form of existence prior to that birth.[25] Furthermore, Paul's use of γενόμενος both in terms of lexical choice (not γεννάω) and syntax (posterior to the main verb, rather than antecedent) suggest preexistence.[26] Again, these points are less than convincing. Equivalent phrases are found in the LXX (1 Chr 2:18; 8:8; Job 11:2; 14:1; 15:14; 25:4) and elsewhere to refer simply to the birth of a human being.[27]

To this may be added the more positive observation, which we will see is a feature of all occurrences of the formula: that Paul's use of the sending motif takes its significance from the soteriological scheme implied in his wider argument. This scheme is evoked by the language of "redemption" (ἐξαγοράζω) and "adoption as sons/children" (υἱοθεσία) in 4:5. The sending of the son in this verse is quite clearly oriented towards the divine redemptive purpose that, in Paul's theology more broadly, is always focused on the event of Christ's saving death (cf. Gal 2:20: "the son of God who loved me and gave himself for me").[28]

To be clear, this is not to say that Paul does not, in other places and with other forms of articulation, espouse some kind of divine Christology

---

15:10 (LXX); Jdt 16:14; Odes Sol. 1:10; Wis 9.17.

22. "Πνεῦμα κυρίου ἐπ᾽ ἐμέ . . .εὐαγγελίσασθαι πτωχοῖς ἀπέσταλκέν με" (Isa 61:1 LXX). Cf. Luke 4:18.

23. For the alternative view see Keener, *Galatians*, 336.

24. Gathercole, *Preexistent*, 29.

25. Fee, *Pauline Christology*, 214–215, 509–510.

26. Fee, *Pauline Christology*, 215–16.

27. Cf. Jub 11:14 and the phrase ילוד אשה in 1QS 11:21; 1QH 5:31; 21:2; 4Q264 fr1:8; 4Q482 fr1:4; 4Q501 fr1:5.

28. So Dunn, *Christology*, 41–42.

or notion of preexistence.[29] Yet, in my view the exegetical arguments supporting the claim that we should interpret Paul's language as connoting something other or more than the idea that Jesus is God's decisive and unique messenger are not compelling.

Romans 8:3

Romans 8 also opens with language that contributes to what Wesley Hill has called the "exegetical roots" of trinitarian theology.[30] Those who are "in Christ" are set free from "law of sin and death" by means of the "law of the Spirit of life" (8:2). This deliverance is nothing less than the action of God, made possible by God's "sending his own Son in the likeness of sinful flesh" (8:3). Gordon Fee asserts that preexistence is the natural "presupposition" of Paul's language here, in that it implies that the one who took flesh had an existence prior to that fleshy experience.[31] The key exegetical question is whether the combination of motifs referring to the (a) intimacy of the relationship with the Father (τὸν ἑαυτοῦ υἱὸν) and (b) the fact of Jesus' human existence (ἐν ὁμοιώματι σαρκὸς ἁμαρτίας) are sufficient to warrant the conclusion that "we are up against strong evidence of the presence of the doctrine of the Incarnation in Paul's thought."[32]

In both cases, this is to read too much into Paul's language. The language of "God's own son" is simply emphatic and anticipates the evocation of the *Aqedah* at Romans 8:32 ("ὅς γε τοῦ ἰδίου υἱοῦ οὐκ ἐφείσατο").[33] Overall, Romans 8:3 is syntactically awkward, perhaps because of the insertion of the formula.[34] The phrase "ἐν ὁμοιώματι σαρκὸς ἁμαρτίας," used in relation to Jesus, is matched and adequately explained by the soteriological formulation that follows: "περὶ ἁμαρτίας κατέκρινεν τὴν ἁμαρτίαν ἐν τῇ σαρκί." It describes Christ's "entering the condition of Adam" to the point of identification with the Adamic condition of enslavement to the powers of sin and death.[35] The same sentiments lie behind Philippians 2:7: "ἐν ὁμοιώματι ἀνθρώπων γενόμενος." Brendan Byrne is right to state that the phrase means

29. See, of course, Philippians 2:6–11 and the discussion of the wider question in Tilling, *Paul's Divine*.

30. Hill, *Paul*, 171.

31. Fee, *Pauline Christology*, 246–247; 510.

32. Cranfield, "Some Comments," here 271.

33. Cranfield, *Romans*, I, 379.

34. So Keck, "Law," 43–44.

35. Hooker, *From Adam*, 32. Cf. Dunn, *Christology*, 45. The scheme overall is captured well in Hooker's notion of salvific "interchange."

something like "the concrete, palpable form proper to human existence," but what drives that assertion for Paul is the notion that *as* one like us, immersed *in* the human condition of weakness and servitude, Christ is able to deliver us from that enslavement.[36]

IV   The Johannine Evidence

John 3:17

It goes without saying that, when viewed as a whole, the Gospel of John offers an account of the relationship between the Father and the Son in terms that imply preexistence.[37] The Johannine presentation of the incarnation of the divine λόγος in 1:14 is associated directly with the revelation of the identity of "a father's only one, full of grace and truth" (cf. 1:18).[38] Undoubtedly, this initial association between the pre-existent Word and the commissioned Son provides the reader with a lens through which to view the subsequent language of sending. Nevertheless, the issue is whether pre-existence is itself in view in the occurrence of the formula in John 3:17. Barrett insists that, here, the "stress does not lie on the theological relations between the Father and Son implied by the process of sending, but on the purpose of the mission."[39] This seems to be established by 3:18 where the language is of God's "giving" of the only son ("τὸν υἱὸν τὸν μονογενῆ ἔδωκεν") through love.[40] On the other hand the phrase "into the world" can connote, in the Johannine symbolic universe, ideas of incarnation (see 1:9; 16:28; 17:18).

Yet not exclusively so. Texts like John 6:14; 10:36; 11:27 speak of Jesus' coming into the world as prophet and/or Messiah. Similarly here, the notion that Jesus is "sent into the world" in order bring salvation may well convey

36. Byrne SJ, *Romans*, 243 and see the extended discussion in Byrne, *"Sons of God,"* 198–205. Like a number of others, Byrne suggests the preexistence is implied by Romans 8:3 under the pressure of texts like Philippians 2:7 and 2 Corinthians 8:9. Reading Philippians 2:7 in terms of preexistence is entirely dependent on the interpretation of Philippians 2:6, and 2 Corinthians 8:9 should probably be read causally as a reference to Christ's generosity in self-giving, rather than concessively and primarily in terms of incarnation: see Barclay, "'Because.'"

37. I say "imply" because of John is careful to use language other than that of "son" when talking about preexistence.

38. Even here in the Prologue, John's language of μονογένης is anticipatory in relation to the specific title of 'son of God' that begins at 1:34.

39. Barrett, *John*, 216.

40. Again, I detect a likely allusion to Genesis 22 here, raising the possibility that this text helped to shape the particular form of Jesus memory visible in the sending formula.

little more (or less) than the claim that Jesus has been commissioned by God as prophet and Messiah. John 3:17 says that divine salvation is "through" the Son ("δι᾽ αὐτοῦ") referring to his role as Revealer, God's agent who brings the light of divine judgment into the world.

Finally, the most important reason to be reluctant to read John's full-blown doctrine of preexistence into these sentiments is not exegetical but theological. Stated briefly, the λόγος is not "sent" by God and doesn't need to be. The λόγος self-determines to become "flesh" and so is the subject of the main verbs in 1:14.

1 John 4:9–10, 14

First John 4 uses variations of the "sending of the Son" formula as a way of describing the revelation of divine love (4:9), with a view to establishing God's love as the source and motivation for the call to love one another (4:11).[41] In contrast to John 3:16–17, the "world" here functions merely as a description of the location of that revelation in the sending of the Son, rather than as the object of divine love *per se*. The focus of the statements throughout, as the language of life (ζάω 4:9), atoning sacrifice (ἱλασμός 4:10), and savior (σωτήρ 4:14) makes clear, is on the soteriological events that ground the ethical call to mutual love. While it is tempting to read a theology of preexistence into the use of μονογενής in 4:9, that term cannot bear that kind of Christological weight. To affirm the uniqueness of Jesus' "sonship" is not the same thing as determining the eternal or pre-temporal nature of that filial identity.[42] The use of ἱλασμός in 4:10 clearly locates God's saving work in Jesus' crucifixion rather than in the incarnation.

In summary, the arguments in support of the claim that Paul and John's reference to the sending of the Son presuppose the notion of the Son's preexistence are not robust enough. In both traditions, while the notion of preexistence might be a feature of the wider theological picture, it is not a necessary category for making sense of the sending formula itself. The evidence suggests that Paul and the Johannine authors use the formula to articulate the eschatological and soteriological significance of Jesus' messianic vocation and especially his saving death, rather than the relationship

---

41. The repeated ἐν τούτωι in 4:9–10 sets up the εἰ οὕτως of 4:11. In 4:9, the unnecessary repetition of θεὸς suggests the use of a pre-established formula. See Lieu, *I, II, & III John*, 180.

42. See the discussion in Brown, *Epistles*, 516–17.

between divinity and humanity in the person and story of Jesus. As Michael Peppard has quipped, "God sent [the Son] to Golgotha—not Bethlehem."[43]

V   The Historical Jesus

Rather than explaining the "sending of the Son" formula by reference to antecedent philosophical/theological traditions or subsequent developments in Christian doctrine, I propose that the primary impulse for Paul and John's usage is an enduring memory tradition relating to the historical Jesus' self-understanding.[44] The sending of the son formula is, to use Chris Keith's term, an instance of "Jesus-memory" for which the historian can try to give an account.[45] In other words, the formula, when laid alongside a data-set of related traditions, invites us to "posit an actual past that best explains the existence of early Jesus-memories in light of the contexts of remembrance in early Christianity."[46] By formulating the issue in this way, it is crucial to remember that the Pauline and Johannine traditions outside of the gospel genre are nevertheless valuable witnesses to the developing Jesus tradition, or emerging trajectories of "remembering Jesus."[47]

It remains to consider the additional data that connects most closely to the form of Jesus-memory preserved in the sending of the Son formula. At the most general level, we observe that the notion of Jesus being somehow "sent" by God for his work occurs at several points within the early Jesus traditions. We can only provide an incomplete summary of this evidence, without detailed analysis.

1. The logion preserved in Matthew 10:40–41//Luke 10.16 and Mark 9:37//Matthew 18://Luke 9:48, referring to the welcome afforded to the disciples/children, Jesus, and the "one who sent me." The collocation of this saying with that about the welcoming of the "prophet" or "righteous person" in Matthew suggests some form of prophetic

---

43. Peppard, *Son of God*, 138.

44. Cf. Dunn, *Christology*, 40.

45. Keith, *Jesus' Literacy*, 66. The summary of the 'Jesus-memory' approach to the tradition on pp.50–68 is developed in greater detail in Keith, "Social Memory (Part One)," 354–76; Keith, "Social Memory (Part Two)," 517–42.

46. Keith, *Jesus' Literacy*, 67.

47. One of the significant strengths of more recent approaches to the study of the historical Jesus, informed by the insights of social memory theory and contemporary historiography, lies in its capacity to integrate the data from Paul and John (and other non-Synoptic early traditions) without making the 'authenticity' of those traditions the primary focus of concern.

vocational self-understanding, a motif also found in Matthew 23:34 (with specific reference to crucifixion); 23:37; Luke 11:49.

2. Similar sentiments are preserved in the logion embedded in Matthew 15:24: "I was sent only to the lost sheep of the house of Israel."

3. The centrality of the language of sending in Luke's programmatic account of Jesus initial preaching in the Nazareth synagogue is relevant (Luke 4:16–30). The dynamics of this text revolve around Jesus' general claim (4:18–19) that the promise of Isaiah 61:1–2—of one whom God has "anointed" ("ἔχρισέν με") and "sent" ("ἀπέσταλκέν με")—has been fulfilled (4:21). This vocation is then framed in explicitly prophetic terms by reference to the "sending" of Elijah in 4:26 and undoubtedly informs the vocational statement in Luke 4:43.

4. The parable of the workers in the vineyard (Mark 12:1–12//Matthew 21:33–46//Luke 20:9–19//G.Thom 65–66), whatever its likely origins, clearly reaches some form of dramatic climax in its reference to the final sending of the "(beloved) son."[48] James Dunn says of this text that "[t]here is no more immediate parallel to Galatians 4:4 or more obvious allusion intended than that provided by Jesus' own manner of speaking about himself and by his parable of the dishonest tenants."[49] Whatever one's views about the likely authenticity of the parable, the close connection between its language and the "sending formula" find a fitting explanation in the hypothesis that both preserve forms of early Christian memory generated out of Jesus' filial and vocational self-understanding.[50]

5. Jesus is remembered as sending his own disciples on mission in terms that explicitly connect that mission with his own: see Matthew 10:1–15 cf. 5:23 and 15:24//Mark 3:13–19; 6:7–13//Luke 6:12–16; 9:1–6; cf. the

---

48. The use of υἱός ἀγαπητός in Mark 12:6 and Luke 20:13 clearly strengthen the christological force of this element of the parable, although it remains a story focused on the relationship between the tenants and the owner of the vineyard. Matthew's lack of ἀγαπητός in his reference to the son is striking, though even without this level of Christological specificity, the parable in its Synoptic narrative contexts invites a reading in terms of Jesus' indirect self-reference. GThom continues this trajectory of muting the parable's implicit Christology. In an essay in honor of Dorothy Lee it is, perhaps, fitting to eschew citation of the major works of scholarship on this parable in favor of a reference to the short note by one of her (and my) predecessors: McCaughey, "Two Synoptic Parables," 24–28

49. Dunn, *Christology*, 40 (emphasis removed)

50. John P. Meier argues for the authenticity of the parable based on the criterion of embarrassment in Meier, *Marginal Jew: Parables*, 240–53. On the parables as media of early Christian memory, see Zimmermann, *Puzzling*, 76–99.

logion in Matthew 10:16. See also the programmatic John 20:21 and the emerging "apostolic" self-understanding/office in the early Jesus movements.

6. References to the sending of God's Messiah/servant occur in accounts of early Christian proclamation in Acts: see Acts 3:20, 26.

7. The significant and weighty Johannine sending motif mentioned in section I above.

Wider and deeper analysis of early Jesus traditions relating to sending, sonship, and the relationship between them would clearly be valuable here. Yet, this initial gathering of evidence is sufficient to invite an explanation by the hypothesis that the historical Jesus regarded himself as one who was "sent by God" for his mission, described himself as such, invited others to share that self-understanding, and so created a form of "Jesus memory" that was profoundly "apostolic" in character. It is to this memory trajectory that the sending of the son formula belongs.

VI   Conclusion

In the *Epistle to Diognetus* we read that:

> The all-powerful and all-creating one, the invisible God. . . did not send, as one might imagine, some kind of servant, or messenger to humanity. . . but the designer and creator of all things . . . by whom all things have been determined, distinguished, and subjected: heavens and the things in heaven; earth and things in the earth; sea and the things in the sea; fire; air; abyss; things in the high place; things in the deep; things in the inbetween — this is the one that he sent to them. He sent him in kindness and gentleness, as a king sends a son. He sent [him] as God, as a human to humanity. (*Ep. Diog* 7:1–4)[51]

This quotation makes it clear that, by the middle of the second-century, the motif of the sending of the Son was embedded into the more expansive Christological categories of preexistence and incarnation. While it is, of course, possible that the sending of the son formula emerges from an earlier stage of such belief, and while it is also true that both Paul and John elsewhere provide the raw materials for the development of the doctrines

---

51. Translation and emphasis mine. The whole section from 7:1–5 is even more rhetorically decorative than this selection would suggest.

of preexistence and incarnation (Phil 2:6–11 and John 1:1–18 as the most explicit examples), the formula itself does not require those categories to be comprehensible in terms of its constituent terms, structure, and discursive locations in Paul and John. Once this point is granted, it seems to me that the formula itself, as it appears in New Testament writings, need not be interpreted within any other framework than that of divine appointment and commissioning. The categories of sending and sonship in combination do not require the notion of preexistence in order to be fully understandable.

Perhaps the most interesting feature of the formula, then, is not its preparatory role in relation to the development of the doctrines of preexistence and incarnation, but its commemorative role in relation to the self-understanding of Jesus of Nazareth. The "Jesus memory" approach to such material provides us with ample possibilities for theological and Christological reflection, without the need for overconfident but ultimately anachronistic claims about the presence of subsequent doctrinal ideas in the pages of the New Testament. After all, what is more significant for Christian faith? That Paul and John use this formula to clearly and effectively espouse a theology of preexistence well in advance of (and as the biblical foundation for) later Christological orthodoxy? Or that the emerging orthodoxy of the second through fourth centuries belongs clearly to a trajectory of Jesus memory that goes back to the self-understanding and self-description of Jesus of Nazareth?

Bibliography

Barclay, John M. G. "'Because He Was Rich He Became Poor': Translation, Exegesis, and Hermeneutics in the Reading of 2 Cor 8:9," Pages 331–344 in *Theologizing in the Corinthian Conflict: Studies in the Exegesis and Theology of 2 Corinthians.* Edited by Reimund Bieringer, Marilou S. Ibita, Dominika A. Kurek-Chomycz, and Thomas Vollmer. Vol. 16 of *Biblical Tools and Studies.* Leuven: Peeters, 2013.

Barrett, C. K. *The Gospel According to St John: An Introduction with Commentary and Notes on the Greek Text.* 2nd ed. London: SPCK, 1978.

Brown, Raymond. *Epistles of John.* Anchor Bible series. New Haven: Yale University Press 1995.

Byrne, Brendan. *"Sons of God"—"Seed of Abraham": A Study of the Idea of the Sonship of God of all Christians in Paul against the Jewish Background.* AnBib 83. Rome: Biblical Institute, 1979.

Byrne SJ, Brendan. *Romans.* SP 6. Collegeville: Michael Glazier, 1996.

Cranfield, C. E. B. *A Critical and Exegetical Commentary on the Epistle to the Romans.* 2 vols. Edinburgh: T & T Clark, 1975, 1979.

Cranfield, C. E. B. "Some Comments on Professor J. D. G. Dunn's Christology in the Making with Special Reference to the Evidence of the Epistle to the Romans," *The Glory of Christ in the New Testament: Studies in Christology in Memory of George*

Bradford Caird. Edited by L. D. Hurst and N. T. Wright. Oxford: Oxford University Press, 1987, 267–280.

de Boer, Martinus C. *Galatians: A Commentary*. NTL. Louisville: Westminster John Knox, 2011.

Dunn, James D. G. *Christology in the Making: An Inquiry into the Origins of the Doctrine of the Incarnation*. Second ed. London: SCM, 1989.

Dunn, James D. G. "Under the Law," *Paul, John, and Apocalyptic Eschatology: Studies in Honour of Martinus C. de Boer*. Edited by Jan Krans, Bert Jan Lietart Peerbolte, Peter-Ben Smit, and Arie Zwiep. Vol. 149 of *Supplements to Novum Testamentum*. Leiden: Brill, 2013, 48–60.

Fee, Gordon. D. *Pauline Christology: An Exegetical-Theological Study*. Peabody: Hendrickson, 2007.

Gathercole, Simon J. *The Preexistent Son: Recovering the Christologies of Matthew, Mark and Luke*. Grand Rapids / Cambridge: Eerdmans, 2006.

George, Roji T. "'God Sent His Son: Born of a Woman' (Gal. 4:4): The Idea of Incarnation, its Antecendents, and Significance in Paul's Theology." *Doon Theological Journal* 5 (2008) 65–85.

Harding, Mark. "Kyrios Christos: Johannine and Pauline Perspectives on the Christ Event." *Paul and the Gospels: Christologies, Conflicts and Convergences*. Edited by Michael F. Bird and Joel Willitts. Vol. 411 of *Library of New Testament Studies*. London: Bloomsbury, 2011, 169–196.

Hill, Wesley. *Paul and the Trinity: Persons, Relations and the Pauline Letters*. Grand Rapids: Eerdmans, 2015.

Hooker, Morna D. *From Adam to Christ: Essays on Paul*. Cambridge: Cambridge University Press, 1990.

Josephus. *The Jewish War*. Translated by H. St. J. Thackeray. Loeb Classical Library 210. Cambridge, MA: Harvard University Press, 1928.

Keck, Leander E. "The Law and 'The Law of Sin and Death' (Rom 8:1–4): Reflections on the Spirit and Ethics in Paul." *The Divine Helmsman: Studies on God's Control of Human Events, Presented to Lou H. Silberman*. Edited by James L. Crenshaw and Samuel Sandmel. New York: Ktav, 1980, 41–56.

Keener, Craig S. *Galatians: A Commentary*. Grand Rapids: Baker Academic, 2019.

Keith, Chris. *Jesus' Literacy: Scribal Culture and the Teacher from Galilee*. LNTS 413 / Library of Historical Jesus Studies 8. London: Bloomsbury, 2011.

Keith, Chris. "Social Memory Theory and Gospels Research: The First Decade (Part One)." *Early Christianity* 6 (2015) 354–376.

Keith, Chris. "Social Memory Theory and Gospels Research: The First Decade (Part Two)." *Early Christianity* 6 (2015) 517–542.

Kramer, Werner. *Christ, Lord, Son of God*. Translated by Brian Hardy. Vol. 50, SBT. London: SCM, 1966 [1963].

Kruse, Colin G. "Paul and John: Two Witnesses, One Gospel," Pages 197–219 in *Paul and the Gospels: Christologies, Conflicts and Convergences*. Edited by Michael F. Bird and Joel Willitts. Vol. 411 of *Library of New Testament Studies*. London: Bloomsbury, 2011.

Kuschel, Karl-Josef. *Born Before All Time: The Dispute Over Christ's Origin*. Translated by John Bowden. London: SCM, 1992 [1990].

Lee, Aquila H.I. *From Messiah to Preexistent Son*. Vol. 192. WUNT2. Tübingen: Mohr Siebeck, 2005.

Lieu, Judith M. *I, II & III John*. NTL. Louisville: Westminster John Knox, 2008.

McCaughey, J. D. "Two Synoptic Parables in the Gospel of Thomas." *Australian Biblical Review* 8 (1960) 24–28.

Meier, John P. *A Marginal Jew, Volume V: Probing the Authenticity of the Parables*. New Haven: Yale University Press, 2016.

Peppard, Michael. *The Son of God in the Roman World: Divine Sonshiop in its Social and Political Context*. New York: Oxford University Press, 2011.

Philo. *On the Confusion of Tongues. On the Migration of Abraham. Who Is the Heir of Divine Things? On Mating with the Preliminary Studies*. Translated by F. H. Colson, G. H. Whitaker. Loeb Classical Library 261. Cambridge, MA: Harvard University Press, 1932.

Schweizer, Eduard. "Zum religionsgeschichtlichen Hintergrund der 'Sendungsformel' Gal 4 4f. Rom 8 3f. Joh 3 16f. I Joh 4 9." *Zeitschrift für Neutestamentliche Wissenschaft und die Kunde der Älteren Kirche* 57 (1966) 199–210.

Seeberg, Alfred. *Der Katechismus der Urchristenheit*. TB Neues Testament 26. Munich: Chr. Kaiser, 1966.

Tilling, Chris. *Paul's Divine Christology*. Grand Rapids: Eerdmans, 2015 [2012].

Zimmermann, Ruben. *Puzzling the Parables of Jesus: Methods and Interpretation*. Minneapolis: Fortress, 2015.

9.

Live and Let Live

Paul's Advice on Ethical Diversity to the "Weak" and the "Strong" in Rome (Romans 14:1–15:5)

FERGUS J. KING

Introduction

Romans 1:26–27 has provided a text whose exegesis appears intractable amidst the debates over human sexuality which beset modern Christian life. Several exegetical and interpretive steps contribute to this. It has proven impossible to reach either a definitive conclusion or agreement about the sexual activities Paul has within his sights,[1] about whether his remarks may be taken to apply what are often differentiated as behaviors or orientations,[2] or whether his identification of these as symptomatic of idolatry, or ignorance about God (the fundamental issue rather than its symptoms)[3] remains applicable. The tendency to atomize and/or use short texts as proof texts has further meant that attention has focused exclusively on sexual behavior.[4] Yet, the behaviors listed in Rom 1:29–31 are equally indicative of an

---

1. Loader, *The New Testament*, 309–311.

2. Loader, *The New Testament*, 321–326; Martin, "The Possibility," 65–66.

3. Loader, *The New Testament on Sexuality*, 297–298.

4. See, for example, Sherlock, "Reading Romans."

idolatrous disposition or rebellion against God which "culminates in despair,"[5] and part of a longer argument (Rom 1:16–3:20), which culminates in recognition of the brokenness of the entirety of humanity[6] rather than highlight the shortcomings of a subgroup for exceptional treatment.[7] As a result, there is a massive distortion of the significance of sexual as opposed to other antisocial behaviors which Paul has included in his critique of idolatry and the human condition. An exclusive focus on sexual mores undermines the thrust of Paul's argument, which is that all of humanity falls short of the behavior desired by God.

When Paul turns his attention to paraenesis in Romans 12–15, he sets out his views on living well which will reveal the aspirations, aims and values which are appropriate to the message he has delineated. However, his attention does not return to matters of sexual mores. Instead, Paul focuses on an issue which was deeply contentious for the new Christian congregations: the question of food. He makes a case for communal living which offers an opportunity for those holding different views to be able to live together.[8]

Three factors appear to shape his argument: a focus on orthodoxy as grounded in belief in the Risen Christ rather than evaluated on a particular behavior, the ethical category known in antiquity as ἀδιάφορον, and the contemporary discussion of food and purity by Jewish teachers. The intercultural dimensions of his approach should not come as a surprise: the broad cultural movements identifiable as Graeco-Romanitas and Judaism were not discrete. Paul and his audience were inhabitants of both, and would have operated socially and intellectually in both. Above all else, they should not be seen as pioneers in some independent new third way: that would come later.

If Romans cannot resolve the question of the value of sexual practice, it might at least offer a strategy for those whose views differ on a substantive and divisive issue to maintain a common life.

Food: An Ethical Crux for the Early Church

One of the greatest challenges that faced the new Christian congregations was the degree to which Judaic practice and customs had to be adopted, particularly by those who came from non-Jewish backgrounds. Food and

5. Johnson, *Reading Romans*, 32.

6. Matera, *Romans*, 41–42; Stendahl, "The Apostle Paul," 200–202.

7. Loader, *The New Testament*, 294.

8. The discussion of food is considered by some to be a hypothetical rather than a historical issue, see Johnson, *Reading Romans*, 209–212.

associated behaviors about preparation and consumption had long been a part of Judaic life,[9] rooted in the descriptions of both the Noahic (Gen 9) and Mosaic covenants (e.g. Lev 17–18).[10] They continued to be the focus of much debate within Second Temple Judaism. Emerging Christianity, which located itself within the boundaries of Judaism, added even more variety to the debate. Paul's own writings provide glimpses of the issues involved, particularly in Gal 2:11–14, and its account of Paul's dispute with Peter at Antioch.

As a result, what has emerged is—to use David Rudolph's phrase—a "traditional view," in which passages like Rom 14:14, 20 are read as though Jewish food laws are redundant.[11] However, such a verdict is not straightforward. Other debates within emerging Christianity are distracting. The pronouncements of the Jerusalem Council (Acts 15:20, 29; 21:25) appear to address issues of dietary practice and purity, and suggest a degree of compliance, but this is misleading. Their proscriptions, all of which are related to idolatry, are better understood as forbidding participation in the meals associated with Graeco-Roman religious practice (cf. 1 Cor 8, 10) than adherence to *kashrut* and Judaic dietary practice.[12]

The issue is further complicated by the apparent absence of a precise ruling or example which might be directly attributed to Jesus.[13] In the absence of a clear dominical statement, it becomes the work of the evangelists to interpret what he intended. Thus, Mark 7:19, that all foods are clean, is well described as "a parenthetical comment."[14] Adding such clarifications suggests that these issues had not been resolved by the time of the gospel's composition, and that the controversy had persisted long after Paul's writing to the Galatians and the Romans. Coupled with this is the possibility that Jesus did not contravene the food laws: Ed P. Sanders has identified many of Jesus' controversial statements and actions, including those about eating, as disagreements over the interpretation of the Law, sometimes from the perspective of the evangelists retroverted into Jesus' own context, rather than a rejection of the Law itself.[15]

The persistence of the debate about dietary practice indicates that these matters had still not been resolved after the writing of Romans. It is this issue which Paul addresses in the most detailed section of his paraenesis

9. Keener, *Romans*, 161–162.

10. King, "Of Blood," 192.

11. Rudolph, "Paul," 152.

12. King, "Of Blood," 196–197.

13. King, "Of Blood," 193.

14. Beavis, *Mark*, 117.

15. Sanders, *Jesus*, 209–210; 264–269.

(Rom 14:1–15:5), not sexual mores, which merit only brief comments in general proscriptions based on the commandments and vice-lists (Rom 12:8–14).[16] However, as the above remarks have indicated, it will be seen that the traditional view stands in need of refinement.

The Situation in Rome

Eating might well have been a problem in Rome because of the nature of the congregation. Even if Paul is addressing a hypothetical situation, it is nonetheless a likely scenario. As James A. Harrison has recently pointed out, the Christians at Rome would have included people from both Judaic and non-Judaic contexts who had co-existed within the congregation for years. Claudius' expulsion of the Jews from Rome in 49 CE was not permanent. Disagreements about food laws are unlikely to have arisen because of a sudden return of Jewish Christians to the city and congregation, but rather reflect long-running disputes about culture and identity in which non-Jewish and Jewish Christians alike disparaged their opponents on cultural grounds.[17] Food is an issue around which such arguments might easily coalesce.[18] Paul shows the futility of such arguments by undermining the use of categories like "weak" and "strong" in claiming superiority. In this respect, his remarks simply re-iterate his earlier contention: all humanity is sinful (Romans 1:18–3:20). Instead, he advocates an approach to community life which sets aside claims for superiority in favour of one which allows different practices to co-exist: live and let live.

The foundation for his approach is seen particularly in his view that both Jew and non-Jew have rebelled against God, the nature of faith, and its focus on the Risen Christ. This leads into a reflection on how faith is to be lived in which Paul will outline an "live and let live" ethic which, given the intercultural dimensions of the Roman church, will potentially be informed by thinking about ethics from both Graeco-Roman and Judaic traditions.

A Sense of Proportion: Faith in the Risen Christ

Consideration must be given to what Paul has already described as effecting salvation. This has two parts: the first is the content or substance, the stuff of faith, which he identifies with Jesus, who is recognized as the risen Christ.

16. Porter, "Paul," 377.

17. Harrison, *Reading Romans*, 329–331.

18. Elliott, "Asceticism," 239–241.

In its most basic form, this is the confession that Jesus is Lord (Romans 10:9), It is a metonymy, giving a specific meaning to a word (κύριος) which notoriously may embrace a wide range of honorifics. It also stands for the gospel whose ten stages from pre-existing Son of God to ruling final judge may be summarized as "Jesus is the saving king."[19] It is this, and this alone, on which Paul grounds claims for salvation, which is appropriated through faith patterned on Abraham. In the steps which precede this, the Law has been stripped of any salvific function (Rom 3:20, 8:3).

Salvation is mediated by Christ (Rom 8:2–3). Faith is the means through which salvation becomes possible (Rom 4:16). It is exemplified by Abraham, perhaps invoking the ancient trust in *antiquitas* (that what is ancient is venerable and reliable).[20] It is thus considered superior to Moses, circumcision, and the Law because it marks an older tradition within the mythic narrative of Israel. This venerable quality is seen also in Gal 3:15–22, which further limits the Law to an interim educative function until the coming of the Messiah.[21] It is intimately linked to the gifting of the Spirit (Romans 8:9–17). However, the Law is not rejected entirely (Rom 7:14). It enters a greyer area in which is it useful, even valuable, inasmuch as it identifies sin,[22] but useless in its ability to effect salvation or reconciliation with God. Yet, its role in identifying sin is still recognized as helpful, even if adherence to it does not result in any teleological benefit.

Given the focus on faith which has emerged within the subsequent interpretation of Romans, it must be remembered that faith in the time of Paul was a different beast from faith in the time of Luther. In the ancient world, faith was not primarily intellectual or epistemic, personal or introspective.[23] Teresa Morgan has highlighted that it further included both relationship and allegiance.[24] It was further shaped by concepts like covenant, which demanded that faith included not just intellectual assent, but also appropriate accompanying behaviors.[25] Faith could not have been a solely intellectual exercise, even if the subsequent portrayal of Paul's thinking as "justification by faith" may have given that impression. Certainly, Paul is of a mind that keeping the Law cannot deliver salvation or righteousness, but this never

19. Bates, *Gospel Allegiance*, 86–87.

20. Pilhofer, *Presbyteron*, 58, 130–131.

21. Stendahl, "The Apostle Paul," 206–207, who further notes that a failure to read Romans in the context of the cultural divide has contributed to the focus on introspection.

22. Stendahl, "The Apostle Paul," 212.

23. Stendahl, "The Apostle Paul," 200, 205.

24. Morgan, *Roman Faith*; Bates, *Gospel Allegiance*, 57–83.

25. Bates, *Salvation*; Keener, *Romans*, 127.

signals a complete disinterest in appropriate behavior for those who have faith. Peter Oakes sums it up well:

> The "trust," *pistis*, Paul has in mind is far from being, say, a detached assent to intellectual propositions. Such *pistis* is an attitude and/or action that involves joining to Christ. This is bound to involve belief in claims made about Christ, but it must always include a change of life.[26]

If a hermeneutical lens like "justification by faith" concludes that all human behavior is irrelevant to faith and salvation, the baby has gone out with the bathwater. The mere presence of paraenetic material designed to shape appropriate Christian behavior in Paul's writing is evidence of this:

> Romans 12:1–15:13 is central to how believers understand the relationship between justification by faith and the morally good life that expresses itself through love.[27]

Paul did not consider behavior, as opposed to Law, to be distinct from faith.

The material about the "weak" and the "strong" (Rom 14:1–15:5) reveals how Paul may have presented the continuing value of the Law. His advice is not general paraenetic comment, but appears directed to a particular issue which has arisen.[28] At its heart lie "real tensions between Roman Christians who are more and less scrupulous in their observance of Jewish dietary practices and of 'days' (14:5.6)."[29] However, the precise identification of the two groups, the "weak" and the "strong" has long vexed interpreters, and risks either giving support to anti-Judaic tendencies or permeating a the superiority of one group over the other.[30] Neither is right. As Mark Nanos has observed, Paul wishes those who would identify as "strong":

> to recognize that the practices of the 'weak' are just as valid before God as those of themselves, and that they spring from the same faith and thanksgiving towards God as their own practices (14: 3–13, 14 ff).[31]

To make his case, Paul appears to draw first, on the Graeco-Roman moral category known as the ἀδιάφορον, and second, on discussion of

---

26. Oakes, *Galatians*, 114–115.

27. Matera, *Romans*, 3.

28. Elliott, "Asceticism," 231–232.

29. Elliott, "Asceticism," 232; Matera, *Romans*, 305–309 notes this is a majority view, but is cautious of making this controversy the sole reason for the writing of the epistle.

30. Elliott, "Asceticism," 232–239.

31. Nanos, *The Mystery*, 96–97.

food, purity and eating within the debates of contemporary Second Temple Judaism.

Paul's Advice 1: Ἀδιάφορον

Greek moral theories of this period focused on living well, and the major philosophical traditions provided rationales for their preferred behaviors.[32] These delineated what was deemed beneficial/good/virtuous, harmful/bad/vicious, or neither. These last were called ἀδιάφορον. As Pierre Hadot summarizes:

> The right moral attitude consists in recognizing only as good or evil that which is morally good or evil and considering as neither good nor bad, and therefore indifferent, that which is neither good nor bad.[33]

Whilst they might be termed neutral, this is complicated by some being viewed as "preferred," even if not ultimately viewed as beneficial. Thus, for example, health and wealth might be preferable, or valued more highly that sickness and poverty, but "all are indifferent, because they do not depend on us."[34] Even life and death were considered ἀδιάφορα (Diogenes Laertius, *Vitae*, 7.104; 189).[35]

This category was associated particularly with Stoicism, which might well have informed the understanding of Roman Christians. Firstly, Stoicism was recognisably present in Neronian Rome (54–68 CE), not least in the persons of major Stoic thinkers like Seneca and Musonius Rufus within the imperial household. James A. Harrison's research posits tantalizing links between the Roman congregation and the imperial household, which would indicate links between the Christian congregation and the Stoic court.[36] Secondly, Stoicism was not an elitist philosophy, but one which, like Epicureanism, popularized its views in a variety of ways, including ἐπιτομαί (summaries of key doctrines). Seneca (*Ep.* 33.5–7) criticizes Lucilius for asking for such summaries, which, nevertheless, is evidence for the practice.[37] The appearance of Stoic teaching in public spectacles like Seneca's

---

32. Hadot, *What is Ancient Philosophy?*, 2–4.

33. Hadot, *What is Ancient Philosophy?*, 132.

34. Hadot, *What is Ancient Philosophy?*, 133.

35. Jaquette, "Life and Death," 31.

36. Harrison, *Reading Romans*,

37. MacGillivray, "Epitomizing Philosophy," 24.

tragedies[38] offers the possibility that it was part of the "visual exegesis" of Roman citizens.[39] Will Deming additionally notes a wide popular use of the category in the 150 BCE–150 CE period outwith Stoicism.[40]

Other Pauline writings (Phil 1:21–26;[41] 1 Cor 7: 18–19, 20–23, 25–38;[42] 1 Thess 5:9–10)[43] suggest that Paul was acquainted with the category. The Corinthian material may provide a significant insight for a potential use of the category in Romans. For, if Paul can designate circumcision as an ἀδιάφορον there,[44] it is not beyond the bounds that food laws could be identified thus in Romans. Significantly, use of the category appears in Rom 8:38–39 in which both life and death are viewed as incapable of separating the believer from God.[45]

Let us consider how Paul might use the category to advise the Romans about dietary practice. The proposed line of thought starts with a re-alignment of what is "morally good." The Law is not morally good because it cannot deliver what is ultimately good or beneficial. Paul identifies the morally good with faith in the Risen Jesus (Rom 10:9–10). This, of course, indicates a major departure from Stoicism, whose benefits ultimately derived from a rational realising of harmony with the Logos and creation.[46] Paul is not advocating that Stoic conceptions of the morally good be adopted. Stoicism provides the categories, but not their content. In this regard, with James L. Jaquette is right to reject Ernst Käsemann's resistance to a "doctrine of ἀδιάφορα":[47]

> Certainly the apostle is not explicitly creating a hierarchy of values on the model of the Stoics. But Paul's assessment of dietary laws as irrelevant (οὐδὲν κοινὸν δι' ἑαυτοῦ, 14:14, cf. 14:20) does relegate such actions to the catagory [sic] of ἀδιάφορα.[48]

38. Nussbaum, *The Therapy*, 439–483.

39. Harrison, *Reading Romans*,

40. Deming, "Paul and Indifferent Things," 62.

41. Jaquette, "Life and Death," 33–38.

42. Deming, "Paul and Indifferent Things," 55–60.

43. Jaquette, "Life and Death," 38–42.

44. Deming, "Paul and Indifferent Things," 60–62.

45. Jaquette, "Life and Death," 42–46.

46. DeBrabander, "Psychotherapy," 201; Hadot, *What is Ancient Philosophy?*, 204–205, 209–211; A.A. Long, *Stoic Studies* (Berkeley CA: University of California Press, 2001) 203.

47. Käsemann, *A Commentary*, 375.

48. Jaquette, "Life and Death," 49. For the more recent adoption of *adiaphoron*, see also Keener, *Romans*, 167, fn.35; Seifrid, "Romans," 684.

Given Nanos' comments on the validity of the practices of both the "weak" and the "strong," it might be better to substitute "irrelevant" with a phrase like "no basis for claiming superiority." This ensures that the comment does not accidentally consolidate the claims of the "strong" by implying that a concern with dietary laws is "irrelevant." In line with Nanos' verdict, he resists non-observance being used to claim superiority. Paul himself rejects any such conclusion, recognizing the value of the practice of the "weak" (Rom 14:6),[49] and ultimately encouraging the strategies of both parties.[50] Paul's delineation of matters such as observance of the Law, dietary practice and "days," as ἀδιάφορα employs a moral category which allows for this.

However, a verdict on the behaviors themselves is not the end of the matter. These have social consequences and ramifications which need not be ἀδιάφορα: "[ἀδιάφορα] must be used carefully, because their use is not a matter of indifference."[51] This means that their choice and practice should not disrupt the life of the community. Disputes over ἀδιάφορα should not compromise what is ultimately beneficial or good, but rather be exercized without causing a lack of harmony.[52] Whilst this is a preferred outcome which would seem to be rooted in a Graeco-Roman philosophical attitude, it also finds traction within the debates about dietary practice which were found within contemporary Judaism.

Paul's Advice 2: Jewish Dietary Practice

The suggested use of the ἀδιάφορον might suggest that Paul is primarily addressing non-Jewish members of the congregation by using a category familiar from Stoicism. Of course, the fact that Paul, himself a Jew, both knows and manipulates this philosophical trope reveals that it was known to Jewish thinkers, and could engage with their worldview and practice. However, Paul's argument potentially engages with the thinking of his Jewish contemporaries about dietary practice. It is a reminder that Judaism of this period was neither monochrome or uniform, and that it embraced a variety of approaches to *kashrut*, or dietary practice. These included approaches which might be ascetic, as seen in Pharisaic practice or Philo Judaeus' descriptions of the Therapeutae (*De Vita Contemplativa*).[53]

49. Elliott, "Asceticism," 243.

50. Elliott, "Asceticism," 244.

51. Epictetus, *Diss.* 2.5.7, cited in Jaquette, "Life and Death," 50.

52. Jacquette, "Life and Death," 50–53.

53. Elliott, "Asceticism," 240. For Philo's account as an idealisation, see Engberg

The arguments which Paul uses show the weakness of the traditional view. The first point is that Jewish dietary practice—and we have already noted that it varied within its implementation within Judaism—was not "monolithic."[54] Indeed, it was not incumbent on non-Jews to follow Judaic dietary practice: the Levitical tradition only demands this of "Jews in their relationship with God."[55] This indicates an understanding of community and identity which can tolerate a diversity over contentious issues. Furthermore, within the diversity of dietary practice, Paul uses the word κοινός which "was likely coined in Second Temple Jewish literature to refer to halakhic grey areas related to impurity that did not fit neatly into the category of ἀκάθαρτος, such as food prepared by gentiles."[56] Purity as a construct is based on "personal decisions."[57] Paul, then, may be described as "something of a first century halakhic pluralist who favored the Hillelite emphasis on personal intention when it came to issues of purity."[58]

This is a radically different reading from that of Luke Timothy Johnson who considers purity to be linked to qualities, and that Paul's words here mark a "stunning step" away from Pharisaism.[59] But is this really the case? Martin Hengel has shown that Paul retained much of his Pharisaism, but refocused it on the person of Jesus.[60] Rudolph's description tallies with this: Paul remains a product of his upbringing rather than performing a *volte-face*. Rather than presenting arguments which would clash with those of the "weak," he uses shared categories. That makes the likelihood of their accepting his advice more plausible: a "stunning step" would offer much less traction.

The examination of terms like καθαρός and κοινός as used both in earlier Jewish discussion and by near contemporaries of Paul like Yochanan be Zakkai shed light on the statement that "nothing is unclean in itself" (Rom 14:14a).[61] These suggest that Paul is correcting the "weak" by pointing out that discussions of purity are not founded on "objective ontological realities,"

Pedersen, "Philo's *De Vita Contemplativa*." Taylor, *Jewish Women Philosophers*, 8 notes that this need not demand a "binary opposition between rhetoric and historical reality." For a stunning reinforcement of that insight, see. Templeton, *The New Testament*, 2004.

54. Rudolph, "Paul and the Food Laws," 156.

55. Ehrensperger, "'Called to be Saints,'" 105–108, quotation from 106; Rudolph, "Paul and the Food Laws," 153–154.

56. Rudolph, "Paul and the Food Laws," 155–156.

57. Rudolph, "Paul and the Food Laws," 156.

58. Rudolph, "Paul and the Food Laws," 159.

59. Johnson, *Reading Romans*, 215.

60. Hengel, *The Pre-Christian Paul*.

61. Rudolph, "Paul and the Food Laws," 159–160.

but rather on "intention."[62] Johnson would agree with this: he differs from Rudolph only in viewing Paul as an innovator.[63] This grounding in intention obviates the need for uniformity in dietary practice within the life of the congregation.[64] To argue for it is unnecessary and simply harmful. Differences in practice should be tolerated rather than become vehicles to claim virtue.

Does this interpretation clash with the earlier claim that Rom 14:14a be identified as an ἀδιάφορον? Perhaps. Alternatively, it indicates that two interpretations are possible, and that this argument may be polyvalent. The text may carry an ambiguity: that Paul is using a term (κοινόν) which may bear different meanings to address the various opinions of members of the congregation. It allows him both to challenge views about purity which are based on ontological categories rather than intention, as well as to shift the status of dietary practice from the centre to the periphery, or, at least, to the indifferent. It allows him to critique both the "weak" and the "strong."

Paul's use of vocabulary which could function within Graeco-Roman and Judaic arguments alike speaks to both Jew and non-Jew, as well as those who were, like himself, immersed in both traditions. Paul allows neither to think that his advice is directed to the other: he speaks to both. He thus avoids playing favourites, or giving the impression that any onus to change is placed with either the "weak" or the "strong." Neither group need change their preferred practice, but both should stop being judgmental.[65] Judgments should be avoided because they alienate and cause others to stumble or lose faith.[66] Whether rooted in Graeco-Roman or Judaic tradition, the outcome is the same: that differences over a vexed ethical choice—in this case dietary practice—are not to become a source of division, as they are peripheral to the faith in the Risen Christ shared by all.

Concluding Remarks

Whether his remarks are couched in the ἀδιάφορον of Stoicism or the intentional dietary practice of Judaism, Paul advises the congregation at Rome that such matters are ultimately secondary to the stuff of salvation,

62. Rudolph, "Paul and the Food Laws," 162.

63. Johnson, *Reading Romans*, 215.

64. Keener, *Romans*, 162 reaches a similar conclusion without this focused argument, referring rather to choices being viewed as "religiously profitable."

65. Keener, *Romans*, 163.

66. Keener, *Romans*, 166–169.

reconciliation, and communal life. These are, rather, anchored in faith in the Risen Christ, which is held and agreed by all the congregation:

> The crucified and risen Christ rules in such a way that our sin, our death, our weakness, our errors have been defeated and overcome, whether we are counted among the "weak" or the "strong."[67]

This reality is to be lived out and expressed by the Christians at Rome. No matter how significant dietary issues may have seemed to be, they give no grounds for division, claims for superiority or judgmentalism. Paul has taken great pains to advise the Romans that no human is intrinsically righteous or good; all have rebelled against God. To introduce a hierarchy of virtue would undermine the fundamental narrative of Rom 1:18—3:20, "that God's righteousness comes by gift."[68]

Christians of the twenty-first century do not need to grapple with the issues of dietary practice with which Paul dealt. However, they do face divisive issues which raise analogous threats to the unity of Christian communities. Paul has not addressed the issues of today, but of their counterparts in his own time. To use Clodovis Boff's distinction, Romans will not give modern Christians a *what* (an immediate answer to their controversies) but, it will give them a *how* (a way to negotiate their problems).[69] To think about the structure of their ethics: about intention and integrity rather than objective categories, about what really matters and the peripheral or indifferent, about gift and virtue. About whether the centrality of confessing Jesus as Lord as the benchmark of faith has been replaced by other statements, no matter how worthy they are adjudged by their advocates. Whether the Romans heeded Paul's advice on a deeply divisive matter remains a mystery. Whether or not Paul's *how* is medicine which today's Christians might take remains to be seen.

Bibliography

Bates, Matthew W. *Gospel Allegiance: What Faith in Jesus Misses for Salvation in Christ.* Grand Rapids MI: Brazos Press, 2019.

———. *Salvation by Allegiance Alone: Rethinking Faith, Works, and the Gospel of Jesus the King.* Grand Rapids MI: Baker, 2017.

Beavis, Mary Ann. *Mark.* Paideia Commentaries on the New Testament. Grand Rapids MI: Baker Academic, 2011.

67. Seifrid, "Romans," 684.

68. Johnson, *Reading Romans*, 32.

69. Boff, *Theology*, 149.

Boff, Clodovis. *Theology and Praxis: Epistemological Foundations.* Translated by Robert R. Barr. Maryknoll NY: Orbis, 1987.

DeBrabander, Frimin. "Psychotherapy and Moral Perfection: Spinoza and the Stoics on the Prospect of Happiness." Pages 198–213 in *Stoicism: Traditions and Transformations.* Edited by Steven K. Strange and Mark Zupko. Cambridge: Cambridge University Press, 2004.

Deming, Will. "Paul and Indifferent Things." Pages 48–67 in *Paul in the Greco-Roman World: A Handbook Vol. II.* Edited by J. Paul Sampley. Rev'd ed. London: Bloomsbury/ T&T Clark, 2016.

Ehrensperger, Kathy. "'Called to be Saints'- The Identity Shaping Dimensions of Paul's Priestly Discourse in Romans." Pages 90–109 in *Reading Paul in Context: Explorations in Identity Formation. Essays in Honour of William S. Campbell.* Edited by Kathy Ehrensperger and J. Brian Tucker. Library of New Testament Studies. London: Bloomsbury/T&T Clark, 2010.

Elliott, Neil. "Asceticism among the 'Weak' and the 'Strong' in Romans 14–15." Pages 231–251 in *Asceticism in the New Testament.* Edited by Leif E. Vaage and Vincent L. Wimbush. London: Taylor and Francis, 1999.

Engberg Pedersen, Troels. "Philo's *De Vita Contemplativa* as a Philosopher's Dream," *Journal for the Study of Judaism* 30 (1999): 40–64.

Hadot, Pierre. *What is Ancient Philosophy?* Translated by Michael Chase. Cambridge MA/London: Belknap Press of Harvard University Press, 2002.

Harrison, James R. *Reading Romans with Roman Eyes: Studies on the Social Perspective of Paul.* Lanham MD: Lexington/Fortress, 2020.

Hengel, Martin *The Pre-Christian Paul.* Translated by John Bowden. London: SCM, 1991.

Jaquette, James L. "Life and Death, Adiaphora, and Paul's Rhetorical Strategies," *Novum Testamentum* 38/1 (1996): 30–54.

Johnson, Luke Timothy. *Reading Romans: A Literary and Theological Commentary.* Reading the New Testament. Macon GA: Smyth & Helwys, 2001.

Käsemann, Ernst. *A Commentary on Romans.* Translated by Geoffrey W. Bromiley. Grand Rapids MI: Eerdmans, 1980.

Keener, Craig S. *Romans: A New Covenant Commentary.* New Covenant Commentary Series. Cambridge: The Lutterworth Press, 2009.

King, "Of Blood and Black Puddings: Learning of the Importance of Contextual Biblical Reading from the Anglicans of Tanzania." Pages 189–200 in *Nuru na Uzima: Essays Celebrating the Golden Jubilee of the Anglican Church of Tanzania, 1970-2020.* Edited by Fergus J. King, Emmanuel Mbennah, Mecka Ogunde and Dorothy Prentice. North Augusta SC: Missional University Press, 2021.

Loader, William. *The New Testament on Sexuality.* Attitudes towards Sexuality in Judaism and Christianity in the Hellenistic Greco-Roman Era. Grand Rapids MI: Eerdmans, 2012.

Long, A.A. *Stoic Studies.* Berkeley CA: University of California Press, 2001.

MacGillivray, Erlend D. "Epitomizing Philosophy and the Critique of Epicurean Popularizers," *Journal of Ancient History* 3/1 (2015): 22–54.

Martin, Dale B. "The Possibility of Comparison, the Necessity of Anachronism, and the Dangers of Purity." Pages 63–77 in *The New Testament in Comparison: Validity, Method, and Purpose in Comparing Traditions.* Edited by John M.G. Barclay and

Benjamin G. White. Library of New Testament Studies, vol. 600; London: T&T Clark, 2020.

Matera, Frank. *Romans*. Paideia Commentaries on the New Testament. Grand Rapids MI: Baker Academic, 2010.

Morgan, Teresa. *Roman Faith and Christian Faith: Pistis and Fides in the Early Roman Empire and Early Churches*. Oxford: Oxford University Press, 2015.

Nanos, Mark D. *The Mystery of Romans: The Jewish Context of Paul's Letter*. Minneapolis MN: Fortress, 1996.

Nussbaum, Martha C. *The Therapy of Desire: Theory and Practice in Hellenistic Ethics*. Martin Classical Lectures: New Series, Volume 2. Princeton NJ: Princeton University Press, 1994.

Oakes, Peter. *Galatians*. Paideia Commentaries on the New Testament. Grand Rapids MI: Baker Academic, 2015.

Pilhofer, Peter. *Presbyteron Kreitton: Der Alterbeweis der jüdischen und christlichen Apologeten und seine Vorgeschichte*. Wissenschaftliche Untersuchungen zum Neuen Testament 2 Reihe 39. Tübingen: Mohr-Siebeck, 1990.

Porter, Stanley E. "Paul, Virtues, Vices, and Household Codes." Pages 369–390 in *Paul in the Greco-Roman World: A Handbook Vol II*. Edited by J. Paul Sampley. Rev'd ed. London: Bloomsbury/ T&T Clark, 2016.

Rudolph, David. "Paul and the Food Laws: A Reassessment of Romans 14:14, 20." Pages 151–181 in *Paul the Jew: Reading the Apostle as a Figure of Second Temple Judaism*. Edited by Gabriele Boccaccini and Carlos A. Segovia. Minneapolis MN: Fortress, 2016.

Sanders, Ed P. *Jesus and Judaism*. London: SCM Press, 1985.

Seifrid, Mark A. "Romans." Pages 607–694 in *Commentary on the New Testament Use of the Old Testament*. Edited by G.K. Beale and D.A. Carson. Grand Rapids MI: Baker Academic, 2007.

Sherlock, Peta. "Reading Romans as Anglicans- Romans 1:26–27." Pages 31–45 in *Five Uneasy Pieces: Essays on Scripture and Sexuality*. Edited by Nigel Wright. Hindmarsh: ATF Theology, 2011.

Stendahl, Kirster. "The Apostle Paul and the Introspective Conscience of the West." *Harvard Theological Review* 56/3 (1963): 199–215.

Taylor, Joan E. *Jewish Women Philosophers of First-Century Alexandria: Philo's 'Therapeutae' Reconsidered*. Oxford: Oxford University Press, 2003.

Templeton, Douglas A. *The New Testament as True Fiction: Literature, Literary Criticism, Aesthetics*. London: T&T Clark, 2004.

10.

The Jews, Israel, and Jerusalem in the Book of Revelation

FRANCIS J. MOLONEY, SDB

Introduction

The "John" named as the author of the Book of Revelation (Rev 1:1, 4, 9; 22:8) is almost universally recognized by interpreters as a Jew.[1] It is with delight and a sense of privilege that I offer this reflection on a "John" who should not be associated with the shadowy Beloved Disciple who has inspired Professor Dorothy Lee's life-long commitment to the interpretation of the Fourth Gospel (see John 21:25). Dorothy's approach to the Sacred Scriptures is always fresh, and often surprising. I come away from her published work (not to speak of our conversations) having learnt something new or seeing texts from a different perspective. What follows is an attempt to emulate the freshness of her approach and perhaps contribute something to an important debate.[2]

---

1. For thorough surveys, see Aune, *Revelation*, 1:xlvii–lvi; Beale, *Book of Revelation*, 34–36; Koester, *Revelation*, 65–69; Moloney, *Apocalypse*, 4–6.

2. This essay was originally written as an Excursus ("Die Juden, Israel und Jerusalem in der Offenbarung") in Moloney, *Offenbarung in der Osterzeit*, due for publication in 2023. This English version appears with the approval of the German-language publishers.

The Jewishness of John

There are several reasons for scholarly unanimity on the Jewishness of John the prophetic visionary. He is very familiar with the Sacred Scriptures of Israel. More than any other work in the New Testament, his book is dominated by direct citations and obvious allusions to Israel's Scriptures: especially Daniel, the Torah, and the prophets, with a keen focus upon Ezekiel and Isaiah.[3] Despite his abundant use of these Scriptures, he never mentions which book he is citing. John is so familiar with these texts that he takes it for granted that his audience will know he is referring to their shared sacred Scriptures. Secondly, he wrote in a highly original Greek, often developing his own grammar and syntax, and sometimes using words and expressions unique to his work. Greek was not his native language. He is entirely familiar with the literary form of Jewish apocalyptic literature (found, for example, in the almost contemporary Jewish books known to us as 1 Enoch [200–100s BCE] and 4 Ezra [200s CE]). His entire literary world was Jewish.[4]

Although less certain, as we have no evidence from the text of the Book of Revelation, it appears that he had fled to Asia Minor from Palestine after the disaster of the Jewish Revolt of 65–70 CE.[5] His awareness of the situations and the experiences of the young Christian communities in the cities of Ephesus, Smyrna, Pergamum, Thyatira, Sardis, and Laodicea (2:1–3:22), all located in south-western Asia Minor (today's Türkiye), toward the end of the first-century shows that he was familiar with that part of the world. He writes to those cities from the nearby island of Patmos, about sixty kilometers from the city of Miletus on the south-western coast of Asia Minor. He tells his audience that he finds himself there because of his zeal and preparedness to undergo sacrifice and suffering in his mission to them (1:9).[6]

3. Among many, see Moyise, *Old Testament*. Beale, *John's Use*, suggests that certain passages in Revelation are almost midrash upon Daniel. Moyise argues that John adapts Daniel creatively.

4. As Koester, *Revelation*, 141, comments: "Some unusual aspects of the grammar may reflect Greek translations of the OT or forms of vulgar Greek that were used in Asia Minor, but at points the writer deliberately flouts the accepted forms of grammar, which fits the idea that neither the writer nor the God to whom he bears witness is held captive by social convention."

5. See Aune, *Revelation*, 1:lvi; Pagels, *Revelations*, 7–8.

6. Most interpreters regard the reason John gives in Rev 1:9 for his being on the island of Patmos ("διὰ τόν λόγον τοῦ θεοῦ καὶ τὴν μαρτυρίαν τοῦ Ἰησοῦ") as forced imprisonment. The expression can equally well be rendered as a missionary motivation for his presence in Asia Minor: on account of the Word of God and to render witness

Despite his obvious Jewishness, John's literary dependence upon Israel's sacred Scriptures, and its more apocalyptic writings, the narrative of Revelation has sometimes been interpreted as "anti-Jewish." How valid is this accusation, levelled against a book that is part of Christianity's sacred Scriptures? Our reflections upon this critical question, especially as we read Revelation in our multicultural and multi-faith third millennium, must begin with a description of what has been called "the parting of the ways" between first-century Judaism and earliest Christianity.

The Parting of the Ways

Jesus was a Jew, as were his parents, the Twelve, his first disciples, and the first groups of people (most likely gathering in Jerusalem and Antioch) who accepted that the crucified Jesus of Nazareth was the long-awaited Christ. Although we cannot be certain, most authors who produced early Christian writings (Paul, the authors of the Gospels and the Acts of the Apostles ["Luke" may not have been Jewish],[7] the Letter to the Hebrews, the so-called Catholic Epistles, and Revelation) were Jews. They celebrated a unique ritual meal "in memory" of Jesus' death and resurrection (see 1 Cor 11:23–26; Luke 22:14–20), but they continued their adhesion to the God of Israel, and took part in Israel's ritual traditions (see, for example, Acts 3:1). That ritual meal, however innovative the summons to "remember" may have been, was celebrated according to Jewish traditions.[8] The very early conflict between Christians on the necessity to circumcise Gentile males who became Christians, evidenced most importantly in the Letters to the Galatians (see 5:1–12), to the Philippians (3:2–11), and in the Acts of the Apostles (see 15:1–35), is significant testimony to the pain that separation from Jewish origins generated for the earliest Christians.

The claim of the Christians that the crucified Jesus of Nazareth was the expected Messiah did not lessen their belief in the God of Israel, nor remove them from trust in the promises made to Israel. Nevertheless, as Paul eloquently pointed out about 52 CE, belief that a crucified criminal was the Christ necessarily created tension between them and their fellow–Jews: "We proclaim Christ crucified, a stumbling block to Jews" (1 Cor 1:23. See also Gal 3:13).[9]

---

to Jesus. See Thompson, *Book of Revelation*, 172–73; Corsini, *Apocalisse di Gesù*, 81.

7. Bovon, *Luke*, 1:8–10, helpfully identifies the author of Luke-Acts as a "god-fearer."

8. See the classical discussion of this question by Jeremias, *Eucharistic* Words, 16–41.

9. See Schmid and Schröter, *Making of the Bible*, 182–221. Although the Acts of the Apostles was written much later (toward the end of the first Century), always focusing

Prior to the Jewish War, several Jewish sects understood, lived, and celebrated their Jewishness differently. We know of the Pharisees, the Sadducees, the Essenes, the Zealots, and there may have been others. The earliest Christians formed another Jewish sect. According to the author of the Acts of the Apostles, they were recognized as such by Rabbi Gamaliel. After describing various other sects that had come and gone, he warns the Sanhedrin: "Keep away from these men and let them alone; because if this plan and this undertaking is of human origin, it will fail; but if it is of God, you will not be able to overthrow them" (Acts 5:38–39). The situation changed dramatically after the Jewish War of 65–70 CE.

After 70 CE, the city of Jerusalem and its temple had been destroyed. The land of Israel was entirely under the control of Roman authority. Only the Pharisees, a mobile and dynamic pastoral form of Judaism, were long-term survivors. They did not need the land, the city, and the temple with its priests and sacrifices. Wherever Jewish people gathered, in geographical Israel and beyond, the Pharisees went with the Torah, and reconstituted post-War Judaism from the devastating results of the War. Synagogues, a place where Jewish people "come together," emerged across the Mediterranean world reaching into Asia, Egypt, and Europe. Over the centuries, the Pharisaic Torah-based form of Judaism built a wonderful religious system that continues in today's Jewish life and practice.[10]

Christians also survived. Both Pharisaic Judaism and Christianity withstood the disasters of 70 CE. In many ways, both Christians and Jews were communities in search of an identity. This was especially clear for post-War Judaism that forged a new identity through its pastoral care and the interpretation and living of Torah, with its manifold possibilities. Christianity's identity was intimately associated with Judaism, its sacred Scripture, its beliefs, and traditions. However, the Christian belief that the God of Israel had entered human history in the person of Jesus of Nazareth, understood as the fulfillment of the messianic prophecies and the savior of humankind, necessarily clashed with post-War Judaism.

Gradually a "parting of the ways" marked the relationship between Judaism, now without land, city, temple, priesthood, and sacrifices, and Christianity, moving further and further into a hostile relationship with its parent, Judaism, as they claimed that God's Messiah had come in Jesus of Nazareth. As post-War Judaism focused more intensely upon Torah and its interpretation for its lifeblood, Christians focused more intensely on what

upon a positive outcome to suffering, its early chapters record these tensions (see Acts 4:1–22; 5:17–42; 6:8–15; 8:1–3).

10. See Goodman, *History of Judaism*, 229–88.

they believed God had done for humankind in and through the life, teaching, death, and resurrection of Jesus Christ. Lines between Jews and Christians were not clear cut, and "the parting of the ways" took many forms, advancing at different speeds in different geographical locations across the closing decades of the first-century and into the second.[11] But the die had been cast.

The Inevitable Polemic

Claim and counter claim across the gradually widening divide between Jews and Christians provide one of the essential elements for a sound understanding of the formative background of the emerging first-century Christian literature, known to us as the New Testament. There can be no avoiding the truth that historically conditioned anger lies behind some of that literature. Even though the earliest Gospel of Mark (c. 70 CE) is not as confrontational as Matthew (late 80s CE), Luke (late 80s CE), or John (c. 100 CE), the author has no difficulty in reading Israel's Scriptures as fulfilled in the life, teaching, death, and resurrection of Jesus Christ. Jesus' coming fulfills the prophecies of Isaiah and Malachi (Mark 1:2–3); he is the historically identifiable Son of Man of the prophet Daniel, the Suffering Servant from Isaiah (see, for example, Mark 10:45),[12] and his suffering and death fulfils Psalm 22 (see Mark 15:29, 32, 34). Israel's Scriptures were interpreted through Christian eyes.

The Gospel of Matthew, most likely written in the late 80's of the first-century, is marked by a growing tension (Matt 11:2–16:12) and a sustained hostility against the leaders of Israel, especially the Pharisees (see especially Matt 23:1–36). Only in Matthew do we find the terrible cry from the Jerusalem crowd during Jesus' Roman trial: "His blood be on us and on our children" (27:25). Such words were most likely never uttered, but the Gospel of Matthew developed them in a hostile situation of claim and counter claim. This anger shaped the way Matthew reacts to what he regarded as a false Jewish narrative. For example, he reports what he regards as a lie concocted

---

11. See Wilson, *Related Strangers*; Lieu, *Image and Reality*. It is difficult to date the addition of the Twelfth Benediction (the so-called *Birkat ha-Minim*) to the Synagogue prayer of the Eighteen Benedictions (the *Shemoneh Esrei*). It is equally difficult to assess its implementation. It is safer to regard it as symptomatic of the parting of the ways, not its cause. See Schmid and Schröter, *Making of the Bible*, 222–28. For a good summary of the debate, see Van Der Horst, "Birkat ha-minim in Recent Research," 363–68. See also the provocative contrasting studies of Marcus, "*Birkat Ha-Minim* Revisited," 523–51, and Reinhartz, *Cast out of the Covenant*.

12. See Moloney, *Mark*, 212–14.

by Jewish leadership about Jesus' disciples stealing Jesus' crucified body (28:11–15), concluding: "This story is still told among the Jews to this day" (28:16. See 27:57–28:20).[13] Matthew outstrips Mark in understanding Jesus as the fulfillment of Israel's Scriptures (see 1:22–23; 2:5–6, 15, 17–18, 23; 3:2, 4:14–16; 8:17, etc.).

For Matthew, Jesus and his teaching "perfects" the Law and the prophets (see 5:17–20). As his story closes, the risen Jesus commissions his disciples for a mission that flies in the face of central beliefs and practices of post-War Judaism. Jesus is the Lord of creation, and all authority has been given to him. Subsequently, the disciples are to take the Gospel to all nations (not just the Chosen People), baptize them in the name of the Father, Son, and Holy Spirit (abandoning circumcision as an initiation rite), teaching them to observe all that Jesus has taught (and not Torah) (28:16–20).

The two volumes of Luke-Acts are more subtle, but the same mindset continues.[14] The author of Luke-Acts is especially heavy-handed in the speeches of Peter, Stephen, and Paul reported in the Acts of the Apostles. They lay the blame for the execution of Jesus upon the Jews (see, for example, Acts 2:36; 4:11–12, 25–27; 7:51–53; 10:39–43, etc.). Consequently, for this early Christian author (who composed these speeches late in the first-century), the Jews systematically reject the preaching of the good news about Jesus. "The apostles" turn away from them to "bring salvation to all the earth" (13:47, see 13:46–52).

The Gospel of John notoriously and consistently uses the expression "the Jews" to describe the characters in his story who reject Jesus, and his disciples. The only credible explanation of this phenomenon lies in the apparent decision on the part of Israel's leadership to expel from the Synagogue anyone who believed and confessed that Jesus was the Christ (John 9:22; 12:42; 16:2). We cannot be sure of when and how that happened, but the animosity between Jesus, his followers, and "the Jews" in the Fourth Gospel is perhaps the most severe form of anti-Jewish rhetoric in the New Testament (see especially 8:44, where Jesus says to "the Jews": "You are from your father the devil"). Jesus accuses them to have lost sight of the manifestation of the glory of God in the person of Jesus because they were too concerned with the superficiality of their own importance (12:43).[15]

---

13. This passage indicates an anti-Christian polemic among post-War Jews. However, there is little evidence of such polemic. The pillars of Rabbinic Judaism (the Mishnah and the Talmudim of Jerusalem and Babylon) largely ignore Christianity and its claims. See Weiss-Rosmarin, ed., *Jewish Expressions on Jesus*. See especially pp. 1–98: Lauterbach, "Jesus in the Talmud."

14. Sanders, *Jews in Luke-Acts.*

15. On the issue of "the Jews" in the Gospel of John, see Moloney, "Israel, the People,

Perhaps the best summary of the early church's self-understanding as transcending its Jewish origins is stated as a Christian author from late in the first-century begins what we call the Letter to the Hebrews:

> Long ago God spoke to our ancestors in many and various ways
> by the prophets, but in these last days he has spoken to us by a
> Son whom he appointed heir of all things, through whom he
> also created the worlds (1:1)

Overwhelmed by their belief in the centrality of the person, teaching, death, and resurrection of Jesus of Nazareth, it was inevitable that early Christians would arrive at this point.

They arrived there in a time of religious and social conflict with their parent, Israel. Two major witnesses manifest their unhappiness with this situation. At the end of his story of Jesus' ministry, the evangelist John wonders why "the Jews" had not accepted Jesus as the one who makes God known. But he has no adequate response (John 12:37–43).[16] Even more poignantly, Paul asks how God's chosen people came to reject Jesus, and he—in great personal anguish (see 9:1–5)—insists that they retain their unique place in God's saving history (Rom 9–11). Like John, but more eloquently, he closes his reflections by leaving this mystery with God: "O the depth of the riches of the wisdom and knowledge of God! How unsearchable are his judgments and how inscrutable his ways!" (11:33).[17]

And there we must leave it, recognizing our obligation to step out of the conflict that must remain within the time-warp of the late first-century. Judaism is the parent of Christianity, and Jews are our brothers and sisters. John Ashton helpfully pointed us in the right direction as he summarized the situation late in the first-century: [One must] "recognize in these hot-tempered exchanges the type of family row in which the participants face one another across the room of a house which all have shared and all call home."[18]

Writing of the Johannine presentation of "the Jews," David Rensberger articulates a serious warning that applies to much early Christian literature, including the New Testament: it "serves as a very sobering reminder that words once written leave their writer's control, and that no one can expect to utter violent words without facing a violent consequence."[19] Despite the

---

and the Jews in the Fourth Gospel," 93–115.

16. See Moloney, *Gospel of John*, 363–69 for this assessment of John 12:37–43.

17. See Byrne, *Romans*, 358–62.

18. Ashton, *Understanding*, 151.

19. Rensberger, "Anti-Judaism and the Gospel of John," 152. See a parallel Jewish reflection by Jules Isaac, especially in the light of the Christian reception of Matthew

tragedies of Christian treatment of our Jewish brothers and sisters in the past, especially (but not only) the recent past, Jews and Christians come from the same home; we are all children of Abraham, called to an unconditional love of the one true God of Israel (see Deut 6:1–4).[20]

The Polemic in John's Revelation

Like all early Christian witnesses, John regards the death and resurrection of Jesus Christ as crucial to an understanding of God's way with humankind. This view necessarily renders his own Jewishness different from that of the established Jewish communities in Asia. However, he has a distinctive view of the role and effects of Jesus Christ's death and resurrection that separates him from the early Christian authors described above. Two associated issues determine John's unique presentation of Israel, the Jews, and Jerusalem. They are both intimately linked with his understanding of God's sacred history, and the sequence of events that determine that history.

Most interpreters and translators of Revelation refuse to render accurately the Greek of Revelation 13:8. John is describing those who give allegiance to the beast from the sea (see 13:1). A literal translation of the original states that their "name has not been written in the book of the life of the Lamb that was slaughtered from the foundation of the world" ("οὗ γέγραπται τὸ ὄνομα αὐτοῦ ἐν τῷ βιβλίῳ τῆς ζωῆς τοῦ ἀρνίου τοῦ ἐσφαγμένου ἀπὸ καταβολῆς κόσμου;" v. 8). Most critics claim that it is illogical and historically irresponsible to suggest that the Lamb was slain "from the foundation of the world."[21] They thus translate the expression as a description of the absence of the names of the sinful "from the foundation of the world in the book of life." This is a misunderstanding of one of John's major contributions to emerging Christian thought.

Secondly, John regularly refers to "the saints" who have suffered and died, sometimes associating them with those who have kept the word of God and listened to the prophets (see 5:8–10; 6:10; 8:3–4; 11:18; 13:7, 10; 14:12; 16:5–6; 17:6; 18:20, 24; 20:9). The expression "the saints" came to John from the Book of Daniel. The author of Daniel uses it for those in Israel

---

27:25: "Crime of Deicide. Proposition 16," 253–83.

20. Dedicated to the characterization of the leaders of Israel in the Gospel of Matthew, *mutatis mutandis* the urgent pastoral need to understand this fundamental truth has been well articulated by Brendan Byrne, *Lifting the Burden. Reading Matthew's Gospel in the Church Today*, 1–8.

21. See Aune, *Revelation*, 2:747; Koester, *Revelation*, 575. See also NRSV. The translation of the Greek endorsed above is provided in the margin of the NRSV.

who withstood the Seleucid persecution of Antiochus IV and maintained their adhesion to the God of Israel, cost what it may. They are victorious over the forces of evil (see especially Dan 7:18, 22, 27). John does not use the expression to refer to Christians who have suffered under Diocletian, as is widely assumed. There was no systematic persecution of Christians or forced emperor-worship at the end of the first-century.[22] As Ramsay MacMullen puts it: "Had the church been wiped off the face of the earth at the end of the first-century, its disappearance would have caused no dislocation in the empire, just as its presence was hardly noticed at the time. . . . Simply, it did not count."[23] In his search for models that will serve him in his instruction of the Asian churches, John looks back across Israel's history, singling out the "holy ones" who have persevered, lived by the word of God, and listened to the messianic prophecies.

For John, Israel's entire history has been marked by saints who have lived by the law and the prophets. No matter "when" they have lived and died, they have been saved by the death and resurrection of Jesus. The saving effects of the death and resurrection of Jesus must not be tied to the chronological time in history when it took place (e.g., 33 CE). They have been perennially present. However strange it may appear to a modern mind, *from all time* the holy ones in Israel have been swept up into the saving effects of the Lamb "slain before the foundation of the world" (13:8).[24] Various moments of God's saving history must not be separated: the story of Israel with its Law and Prophets, and the story of the Christian church form one sacred story. The death and resurrection of Jesus Christ is the swivel around which they move, and it makes sense of both! Jews and Christians are not enemies.

The saints from the period of the Seleucid persecutions kept the word of God and listened to the prophets. They serve as models for the Asian churches. The suffering of the saints did not begin with the Christian church. As the Book of Daniel regularly points out, it has marked the whole of Israel's history: Assyria, Babylon, the Medes, Persia, and Rome (see especially Daniel 7:1–8).

When the Lamb opened the fifth seal, John saw "the souls of those who had been slaughtered for the word of God and for the testimony they

22. This is almost universally accepted by historians. See the summary in Thompson, *Book of Revelation*, 95–115.

23. MacMullen, *Christianizing the Roman Empire*, viii.

24. The notion of the perennial presence of the saving effects of Jesus' death and resurrection "from the foundation of the world" is central to John's thought, but it is also present in other New Testament witnesses. On this, see Moloney, *Apocalypse*, 199–204. Beyond the texts considered there, see also Matt 13:35; 25:34.

had given" (6:9). They are to wait until their number is "complete" (v. 11: "ἕως πληρωθῶσιν"). The opening of the sixth seal presents one hundred and forty-four thousand "sealed out of every tribe of Israel" (7:4–8). They are joined by "a great multitude that no one could count" (v. 9) who have access to the throne because of the blood of the Lamb (vv. 13–15). For *both* groups "the Lamb at the centre of the throne will be their shepherd, he will guide them to springs of the water of life, and God will wipe away every tear from their eyes" (v. 17). The same double-staged access to life through the perennial saving effects of the death and resurrection explains the temple and the witnesses in 11:1–13. John's understanding of Israel and Christianity as part of a continuous story, determined by the perennial saving effects of the Lamb slain before the foundation of the world (13:8) is fundamental to his argument. As such, it throws light upon his explicit references to the Jews, Israel, and Jerusalem.

The Jews

In the letters to Smyrna (2:8–11) and to Philadelphia (3:7–13), John identifies what was most likely a regular experience for Christians in those cities: opposition from the Jewish community. Given John's understanding of the Jewish people as an integral part in a long saving history, on both occasions he accuses these opponents of not really being Jews. If they had been, they would courageously live by God's word, and accept the promise of the messianic prophecies. In John's judgment, they have not done so. On the contrary, they adhere to God's archenemy: Satan, "the deceiver of the whole world" (see 12:9; 20:2, 7). From John's perspective, authentic Jews were "saints" who hold to the word of God and listen to the messianic prophecies. In Smyrna (2:9) and Philadelphia (3:9), this has not happened. Some ethnic Jews have transferred their allegiance from the word of God and the messianic prophecies to collude with the powers of evil (Satan). John can thus claim that they are not Jews like the saints who went before them, whatever their ethnicity. They belong to the Synagogue of Satan. These are the only times in Revelation that "the Jews" are mentioned.

Israel

The nation Israel is presented in the same positive light. The letter to Pergamum (2:12–17) uses the background story of God's presence to his people during their period of wandering in the desert. Names are applied to two figures, Balaam and Balak, who cannot be identified in any first-century time and place, least of all in Pergamum. John uses those names to recall the episode in the desert where the Lord overcame collusion between them "to put a stumbling block before the people of Israel" (v. 14). They seek to deceive the Israelites into eating food sacrificed to idols and thus to practice fornication, a temptation that is overcome (Num 22:1–24:25). We have already seen that the first fruits of the saving effects of the death and resurrection of Jesus Christ are "one hundred forty-four thousand, sealed out of every tribe of the people of Israel" (7:4). The walls of the New Jerusalem are penetrated by twelve gates, inscribed "with the names of the twelve tribes of the Israelites" (21:12), and built on twelve foundations bearing the names of the twelve apostles (v. 14). John's sparse use of the name of the nation "Israel" demonstrates the continuity that exists between Israel and the church, the New Jerusalem, determined by the death and resurrection of Jesus Christ.

Jerusalem

At first sight, John could be seen as critical of the historical Jerusalem. He regards it not only as the place where Jesus was executed (11:8), but as the seat of corrupt political and religious authorities that colluded with another corrupt political and religious authority to promote that execution. This affirmation depends upon the identification of "Babylon" with the political and religious leadership in Jerusalem (14:8; 16:19; 17:5; 18:2, 10, 21). John develops a narrative that portrays two beasts, one from the sea and the other from the land (13:1–18), as the corrupt political and religious agents of Satan. It is with these agents that corrupt political and religious agents in Jerusalem collude to execute Jesus Christ. This collusion is developed in 17:1–18. For John, the wicked collusion between Rome and the evil leaders of Jerusalem, dramatically portrayed as a whore mounted on the beast, led to the destruction of the whore in a way that recalls the destruction of Jerusalem in 70 CE: "They will make her desolate and naked; they will devour her flesh and burn her up with fire" (v. 16). It leads to the fall and disappearance of Babylon (18:1–24) , the great city (v. 18) where the Lord was crucified (11:8), the whore (see Ezek 16). At the end of the first-century, only of a corrupt and sinful Jerusalem can it be said: "And in you was found the blood of the prophets and of saints" (v. 24. See Mark 12:1–12; Matt 22:1–14).[25] Rome destroyed her corrupt ally in 70 CE. The beast (Rome) destroys the whore (Babylon/Jerusalem).

---

25. Anachronistic reference to the later Roman practice of Christian martyrdom (third and early fourth Century) must be avoided. See Frend, "Persecutions: Genesis and Legacy," 503–23.

But this destruction was not the end of God's holy city. For John, the political and religious authorities in Jerusalem who colluded with such Roman authorities were the sinful face of Jerusalem. Like the Jews who are no longer Jews but a Synagogue of Satan (2:9; 3:9), corrupt Jerusalem leadership should not be recognized as the city of "Jerusalem." That is why John calls the city, its leaders, and all the sinful people and practices that dwell there "Babylon" (see 18:1–24). The death of Jesus brings that "Babylon" to an end (15:1—16:21) and leads to Rome's destruction of the city (17:1—18:24). Judgment follows (19:1—20:15); a New Heaven, a New Earth, and a New Jerusalem emerge (21:1—22:5).

The narrative of Revelation matches the Gospel accounts of the collusion between Roman and Jewish leadership that led to the death of Jesus (see Mark 3:6; 15:1–20; Matt 12:14; 27:1–31; Luke 6:11; 23:13–25; John 11:45–53; 18:28–19:16). Jewish leadership (Babylon, the whore) sold out to the powers of evil. But John never condemns the city of Jerusalem. The death and resurrection of Jesus sees to the continuation of Jerusalem in the New Jerusalem. As there was once "Jerusalem," there is now a "New Jerusalem." Because of the death and resurrection of Jesus, the New Jerusalem has no temple "for its temple is the Lord God the Almighty and the Lamb" (21:22).

John makes it clear, however, that the New Jerusalem is not an otherworldly reality. Despite the hyperbolic descriptions of the city, its walls, its gates, and its interior, all the promises made to the seven churches in 2:1–3:22 are fulfilled in the New Jerusalem which is a gift from heaven ("the holy city of Jerusalem coming down from heaven and God" [21:10]). The "ideal" described in the promises to the stumbling churches of Asia (2:7; 2:17; 3:21) becomes "real" in the New Jerusalem, the Christian church (22:2; 21:18–21; 22:1–2).[26] But there can be no escaping the ambiguity of the human condition and human communities. Those who dwell in the New Jerusalem continue to live in an ambiguous situation: "Let the evil doer still do evil, and the filthy still be filthy, and the righteous still do right, and the holy still be holy" (22:11; see also v. 15).

Conclusion

As with his allusions to the Jews (2:9; 3:9), to the nation Israel (2:14; 7:4; 21:12), so also with his stunning transformation of Jerusalem into the New Jerusalem (17:1–22:5) John does not replicate the antagonism between Jews and Christians found elsewhere in the New Testament. For John, the perennial saving effects of the death and resurrection of Jesus Christ have

---

26. For more detail, see Moloney, *Apocalypse*, 343–44.

generated a God-designed continuity between Israel's sacred history and the life and practice of the Christian church.

These reflections opened with a recognition of John's deep association with—even embodiment of—the sacred Scriptures of Israel (see 19:10; 22:9). In the epilogue to his book (22:6–21), he issues a warning that has long troubled interpreters. He threatens dire punishment for anyone who "adds to" the prophecy of this book (v. 18), or "takes away from the words of the book of this prophecy" (v. 19). Can John be so arrogant that he regards his own book as an untouchable word of God? If so, he is the only author in the New Testament to make such a claim.

It all depends upon what John means when he refers to "this book." He is not writing of his own book, but the sacred Scriptures of Israel that must never be altered in any way.[27] They tell the story of God's care for humankind with God's Law, and they are filled with the messianic promises of the prophets. John's book only makes sense because of the unchangeable truths that have come to him from his Jewish life and practice, enlightened by the unchangeable and perennial truths announced in Israel's sacred Scriptures. John's book makes sense because of "this book." For him, only the word of God articulated in Israel's Scriptures stands forever (see Isa 40:8; 1 Pet 1:23–25).

Bibliography

Ashton, John. *Understanding the Fourth Gospel.* Oxford: Clarendon Press, 1991.

Aune, David E. *Revelation.* 3 vols. Word Biblical Commentary 52A–C. Dallas, TX: Word, 1997–1998.

Beale, G. K. *John's Use of the Old Testament in Revelation.* Library of New Testament Studies 166. London: Bloomsbury, 1999.

Beale, G. K. *The Book of Revelation,* New International Greek Testament Commentary. Grand Rapids, MI: Eerdmans, 1999.

Bovon, François. *Luke.* Translated by Christine M. Thomas. 3 vols. Hermeneia. Minneapolis, MN: Fortress, 2002–2012.

Byrne, Brendan. *Lifting the Burden. Reading Matthew's Gospel in the Church Today.* Collegeville, MN: Liturgical, 2004.

————. *Romans.* Sacra Pagina 6. Collegeville: Liturgical Press, 1996.

Corsini, Eugenio. *Apocalisse di Gesù secondo Giovanni.* Sestante. Torino: Società Editrice Internazionale, 2002.

Frend, W. H. C. "Persecutions: Genesis and Legacy." Pages 503–23 in Margaret M. Mitchell and Francis M. Young, eds. *The Cambridge History of Christianity. Volume 1: Origins to Constantine.* Cambridge: Cambridge University Press, 2006.

Goodman, Martin. *A History of Judaism.* Milton Keynes: Penguin Random House, 2017.

27. See Moloney, *Apocalypse John,* 358–62.

Isaac, Jules. "The Crime of Deicide. Proposition 16." Trude Weiss-Rosmarin, ed. *Jewish Expressions on Jesus. An Anthology.* New York: Ktav, 1977, 258–83.

Jeremias, Joachim. *The Eucharistic Words of Jesus.* Translated by Norman Perrin. London: SCM Press, 1966.

Koester, Craig R. *Revelation*, The Anchor Yale Bible 38A. New Haven, CT: Yale University Press, 2014.

Lauterbach, Jacob Z. "Jesus in the Talmud." Pages 1–98 in Trude Weiss-Rosmarin, ed. *Jewish Expressions on Jesus. An Anthology.* New York: Ktav, 1977.

Lieu, Judith M. *Image and Reality: The Jews in the World of Christians in the Second Century.* Edinburgh: T. & T. Clark, 1996.

MacMullen, Ramsey. *Christianizing the Roman Empire (AD 100–400).* New Haven: Yale University Press, 1984.

Marcus, Joel. "*Birkat Ha-Minim* Revisited," *New Testament Studies* 55 (2009) 523–51.

Moloney, Francis J. "Israel, the People, and the Jews in the Fourth Gospel." *Johannine Studies 1975–2017.* Wissenschaftliche Untersuchungen zum Neuen Testament 372. Tübingen: Siebeck, 2017, 93–115.

———. *Offenbarung in der Osterzeit.* Sankt Ottilien: EOS Editions, 2023.

———. *The Apocalypse of John. A Commentary.* Grand Rapids, MI: Baker Academic, 2020.

———. *The Gospel of John.* Sacra Pagina 4. Collegeville, MN: Liturgical Press, 1998.

———. *The Gospel of Mark. A Commentary.* Grand Rapids, MI: Baker Academic, 2002.

Moyise, Steve. *The Old Testament in the Book of Revelation*, Journal for the Study of the New Testament Supplement Series 115. Sheffield: Sheffield Academic, 1995.

Pagels, Elaine. *Revelations: Visions, Prophecy, and Politics in the Book of Revelation.* New York: Viking, 2012.

Reinhartz, Adele. *Cast out of the Covenant. Jesus and Anti-Judaism in the Gospel of John.* Lanham, MD: Lexington Books/Fortress Academic, 2018.

Rensberger, David. "Anti-Judaism and the Gospel of John." William F. Farmer, ed. *Antijudaism and the Gospel.* Harrisburg, PA: Trinity Press International, 1999, 130–37.

Sanders, Jack T. *The Jews in Luke-Acts.* London: SCM, 1987.

Schmid, Konrad and Jens Schröter. *The Making of the Bible. From the First Fragments to Sacred Scripture.* Translated by Peter Lewis. Cambridge, MA: Harvard University Press, 2021.

Thompson, Leonard L. *The Book of Revelation: Apocalypse and Empire.* New York: Oxford University Press, 1990.

Van Der Horst, Pieter. "The Birkat ha-minim in Recent Research," *The Expository Times* 105 (1994) 363–68

Weiss-Rosmarin, Trude, ed., *Jewish Expressions on Jesus. An Anthology* (New York: Ktav, 1977).

Wilson, Stephen G. *Related Strangers. Jews and Christians 70–170 C. E.* Minneapolis: Fortress, 1995.

Women, and Ecclesiology

11.

Daughter-in-law of Eli, Wife of Phinehas, and Mother of Ichabod

An Unnamed Woman in the Theology and Politics of 1 Samuel

RACHELLE GILMOUR

Introduction[1]

The narrative of 1 Samuel is dominated by the institution of the monarchy over Israel, the rise and fall of Saul, Israel's first king, and the anointing of King David in his stead. However, the first seven chapters of 1 Samuel contain only faint allusions to the monarchy that will be established and focus instead on the beginnings of the prophet, judge, and priest Samuel, and the end of the priestly house of Eli.

The offices of priest and king were reserved only for men in ancient Israel and so it might follow that these opening narratives in 1 Samuel were restricted to the domain of male characters. Instead, 1 Samuel begins with the story of a woman, Hannah, including her remarkable prayer in 1 Samuel

---

1. In 2020, Professor Dorothy Lee and I co-taught a unit "Women and the Bible" in which one of the class topics was "Unnamed Women of the Bible." I offer this essay in honor of Dorothy's inspiring teaching and research on overlooked women of the New Testament.

2:1–10 that will prove programmatic for the theology of 1–2 Samuel.[2] According to the authors and redactors of the Book of Samuel, a woman's grief and distress at being unable to bear a child is the fitting introduction to a story of priests and kings.

This essay turns to the story of a second, unnamed woman whose distress regarding the birth of a child is narrated in 1 Samuel 4:19–22. The stories of Hannah and the unnamed woman frame the fall of the house of Eli, suggesting the latter, even if unnamed, is also significant to the theology and politics of 1 Samuel. Attention to the unnamed woman reveals critical connections between the fall of the house of Eli and the house of Saul; and provides insight into the broader narrative role of women as political actors in ancient Israel. After considering the literary context for this unnamed woman, this essay will examine the ways in which this woman's story contributes to the national story of Israel through her positioning as daughter-in-law of Eli, wife of Phinehas, and mother of Ichabod respectively.

The unnamed woman in context

The opening drama in 1 Samuel 1 centers on the house of the LORD in Shiloh. The ark of the covenant, the presence of God,[3] is located there and the priest Eli and his two sons, Hophni and Phinehas, serve before it. A woman, Hannah, prays before the ark for a child (1:11). She is seen by the priest Eli who, after first mistaking her for being drunk, tells her that her petition will be granted (1:17). Hannah duly gives birth to a son Samuel (1:20), and after he is weaned, Samuel enters priestly service with Eli (1:24–28).

Throughout the following chapters, the boy Samuel and the sons of Eli are compared and contrasted.[4] All are priests; but whereas Samuel continues to grow in favor with God (2:26), and the LORD is reportedly "with him" (3:19), Eli's sons are corrupt. According to 1 Samuel 2:12–17, they take

2. See Gilmour, *Representing the Past*, 102–13, for an overview of links between Hannah's song and the song of David that concludes the book of Samuel in 2 Sam 22:1—23:7, and on the commentary of Hannah's song on the theology of the book of Samuel as a whole.

3. Note that there are different conceptions of the ark throughout the biblical traditions. In Deuteronomistic traditions (primarily Deuteronomy to 2 Kings), the ark is usually understood as a container for the tablets of the covenant, whereas in the Priestly traditions in the Pentateuch, the ark is God's throne. See McCormick, 'From Box to Throne," 174– 86. For the argument that the ark in 1 Samuel is associated with the actual presence of God, not just a container for the stone tablets, see Gilmour, *Divine Violence*, 167–74.

4. On the juxtaposition of Samuel and Eli's sons, Garsiel, *First Book of Samuel*, 37– 41.

offerings at the house of the LORD dishonestly and according to 2:22, they lie with the women at the entrance to the sanctuary.[5]

Consequently, oracles of divine judgment are delivered to Eli. In 1 Sam 2:27–36, an unnamed man of God comes to Eli and announces that his house will no longer be priests but will be despised and cut off. Moreover, his two sons Hophni and Phinehas will die on the same day as a sign to Eli (2:34). Those who are left of his family will beg for bread (2:36), a retributive reversal of his sons' sin of stealing meat from offerings in the sanctuary. A second oracle to Eli through the mouth of Samuel in 1 Sam 3 reiterates that God will "judge" Eli's house forever (3:13), another ironic reversal of Eli's role as "judge" over Israel (4:18).

In 1 Sam 4, events are initiated that will bring about the foretold divine judgment. The Philistines and Israelites are at war, and the ark of the covenant is brought into battle by Hophni and Phinehas in the hope of bringing success for Israel (4:4). Instead, the Israelite army is defeated (4:10), the ark is captured and taken to the cities of the Philistines, and Hophni and Phinehas die (4:11). When Eli hears the news, he falls from his seat and dies also (4:12–18).

At this point in the narrative, an unnamed woman dies in childbirth. She is the daughter-in-law of Eli, the wife of Phinehas and, shortly before her death, she becomes the mother of Ichabod. Her story is told with anguish: she bows down and gives birth when the pains of childbirth overwhelm her,[6] and her physical pain embodies the disastrous news that the ark is captured, and her father-in-law and husband have died (4:19). Those attending her tell her not to fear, for she has had a son; but 4:20 reports that "she did not answer or set her heart" on this. She evidently hears that she has had a son, for she names him (4:21), and so it is the injunction not to fear that she chooses to ignore. Her reason for fear is encapsulated in the name of the child and the narrator's explanation for this name: Ichabod, "'The glory has gone into exile from Israel,' for the ark of God had been captured and for her father-in-law and her husband" (4:21).

5. It is unlikely that these women were understood as temple prostitutes, but rather women who worked in the temple and were abused by Hophni and Phinehas. See Campbell, *1 Samuel*, 49; and Tsumura, *First Book of Samuel*, 161.

6. Bowed down on the knees was probably the usual position for labor. See Hertzberg, *I & II Samuel*, 50. However, the qualifying phrase "for her distress overwhelmed her" suggests the double meaning that both pain of childbirth and pain of the news bowed her down.

The daughter-in-law of Eli and the end of Shiloh

The significance of this short narration of an unnamed woman for the whole house of Eli is indicated by the introduction of the woman in 4:19 first as "[Eli's] daughter-in-law" and only second as "the wife of Phinehas." The accounts of the deaths of Eli in 1 Sam 4:12–18 and the woman in childbirth in 1 Sam 4:19–22 are juxtaposed and paralleled. Each of them "hears" the news of the battle (4:14; 19), and, in this news, the capture of the ark is foregrounded over the deaths of Eli's sons. Eli falls pointedly at the mention of the ark (4:18) and the woman hears of the capture of the ark, then the deaths of her father-in-law and husband secondarily (4:19).[7] Eli is old, ninety-eight according to 4:15, and therefore vulnerable to death; so also the woman is in childbirth, and physically vulnerable to death. Eli's *"heart* trembled" ("לִבּוֹ חָרֵד") in 4:13, the word translated "trembled" usually associated with trembling with fear; and when the woman is told "do not fear" in 4:20 she "did not set it to her *heart* (לְבָּהּ)," meaning she did not heed. The death of this woman, therefore, compounds and completes the tragedy of the fall of the house of Eli.[8]

However, the unnamed woman's role in the narrative extends beyond being another casualty in God's judgment against Eli. In naming her child, this woman augments the two earlier prophecies against her father-in-law, explicating the significance of what has taken place. These earlier prophecies indicated the end of Eli's priestly house, but now the woman associates the end of the house of Eli with the end of Shiloh as the sanctuary and location of the ark of the covenant.

This association is communicated through the name that she gives her child, Ichabod. The act of naming is associated with theological commentary throughout the Hebrew Bible and, as Meir Sternberg points out, naming is usually more about the name giver than the recipient, in this case, the context of the name giver.[9] For example, in Gen 29:31–35, Leah offers a

---

7. When the explanation for Ichabod's name is repeated in v. 22, the deaths of her male relatives are forgotten altogether and only the loss of the ark is in view.

8. Note too that the woman's death contrasts the other deaths in the house of Eli because she is not personally culpable. See Dietrich (*1 Sam 1–12*, 243) for the proposal that 1 Sam 4:19–22 was part of an earlier tradition where the Elides were victims, not culpable recipients of divine judgment. In this case, the pathos of her death epitomized the undeserved devastation of Eli's house.

9. Sternberg, *Poetics of Biblical Narrative*, 330. Fuchs ("Literary Characterization," 165) argues that the "procreative context" is the only one in which women have direct communication with God. Although the unnamed woman in 1 Sam 4 does not reportedly have direct communication from God, it follows that the context of childbirth is linked to her theological insight into the end of the house of Eli.

commentary on God's favor for her, despite Jacob's favor for Rachel, through wordplays on her sons' names: Reuben (רְאוּבֵן), "the Lord has seen (רָאָה) my affliction"; Simeon (שִׁמְעוֹן), "the Lord has heard (שָׁמַע) that I am hated;" and so on. Leah's assertion that God has blessed her and compensated her for being unloved has wider significance, foreshadowing the blessing to Judah (49:8–12), and his line of Davidic kings. In a similar way, the naming of Ichabod in 1 Sam 4:19–22 offers a commentary on the downfall of the house of Eli.

The meaning of the name Ichabod ("אִי־כָבוֹד") is probably "where is glory" or "alas for glory."[10] As is common in biblical naming, an explanation is given for the name in the narrative that explains the reason for the name but is not a precise etymology. The woman says in 4:21, "Glory (כָבוֹד) has gone into exile from Israel," suggesting that "where is glory" is abbreviated from the longer explanation. The word "glory" (כָבוֹד), found in both name and explanation, is the term for the divine presence associated with the tabernacle and ark (e.g. Exod 40:34–35) and is therefore a direct allusion to the ramifications of the capture of the ark: the divine presence has also departed from Shiloh in Israel. The woman's concern with the loss of divine presence explains her response to the women who say "do not fear" in 4:20. "Do not fear" is a conventional component in accounts of encounters with divine presence, whether at Sinai or visitation from angels and divine figures.[11] The unnamed woman's refusal to heed aligns with her insistence that there is now no divine presence in Israel. The birth of a son is not compensation for the loss of the ark from the care of the Elides at Shiloh.

The use of the term "glory" (כָבוֹד) is also a less direct allusion to the loss of her father-in-law. Indeed, the deaths of her father-in-law and husband are listed after the ark in v. 21 as the reason for her choosing the name and, like the ark, they have, in a sense, departed. Throughout 1 Samuel 1–4, the Hebrew root כבד, from which the term "glory" comes, is frequently applied to Eli with a number of different meanings. In 1 Sam 2:29–30, the root is used meaning "to honor": God asks Eli "why honor (וַתְּכַבֵּד) your sons more than me" leading to God's declaration "those who honor me (מְכַבְּדַי) I will honor (אֲכַבֵּד)." When Eli dies in 4:18, the narrative says, "for the man was old and heavy (וְכָבֵד)," again using the same root as "glory" now with the meaning "heavy."

Neither of the judgment oracles to Eli in 1 Sam 2:27–36 and 3:11–14 mention that the end of the house of Eli would also entail the loss of the

---

10. McCarter, *I Samuel*, 115–16. Josephus *Ant* 5.360 explains the name as ἀδοξίᾳ "inglorious," possibly deriving אי as an abbreviation of אין meaning "there is no."

11. Cf. Campbell, *1 Samuel*, 68.

ark and divine presence in Shiloh; and the unnamed woman is the first to articulate this connection. Moreover, the articulation made is at the naming of a descendent of Eli, one who by rights should be priest after him, and so the child embodies the fact that the ark has left the care of Eli's descendants: Ichabod is the first generation of the Elides who may ask "where is glory?"

The political significance of the physical departure of the ark, not just the cessation of the Elide priesthood, is revealed in the broader narrative of Samuel. The ark remains with the Philistines for only a short period of time before it is returned to Beth-shemesh and then taken to Kiriath-jearim in 1 Sam 6:19—7:2. This location is also temporary until David retrieves the ark and brings it to Jerusalem in 2 Samuel 6. Therefore, the end of the Elides is not only theologically significant as a punishment for their sin; it has a political dimension that the ark moves from Shiloh, where Eli ruled Israel as judge, to Jerusalem, the seat of Davidic power. The divine presence in Jerusalem endorses Davidic monarchy and relegates the priesthood to being under monarchic power. This dimension is foreshadowed in the oracle to Eli in 1 Sam 2:35, when the unnamed prophet says of the priest to replace Eli, "he shall go in and out before my anointed one forever." This prophecy is fulfilled by the replacement of the Elides by the priestly house of Zadok who serve in the Jerusalem sanctuary under the Davidic kings.[12]

In the explanation of Ichabod's name, the term "go into exile" (גָּלָה) may simply mean "to leave, disappear" describing the departure of the ark; and a pre-exilic dating of the text points to this interpretation.[13] Nevertheless, the term would have resonated in later periods of Israel's history, particularly the post-monarchic period when the book of Samuel was still undergoing composition and redaction. Indeed, there are a number of parallels between Israel's experience of exile and the sojourn of the ark among the Philistines in 1 Samuel 4–6.[14] In an exilic period, the words of the unnamed woman take on even broader theological and political significance as the community mourns the loss of God's presence in the temple;[15] and,

---

12. Note that Zadok is possibly descended from the Elides in at least one tradition. According to 1 Sam 14:3, Ahitub is the brother of Ichabod, and according to 2 Sam 8:17, Zadok is the son of Ahitub. However, Blenkinsopp (*Sage, Priest, Prophet*, 76) argues that 2 Sam 8:17 is either corrupt, or a different Ahitub is meant. Cf. in the context of 1 Sam 2–3, the Elides' replacement is apparently Samuel who is compared favourably to Eli's sons (see Eslinger, *Kingship of God*, 135– 37), but Samuel does not ultimately establish a priestly house.

13. Miller and Roberts, *Hand of the Lord*; McCarter, *I Samuel*, 23–26.

14. See Smelik, "Ark Narrative Reconsidered," 128– 44. Note that Smelik also assigns an exilic date to the ark narrative.

15. Note the use of the term "temple" הֵיכַל in 1 Sam 3:3 to describe the sanctuary in Shiloh, strengthening the connection to the destruction of the temple in Jerusalem.

so too, the woman's anguish would reflect the trauma of the destruction of Jerusalem and experience of exile.

The wife of Phinehas and matriarchal powerbrokers

According to the oracle against Eli in 1 Sam 2:33, only one of Eli's descendants will remain to weep over Eli's life and all the other members of his household will die by human hands. Although another sole descendent of Eli, Abiathar, will feature later in the Samuel narrative,[16] the birth of Ichabod is narrated in such a way that no other descendants are in view. At this point in the narrative, it appears he will be the sole survivor. After the death of Phinehas, the pregnancy of his wife in v. 19 suggests a hope for the continuance of his line, a posthumous successor to his priesthood. Indeed, when the women say "do not fear" in 4:20, presumably they believe the unnamed woman is afraid that the child will also be dead, along with her father-in-law and husband. Instead, they reassure her that she has given birth to a son, who is alive, and will grow up to continue the line extinguished with the death of her husband and herself.

The hope of a male priestly successor to Phinehas is dashed by the unnamed woman's insistence that the glory has gone into exile from Israel. The birth of Ichabod is a sign not of hope for the line of Eli, but a sign of its end in accordance with 1 Sam 2:33. She has had a son but in her naming of the child, she has indicated that he will not serve before the ark, for the ark is gone.

Insight into the unnamed woman's position as wife of Phinehas can be gained from an essay by Sarah Shectman, "Israel's Matriarchs: Political Pawns or Powerbrokers," on the role of matriarchs in the politics of Genesis. Shectman observes "the majority of the *patriarchal* drama in Genesis relates to interactions with neighbors and especially to the finding, digging, or defending of wells."[17] In contrast to these interactions with outsiders, the matriarchs in Genesis are involved in determining their sons' futures; and they are concerned with who will be their husband's heir and who will receive his inheritance. Shectman writes, "the matriarchs perform an important political task not only narratively but also historically focusing Israelite

16. Alongside the question of whether Zadok was descended from Eli (see n. 12), another surviving descendent will be revealed in 1 Sam 22:20 from among the priests at Nob. The descendants of Eli remained at the sanctuary at Nob, and, after Saul slaughters the priests there, Abiathar son of Ahimelech, son of Ahitub, Ichabod's brother survives.

17. Shectman, "Israel's Matriarchs," 153.

lineage through specific male lines that they beget and protect."[18] For example, Abraham wants an heir and is willing for this heir to be Ishmael (Gen
17:28); but the drama of choice between Isaac and Ishmael is governed by
the rivalry of Sarah and Hagar (Gen 16, 21:8–21). In the same way, Rebekah,
not Isaac, is key to Jacob's advancement over Esau (Gen 27).[19] In a similar
dynamic, the actions of Phinehas have led to the judgment against Eli, but
his unnamed wife is key to the cessation of the priesthood for his son.[20]

The importance of mothers—over fathers—in determining the political aspirations of their sons is highlighted through the structural parallel
between Hannah's story in 1 Sam 1:1—2:10 and the unnamed woman in
1 Sam 4:19–22. Both women name their child and provide an etymology,
offering their summation of the theological significance of the birth (see
1 Sam 1:20). Both women name a future for their child without the input
of their husband: Hannah's husband Elkanah is not involved in her vow
to bring Samuel to the sanctuary at Shiloh (1 Sam 1:22), nor is Phinehas
present for the naming of his son determining the end of this line of priest.
Both women have a quasi-prophetic role. Hannah's prayer in 1 Sam 2:1–10
foreshadows the theology and politics of the book of Samuel as a whole,
including divine favor for a monarchy (1 Sam 2:10), just as the unnamed
woman points to the end of the ark's presence at Shiloh. Finally, and most
crucially for this argument, both women determine their son's political futures: Hannah's words point to her own son's elevation and service of God
(1 Sam 1:28) and the elevation of a king anointed by Samuel (1 Sam 2:10);
the unnamed woman's words point to her son's impeded future as a priest
because the divine presence is gone.

The unnamed woman's closure of her son's future as priest may also
explain why the woman is unnamed. Immortality in the Hebrew Bible is
conceived, not as life after death, but through memory of a person's name.
For a patriarch, this is usually through a male heir, but can also be ensured through the marriage of his wife to a kinsman after his death (e.g.,

18. Shectman, "Israel's Matriarchs," 163. In the context of Genesis, the primary
political concern is balancing particularist and universalist aspects of Israelite theology in a Persian period context. As I will argue shortly, the primary political concern
underlying the book of Samuel is the establishment and endorsement of Davidic kingship, including David's sanctuary in Jerusalem and a priestly house that is deferential
to the monarchy.

19. An example from Samuel–Kings is found in 1 Kings 1 where Bathsheba plays a
key role in securing the throne for her son Solomon.

20. See also Bridge, "Mother's Influence," 389–400. Bridge argues that the influence
of women in ancient Israelite households is recognized in Biblical stories of women
naming their children, although his study does not extend to the significance of the
name meanings chosen by these women.

Ruth 4:10), or through a monument if he does not have sons (e.g. 2 Sam 18:18). Rachel Havrelock has argued that there is also a concern for female memory and legacy in biblical narrative, but this is realized through a woman overcoming childlessness and naming her children.[21] In light of Shechtman's work, successfully securing her son's political future and blessing as his father's heir might be added as a further way in which a woman's legacy is ensured. Such a female hero is epitomized by Hannah whose name is preserved in the memory of 1 Sam 1–2. As a counterpoint, the woman in 1 Sam 4:19–22 remains unnamed. She is attributed no such triumph over childlessness, and she names her child to realize the end of a priestly house, not the beginning of one.

The mother of Ichabod and the end of the house of Saul

In light of the high maternal mortality rate in the ancient world, it is something of a surprise that there are only two narrative references to a mother dying in childbirth in the Hebrew Bible: the unnamed woman in 1 Sam 4:19–22 and Rachel at the birth of Benjamin in Gen 35:16–21. There are several connections between the stories: both women experience difficult childbirth, although different terminology is used (Gen 35:17); both women are told "do not fear" by those attending them (Gen 35:17); and both women name their son before they die (Gen 35:18).[22]

The close correspondence between Benjamin's birth to Rachel and Ichabod's birth to the unnamed woman suggests an allusion to Saul, Israel's rejected Benjaminite king, in 1 Sam 4:19–22.[23] The tragic death of this unnamed woman foreshadows the tragic fall of Saul, the most significant

21. Havrelock, "Myth of Birthing the Hero," 154–78. Havrelock notes that childbirth is not the only way in which women demonstrate strength in the Hebrew Bible, and makes clear that maternity does not equal female power (156–57).

22. The stories differ, however, by the presence of Rachel's husband, Jacob: Rachel names her son Ben-Oni, meaning "son of my affliction," but his name is changed to Benjamin "son of my right hand" by Jacob. The name change offers further evidence that a mother's naming could determine that child's future as in the case of Ichabod. Cf. De-Whyte, *Wom(b)an*, 122. De-Whyte suggests such a name would draw sympathy for the bearer but potentially also prejudice, and thus Jacob renames the child.

23. There are a number of parallels between the prophetic rejections of Saul and of Eli as leader in Israel (see Gilmour, *Divine Violence*, 140–49); and a number of veiled references to Saul throughout the Elide narratives. The Hebrew root of Saul's name ("שָׁאוּל") "to ask" שאל is repeated throughout 1 Sam 1, including in the naming of Samuel in 1 Sam 1:20, "She named him Samuel, for she said, 'I have asked him of the LORD.'" Note also that a Benjaminite appears in the narrative as a messenger to Eli in 1 Sam 4:12, again linking his death with the Benjaminite king.

Benjaminite of biblical narrative. Just as Ichabod represents the end of the house of Eli as priests in Israel, and the departure of divine presence, so also Saul will fail to establish a dynasty in Israel and the spirit of God will depart from him (1 Sam 16:14).

An additional link between this short narrative and the house of Saul is between Ichabod, Eli's last surviving descendent and Mephibosheth, Saul's last surviving descendent. Mephibosheth is five years old when news of his father's and grandfather's deaths arrive in 2 Sam 4:4. Although it is not stated explicitly that Mephibosheth's mother has died, it is narrated that his nurse flees with him, implying his mother is absent. Thus Mephibosheth's mother is not just unnamed but unmentioned. Just as the oracle to Eli promises a surviving descendent to look upon the disgrace and fall of the Eli's house, so Mephibosheth is the sole descendent eating at David's table after the fall of the house of Saul (2 Sam 9:13).

In this way, the unnamed woman contributes to the broader political interests of 1 Samuel: the rejection of Saul in favor of David. The ark is in exile from Shiloh and will return to David's capital, Jerusalem; the house of Eli has come to an end in favor of the Zadokites who will serve David's sanctuary in Jerusalem; and the house of Saul, the Benjaminite, comes to an end in favor of David's enduring dynasty.

Conclusion

The designation of this unnamed woman in relation to her father-in-law, husband, and son points to the different dimensions of her character's significance in the narrative. This woman suffers the ramifications of the sins of her husband and brother-in-law, and the failings of her father-in-law. She interprets the significance of God's judgment against the Elides, augmenting the oracles of the man of God (1 Sam 2:27–36) and Samuel; but, unlike these messengers, she dies a tragic death as the culmination of downfall of this house.

Despite the theological and political dimensions of the unnamed woman's story, the framing of the unnamed woman only in terms of her male relatives suggests an opening for feminist critique. However, perhaps this very critique is embedded in the structure of 1 Sam 1–4. The narrative begins with the agency and theological insight of Hannah, a woman whose husband is in a supporting role as she determines the future of her son Samuel. Over the following chapters, the sins of the Elides impoverish Israel: stealing at the house of the LORD, laying Israel open to the outside threat of the Philistines, and, finally, their responsibility for the loss of the ark. The death of an unnamed woman in childbirth is the tragic ending to this downward spiral, and a sign that all is not as it should be.[24]

Bibliography

Blenkinsopp, Joseph. *Sage, Priest, Prophet: Religious and Intellectual Leadership in Ancient Israel*. Library of Ancient Israel. Louisville, KY: Westminster John Knox Press, 1995.

Borgman, Paul. *David, Saul, and God: Rediscovering an Ancient Story*. Oxford: Oxford University Press, 2008.

Bridge, Edward J. "A Mother's Influence: Mothers Naming Children in the Hebrew Bible." *VT* 64 (2014) 389–400.

Campbell, Antony F. *1 Samuel*. FOTL 7. Grand Rapids, MI: Eerdmans, 2003.

De-Whyte, Janice P. *Wom(b)an: a Cultural-Narrative Reading of the Hebrew Bible Barrenness Narratives*. Leiden: Brill, 2018.

Dietrich, Walter. *1Sam 1–12*. BKAT 8.1. Neukirchen-Vluyn: Neukirchener Theologie, 2010.

Eslinger, Lyle M. *Kingship of God in Crisis: A Close Reading of 1 Samuel 1–12*. Decatur, GA: Almond Press, 1985.

Fuchs, Esther. "The Literary Characterization of Mothers and Sexual Politics in the Hebrew Bible." *Semeia* 46 (1989) 151–66.

Garsiel, Moshe. *The First Book of Samuel: A Literary Study of Comparative Structures, Analogies and Parallels*. Ramat Gan: Revivim, 1985.

———. *Representing the Past: A Literary Analysis of Narrative Historiography in the book of Samuel*. VTSup 143. Leiden: Brill, 2010.

———. *Divine Violence in the Book of Samuel*. New York: Oxford University Press, 2021.

Havrelock, Rachel. "The Myth of Birthing the Hero: Heroic Barrenness in the Hebrew Bible." *BI* 16 (2008) 154–78.

Hertzberg, Hans W. *I & II Samuel: A Commentary*. Translated by J.S. Bowden. OTL. London: SCM, [1960] 1964.

McCarter, P. Kyle. *I Samuel: A New Translation with Introduction, Notes, and Commentary*. AB 8. New York, NY: Double Day, 1980.

McCormick, Clifford M. "From Box to Throne: The Development of the Ark in DtrH and P." Pages 174–186 in *Saul in Story and Tradition*. Edited by Carl S. Ehrlich and Martha C. White. FAT 47. Tübingen: Mohr Siebeck, 2006.

Miller Jr., Patrick D., and J.J.M. Roberts. *The Hand of the Lord: A Reassessment of the "Ark Narrative" of 1 Samuel*. Atlanta, GA: Society of Biblical Literature, 2008.

Shectman, Sarah. "Israel's Matriarchs: Political Pawns or Powerbrokers?" Pages 131–48 in *The Politics of the Ancestors*. Edited by M.G. Brett and J. Wöhrle. Tübingen: Mohr Siebeck, 2018.

24. Compare the placement of the narrative of the unnamed concubine in Judges 19 at the conclusion of the book of Judges. It is widely accepted that this tragic narrative indicates disintegration and disunity in Israel, particularly when compared to the positive treatment of a woman, Achsah, in Judges 1. On similarities between Judges 19 and the mother of Ichabod, see Borgman, *David, Saul, and God*, 97–119.

Smelik, Klaas A.D. "The Ark Narrative Reconsidered." *New Avenues in the Study of the Old Testament*. Edited by A.S. van der Woude. OtSt 25. Leiden: Brill, 1989, 128–44.

Sternberg, Meir. *The Poetics of Biblical Narrative: Ideological Literature and the Drama of Reading*. Bloomington, IN: Indiana University Press, 1985.

Tsumura, David Toshio. *The First Book of Samuel*. NICOT. Grand Rapids, MI: Eerdmans, 2007.

12.

Jesus and the Syro-Phoenician Woman
A Story of Inclusion?

MICHAEL F. BIRD[1]

Introduction

Several years ago, blogger and author Rachel Held Evans, who passed away quite suddenly and sadly, tweeted about Jesus and the Syro-Phoenician/Canaanite woman and how she changed Jesus' racial bias (see Mark 7.24–30 and Matt 15.21–28). Evans wrote:

> It's fear of Jesus' humanity, I think, that keeps us from interpreting the story of the Syrophoenician/Canaanite woman as a story about a man changing his mind about his racial bias when confronted with the humanity (and chutzpah!) of another person. But that's a tricky one . . .[2]

Evans was not a biblical scholar; however, her remarks on this point are not exactly out of left field. The notion that Jesus had his mind changed, that he had his preconceptions and prejudices challenged by the encounter

1. I consider it an honor to contribute to Prof. Dorothy Lee's festschrift as Prof. Lee is an internationally recognized and celebrated Gospels scholar, she has been a wonderful sparring partner in the quest for unity, catholicity, and love in the Anglican Communion, and she is a fellow redhead who knows the trials of being an antipodean "ranga."

2. Evans, Twitter, 1:14 a.m., 20 Nov 2018.

with the Syro-Phoenician/Canaanite woman, can be found in scholarship and even in some Jesus movies.[3] One must acknowledge that in an age (now) and places (like America and Australia) where ethnic and racial prejudices abound, where historical, systemic, and institutional racism continues unabated, there is something attractive about the interpretation, "See, even Jesus was cured of his prejudices by a woman with courage and wit."

The implications this has for contemporary Christians is that to test one's own biases and be willingly to abandon one's own prejudices has christological precedent! "Here Jesus is a paradigm," says James McGrath, "for what he calls his followers to be and do, namely being humble in the practical way of being open to correction and learning."[4] The argument for the post-prejudice Jesus is attractive, but it can elicit the apologetic knee-jerk push-back that the sinless Jesus harbored no prejudices, discriminations, or ethno-tribal rivalries. As keen as some are to portray Jesus as freed from his ethno-religious biases, others are equally eager to dispel the notion that Jesus had any biases in the first place.

But then again, all of this might be well just missing the point that the Evangelists Mark and Matthew are making when they recount the story of the encounter Jesus had with a Gentile woman. According to Dorothy Lee:

> Jesus' words about dogs and children are not a literal description but a parable, with typical characteristics: a fictional and realistic narrative, centering on a metaphor that takes on symbolic meaning. The parable narrates an imaginary but realistic scenario of dogs scavenging food from the table while the family eats, where the children have priority of access. The parabolic reading is confirmed in the woman's response. Far from taking umbrage, the woman takes the parable further and, in a sense, completes it. Keeping to the spirit of things, she adds a typical element: the dogs are fed the leftovers. Jesus concedes the point and grants the woman's request. . . . The parable thus elicits the woman's faith, acting ironically to connect the two characters. The female outsider displays an exemplary faith in contrast to the insiders, Jesus' disciples, who have so often failed to grasp his parables (Mark 4:10).[5]

I find myself largely in agreement with Lee on this point, but I would like to fill out some details to show that, at least concerning the Marcan Jesus and

3. See McGrath, *What Jesus Learned from Women*, 87–107.

4. McGrath, *What Jesus Learned from Women*, 100.

5. Lee, *Ministry of Women in the New Testament*, 19–20.

the Syro-Phoenician woman, the point is not prejudice but a parable of faith in unexpected places by unexpected people.[6]

Jesus, Mark, and the Gentiles

> From there he set out and went away to the region of Tyre. He entered a house and did not want anyone to know he was there. Yet he could not escape notice, but a woman whose little daughter had an unclean spirit immediately heard about him, and she came and bowed down at his feet. Now the woman was a Gentile, of Syrophoenician origin. She begged him to cast the demon out of her daughter. He said to her, "Let the children be fed first, for it is not fair to take the children's food and throw it to the dogs." But she answered him, "Sir, even the dogs under the table eat the children's crumbs." Then he said to her, "For saying that, you may go—the demon has left your daughter." So she went home, found the child lying on the bed, and the demon gone (Mark 7:24–30 [NRSV]).

While I remain confident that the story of Jesus and the Syro-Phoenician woman is historically authentic, nonetheless, Mark's redactional hand is detectable in his editing of this material. The location of the story in Mark 7–8 shows that it has been curated to fit with Mark's pro-Gentile interests. There is evidence of the Marcan "messianic secret" with Jesus absconding to Tyre to avoid the crowds as "he did not want anyone to know he was there" (Mark 7:24). The story evidences Mark's belief that the Jews are "first" and the Gentiles second, and so assumes a particular scheme of redemptive-history which accords with a missional interest (Mark 7:27; 13:10) and might even be indicative of Pauline influence (see Rom 1:16; 15:7). Plus, there is an accord with Mark's overall emphasis on "faith," including faith exhibited by Gentiles (see Mark 5:19–20). Matthew includes the story in his Gospel, but effectively re-Judaizes it and does not follow Mark by deploying the story in order to furnish his pro-Gentile concerns. Luke omits the story probably because he wishes to defer the majority of his Gentile material to the Book of Acts.

The story of Jesus' encounter with the Syro-Phoenician woman (Mark 7:24–30) is situated in a context where issues of religious authority, demonstrations of faith, and crossing boundaries are central. In a preceding pericope (Mark 7:1–23), we find that Jesus' parabolic teaching about food

6. See my earlier argument set forth in Bird, *Jesus and the Origins of the Gentile Mission*, 112–16.

and impurity are issued as a direct challenge to the popular interpretation of the Pharisees. Jesus here does not abrogate the Torah but intends, like other teachers of his time, to illustrate the weightier aspects of the Torah in terms of a hierarchy of commands. In this case, Jesus' point is that the demands of morality typically should trump concerns for cultic (im)purity.[7] What is more, the Marcan gloss, "Thus he declared all foods clean" (Mark 7:19c) is probably given for Mark's Gentile audience, to the effect that, for you Gentiles, all foods are clean (an editorial remark that is noticeably absent from Matthew's version written, as it probably, was for Jewish Christian consumption). The Gentile motif is continued in what immediately follows with a healing story unique to Mark that takes places in the non-Jewish territory of the Decapolis (Mark 7:31–37) and the feeding of the four thousand on the Gentile side of the Sea of Galilee also takes place in the Decapolis (Mark 8:1–10).

Thus Mark's interest in Gentiles is quite pronounced: Mark's Jesus relativizes the Torah as the barrier between Jews and Gentiles (Mark 7:1–23), Mark includes the story of a Gentile woman as an exemplar of faith (Mark 7:24–30), the Marcan Jesus heals a deaf and mute Gentile man to the astoundment and approval of the crowd (Mark 7:31–37), and Jesus performs a feeding miracle for Gentiles just like the one performed for the Jews (Mark 8:1–10). Mark affirms both the salvation-historical priority of the Jews (Mark 7:27), yet also that that there is enough "bread" for Jews and Gentiles (Mark 8:19–21), and what counts is "faith" (Mark 7:29) and excitement about Jesus (Mark 7:36–37) which Gentiles demonstrate. All of this illustrates that Mark has a Gentile audience in mind since he writes about Gentile characters, in Gentiles places, who exhibit faith, are supplicants of healing, and witness multiple mighty acts by Jesus.

Jewish and Syro-Phoenician Relations

In the story, Jesus retreats to the coastal city of Tyre, a journey which, despite some howling protests by scholars, is not historically implausible. Mark as narrator has also indicated that news about Jesus has already spread as far as "beyond the Jordan, and the region around Tyre and Sidon" (Mark 3.8). Jesus may have wanted respite from crowds and attention that would, inevitably, force Galilean and Judean security instruments to seize him. In addition, it helps if we remember that upper Galilee was economically orientated towards Tyre and Sidon as two significant and nearby urban

---

7. See Bird, "Jesus the Law-Breaker," in *Who Do My Opponents Say That I Am?* 12–24.

centers.[8] Indeed, the reference to giving "bread" to "dogs" may play on the reality that north Galilean wheat was often exported to Tyreans and Sidonian markets even if it meant that grain destined for Galilean villages was exported rather than consumed locally.

Luke reports that Herod Agrippa I, despite harboring some hostility against the two cities, won their accolades by assisting them during a time of famine (see Acts 12:20–23). In which case, the Marcan story would be playing on known socio-economic inequalities between rural Galileans and urban Syro-Phoenicians.[9] In addition, Tyre was a Gentile city yet had a sizable Jewish population. This put the Jewish minority in a perilous state because of the traditional ethno-regional rivalry between Syrians and Judeans (Josephus, *Ant.* 14.313–21; *Apion* 1.69–72) and the Jewish population of Tyre was massacred during the Judean revolt against Rome (Josephus, *War* 2.478). The bite of the story is that it plays on local grievances, that is, it rehearses the well-known economic inequalities whereby Galilean grain went to feed Tyrean bellies as well as the historical enmity between Jews and Syro-Phoenicians.

The Parable of Bread, Children, Dogs, and the Witty Woman

The context and scenery prompt so many questions that we cannot answer. Why did Jesus go to Tyre? Did Jesus have the disciples with him? Whose house was he in? Who is this unnamed woman? Is she rich or poor? Is she a widow? We do not know! In the end, it is the banter between Jesus and the Syro-Phoenician woman that draws the attention of readers. The woman, described as Greek by language and culture, and Syro-Phoenician by genealogy and ethnicity, presents a request, as others have (Mark 5:21–43), for Jesus to expel a demon from her sick daughter. Jesus, either expectedly or unexpectedly—depending on the reader—rebuffs her request on the grounds that it is not "fair" to help her while his own people remain in need; that would be like giving the family bread to dogs ahead of the children. Notably, the imagery assumes the priority of Jesus' mission to Israel (see Matt 10:5–6; 15:24; Rom 15:8), plays on the economic inequalities about bread between Galilee and Syro-Phoenician, and trades in the trope of Gentiles as unclean "dogs" (see Exod 22:31; Prov 26:11; 1 Kgs 21:23; 22:38; 2 Kgs 9:36).

In a fair and rank analysis of the passage, there is no way spin it. Jesus' answer to her desperate request appears merciless as he refuses to help her and he is derogatory in that to label or compare someone to a dog, in nearly

8. Horsley, *Galilee: History, Politics, People,* 162.

9. Theissen, *Gospels in Context,* 72–75.

any culture, is an insult.[10] To imagine that Jesus' harsh words are blunted by the use of the diminutive Greek word for dog, "κυνάριον," i.e., puppy, does not dull the sense of offense for the reason that to label her a "little bitch" is hardly an improvement on "bitch."[11] In fact, Joseph Klausner notes that the statement is "so brusque and chauvinistic that if any other Jewish teacher of the time had said such a thing Christians would never have forgiven Judaism for it."[12]

What happens next, however, is indeed striking. The Syro-Phoenician woman neither protests the unfairness of Jesus' stinging reply nor shrinks away in defeat; instead, she dares to play the word game with Jesus . . . and wins![13] She doesn't rebuff the derisive designation of a "dog," but plays on it to turn the tables on Jesus. She does not deny her outsider status as a Gentile "dog," but takes the imagery into a new direction. Instead of dogs being unclean scavengers who are a cipher for Gentiles, she presents dogs as supplicants in a lower place in the hierarchy of power, yet they are still deserving of compassion. In other words, she acknowledges her lower place as a "dog" before Jesus or the Jews, but pivots towards the picture of a household dog who is inferior, yet also dependent, one who is part of the household, and who eats the same bread as the children. The fact that Jesus grants her request because of her answer shows that in the game of words she has won. The woman may be "other," even a regional rival to the Galileans, an idolator in Jewish metrics, but her expression of faith through wit makes her deserve an act of mercy for her sick daughter. She is clever and shrewd and persuades Jesus into granting her request. Susanna Asikainen notes that, "The Syrophoenician woman is an exceptional figure, because she is the only person in the Synoptic Gospels to best Jesus in a dispute."[14]

Several scholars suppose that the conversation that Jesus had with the Syro-Phoenician woman changed his mind on the issue of the Gentiles, curing in effect his chauvinism and ethnic prejudice.[15] Reinhard Feldmeier comments:

> In any case, the event is authentic in that it does not reflect the glorified image of the infallible religious hero. The same evangelist who proclaims Jesus as the Son of God and Messiah of

10. See McGrath, *What Jesus Learned from Women*, 97–100.

11. Levine, "Matthew's Advice to a Divided Readership," 32.

12. Klausner, *Jesus of Nazareth: His Life, Times, and Teachings*, 294–95.

13. See Ringe, "Gentile Woman's Story Revisited," 90–92.

14. Asikainen, "Women out of Place," 183.

15. See e.g. Rhoads, "Jesus and the Syrophoenician Woman in Mark, 361; Feldmeier, "Die Syrophonizierin," 223–24; Marcus, *Mark 1–8*, 468.

> Israel, who shows how his divine authority is reflected in all of his works and deeds, paints here a picture of a Jesus who is willing to modify and even correct the presuppositions of his self-understanding on the basis of the arguments made by a Gentile woman.[16]

The problem is that such a view includes some kind of psychologizing of Jesus, and Morna D. Hooker correctly advises that we lack the kind of evidence to trace such a development in Jesus' thought as to how he might have shifted his attention from the Jews to the Gentiles in the way like Paul is reported to have done in Acts 18:6.[17] In addition, while it is attractive to imagine that the woman changed Jesus' mind about Gentile inclusion in his mission, so that the Jewish crumbs that feed Gentile dogs in 7:28 soon turns into the abundance of bread in the feeding miracle for Gentiles in 8:8–10, that will not work either. That is because, to state the blinding obvious, Jesus has already engaged in mission on Gentile territory and to Gentiles during his time in the region of the Decapolis and to the Gerasene demoniac (Mark 4:35–5:20).[18]

I find it more likely that Jesus' dismissive remark towards the woman is premised on the focus of Israel in his mission and deliberately attempts to elicit an animated response from her.[19] Thus, it could be possible that Jesus deploys a type of "peirastic irony" which is a challenge disguised as an insult to draw out one's interlocutor.[20] In which case, Jesus' seeming mistreatment is a test of faith. Jesus has, after all, tested, or at least critically conversed with, other supplicants such as the leper (1:40–45), the paralytic man (2:1–5), Jairus, the bleeding woman (5:21–43), and, later, the demoniac's father (9:17–19), and Bartimaeus (10:46–52). In Marcan narration, refusal and rejoinder are part of Jesus' normal engagement with characters who need his healing powers.[21]

---

16. Feldmeier, "Die Syrophonizierin," 224 (my translation). Original German: "Die Begebenheit ist in jedem Fall darin authentisch, dass sich in ihr nicht das verklärte Bild des unfehlbaren religiösen Heroen spiegelt. Von denselben Evangelisten, die Jesus als den Gottessohn und Messias Israels verkündigen, die zeigen, wie sich dessen göttliche Vollmacht in allen seinen Werken und Taten spiegelt, wird hier das Bild eines Jesus vor Augen gemalt, der bereit ist, eine Voraussetzung seines Selbstverständnisses aufgrund der Argumente einer heidnischen Frau zu modifizieren, ja zu korrigieren."

17. Hooker, "Uncomfortable Words: X," 364.

18. Malcolm, "Did the Syrophoenician Woman Change Jesus's Mission?" 177–80.

19. A view I first learned from Caird, *New Testament Theology*, 395.

20. Iverson, *Gentiles in the Gospel of Mark*, 52.

21. Rhoads, "Jesus and the Syrophoenician Woman," 350.

I am intrigued yet not fully persuaded by the possibility that peirastic irony is deployed in this pericope. Instead, I prefer to see Jesus' words as straightforwardly parabolic, because Jesus speaks in parables to outsiders (Mark 4:10–13) and Jesus' preceding speech across 7:1–23 is parabolic even though the word "parable" is not explicitly used.[22] What is more, Jesus' parables, including this parable about children, bread, and dogs, is intended to elicit faith. First, her behavior designates her as an ideal figure of faith, combining both prostration ("she came and bowed down at his feet") and persistence (the imperfect "ἠρώτα" is iterative, she kept on asking him to heal her daughter). Second, she does not object to the harsh language of the parable even with its degradation of her status as a Gentile; rather, she plays the word game to her advantage. The woman grants Jesus' premise of the priority of the Jews, she accepts her outsider status as a Gentile "dog," yet she turns the language of children, dogs, and bread to her advantage: even dogs eat the crumbs that children give them.

The irony is that by recognizing her outsider status, she makes herself an insider, i.e., one who has faith in Jesus. She exercises faith in Jesus as a healer and recognizes Jewish priority in order to be the recipient of healing from a Jewish healer/exorcist. Jesus in turn acknowledges the cleverness of her reply that Israel's blessings can, even in limited ways, extend to Gentiles, a theme found elsewhere in the Jesus tradition (e.g., Luke 4:25–27). Israel's priority does not negate the opportunity for Gentiles to also be "fed" with messianic compassion in the here and now. In the end, she does not change Jesus' mind about Gentiles, but she does change Jesus' mind about healing her daughter.[23]

In the Marcan scheme, blessings, mercy, and healings for Gentiles are now available to Gentiles as the sequel to Israel's restoration and rescue. There is messianic bread and abundance for both Israel (Mark 6:30–44) and Gentiles (Mark 8:1–10) right now. There is an eschatological "now" that appears to undergird the Marcan Jesus' ability and willingness to heal a Gentile. David Rhoads paraphrases the woman's response: "*Even now* I and my daughter at the margins (should) benefit from just one exorcism from among the many benefits for the Jews."[24] In the progression of the narrative, as the children of Israel are being fed, crumbs are *now already* falling for the dogs. Mark deploys the story to accent this notion, that as Israel's restoration becomes more and more of a reality, it becomes ever more possible

22. I confess to having my mind changed on this point by Shively, "Identity and Inclusion: Jesus and the Syrophoenician Woman in Mark's Gospel."

23. Shively, "Identity and Inclusion."

24. Rhoads, "Jesus and the Syrophoenician Woman," 357 (italics original).

and perhaps even necessary for Gentiles to experience the blessing of its fulfillment. This means that the daughters of Jairus and the Syro-Phoenician can both be healed, or, to use the digestive metaphor, fed to the point of satisfaction. Mark believes that the restoration of Israel, even in nascent form, carries with it incipient eschatological benefits for the Gentiles who find themselves confronted with the compassion of God's messianic leader. As the children of Israel are fed, it is *now* possible for the dogs (i.e., Gentiles) to be healed because of Israel's dawning restoration.

Conclusion

So, then, did the Syro-Phoenician woman change Jesus' mind about the inclusion of Gentiles in God's redeeming mercy? Well, at the level of the Marcan narrative, the answer must be "no" simply because Mark 5 precedes Mark 7. That said, Mark does construct a chain of pericopae that show that Jesus is interested in crossing boundaries and bestowing his divine healing power on Gentile supplicants. His banter with the Syro-Phoenician woman is, it would appear to me, to be typical of his parables and the critical interaction he has with supplicants of healings that illustrates and draws out the true nature of faith. In the case of the Syro-Phoenician woman, she is, in every respect, an exemplar of faith. She is the one who rightly asks for eschatological crumbs of salvation (Mark 7:27) even while the disciples become befuddled about whether there is enough literal bread for Jews and Gentiles (Mark 8:14–21). The point is that, because of her faith, Jesus consents to heal her daughter. Thus, Jesus himself goes from being antagonistic to agreeable, from refusal to receptive, from dismissive to inclusive . . . just as he intended to!

Bibliography

Asikainen, Susanna. "Women out of Place: The Women Who Challenged Jesus." *NeoT* 52 (2018) 179–93.

Bird, Michael F. *Jesus and the Origins of the Gentile Mission.* LNTS 331; LHJS; Edinburgh: T&T Clark, 2006.

———. "Jesus the Law-Breaker." Pages 12–24 in *Who Do My Opponents Say That I Am? An Investigation of the Accusations Against Jesus.* Edited by Joseph B. Modica and Scot McKnight. LHJS; London: T&T Clark, 2008.

Caird, George B. *New Testament Theology.* Ed. L.D. Hurst; Oxford: Clarendon, 1994.

Feldmeier, Reinhard. "Die Syrophonizierin (Mk 7,24–30)—Jesu ‚verlorenes' Streitgesprach." Pages 211–17 in *Die Heiden: Juden, Christen und das Problem des Fremden.* Edited by Reinhard Feldmeier and Ulrich Heckel. Tübingen: Mohr/ Siebeck, 1994.

Hooker, Morna D. "Uncomfortable Words: X. The Prohibition of Foreign Missions (Mt 10$^{5-6}$)." *ExpT* 82 (1971) XX.

Horsley, Richard H. *Galilee: History, Politics, People.* Valley Forge, PA: Trinity, 1995.

Iverson, Kelly. *Gentiles in the Gospel of Mark: "Even the Dogs under the Table Eat the Children's Crumbs."* London: T&T Clark 2007.

Josephus. *The Jewish War*, Volume I: Books 1–2. Translated by H. St. J. Thackeray. Loeb Classical Library 203. Cambridge, MA: Harvard University Press, 1927.

———. *Jewish Antiquities*, Volume I: Books 1–3. Translated by H. St. J. Thackeray. Loeb Classical Library 242. Cambridge, MA: Harvard University Press, 1930.

———. *The Life. Against Apion.* Translated by H. St. J. Thackeray. Loeb Classical Library 186.Cambridge, MA: Harvard University Press, 1926.

Klausner, Joseph. *Jesus of Nazareth: His Life, Times, and Teachings.* Trans. Herbert Danby; London: Allen & Unwin, 1929

Lee, Dorothy A. *The Ministry of Women in the New Testament: Reclaiming the Biblical Vision for Church Leadership.* Grand Rapids, MI: Eerdmans, 2021.

Levine, Amy-Jill. "Matthew's Advice to a Divided Readership." *The Gospel of Matthew in Current Study.* Edited by David E. Aune. Grand Rapids, MI: Eerdmans, 2011, 22–41.

Malcolm, Matthew. "Did the Syrophoenician Woman Change Jesus's Mission?" *BBR* 29 (2019) 174–86.

Marcus, Joel B. *Mark 1–8: A New Translation with Introduction and Commentary.* ABYRL; New York: Doubleday, 1999.

McGrath, James F. *What Jesus Learned from Women.* Eugene, OR: Cascade, 2021.

Rhoads, David. "Jesus and the Syrophoenician Woman in Mark: A Narrative-Critical Study." *JAAR* 62 (1994) 343–75.

Ringe, Sharon H. "A Gentile Woman's Story Revisited: Rereading Mark 7.24–31." *A Feminist Companion to Mark.* Edited by Amy-Jill Levine with Marianne Blickenstaff. Sheffield: Sheffield Academic Press, 2001, 79–100.

Shively, Elizabeth, "Identity and Inclusion: Jesus and the Syrophoenician Woman in Mark's Gospel," *Figuring the Enemy: Socio-Scientific Approaches to Religious Enmity,* Edited by Christopher Porter, Elizabeth Shively, Kenneth Mavor. Routledge, forthcoming.

Theissen, Gerd. *The Gospels in Context: Social and Political History in the Synoptic Tradition.* Trans. Linda M. Maloney; Minneapolis: Fortress, 1991.

13.

The Queen's funeral service and the Book of Common Prayer

COLLEEN O'REILLY AND MURIEL PORTER

Introduction

It was anticipated that at least four billion people would watch the funeral of Queen Elizabeth II.[1] It will never be known how many people around the world tuned in briefly or stayed for the whole telecast, but there can be little doubt this must have been one of the most observed Christian services ever held. Many viewers from the English-speaking world, and particularly those from an Anglican heritage, would have recognized in the funeral liturgy the language and formality of the sixteenth-century *Book of Common Prayer* (BCP), best known in its final revision of 1662. The BCP style in the order of service was so potent that public commentary assumed that the service was in fact the funeral service from the BCP.

---

1. In Australia— where the Queen was head of state and the funeral aired live in the evening— *The Sydney Morning Herald* estimated that, based on viewing figures published overnight, a peak audience of 5.17 million viewers tuned into the funeral, approximately one-fifth of the country. Karl Quinn, "Did Four Billion People Really Watch the Queen's Funeral?"

Writing in the *Guardian* newspaper, Harriet Sherwood, noting that the Queen was "said to be devoted to the Book of Common Prayer," stated that "the service was taken from the 1662 Book of Common Prayer . . . largely displaced in recent decades by those seeking a more modern style of worship."[2] Perhaps her view was shaped by a comment made before the funeral by the former Archbishop of York, John Sentamu, who had been quoted as saying the funeral would be the "best of funeral services, the prayer book service, the words which were an inspiration to Shakespeare."[3] Other commentators made the same assumption,[4] and anecdotal evidence suggests many viewers thought likewise.

The reality, however, is that if the Queen's funeral had been the actual BCP service, viewers would no doubt have been shocked by a spare, austere liturgy in which the deceased is not named, but merely referred to as "the corpse." It would be surprising if even the most devoted aficionado of the BCP chose that rite exactly as it is in the BCP. While the Queen's funeral used the now archaic English used in the BCP, and borrowed some elements from it, it was in fact a hybrid liturgy, as is the case with almost all contemporary Anglican funeral rites. This discussion concerns the State Funeral of the late Queen held in Westminster Abbey in the light of the BCP funeral service from its origins in the sixteenth-century and its development since then. It then reflects on the relationship of the Queen's funeral to contemporary funeral practices.

Anglican funeral rites

Current Anglican funeral rites have a history reaching back into the sixteenth-century's reforms of English worship, and the theological disputes which formed part of the complex politics of those times. It is remarkable that those turbulent times eventually gave Anglicans, and English-speaking peoples everywhere, a settled book of services for the whole of life in Christ which has endured in use until today. For the better part of four hundred years, except for the disruption of the Cromwellian Commonwealth from 1649 to 1660[5] when the Elizabethan BCP was suppressed, the Anglican

2. Sherwood, "'We Will Meet Again.'"

3. Sherwood, "Queen Did Not Want 'Long, Boring' Funeral, Says Former Archbishop of York."

4. See for example Mammana, "An American's Guide to the State Funeral of Her Majesty Queen Elizabeth II."

5. Following the execution of King Charles I in 1649, England became a Puritan Commonwealth led by Oliver Cromwell. The BCP, along with the Episcopate, was suppressed. Both were restored following the return of the monarchy in 1660.

liturgical "playbook" of scripts has been the bedrock from which all modern revisions have emerged.

There were five versions of the BCP.[6] The original version of 1549, though it emerged during the first years of the reign of Edward VI (reigned 1547–1553), was soon deemed too Catholic for the Protestant king and his advisers; it was replaced by the more Protestant 1552 version. The death of the young king and the accession of his Catholic sister Mary meant that that version lasted only briefly as well. It was restored with minor variations with the accession of Elizabeth I in 1559. King James I (reigned 1603–1625) ordered some changes, principally to the Catechism, resulting in a 1604 version. The 1662 BCP, the revision adopted following the restoration of the monarchy in 1660, is fundamentally the 1559 version. It remains the official prayer book of the Church of England, and so has become the BCP standard usually meant in references to the BCP. The three principal versions—1549, 1559, and 1662—offer a fascinating glimpse into the profound theological shifts that occurred over those 113 years.

The BCP's "The Order for the Burial of the Dead" is one of the most severe liturgies devised by the sixteenth-century reformers, who reduced the medieval funeral liturgies that had developed over the centuries to one spare service. Funeral rites were dramatically simplified to correct what the reformers deemed to be theological errors in the existing rites.

By the time of Henry VIII, who reigned from 1509 to 1547, funerals in the western Latin church, of which the English church was part, were elaborate liturgies. They were part of the rituals of the Roman church that constituted a yearly cycle of feasts and fasts, enacted by processions and symbolic acts as well as spoken words. By far the most familiar rites to people of any rank, apart from the central one of the mass or Eucharist, was the Office of the Dead.

For several hundred years, the English liturgical tradition had been the use of Roman rites, predominantly in Latin, but adapted according to slightly differing customs known as "uses" by the many religious communities, by regional custom that had developed in parish churches, or in cathedrals.[7] The "use" from which elements of the reformed funeral service were drawn was that used in Salisbury Cathedral, known by the Latin name, Sarum.

6. A concise history of the five editions of the BCP can be found in Cummings, ed., *Book of Common Prayer*, ix–lii.

7. England had many religious houses for members of the Carthusian, Benedictine and Cistercian orders, as well as the newer orders of friars such as the Franciscans, and cathedrals had distinctive liturgical "uses." The BCP brought these differences to an end while also making the vernacular English the new language of worship.

The "use" of Sarum had dominated the English church by the thirteenth-century.[8] The elaborate sequence of funeral services included burial, but so much more, both before and following the burial. It was the teaching of purgatory that drove this elaboration, and rejection of this teaching that drove the reformers.

The doctrine of purgatory had arisen in response to an anxiety about admission to heaven. It claimed that most Christians would ultimately be saved, but that few would die in a state of sufficient grace to be admitted immediately to the beatific vision of heaven. So, the assumption of the need for a place of post-mortem suffering and preparation, a place of the purgation of sin that had been carried into the next life, created the idea of purgatory.[9] In turn, this encouraged prayer for the dead, to support or shorten the time souls spent in purgatory. Attendance at masses for which indulgences—which granted remission of time in purgatory— and masses specifically for the dead, created the need for chantries[10] in chapels and colleges where the clergy spent their time saying multiple masses for the departed, according to the pecuniary provisions of their wills. For instance, Henry VIII made ample provision in his will for this practice.[11]

By the later Middle Ages, indulgences had become the subject of abuse, when professional "pardoners" sold them indiscriminately. This practice was a factor in the Reformation, when the whole doctrine of purgatory, and the notion that the living could by prayer affect the destiny of the departed, came under intense scrutiny.[12] At first, the Protestant reformers allowed some prayer for the dead until the practice came to be denounced as un-scriptural.[13] That they struggled with the issue can be seen in the evolution of the BCP burial service, though from the outset the English reformers

8. Krick-Pridgeon, "'Nothing for the godly to fear': Use of Sarum Influence on the 1549 Book of Common Prayer," 10.

9. Cross & Livingstone, *Oxford Dictionary of the Christian Church*, 1349

10. This English word is derived from the Latin *cantaria* meaning a place for sing-ing. It was based on the convention that Masses were sung. People of modest means might employ one priest for a short period of time, but the wealthy were able to access permanent arrangements through guilds or the universities of Oxford and Cambridge. For further information about the elaboration of a system of prayers and good works, see MacCulloch, *Reformation*, 11–15.

11. Henry VIII's will ordered that an altar in St George's Chapel, Windsor Castle "be furnished for the saying of daily Masses while the world shall endure." Further, among other disbursements for prayer for his soul, the will ordered the distribution of 1,000 marks "in alms to the poor (common beggars, as much as may be, avoided) with injunctions to pray for his soul." "Henry VIII: December 1546, 26–31."

12. Cross & Livingstone, *Oxford Dictionary of the Christian Church*, 830

13. Cross & Livingstone, *Oxford Dictionary of the Christian Church*, 457

dispensed with the elaborate ceremonials of death that had depended on the need for constant prayer for the departed. Their reduction of the death rites to one simple burial service was surely an unsettling change for people accustomed to so much more.

Cranmer's reformed funeral of 1549

There is no evidence that the English reformers tried to abolish the funeral completely. In general, the 1549 BCP "retained many traditional practices in order not to offend the conservative inclinations of the bulk of churchgoers."[14] Nevertheless, the BCP "represented a shift in attitudes towards the dead and in their memorialization . . . The focus shifted from remembrance of the deceased to using the death of someone to remind oneself that self-reliance was the maintenance mechanism of a healthy soul."[15] It drove a wedge between living and departed and in the order for burial only speaks *about* the deceased, no longer *to* them.

Thomas Cranmer's first reformed funeral service in the proposed prayer book of 1549 was conservative. It retained a fourfold scheme of a procession to the church or place of burial, the burial itself, a brief office for the dead, and an optional funeral Eucharist. It seems that burial could take place before the office and the Eucharist if being celebrated. Allowing for either may have been to provide for the immediate burial of anyone dying of an infectious disease, thus reducing the risk of infection to mourners and clergy. The emphasis in each edition of the BCP was on the burial rather than on a rite conducted in the church building, the latter being treated as optional.

The service begins with the singing of sentences of Scripture designed to accompany the procession of the body either into the church or to the place of burial. The first "Sentences" are John 11:24 and Job 29:25 from the old offices of the dead, and Matins and Lauds. Then follows a third, an original combination of 1 Timothy 6:7 and Job 1:21:

> We brought nothyng into the worlde, neyther may we carye anything out of this worlde. The Lorde geveth, and the Lord taketh away. Even as it pleaseth the Lorde, so cummeth thynges to passe: blessed be the name of the Lorde.[16]

14. Benedict, *Christ's Churches Purely Reformed*, 237

15. Krick-Pridgeon, "'Nothing for the godly to fear,'" 231

16. Cummings, ed., *Book of Common Prayer*. 82. The 1549, 1559 and 1662 editions of the BCP are printed in full in this volume. All references to the text of these editions is taken from here.

Other sentences, many of them antiphons to psalms, and psalms familiar from the pre-Reformation services, then follow. One, commencing "Man that is borne of a woman," was a series of Scriptural citations forming a textual sequence unique to the Sarum rite, that is, it was not in the Roman rite.[17] Then follows a prayer, again from Sarum, beginning "I commende thy soule to God the father almighty," addressed to the corpse. This hangover from medieval rites was clearly anathema to stricter reformers, who changed it in the 1552 BCP, so that the words are addressed instead to the congregation.[18] Two prayers follow, commending the departed to God's mercy and giving thanks that they have been delivered "from the miseries of this wretched world, from the body of death and all temptacion."[19]

Then follows a shorter Office of the Dead, the third component, which is to be said in the church, and may be before or following the burial. The psalms set to be recited begin with Psalm 116, its Latin superscription *Dilexi, quoniam*,[20] speaking of the comfort of having been heard and delivered "when the snares of death compassed me round about."[21] Next comes a large portion (38 verses) of chapter 15 from Paul's first letter to the church in Corinth, a chapter concerned with the nature of the resurrected body. After the petition known as the Kyries (after the original Greek), and the Lord's Prayer, the brief litany that follows contains a petition, "deliver theyr soules, o lorde," which has been described as "an unequivocal prayer for the souls of the dead."[22] The concluding prayer of this section draws on phrases from the Sarum rite. The final provision, the fourth element, is a celebration of the Eucharist which retains familiar words and the epistle reading from 1 Thessalonians 4:13–18 from the Sarum requiem for use when the body is present and in use by many Lutherans at that time.[23]

This continuity with the former rites is striking given the repudiation of the doctrine of purgatory and the belief that praying for the dead was of any assistance to them since there was no scriptural warrant to do so. It is worth considering Cranmer's purpose in continuing some elements of the custom that was both embedded in popular piety, and that provided an income for chantry priests. Could it be that pastoral considerations were a

17. Cummings, ed., *Book of Common Prayer*, 718

18. Cummings, ed., *Book of Common Prayer*, 718

19. "The Ordre for the buriall of the Dead," 1549 BCP, in Cummings, ed., *Book of Common Prayer*, 83

20. The psalms in BCP all have a Latin superscription of the opening words. "*Dilexi quoniam*" translates as "I am well pleased since." . . the Lord has heard my voice.

21. Cummings, *Book of Common Prayer*, 83.

22. Cummings, *Book of Common Prayer*, 718.

23. Rowell, *Liturgy of Christian Burial*, 85–98

factor in the retention of some of the familiar psalms and prayers? Did the English reformers initially intend to keep what may have been a source of comfort to mourners in an unsettling time when other old practices were being questioned or abandoned? Perhaps they intended that the people should be better instructed in the meanings of those ceremonies and prayers which were retained and did not have a zeal to reject all previous patterns. Perhaps they were also aware that in matters relating to death, change is slowly embraced and may even be resisted to the point of losing the acceptance of other reforms.

The further reform of 1552

In 1552, during the reign of Edward VI, even this reduced order was further shortened. The text is half the size of the 1549 service.[24] A more Protestant influence is evident in the removal of the psalms and the Eucharist. The opening "Sentences" are retained, as is the reading from I Corinthians. Where the 1549 service had the priest alone "casting earth upon the Corps," in the 1552 service the earth is thrown onto the body "by some standying by." The prayer accompanying this action, from the 1549 service, is given a new introductory phrase, "Forasmuche as it hath pleased almightie God," emphasizing "God's sovereignty in the passage from life to death."[25] That short phrase introduces an element of the German reformation; it is taken from *A Simple and Religious Consultation* by Hermann von Wied, the Archbishop of Cologne who was so convinced by the reformers that he died a Lutheran. It was published in English in 1547.[26] Further, the priest's role is diminished by the use here of the plural pronoun "we" in committing the body to the ground, and note it is the body committed, not the soul commended.[27]

After the reading from 1 Corinthians, only the Kyries and the Lord's Prayer remain from the Office of the Dead, followed by two prayers from the 1549 service. The first, commencing "Almightie God, with whom do live the spirites," was altered to exclude direct prayers for departed, while the final prayer, with some small variations, was originally the collect for the now-removed requiem Eucharist.

24. The 1552 BCP in the modified version of 1559 is reprinted in full in Cummings, ed., *Book of Common Prayer,* 99–181

25. Cummings, ed., *Book of Common Prayer,* 743

26. Jasper and Cuming, *Prayers of the Eucharist: Early and Reformed,* 219

27. Cummings, ed., *Book of Common Prayer,* 743.

It is this briefer form of burial service that was restored by Elizabeth I in 1559. Mary I, Elizabeth's older half-sister, had brought back the old Roman rites during her previous short reign but Elizabeth needed to settle the nature of the English church in both continuity with its past and in conformity to its reformed future.

The burial service of 1662

The burial service in the 1662 BCP is almost entirely the service from 1552/1559. It begins with the "Sentences" as the others do, but restores two psalms, this time Psalms 39 and 90, before the 1 Corinthians reading. The prayer "Man that is borne of a woman," found in the earlier services, is moved to a position following the reading, as is the ritual of casting earth on the body. Then follows the two last prayers, with minor variations, from the 1552/559 service, with one new final addition—the prayer that closes the second letter to the Corinthians: "The grace of our Lord Jesus Christ, and the love of God, and the fellowship of the holy Ghost, be with us all evermore. Amen."[28]

The 1662 "The Order for the Burial of the Dead" is the final BCP funeral service and as such, remains an official authorized service of the Church of England. As noted earlier, it is a spare, austere service, resolutely adhering to the Reformation anxieties about praying for the dead. It would be utterly surprising if more than a few today, even the most devoted supporter of the continuing use of the BCP, chose this service as it is printed for their funeral, or for that of a loved one. Instead, by using a few elements from it and adopting the language style of the BCP in additional material, BCP devotees no doubt can comfort themselves that they are using their beloved prayer book. This is what it seems has happened for the funeral of Queen Elizabeth II.

The funeral of Queen Elizabeth II

The Queen's funeral was always going to be a Church of England service, given that the monarch is by law required to be a member of the Church of England.[29] Since the British monarch is Supreme Governor of the Church of England, the highest-ranking clergy led the services and religious

---

28. 2 Corinthians 13:13.

29. The Sovereign must "be in communion with the Church of England and must swear to preserve the established Church of England." The Royal Household, "Succession."

ceremonies associated with the Queen's death. The service had been planned over many years, beginning in the 1960s, when the plans for all the events following her death were given the code name "London Bridge"; the plans were frequently revised,[30] with the Queen reportedly choosing every aspect of the service.[31]

Designated a State Funeral and not simply a Royal Funeral, the Queen's funeral was the highest honor that the British parliament could confer. The expenses associated with this funeral were paid from government revenue. State funerals in the United Kingdom are rare, normally reserved to sovereigns, though occasionally notable citizens will be accorded this honor. The last State funeral was following the death of Sir Winston Churchill in 1965. The funerals of other members of Queen Elizabeth's family have been Royal and ceremonial, but not State funerals. The difference may not appear much to an observer, except for the conveyancing of the gun carriage which in a ceremonial funeral is pulled by horses, not young men and women of the Royal Navy. Behind the scenes, the difference matters significantly. The person who is responsible for arranging a Royal funeral is decided by its status. The Earl Marshall[32] arranges State funerals while it is the duty of the Lord Chamberlain[33] to organize those of the Royal family.

The Queen's funeral service in Westminster Abbey began with "The Sentences," which introduced each of the BCP funeral services. At the Queen's funeral, the Sentences were sung to the 1724 setting by William Croft, including William Purcell's 1695 anthem, "Thou knowest, Lord, the secrets of our hearts." This compilation has been standard across English royal and state funerals.[34] The inclusion of the Purcell anthem already constitutes a variation on the BCP service.

Next came a "bidding" prayer, clearly written for the occasion, and not in any sense redolent of the BCP. It was followed by the "The Collect" from the BCP—"O merciful God . . ." —normally found at the end of the BCP

30. Knight, "'London Bridge Is Down.'"

31. Rieden, "Royal Funerals Are Never the Same — but We'll See One Famous Scene Repeated."; Westminster Abbey, "The State Funeral of Her Majesty Queen Elizabeth II."

32. This hereditary office is held by the Dukes of Norfolk, the senior peer in the United Kingdom. The current Duke is Edward Fitzalan-Howard, 18th Duke of Norfolk, who inherited the position in June 2002. The family has remained Roman Catholic since the English church broke from the jurisdiction of Rome in 1534.

33. The Lord Chamberlain of the Household is the most senior officer of the Royal Household of the United Kingdom. It is not an hereditary office and since 1924 the person is appointed by agreement between the sovereign and the prime minster. The appointee is always a peer or a privy councilor.

34. "The Queen's Music • Andrew Ford."

service. After a hymn[35] came a reading from a portion of 1 Corinthians 15, but at just 10 verses, a much shorter portion than the 38 verses set in the BCP service. A sung setting of Psalm 42 (not a psalm that appears in any of the BCP funeral services) followed. After another hymn came a second reading, this time from the fourteenth chapter of John's Gospel, a reading much more common in contemporary Anglican funerals than the selection from 1 Corinthians, but again not found in any of the BCP services. Then came another hymn, a sermon, and an anthem—all elements not found in any BCP funeral service.

Lengthy intercessory prayers came next, voiced by representatives from across the Christian churches in Britain. They have no origin in the BCP, but cleverly used BCP-style language and construction—"thee" and "thy" proliferated. The opening prayer,

> O GOD, from whom cometh everything that is upright and true: accept our thanks for the gifts of heart and mind that thou didst bestow upon thy daughter Elizabeth, and which she showed forth among us in her words and deeds; and grant that we may have grace to live our lives in accordance with thy will, to seek the good of others, and to remain faithful servants unto our lives' end; through Jesus Christ our Lord. Amen.

was a prayer issued by the Archbishops of Canterbury and York "for use by individuals and churches" following the death of Queen Elizabeth the Queen Mother in 2002, with one small change: the Queen was referred to as God's daughter, rather than servant, as it was in the original version.[36]

The next prayer, a prayer for the bereaved beginning "Almighty God, Father of all mercies and giver of all comforts," comes from the failed proposed 1928 revision of the BCP.[37] The prayer for the royal family comes straight from the BCP services of morning and evening prayer, while prayers for the nation and the Commonwealth look to have been written specifically for the Queen's funeral. The next prayer, the prayer for the church, is the BCP Collect for the Twenty-Second Sunday after Trinity, beginning "Lord, we beseech thee to keep thy household the church in continual godliness."

---

35. There was no provision for hymnody in the BCP services; hymns as we know them were not introduced into post-Reformation Anglican worship until the early nineteenth century: Cross & Livingstone, 810–811.

36. "Prayers Offered at a Time of Mourning—Prayer & Worship—Thisischurch.Com."

37. *Book of Common Prayer with the additions and deviations proposed in 1928*, 434. This revision failed to pass the British Parliament, as is required for legislation of the Church of England. However, it was widely used throughout the Anglican Communion, particularly in Anglo-Catholic churches, until contemporary prayer books emerged in the late twentieth century.

The final prayer, "Bring us O Lord into our last awakening . . .," does not come from any version of the BCP, but is a prayer written by the poet priest John Donne (1572–1631).

Then followed an anthem, the Lord's Prayer (in traditional language), and a hymn before the commendation, which amounted to just two prayers. The first does not appear to come from any of the standard Church of England funeral liturgies, old or new:

> HEAVENLY Father, King of kings, Lord and giver of life, who of thy grace in creation didst form mankind in thine own image, and in thy great love offerest us life eternal in Christ Jesus; claiming the promises of thy most blessed Son, we entrust the soul of Elizabeth, our sister here departed, to thy merciful keeping, in sure and certain hope of the resurrection to eternal life, when Christ shall be all in all; who died and rose again to save us, and now liveth and reigneth with thee and the Holy Spirit, in glory for ever. Amen.

While it contains the phrase "in sure and certain hope of the resurrection" used in the 1662 prayer to be said while the body is being sprinkled with earth, the rest of the prayer seems to have been written either for the Queen's funeral or for some other from which it has been borrowed. Nevertheless, it conforms to the archaic style of sixteenth-century English, perhaps giving the sense that it is a BCP prayer, but it differs from the 1662 service in one striking particular. The "soul" of the Queen is entrusted to God, whereas the 1662 service deliberately avoids prayer for the departed. The BCP service gives no such license to the officiating priest; rather, it acknowledges that God had the agency in taking "unto himself the soul of our dear *brother* here departed."

The final prayer, before another anthem, the blessing, the last post, the reveille, the national anthem and a piper concluded the service, has an interesting history. The prayer, beginning "Go forth, O Christian soul, from this world," known as the *Proficiscere*, possibly originated in France in the eighth-century, but disappeared in English use after the Reformation.[38] It came back into prominence when it was used by John Henry Newman in his 1865 poem, *The Dream of Gerontius*, inspiring a choral work by Edward Elgar in 1900. It took a century from Elgar's rendition to find a place in an official Church of England rite; it is an optional prayer in prayers for the dying in the "Ministry at the Time of Death" in *Common Worship*.[39] It

---

38. The prayer is the subject of a book: *Go forth Christian Soul: the Biography of a Prayer* by John Lampard: see Rowell, "Go Forth, Christian Soul."

39. *Common Worship*, 2000.

had however already been used in the "Prayers for the Dying" in the 1995 *A Prayer Book for Australia*[40] but not, note, in the actual funeral service in that prayer book. Its placement in the funeral service for the Queen was therefore unusual. This prayer, with its expectation that the departed was in "communion with all the blessed saints, and aided by the angels and archangels and all the armies of the heavenly host," would have been anathema to the theology of the English reformers, including those who revised the BCP in 1662.

The funeral of Queen Elizabeth was then not only most certainly not a BCP service, except for the brief inclusions already noted, but was instead a hybrid service. All the indications are, as noted, that the Queen herself was responsible for its content. As such, it reflects modern Anglican funeral practice, where mourners and the clergy together, sometimes using the pre-advised preferences of the deceased, construct a specific rite. The resulting service can still have strong Anglican content because of the range of alternatives offered in contemporary Anglican prayer books. No such leeway is offered in the BCP funeral rites, however, where an overriding concern was to ensure, through precise choice of words, that there could be little doubt about the Protestant theology of death and dying.

In other respects, however, the Queen's funeral was decidedly out of step with contemporary Anglican funeral services, from the use of archaic English throughout, including in the Bible reading and hymns, to the black clerical vestments and the unrelieved black worn by almost all the mourners in Westminster Abbey. Since modern funeral liturgies were authorized from the 1970s, traditional black or purple vestments have usually given way to white or gold, "denoting the resurrection life given in Christ."[41] Expectation of black dress for mourners at funerals has been absent for decades.

Contemporary funeral services and practices

There was virtually no change to the BCP from 1662, other than in minor details such as the names of the sovereign and members of the royal family, until the twentieth-century. The first major attempt at revision was proposed in 1928, offering a greater variety of services and prayers, but still retaining sixteenth-century English. Although approved by the Church of England, through the clergy convocation and the Church Assembly (forerunners of the General Synod), the legislation authorizing it failed in the Parliament.[42]

40. The Anglican Church of Australia, *A Prayer Book for Australia*, 703.
41. See for example, Charles Sherlock, ed., *An Anglican Pastoral Handbook*, 88
42. See footnote 37

Later revisions did not attempt to supplant the BCP entirely as the 1928 book had tried to do. Revisions in both England and Australia were styled as "alternative" and/or "for use with" the BCP.[43]

Like the Church of England's *The Alternative Service Book 1980* and *Common Worship*, both the 1978 *An Australian Prayer Book* and the 1995 revision, *A Prayer Book for Australia,* provide additional liturgical resources, prayers and readings suitable for death and dying, funerals and mourning. It was not until *A Prayer Book for Australia,* however, that Australian Anglicans had a funeral service suitable for a child, or for an infant who dies near the time of birth, unless they used the English *Alternative Service Book. A Prayer Book for Australia* also provides a Thanksgiving Prayer for use when the funeral is also a service of Holy Communion, something the reformers had eliminated from their service. Modern funeral services provide for a sermon or homily, an opportunity to proclaim the Christian faith's belief in the resurrection. This is a significant change from the sixteenth-century Reformation rites, which trusted the stark words of Scripture to remind mourners of their own mortality and coming judgement.

In 2023, funeral services taken in churches or by clergy elsewhere are increasingly giving way to secular "celebrations of life" in a variety of places. Christian funerals today are usually for committed churchgoers, although some families who have only a slight connection with the church still seek a Christian service for their deceased relative. Funerals are likely to be the last remaining pastoral opportunity to care for the Anglican community beyond regular attenders for decades yet to come. How much longer that continues must be a matter of speculation.

While some elements of the BCP remain foundational, Anglican funeral services and accompanying rituals have changed over the centuries in response to changes in theological understandings of death, resurrection and salvation, and changes in social customs surrounding death and mourning. Nothing could contrast more than the somber funeral provided by the reformers in 1552, with its emphasis on death delivering the deceased to God's judgement, than today's common note of "celebration of a life." People today seem to have little willingness to give voice to lament for the sorrow of loss, or of the limitations of human mortality. Somber mourning dress has been replaced with instructions in some funeral notices to wear bright colors, or to wear a particular color cited as the deceased person's favorite. At the end of a child's funeral—thankfully now a rare occasion— helium filled balloons will often be released to soar into the sky as people "celebrate" the young life.

43. *Alternative Service Book 1980; An Australian Prayer Book*

Memorial services are now held in greater numbers, in which the cremated remains, the ashes, may or may not be present. This is an aspect of the disembodied nature of faith in the western tradition which originated with the reformers' rejection of rituals or bodily actions contributing to faith, which they had come to believe to be dependent upon a person's interior dispositions alone and not external actions. Some families choose a small private funeral in the presence of the deceased with a later memorial service for the wider family and community. During the restrictions on gathering during the COVID-19 lockdowns of 2020–2021 in Melbourne, Australia, only ten people could attend a funeral. This created difficulties as families had to decide who would be among chosen ten. The livestreaming of services, now commonplace, accelerated during this time to accommodate the changed circumstances.

Until the establishment of private cemeteries in the early nineteenth-century, most ordinary English people were buried in their local churchyard. It was one of the ways the dead were kept close in a spiritual community of the living and the departed. Throughout most of Christian history, funeral rites and burial sites were in close proximity, as can be seen from the structure of the BCP burial services. People usually died at home, bodies were prepared for burial at home, and then taken to the local churchyard.

Burial is less common now, especially in cities. Cemeteries are usually some distance from churches so that fewer attend the burial. However, watching the coffin lowered into the ground is both a profoundly human moment and a sobering one. Cremation has become the most chosen means of disposing of the body in Australia. The latest figures available are that of the169,372 deaths recorded in 2019, 65 per cent led to cremation.[44] Most funerals in churches or in funeral directors' chapels no longer involve mourners accompanying the body to the crematorium which is usually some distance away. The convenience of this appeals to clergy who need not make the journey to the crematorium only to conduct the committal service. It also appeals to mourners who can spend time with family and friends at the gathering which follows rather than leaving immediately to follow the hearse. It means that crematoria staff can schedule the work to suit their convenience. When the deceased has lived a long life and their death has been anticipated as inevitable, the "full service" (as it is called in the funeral directors' trade) at the church or funeral chapel is generally adequate. Pastoral wisdom lies in recognizing when it is not and providing more.

44. Australasian Cemeteries & Crematoria Association, "National Cremation Capacity Survey" demonstrates the capacity of crematoria in Australia if the number of deaths was to increase dramatically; a sensible survey during the early stages of the pandemic.

Funerals' ritual work

Funerals must accomplish many functions, and the funeral of a monarch even more, since the succession must be clearly seen. As a rite of passage, every funeral confers new status on both the dead and the living. Anthropologists have identified three stages in a rite of passage: separation, liminality, and re-integration.[45] The deceased person must be declared dead, and the living given the appropriate new status as widow, orphan or more generally, a mourner. Separation begins with the death of someone, which finalizes the first stage of the process of disengaging from them as previously known. That process may have begun days or even weeks before in the case of a terminal illness or come as a sudden break of relationship following an unexpected death. Liminality is a busy time of activity when the funeral is planned, and the many tasks associated with those arrangements are carried out. Re-integration involves assuming daily life in changed circumstances and being accepted back among a person's family, friends, and wider community with the new status.

Conclusion

The funeral of Queen Elizabeth II had much ritual and emotional work to carry out. It was a family funeral and the grief of the Queen's immediate family, while well controlled by them as expected, was evident. It was a national and Commonwealth funeral as the peoples of the United Kingdom were joined by those of the nations of the Commonwealth in observing national days of mourning.[46] It was an international event since the death of the longest ever reigning British monarch was of global significance given the numbers of heads of state and heads of governments Queen Elizabeth II had met or entertained over her seventy years in office.

Yet while the State Funeral of the late Queen was a showcase of ceremonial and traditional music, it was also a simple service of readings and prayers conducted with care for the unnumbered mourners beyond the Abbey that day. It was a tangible link between the reigns of two Queens sharing the name Elizabeth, given that a text known by the first Elizabeth became a small part of a suitable means to give thanks and acknowledge grief when the second Elizabeth died more than five hundred years later.

45. See Victor Turner, *Ritual Process*, Ithaca, NY: Cornell University Press, 1969.

46. In Australia, for instance, a public holiday for a National Day of Mourning was declared by the Commonwealth Parliament for 22 September 2022. A memorial service was held in the Australian Parliament building in Canberra.

Bibliography

An Australian Prayer Book for use together with the Book of Common Prayer, 1662. Sydney: Anglican Information Office, 1980.

Australasian Cemeteries & Crematoria Association. "National Cremation Capacity Survey," October 14, 2020. accaweb.com.au/images/easyblog_articles/45/CREMA TION-CAPACITY-SURVEY-2020_14Oct2020.pdf

Benedict, Philip. *Christ's Churches Purely Reformed: A Social History of Calvinism.* London: Yale University Press, 2002, cited in Krick-Pridgeon.

Church of England, *Common Worship: Daily Prayer*, London: Church House, 2000.

Cross, F. L. & Livingstone, E. A., eds, *The Oxford Dictionary of the Christian Church*, Oxford: Oxford University Press, 3rd edition, 1997.

Cummings, Brian, ed, *The Book of Common Prayer: The Texts of 1549, 1559 and 1662.* Oxford: Oxford University Press, 2011.

Duffy, Eamon, *Royal Books and Holy Bones. Essays in Medieval Christianity.* London: Bloomsbury Continuum, 2018.

Ford, Andrew. "The Queen's Music." *Inside Story*, September 21, 2022. https://inside story.org.au/the-queens-music/.

Full Fact. "Did Several Billion People Watch the Queen's Funeral?" 17:27:31+00:00. https://fullfact.org/news/Queen-funeral-viewing-figures/.

Gairdner, James and Brodie, R. H., "Henry VIII: December 1546, 26–31," in *Letters and Papers, Foreign and Domestic, Henry VIII, Volume 21 Part 2, September 1546-January 1547*, London: His Majesty's Stationery Office, 1910, 313–348, *British History Online* http://www.british-history.ac.uk/letters-papers-hen8/vol21 /no2/313–348.

Jasper, R. C. D. and Cuming, C. J., *Prayers of the Eucharist: Early and Reformed*, Collegeville, Minnesota: Liturgical Press, 1987.

Knight, Sam. "'London Bridge Is down': The Secret Plan for the Days after the Queen's Death." *The Guardian*, March 17, 2017, sec. UK news. https://www.theguardian. com/uk-news/2017/mar/16/what-happens-when-queen-elizabeth-dies-london- bridge

Krick-Pridgeon, Katherine Anne, "'Nothing for the godly to fear': Use of Sarum Influence on the 1549 Book of Common Prayer," Durham theses, 2018, Durham University, 10. http://etheses.dur.ac.uk/12868/

Lampard, John, *Go forth Christian soul: the biography of a prayer.* London: Epworth Press, 2005.

MacCulloch, Diarmaid, *The Reformation: A History*, New York: Penguin, 2003.

Mammana, Richard. "An American's Guide to the State Funeral of Her Majesty Queen Elizabeth II." *Medium* (blog), September 19, 2022. https://medium.com/@richard. mammana/an-americans-guide-to-the-state-funeral-of-her-majesty-queen- elizabeth-ii-2dc2b09f8874.

Quinn, Karl. "Did Four Billion People Really Watch the Queen's Funeral?" *Sydney Morning Herald*, September 20, 2022, Online edition. https://www.smh.com.au/ culture/tv-and-radio/did-four-billion-people-really-watch-the-queen-s-funeral- 20220920-p5bjf9.html.

Rieden, Juliet. "Royal Funerals Are Never the Same — but We'll See One Famous Scene Repeated." *ABC News*, September 18, 2022. https://www.abc.net.au/news/2022– 09-18/queen-elizabeth-ii-state-funeral-plans-different-from-royals/101449874.

Rowell, Geoffrey, *The Liturgy of Christian Burial*, London: Alcuin/SPCK, 1977.

———. "Go Forth, Christian Soul: The Biography of a Prayer." *Church Times*, November 2, 2006. https://www.churchtimes.co.uk/articles/2006/10-february/books-arts/book-reviews/go-forth-christian-soul-the-biography-of-a-prayer.

Sherlock, Charles, ed., *An Anglican Pastoral Handbook: Guidelines for the Administration of Baptism and Pastoral Services in the Diocese of Melbourne*, Canberra: Acorn Press, 1988.

Sherwood, Harriet. "Queen Did Not Want 'Long, Boring' Funeral, Says Former Archbishop of York." *The Guardian*, September 18, 2022, sec. UK news. https://www.theguardian.com/uk-news/2022/sep/18/queen-funeral-service-former-archbishop-of-york-john-sentamu.

———. "'We Will Meet Again': Christian Themes at Heart of Welby's Funeral Sermon." *The Guardian*, September 19, 2022, sec. UK news. https://www.theguardian.com/uk-news/2022/sep/19/justin-welby-sermon-queen-funeral.

The Alternative Service Book 1980: Services authorized for use in the Church of England in conjunction with the Book of Common Prayer, together with the Liturgical Psalter, London: Hodder & Stoughton, 1980.

The Anglican Church of Australia, *A Prayer Book for Australia: for use together with the Book of Common Prayer (1662) and An Australian Prayer Book (1978); liturgical Resources authorised by the General Synod*, Alexandria NSW: Broughton Books, 1995.

The Book of Common Prayer with the additions and deviations proposed in 1928, Oxford: Oxford University Press, n.d.

The Royal Household. "Succession." Accessed May 16, 2023. https://www.royal.uk/encyclopedia/succession.

Turner, Victor, *The Ritual Process: Structure and Anti-Structure*. Ithaca, NY: Cornell University Press, 1969.

Westminster Abbey. "The State Funeral of Her Majesty Queen Elizabeth II." Westminster Abbey, September 19, 2022. https://www.westminster-abbey.org/media/15467/order-of-service-the-state-funeral-of-her-majesty-queen-elizabeth-ii.pdf.

"Prayers Offered at a Time of Mourning—Prayer & Worship—Thisischurch.Com." Accessed May 16, 2023. http://thisischurch.com/prayer_worship/liturgy/queen motherprayers.htm.

14.

The Precarious Church
New and False Tracks on Kenosis and Healing

STEPHEN PICKARD[1]

Introduction: The Logic of a Theological Diagnostic

The ills of the church of God are many and varied. My concern in what follows is an attempt to offer a theological diagnostic of the failures, wounds, and precarious state of the church of Jesus Christ.[2] There are, of course, a variety of approaches to inquire into the problems and challenges that confront the church: sociological, psychological, biblical, missional, pastoral. Curiously enough, an intentional theological diagnostic is not that common. A theological diagnostic can be particularly helpful in that it ought to provide the basis for developing an appropriate theological therapeutic

1. At this point I acknowledge Dorothy Lee's remarkable teaching, scholarly, and writing career. She has been an exemplar of biblical scholarship and imagination, theological vision, and pastoral and missional energy. This has been a great gift to the church of God, both nationally and internationally. In her life and work, she has been a potent and joyful sign of the kenotic pattern of discipleship to which we are called by the grace of God.

2. My reflections arise out my life-long membership of the Anglican Church of Australia and having spent significant periods in ministry beyond Australia in the UK and participation for over two decades in various international Anglican Communion bodies across the globe as well as having taught theology for a number of years in a college of the Uniting Church in Australia.

for the ecclesia. The assumption is that such a therapeutic is directed to the repair and improvement in the practices and purpose of the Body of Christ.

As the title of the essay suggests, I want to probe the meaning and significance of the kenotic pattern of God for a theological diagnostic of the ills of the church, and as a clue to the repair of the church. Such an approach necessarily engages important themes in Christology, anthropology and ecclesiology. The reason being that issues concerning human and societal repair and renewal, in order to be properly theological, need to be undertaken against the backdrop of God's ways with the world in Jesus Christ and the Spirit.

But why a theological diagnostic and therapeutic? Is it really necessary? In the contemporary climate of the West, marked by significant institutional stress, secular skepticism, and declining adherence to Christianity, a certain pragmatism and impatience with matters of the intellect has shown little enthusiasm for, or apparent need of, the distinct vocation of theology in the church. Who needs theological diagnostics when we have so many other tools at our disposal to remind us of the ills, failures and dissolution of the ecclesial body in society? It is also the case that some kinds of theological activity—overly academic, elitist, and irrelevant—might only confirm such popular and well embedded views. If theology occupies a somewhat marginal place in the mind of the church and its leadership, then perhaps this is as it should be. After all, in a management and market driven world, what is the value of theology in the life of the church?

In defense of a theological diagnostic, I want to flag at the outset that while the question of the relevance and importance of theology may be a pressing issue for a limited few today, it is not a new problem. It was a matter once addressed by that famous ex-Anglican John Henry Newman. In his preface to the re-publication of his famous essays on the *Via Media* of the Anglican Church (1879)—first published as the *Prophetical Office of the Church* in 1837—Newman identified theology as one of the three fundamental powers of the church.[3] Theology (Newman's system of philosophy) offered a critical stance in relation to the other two powers, the sacramental and worship tradition (ritual) and ecclesiastical rule (political power). Liturgy and polity required this third power as an essential hermeneutic for the ongoing faithfulness of the church to the gospel. Without this third power, the church, he argued, was easily directed into an unhealthy sacramentalism and/or an unfettered abuse of ecclesiastical power. Church history bore testimony to the conflict that often occurred between these three indispensable elements of the life of the church. Newman considered that the theological vocation was essential to preserve and foster a critical and reforming spirit.

3. Newman, *Via Media of the Anglican Church*, 40–42.

In a time, such as the present, which is dominated by anxiety, rather furtive attempts at re-structuring and rationalizing of resources, financial strains, loss of respect for the institutional church, and a leadership that for the most part echoes such realities, a theological diagnostic cannot but appear otiose and somewhat quaint, certainly not at the cutting edge for the renewal of the church. For the church generally, the condition of theology might be best likened to the bruised outcast on the side of the Jericho road waiting for some good Samaritan to take pity and help.

This essay charts a different course and begins with a brief reflection on the theme of kenosis in Philippians 2:5–11. My concern is to follow the logic of the kenotic pattern of God's ways with the world; in particular the way in which the dynamic that inheres in kenosis reorders and raises all things to their proper place within the economy of God. This provides the basis for identifying the theological reasons why this dynamic is disturbed, resisted and disfigured and what is required to recover the kenotic pattern of God in the life of the church and its mission.

Form of God; Form of a Slave: the Kenotic Pattern of Christ

The British writer, Francis Spufford, describes his jettisoning of atheism in favor of theism in *Unapologetic: why, despite everything, Christianity can still make surprising emotional sense.*[4] The author articulates what he does believe, or think, in the following terms:

> I think that the reason that reality . . . is in some ultimate sense merciful, as well as being a set of physical processes all running along on their own without hope of appeal, all the way up from quantum mechanics to the relative velocity of galaxies by way of 'blundering, low and horribly cruel' biology (Darwin), is that the universe is sustained by a continual and infinitely patient act of love.[5]

Importantly, the clue to Spufford's affirmation of the continual and infinitely patient act of love can be located in the witness of Holy Scripture to the self-giving of God in Christ. It is signaled in the well-known passage from the Apostle Paul's letter to the church at Philippi:

> *Let the same mind be in you that was in Christ Jesus,*
> *who, though he was in the form of God,*
>   *did not regard equality with God*

4. Spufford, *Unapologetic*

5. Spufford, *Unapologetic*, 19, 20.

> *as something to be exploited,*
> *but emptied himself,*
>   *taking the form of a slave,*
>   *being born in human likeness.*
> *And being found in human form,*
> *he humbled himself*
>   *and became obedient to the point of death—*
>   *even death on a cross.*
> *Therefore God also highly exalted him*
>   *and gave him the name*
>   *that is above every name,*
> *so that at the name of Jesus*
>   *every knee should bend,*
>   *in heaven and on earth and under the earth,*
> *and every tongue should confess*
>   *that Jesus Christ is Lord,*
>   *to the glory of God the Father* (Phil 2:5–11)

This passage is, perhaps, one of the most significant texts for New Testament scholarship in the past one hundred and fifty years. While there are a variety of approaches to interpreting this text (often referred to as the "Christ Hymn" of Philippians), the thrust seems to be that relinquishing, divesting, emptying and outpouring is fundamental to the divine life.[6] Importantly, the emphasis is upon emptying of the *self* (my italics). Theological discussion of kenosis in the nineteenth and twentieth centuries concerned the particular traits, powers, etc. that the eternal Son of God divested in assuming human nature. This somewhat tortuous and impossible inquiry has proved fruitless and misguided. The Philippian's text points in another direction. It is the whole self that is given over, poured out for the world. The eternal Son of God, the Second Person of the Trinity, the eternal Logos is humanized; the One who was in the form of God took on the form of a slave (*doulos*). Literally morphed from the eternal God to a human slave. The point being that this second form, in flesh, in time, and in space, does not entail jettisoning the eternal form of God. Both forms belong to the eternal God. Precisely how that is the case is, of course, one of the enduring, beguiling and difficult themes in Christian theology.

The most recent significant and comprehensive discussion of kenosis has been undertaken by the Princeton Reformed scholar Bruce McCormack.[7] McCormack's tour de force of kenoticism is the first in an anticipated trilogy on Christology and trinitarian theology. And the critical first step is

6. Fewster, "Philippians 'Christ Hymn,'" 201.

7. McCormack, *Humility of the Eternal Son of God*.

the doctrine of the incarnation through the lens of kenosis. McCormack's own route through the complexities and difficulties of kenotic theology are via a doctrine of the eternal Logos, for whom enfleshment entails the humanizing of divinity.[8] McCormack argues that the humanity of the Logos is not novel to the Divine life. Rather in the incarnation the Logos eternally "knows what he [sic] already knew but now knows it experientially."[9] McCormack wants to talk about kenosis and the humanizing of the Logos in terms of "'illuminating' (intensifying) the knowledge that is his as divine."[10] McCormack opines "Experience makes more vivid that which is known, giving it depth and 'color' (if you will)."[11] In this morphing of the form of God into the form of a slave the Triune God is not divided, or split though appropriately differentiated. The Logos in flesh, Jesus Christ remains a complex "composite subject."[12]

There are hints here of the incarnation as a form of kenotic enrichment wherein self-emptying is neither diminution nor divestment but expansion and enhancement of what already is.[13] Certainly, some such notion of enrichment is entailed in McCormack's suggestion that "the fact that the Logos can experience humanly the experiential process of deliberation before making a decision gives to divine willing and experiential depth that would otherwise be lacking."[14] A kind of heightened "receptivity" seems to be involved in the joining of the Logos to humanity.[15] In terms of the history of the discussion of the subject McCormack's Reformed Kenoticism is of a kind wherein "power used in 'weakness'" "is a wholly meaningful explanation of 'self-emptying,'" and does not require "divestment" or "depotentiation."[16]

How then does this matter unfold in terms of the life the church and humanity generally? The theology of kenosis has generated increasing theological interest in the area of ecclesiology.[17] Percy discusses this in terms of

8. McCormack, *Humility of the Eternal Son of God*, 263.

9. McCormack, *Humility of the Eternal Son of God*, 260.

10. McCormack, *Humility of the Eternal Son of God*, 260.

11. McCormack, *Humility of the Eternal Son of God*, 260.

12. McCormack, *Humility of the Eternal Son of God*, 264.

13. This quite unique and innovative interpretation of kenosis has been the subject of a major study by Australian theologian, Jacqueline Service. *Divine Self-Enrichment and Human Well-Being*.

14. McCormack, *Humility of the Eternal Son of God*, 260.

15. McCormack, *Humility of the Eternal Son of God*, 260–261.

16. McCormack, *Humility of the Eternal Son of God*, 264.

17. Percy, *Humble Church* lists the following: Connor, *Kenotic Trajectory of the Church*; Brown, *Divine Humanity* McDowell, J. S. Kirkland and A. Moyise eds, *Kenotic Ecclesiology*.

the "self-conscious kenosis of Christ" where self-emptying "is not resigned stoicism" but a "surrender to God."[18] For Percy, who is focused on church leadership in particular, the ecclesial form of the kenotic pattern of Christ resolves itself into leaders whose lives and practices are marked by humility wherein they and the people of God are "bound to an ecology of obedience rather than one of self-preserving resistance."[19] At this point, Christology and ecclesiology are inextricably linked, "kenotic Christology leads us to kenotic ecclesiology: we become the body of Christ when we participate more fully in the reality of Jesus' incarnation."[20]

As suggested above, kenosis is not emptying in the sense of nothing left but rather the very opposite i.e., the way of enrichment, of concentrated abundance and enhanced receptivity through the humanity. Kenotic enrichment is the way of God with the world and, therefore, with human life. This way of God from eternity is a work of the Spirit of God. And it comes to fulfillment on this side of Easter at Pentecost with the outpouring of the Spirit in the concrete, historical realities of time and space.

What we have, then, is the divine life of the infinite Being embracing an expanding universe, unimaginable in extensity. This is the same God of the little things; intimately present to all things; the God of the cracks in our life; like the first light of dawn breaking through the darkness at the edges of the blinds. What kind of God is this? As suggested by Spufford, the gospel is good news precisely because the infinitely patient act of love manifest in the being of the universe is, at the same time, through the self-emptying God, nearer than breath[21] under the form of a slave and the disfigurement of the crucified One made present across time and space through the eternal Spirit.

In so far as the ecclesia of God is called to be an imitator of Christ so too it is called to live and move under the double sign of the form of God and the form of a slave. It prompts some questions. How does this happen? How does the ecclesia of God participate in the kenosis of God? What work does the self-emptying God do in the historical contingencies of time and space? And how does it happen? What activates the ecclesial self-emptying? How is it resisted? What thwarts and/or distorts it?

18. Percy, *Humble Church*, 135.

19. Percy, *Humble Church*, 138.

20. Percy, *Humble Church*, 138.

21. The nearness of God is a fundamental insight of medieval theology typified in Aquinas: '*Deus est in omnibus rebus, et intime* [God is in all things, and intimately]'. See *Summa Theologica*, Part 1, Question 8, first article.

Abduction: Being Drawn into the Purposes of God

Perhaps the critical question arising from the foregoing concerns the work of the kenotic God in the life of the world, and in particular the Body of Christ. The redeeming work of the Lord occurs as people and indeed the whole of creation is drawn into the purposes of God. The word for this is "abduction." Not in the popular sense of being abducted or taken away for nefarious purposes. Theologically it arises from the attraction of all things towards God and can be stated thus:

> "Everything is toward God, attracted to God. All creatures are attracted to God. . . The activity of being attracted is something within every creature, not outside it, it belongs to the creature's very being as created. Creatures have a seed of perfection in them antecedently: a capacity for benevolence, for being attracted and thus for being brought into relation with their creator. Not to be attracted is, against the direction of creation, to be enclosed in one's self-reference. To be attracted is to be drawn beyond oneself to God. It is also to be drawn to others throughout the order of creation. This attraction to others characterizes the inherent sociality of all creation: the irresistible attraction of each creature to others."[22]

Hardy refers to this underlying and ever-present attraction as a given of creation as "sociopoiesis," "the generation and shaping of relations."[23] As such, sociopoiesis belongs to the Triune life of God. This theological reality is often ignored, and humanity is constantly burdened with the task of generating its own sociality "independently of the powers of attraction."[24] This quality of sociopoiesis means it is "abductive," signaling the drawing power of the divine. Hardy refers to Samuel Taylor Coleridge's invocation of the term abduction "to refer to the capacity of our reasoning to be drawn by light, enabling us to 'see' more than perception allows."[25] "Abduction draws on the inner light of reason, *lumina rationale*, generating what Hooker called 'divinely infused rationality.'"[26] Hardy notes that for Coleridge "every knowing and all love involve abduction . . . drawing the whole person ; and

---

22. Hardy, *Wording a Radiance*, 48–49.

23. Hardy, *Wording a Radiance*, 49.

24. Hardy, *Wording a Radiance*, 49.

25. Hardy, *Wording a Radiance*, 49.

26. Hardy, *Wording a Radiance*, 49.

the whole person includes all modes of personal activity: cognition, politics, relations, ethics, economics, and love."[27]

The concept of abduction identified here echoes the Johannine theme of the exaltation of Christ: "And I, when I am lifted up from the earth, will draw all people to myself" (John 12:32). The sense of the Greek (*elkuso*) is variously to draw, to bring near, even to drag! There is here a unity of purpose between the Son and the Father.[28] The abductive power of God in Christ, present antecedently in a creation beloved of God, is now concentrated within a divine kenotic pattern unfolded in successive modes of Christ's self-emptying, abasement, death and exaltation, and Lordship under the agency of God. This dynamic is God's way of non-coercive abduction. The divine kenotic patterning within creation is the inner logic of the drawing power of people towards God.

This kenotic patterning and dynamic is foundational for the establishment and operation of the ecclesial body in all its life: worship, eucharist, scripture, service and mission. The liturgical life of the people of God optimize the capacity for abduction in which God is part of the very process. So too pilgrimage is "an effort to renew one's primordial identity as a creature attracted to God."[29] In short abduction identifies our capacity to turn away from self-engagement, self-absorption, the inertia of self-attraction, being twisted into self. And this occurs when we allow "self-displacement" and enter into the kenotic patterning of God.

Granulation: Healing from Below the Wound

The process of being drawn into the purposes of God; of growing into the image of Christ, is the great project of the Christian life. Call it conversion; sanctification, transformation, whatever you will. The really pressing questions might be put thus: What activates the image of God in our lives? What activates the *imago Dei* in the church of God? I admit it is somewhat unusual to put the matter quite like that, i.e., in terms of activation of the *imago Dei*. Too often, we have become locked into steady state theories wherein for example *imago Dei* is simply a given. The emphasis is on the originative

---

27. Hardy, *Wording a Radiance*, 50.

28. See Barrett, *Gospel According to St John*, 257, 295, esp. 247.

29. Hardy, *Wording a Radiance*, 53–54. Hardy comments: "To enter into pilgrimage is, in some way, to confess one's having strayed from this identity and one's openness to being shown a way back. And what is the source and measure of a communities (and individual's) turning to the path of pilgrimage and healing: Scripture." (54)

character of the gift rather than the dynamics of that gift i.e., what actually reinvigorates the *imago Dei*.

However, if the image of God we bear is also an eschatological reality, or as Pannenberg refers, our destiny,[30] then the critical question becomes, what energizes that process to bring it to full term? The answer cannot be left to generalities but requires a far more concentrated account of the activation of the *imago Dei*. For example, Oliver Davies, argues that it is the exercise of compassion that activates God's image in us.[31] The reason is that compassion requires "undergoing the dispossession of self-entailed by compassion" which is "to align our own 'being' with God's 'being', and thus, performatively, [to] participate in the ecstatic ground of the Holy Trinity itself."[32] From a somewhat less rarefied point of view, and in line with the focus of this essay, what occurs in the process of self-dispossession is a participation and alignment of the self with the kenotic pattern of Christ. This abductive process draws people into the orbit of God's loving work.

This process applies not just to individuals but has an inescapable ecclesial dimension that can be probed in terms of the following questions: how is the ecclesia of God regenerated and thereby enabled to move from self-attraction towards the source of its life and healing? In short, how does the kenotic patterning of God in Christ become operative in the Body of Christ? The text I have in mind as a companion to the Philippians text above is the well-known Johannine passage: "Very truly, I tell you, unless a grain of wheat falls into the earth and dies, it remains just a single grain; but if it dies, it bears much fruit" (John 12:24). Literally "rot in the earth." Clearly, in the text, it is Christ who is the grain which dies, and bears fruit. However, to the extent that we are exhorted to be imitators of Christ, this same pattern of self-dispossession as life giving for self and others is to be a mark of Christ's body the church (1 Cor 12:27).

I'm interested in how this process of falling to the ground, breaking open and being fruitful applies to the ecclesial body; not simply a person's body. To assist discussion, I find the concept of granulation, a medical term, extremely helpful. Granulation "refers to the body's capacity to generate new connective tissue from deep within the flesh, just underneath the diseased tissue that lies above it."[33] Hardy comments that granulation "is a hopeful sign because it shows how the rebuilding of tissue is possible from within

30. Pannenberg, *Anthropology in Theological Perspective*, 54.

31. Davies, *Theology of Compassion*, 252.

32. Davies, *Theology of Compassion*, 52.

33. Hardy, *Wording a Radiance*, 64.

the deepest parts of the human body."[34] In other words, the healing of the body begins just below the wound. In dental work, for example, the body's antibodies begin to deal with infections underneath the wound.

Why is this interesting? Because our concern is with the ecclesial body; the body of Christ. In this context, granulation points to the "capacity of societies and persons to be regenerated from deep within themselves. Communities and persons do lose their way and suffer disease—but their cure emerges from deep within them: from 'underneath' the disease."[35] We might say that the ultimate terrain of human redemption lies deep within us. It means that out of the "very thicket of trouble," despair and wounded-ness "there is an incredible growth of unexpected hope and promise."[36]

Hardy refers to this process of granulation as a kind of temporal abduc-tion; which is remarkably expansive and generative of ever deeper relations with one another and the divine. For this reason, such a process of healing is fundamentally an ecclesial reality and not confined to individuals. It has echoes of what I have in other contexts discussed in terms of slow church.[37] The activation of the ecclesial *imago Dei* comes slowly and often impercep-tibly. "It comes at first as a very slow granulation of new relations, processes and institutions of sociopoiesis: starting directly underneath those that are most troubled and dis-eased. The movement is not individual but emerges as a renewed social ecology: since the rebuilding moves across the whole rather than from out of individual parts, it cannot be measured by instru-ments formed out of separate parts . . . Temporal abduction is measured only by the whole, which means by the ultimate measures that god brings down to earth."[38]

Hardy refers to the story of the woman who reaches out to touch the cloak of Jesus (Luke 8:40–48): "this is a powerful example of how Jesus' heal-ing does not come 'instantaneously as it may appear (as if it were a matter of mere externality), but slowly, as something Jesus has offered her enters into the depths of who she is, working at the core of her being. She becomes aware that something has shifted very deep within her: some deep ameliora-tion ingrained in her being . . . A powerful presence that goes down to the depths, surfaces slowly and attracts a kind of healing."[39]

34. Hardy, *Wording a Radiance*, 64.

35. Hardy, *Wording a Radiance*, 64.

36. Hardy, *Wording a Radiance*, 78.

37. Pickard, *Seeking the Church*, ch. 9.

38. Hardy, *Wording a Radiance*, 78.

39. Hardy, *Wording a Radiance*, 81.

Conclusion: Kenosis as a Theological Diagnostic of Failure and Repair

In this essay, I have briefly outlined the kenotic pattern of God's ways with the world. In doing so I have drawn attention to the ways in which this pattern operates to draw people and the whole of creation towards the nature proper to each. This exaltation (raising up) is an eschatological work of God in the world and to the extent that this abductive process is allowed to occur, possibilities arise for an expanded, rich, and fulsome life together. The theory of granulation is offered as a contemporary comment on the Johannine text regarding the falling of wheat to the ground, breaking open and bearing fruit. In applying this to the ecclesia of God the critical issue to note is that the healing of the body, and—in this case— the Body of Christ, is a slow granulation which begins precisely underneath those parts of the body that are infected, dis-eased, and troubled. In the economy of salvation, this same process can be observed wherein that which is diseased is the very place from whence the healing is begun.

The Patristic tradition is familiar territory for this. Thus, St Gregory of Nazianzus can state: "for that which He has not assumed He has not healed."[40] From another angle Athanasius argues that the very place where immortality was lost becomes the very place where immortality was recovered. All this is by means of the eternal Son of God assuming mortality and corruptibility and bringing healing and repair from within. Here is a kind of granulation within the economy of salvation.[41] In like manner, it is from the place of the wound that we engage in practices that activate healing, regeneration, and repair. It is the pattern of the divine condescension in the incarnation repeated in the ecclesial body to effect repair.

I began this essay by noting that the ills, failures, wounds, and precariousness of the church of God are many and varied. The theological diagnostic briefly outlined in this essay suggests that the ills and wounds the church suffers will usually arise due to a failure to follow and hence embody the patterning of God's ways with the world as captured in the hymn-like passage from the Apostle Paul's letter to the Philippians (2:5–11). The church's ills and wounds both arise and persist when the dynamic of kenosis and exaltation have been avoided, distorted, or truncated. The reasons for this are various. However, importantly at this point, the diagnostics are critical. We need to go beyond the symptoms, which we often mistake for the cause, and instead focus on the cause of the wound. We need to do this otherwise we will spend an inordinate time and a great deal of wasted effort and resources

40. St Gregory's letter to Cledonius, *NPNF*,7:440.

41. Athanasius on the *Incarnation*, *NPNF*, 4:38–43.

responding to the symptoms. We will soon discover that the wounds remain not only unhealed; but become chronic and systemic.

An interesting case in point is the healing of the demoniac in Mark's Gospel chapter five. The story poses a question about the source of the wound. To the extent that the wound is located in the demoniac and assumed to be self-generated we fail to recognize that the community from which he had been excluded played a critical part. Beyond the immediate symptom, the underlying origins of the problem are to be located in another place and people. Is it any wonder that the healed man was reluctant to return to his community and desired the company of Jesus? His exclusion from that community enabled it to excise suspected contagion, keep itself stabilized and mask its own proclivity for violence. Here is a small example of the value of a Girardian analysis as a hermeneutical tool to identify the whence and the why of social and personal suffering and trouble. It is also the case that, when it comes to diagnostics, there is often contestation and hence little consensus about the prognosis.

Disruption to the process of kenotic patterning is evident, from a theological point of view, in a number of different ways. For example, there are mistaken forms of self-emptying generative of significant personal and ecclesial self-harm. This can occur via excessive self-deprecation and subservience within a framework of patriarchy and top-down authority. There is also a natural human predilection to short circuit the kenotic pattern by preoccupation with overt and covert forms of ecclesial and personal exaltation, power, and authority. Church leaders, for want of courage and paralyzed by fear, will sacrifice others, preserve their own reputation, and in the end abandon mercy. This is manifestly not the way of the Son of God into the far country. More generally the church and its agencies simply mimic host cultures that evidence the very antithesis of self-dispossession being more concerned with the enchantments of mammon.[42]

Much more needs to be said regarding these domains of failure and how they manifest themselves in the life of the church and its mission. My chief concern in this essay has been to outline theological criteria for assessment of ecclesial failure and indirectly clarify a theological remedy. To participate in the sufferings of Christ is to bear one another's burdens (foibles, furies, and frailties) in order to bear witness to the gospel of the eternal Spirit of love. This involves nothing less than the recapitulation of the patterning of Christ by means of which the ecclesial body might be drawn deeper into the life of God and the world for which Christ died and was raised.

42. McCarraher, *Enchantments of Mammon*.

Bibliography

Aquinas, Thomas. *Summa Theologica*. Translated by Fathers of the English Dominican Province. New York: Benziger Brothers, 1911–1925.

Barrett, C. K. *The Gospel According to St John: An Introduction with Commentary and Notes on the Greek Text*, second edition, London: SPCK, 1978

Brown, David. *Divine Humanity: Kenosis and the Construction of a Christian Theology*, Waco Texas: Baylor, 2011

Connor, T. *The Kenotic Trajectory of the Church in Donald MacKinnon's Theology*, London: Bloomsbury, 2011

Davies, Oliver *A Theology of Compassion: Metaphysics of Difference and the Renewal of Tradition*, Grand Rapids, Michigan: Eerdmans, 2001

Fewster, Gregory P. "The Philippians 'Christ Hymn': Trends in Critical Scholarship," Currents in Biblical Research 13:2 (2015).

Hardy, Daniel W. w. Deborah Hardy Ford, Peter Ochs and David F. Ford, *Wording a Radiance: Parting Conversations on God and the Church*, London: SCM, 2010

McCarraher, Eugene. *The Enchantments of Mammon: how capitalism became the religion of modernity*, Cambridge, Massachusetts: Harvard University Press, 2019.

McCormack, Bruce. *The Humility of the Eternal Son of God: Reformed Kenoticism and the Repair of Chalcedon*, Cambridge, Cambridge University Press, 2021.

McDowell, J., S. Kirkland and A. Moyise eds, *Kenotic Ecclesiology: Selected Writings of Donald MacKinnon*, Augsburg Minnesota: Fortress Press, 2016.

Newman, John Henry. *The Via Media of the Anglican Church*, 2 volumes (London: Basil Montagu Pickering, 1877), vol 1, *Lectures on the Prophetical Office of the Church Viewed Relatively to Romanism and Popular Protestantism*, 3rd ed

Pannenberg, Wolfhart. *Anthropology in Theological Perspective*, Translated Matthew J. O'Connell, Edinburgh: T&T Clark, 1985

Percy, Martyn. *The Humble Church: renewing the body of Christ*, Norwich, Canterbury Press, 2021

Pickard, Stephen. *Seeking the Church: an introduction to ecclesiology*, London: SCM, 2012

Schaff, Philip and Wace, Henry (eds), *The Nicene and Post Nicene Fathers of the Christian Church*, Second Series, Vol. 7, Edinburgh: T & T Clark, 1989.

———.*Incarnation, Nicene and Post Nicene Fathers*, Second Series, Vol. 4, Edinburgh: T & T Clark, 1995.

Service, Jacqueline. *Divine Self-Enrichment and Human Well-Being: A Systematic Theological Inquiry, with Special Reference to Development and Humanitarian Aid*, unpublished PhD, Charles Sturt University, 2018

———. *Triune Well Being: The Kenotic-Enrichment of the Eternal Trinity*, Fortress Press, 2023.

Spufford, Francis. *Unapologetic: why, despite everything, Christianity can still make surprising emotional sense*, London: Faber and Faber, 2012.

15.

Keep Awake!
Living Eschatologically Here and Now

CHRISTIAAN MOSTERT

Introduction

The Bible, both its Testaments, has always been subject to a range of interpretations, but critical reflection on the process of interpretation, *i.e.* hermeneutics, is of much more recent origin.[1] This is not to suggest that there was no serious reflection on the study of sacred writings in the ancient world. Origen, for example, distinguished between different senses of Scripture—the literal, the moral and the spiritual—and wrote about the effect of these on readers. In Reformation times, Luther and Calvin were well aware of different ways of interpreting the Bible, though they also defended the idea of the clarity of Scripture. However, it was not until the eighteenth-century that the subject of hermeneutics became in any clear sense a discipline. In the nineteenth-century, Schleiermacher reflected on the basis of understanding texts, including what later came to be called the "hermeneutical circle," in which the whole of a text is understood from its parts, yet also in the reverse relation: the parts of a text are also understood from the whole.

Understanding works requires a movement in both directions. Wilhelm Dilthey (in the nineteenth-century) and Martin Heidegger (in the

---

1. For an excellent short article on the subject, see Thiselton, "Hermeneutics," 283–87.

twentieth-century) made significant further contributions to the discipline of hermeneutics in general. Then Bultmann (in the twentieth-century) articulated an "existential" hermeneutics of the New Testament, in which a key element was his program of "demythologization." Myths should not be understood to present "an objective picture of the world as it is, but to express man's understanding of himself in the world in which he lives. Myth should be interpreted not cosmologically but anthropologically, or better still, existentially."[2] One consequence of this approach is Bultmann's reduction of eschatology in anything like its traditional sense to a focus on "eschatological existence," which represents the "emancipation" of the eschatology of Jewish apocalyptic and Gnosticism from its accompanying mythology.[3] On this view, eschatology is no longer about the future of the world and of human beings, but only about our existence *now*. Bultmann undoubtedly contributed to the discussion of hermeneutics, especially in relation to the New Testament, but in the following decades the one-sidedness of his contribution has been seriously criticized. Biblical eschatology cannot fairly be subjected to such radical reductionism.

There is, of course, much to be said about "eschatological existence" or existence in faith; also about the church as being as much an eschatological community as a socio-political institution. There is an important sense in which living *from* faith and *in* faith is *eschatological* existence, but this cannot be abstracted from the great Easter affirmation that "Christ is risen!" and its response, "He is risen indeed!" The whole "economy (*oikonomia*) of salvation" is not about time's relation to eternity but about the relation between the present age, which has a finite future and will conclude with a righteous judgment, and a future age, which will be eternal. Luke's Paul (in the Acts of the Apostles) states that God "now commands all people everywhere to repent, because he will have the world judged in righteousness by a man whom he has appointed, and of this he has given assurance to all by raising him from the dead."[4] The present time is an "in-between" time in which the two ages "overlap,"[5] with the death and resurrection of Jesus at

2. Bultmann, "New Testament and Mythology," 10.

3. Bultmann, "New Testament and Mythology," 20. The cross, then, is "not just an event of the past which can be contemplated, but is the eschatological event in and beyond time." (36) Even more radically, the resurrection is reduced to being "really the same thing as faith in the saving efficacy of the cross." (41) It has no intrinsic objective reality.

4. Byrne, *Paul and the Economy of Salvation*, 1. He cites in particular Acts 17:29–32 and, in Paul's own writings, 1 Thessalonians 1:10 and 5:9–10 and Romans 1:18–2:16. Byrne adds that the motif of the last judgment 'is never far from [Paul's] consciousness in all the letters and should be taken as a controlling element in interpretation.'

5. Byrne, *Paul and the Economy of Salvation*, 3.

the point at which the overlap began. One way or another, the present age will come to an end, but Paul announces "good news": that there is a divine project afoot to set humankind free from its self-centeredness, destructiveness, and idolatry. In addition, the Spirit has been given to believers as the power of the new creation, already operative in their lives to bring them through the judgment that is still to come.

Eschatology in the New Testament

The term "eschatology" denotes the last or final things (the *eschata*) to happen in the cosmos, or the final event (the *eschaton*) to take place in the history of the world, or even the one (the *eschatos*) who will come "to judge the living and the dead" at the end of the age. Its context is religious, mainly Judeo-Christian, though comparable ideas are found in many religions.[6] On the presupposition that history had a beginning, it postulates a corresponding end, not only in a chronological sense but in the sense of a *telos*, a goal reached or a purpose achieved. An integral part of it is the idea of a judgment, with a good outcome for some and a less good or fearful outcome for others. Central for Christians (and monotheists generally) is the reign ("kingdom") of God in and over all things; Christians constantly pray for its coming. Pannenberg describes eschatological ideas as a "rationally lucid projection of the conditions for a final realization of human destiny in the unity of individual existence and social interrelatedness."[7] The teaching and activities of Jesus were clearly eschatological—at various times strongly but not widely disputed—as was the climate of faith and life in the early Christian community.

It would be a formidable challenge to dispute the view that a robust Christian theology must be eschatological in character. The logic of Christian theology, with its paradigm of the death and resurrection of Jesus Christ, implies the breaking of something radically "new" into the "old" order of things, creating a decisive discontinuity within the course of historical events. This, however, is not an undifferentiated claim: the Apostle Paul spoke about a "new creation" already in this present life. (2 Cor 5:17), a proleptic experience or "first instalment" of the full experience of the new reality that is still to come (2 Cor 1:22). The "new" is not an extension of the natural order of things but involves a "radical break with all that has gone

---

6. The detailed content of eschatological hopes and expectations in the period before and after the life of Jesus varied considerably from group to group within Judaism at the time.

7. Pannenberg, "Can Christianity Do without an Eschatology?" 33.

before."[8] In this 'radical disjunction' lies its "salutary power." It is a negation and a judgment as well as a fulfilment.[9]

Eschatological themes are pervasive throughout the New Testament, with very few of its twenty seven "books" the exception. In an extensive Dutch collection of articles on eschatology, including *inter alia* a biblical section, the point is made strongly that:

> the eschatological expectation in the witness of the evangelists and apostles is by no means an appendix but the central theme of New Testament proclamation. The preaching of Jesus and the apostles has an eschatological character, governed by the question of the fulfilment of God's salvific purpose for the world.'[10]

That is, in my view, an entirely justified conclusion to draw. However, on the whole, this was not the view of the Liberal Protestant theology of the nineteenth-century. In any case, this was the least of the reasons for still taking Jesus seriously after almost two millennia.[11] But this view changed drastically by the end of the nineteenth-century. In 1892, Johannes Weiss published his *Jesus' Proclamation of the Kingdom of God*, and changed the course of New Testament scholarship.[12] For him, Jesus is to be understood as a thoroughly eschatological figure, a view reinforced by Albert Schweizer in his survey of the "lives" of Jesus written in the nineteenth-century, which he considered to be anachronistic, failing to see Jesus in his own time. He was emphatic that "Jesus of Nazareth will not suffer Himself to be modernized."[13] Personally, he found this newly discovered Jesus unappealing: to our time he would be "a stranger and an enigma" but he could not be "wrenched loose from the soil of eschatology." For well over a hundred years Jesus has been widely understood as an eschatological prophet, who announced the imminent coming of God's reign.

The majority of scholars, particularly in the English-speaking world, see Jesus in some sense as an eschatological prophet. N.T. Wright says that Jesus lived in a climate of "intense eschatological expectation," probably expecting a "climactic moment in Israel's history."[14] Dale Alison sees Jesus

---

8. Ziegler, *Militant Grace*, 8.

9. Ziegler, *Militant Grace*, 9.

10. Van 't Spijker, *Eschatologie*, 85. My own translation.

11. See Harnack, *What is Christianity?* 54. For Harnack, the kingdom of God was "a still and mighty power in the hearts of men." 54.

12. Weiss, *Jesus' Proclamation of the Kingdom of God*.

13. Schweitzer, *Quest for the Historical Jesus*, 312, 399 & 401.

14. Wright, *Jesus and the Victory of God*, 96f. See also Borg & Wright, *Meaning of Jesus*, ch. 3, in which, in disagreement with Borg, he sees Jesus as a first-century Jewish

as a millenarian prophet, who took up ideas that were part of his heritage: the final judgment, the resurrection of the dead and the restoration of Israel.[15] These views are formed over against the ideas of the North American 'Jesus Seminar,' which understands Jesus not as an eschatological prophet but, in Robert Funk's words, as a teller of "parables and aphorisms" which are non-eschatological.[16] Another prominent member of this group, Marcus Borg, describes Jesus as "a charismatic who was a healer, sage, prophet, and revitalization-movement founder."[17] Jesus did *not* expect a dramatic, future intervention by God, resulting in a drastically new state of affairs for God's people.[18] The kingdom of God is a *present* reality rather than a *future* one. The views of the Jesus Seminar have not been very influential outside North America.

There are several reasons for finding the idea of a non-eschatological Jesus unconvincing. First, the Dead Sea Scrolls confirm that an apocalyptic worldview was part of the climate of Jesus' time and place; second, the preaching of John the Baptist was unmistakably eschatological; third, the gospel of the early Christians too was undeniably eschatological; fourth, prophets were much more likely to live dangerously and attract the attention of the authorities than wisdom teachers. Jesus' mission was to make known the coming reign of God. Mark begins his Gospel by saying that after John's arrest Jesus came to Galilee, proclaiming the good news of God: the time is fulfilled, and the kingdom of God has come near; repent and believe in the good news. (Mark 1:1–15).[19]

He was a prophet of the kingdom of God but gave this message an unexpected twist. The emphasis in his message was the reality of God's merciful forgiveness, especially for those excluded from participation in the religious life of the community. Jesus welcomed into the kingdom people who were regarded as disreputable: he dared to declare God's forgiveness to them. In fact, to be in relationship with Jesus *now* was to be assured of participation in eschatological salvation. But there was a sting in the tail

---

prophet, announcing the kingdom of God and believing that "the kingdom was breaking into Israel's history in and through his own presence and work" (37).

15. Allison, *Jesus of Nazareth*, ch. 2, esp. 170f. See also Allison, "Eschatology of Jesus," 267–302 and Allison, "A Plea for Thoroughgoing Eschatology."

16. Funk, *Honest to Jesus*, 145. Funk suggests that Jesus "may well have been a wisdom teacher—a sage" (70).

17. Borg, *Jesus: New Vision*, 15.

18. Borg, *Jesus in Contemporary Scholarship*, 73f.

19. Matthew follows Mark very closely (Matt. 4:17). Luke reports the return to Galilee and Jesus' teaching in the synagogues but does not mention the content of his teaching.

for those who were presumptuous about their place in the kingdom: others would enter it before them (Matt. 21:31). In short, Jesus' ministry had a strong eschatological flavor: the future reign of God was so near that it was tangible, in both judgment and salvation.

Reference has been made several times to apocalyptic ideas at the time of Jesus: second Temple Judaism. In non-theological usage, "apocalyptic" means something like "violent" or "cataclysmic." In theological usage, it comes from *apocalypsis,* which means "disclosure" or "revelation," e.g. the revelation of hidden things or divine mysteries. "Apocalyptic" can refer to a particular genre of literature or to a particular kind of eschatology. There is no uniformity in apocalyptic, except that its ideas and symbols of a supernatural world are typically arcane and bizarre. Human destiny is influenced by this other world and comes under a final judgment from that world. The last book of the Bible, the *Revelation* (or *Apocalypse*) *to John,* is the clearest example of this kind of literature in the New Testament (see especially Rev.1:1–2)

In an important study of Paul some decades ago, J. Christiaan Beker wrote that "the apocalyptic world view is the fundamental carrier of Paul's thought."[20] E.P. Sanders agreed: Jesus shared the apocalyptic world-view of his time.[21] J. Louis Martyn highlighted the dualism of the two ages of apocalyptic thought, particularly in his work on Paul's letter to the Galatians.[22] Brendan Byrne writes that the Qumran documents bear witness to "a sect or movement apocalyptic in character," in particular its sense of "living at the close of the present age preliminary to a massive divine intervention in which . . . they themselves would play a significant role."[23] What complicates Paul's theology is the sense of living in the "overlap of the ages," which was not a feature of Jewish apocalyptic eschatology at the time. The "fullness of the time" had come (Gal 4:4) and the last judgment may have started, but God had "suspended . . . the full working out of the judgment and created through the sending of the Son a moment and a way for human beings to experience the judgment not as condemnation and ruin but as justification leading to (eternal) life."[24]

20. Beker, *Paul the Apostle,* 181.

21. Sanders, *Jesus and Judaism,* 124, 375f.

22. Martyn, *Galatians,* 37–39.

23. Byrne, *Paul and the Economy of Salvation,* 27.

24. Byrne, *Paul and the Economy of Salvation,* 244.

Staying awake

In Paul's earliest known letter, 1 Thessalonians, Paul responds to anxiety about the arrival of "the day of the Lord" (1 Thess 5:6,10). He clearly "shares with the wider background of Jewish apocalypticism the expectation of a last judgment in which not only the world as a whole but also believers will be held accountable." It is an indication of the sharp eschatological awareness of this early generation of Christian believers. Paul repeatedly addresses his readers "as people living within the horizon of the judgment" and calls them to "righteous behavior in view of the accountability to come."[25] The inference is that, although everything depends on the grace of God, enacted in Jesus Christ, believers must live in a way that is worthy of the gift.

In chapter 4 of this letter, Paul reminds his readers that they know how they should live and how to please God; he compliments them on how well they are doing but he urges them to do so more and more. They should live a holy life, becoming a "sanctified" people. He is quite specific about what this involves. He then gives them advice about the situation of those who have died: they need not worry on their account because, through Jesus, God will bring with him those who had already died. They will not be at a disadvantage compared to those who will be alive when the Lord comes. (At this point Paul clearly thinks that the *Parousia* will come in the foreseeable future. This brings him to the question of "the times and the seasons" in chapter 5.) The colorful image of the day of the Lord coming "like a thief in the night," without warning, prepares the way for Paul's exhortation to his readers to be vigilant.[26] He tells them that they are not in darkness, but in light: there is no need for them to be afraid. They are "children of light, children of the day, not of the night." They should not fall asleep as others do but should "keep awake and be sober." (5:6) They are "daytime" people and must therefore also live sober, self-controlled lives (5:7). Paul says several things here: about being alert to the coming of the day of the Lord and about living a restrained life and so pleasing God.

In the background of this passage in 1 Thessalonians is the story of Jesus urging his disciples to keep watch with him in Gethsemane and their inability to stay awake (Mark 14:32–38, Matt. 26:36–46, Luke 22:39–46). In different contexts, the Synoptic Gospels, written well after Paul's Thessalonian letter, echo the theme of "keeping awake" for the coming of the Son

25. Byrne, *Paul and the Economy of Salvation*, 69.

26. This image is also found in Mark 13:37, again in relation to not knowing the day or the hour when "heaven and earth will pass away" (13:32). They are to keep alert, keep awake, for this could take place at any time.

of Man, the day and hour of which cannot be known (Mark 13:35,37; Matt. 24:36–44 and Luke 12:35–40).

One further passage warrants some reflection: chapter 16 of the Book of Revelation, in which seven angels are told to pour out on earth the seven bowls of the wrath of God. When the sixth angel declares the assigned bowl of wrath, the great river dries up, allowing the kings from the east to come for battle on "the great day of God the Almighty," an allusion to the destruction of the Roman Empire, the perpetrator of great evil. These seven bowls of wrath are code for the woes that are the prelude to the eschatological future. Then a voice breaks in: "See, I am coming like a thief! Blessed is the one who stays awake and is clothed, not going about naked and exposed to shame." (16:15) This is the voice of Christ, speaking to the Christian community. There are echoes here of the words of Paul to the Thessalonians: that the risen Christ challenges the Christian community to re-orient its life, even as the coming eschatological reality is in view. The point is spiritual and practical, not to give speculative information about the future.[27]

The question to be considered is how the relation between the present and the eschatological future might be appropriately described in the cultural and political context of the time. The lenses through which we now read the New Testament are sharply different from those of the early Christian centuries. We are nourished and challenged by the same texts, but what are we likely to filter out as we read these texts? Eschatological texts were likely to be filtered out or marginalized in the culture of the Enlightenment and the "liberal" theologies of the nineteenth-century. The expectation of the *parousia* of the crucified, risen and ascended Christ has continued to characterize "adventist" groups but have a much lower profile in many contemporary Christian circles. It is very hard today to imagine an early adventist community like the eighteenth-century Ephrata Cloister west of Philadelphia and north-east of Lancaster.[28]

At one time, almost 80 celibate Brothers and Sisters formed the nucleus of this Community; they were surrounded by "Householders," families living nearby. They worked hard and spent hours in prayer. They sang hymns, many of them composed by themselves, till the early morning. Informed by the biblical teaching that the Lord would return "like a thief in the night," they thought that he would not come after a certain time; only then would

---

27. Boring, *Revelation*, 178.

28. During a half-year of study leave in 2005, I visited the site of this community, many of whose buildings survive, and learnt something of its life and customs. It was founded by one Conrad Beissel in 1732. The last celibate member died in 1813 and the community closed as late as 1934. They had a great emphasis on the "second coming" which they believed was imminent.

they go to bed. These beds were extremely narrow and uncomfortable, so that they would not sleep too soundly and too long. Their life was extremely disciplined. Their piety and devotion, their discipline and hard life, and the persistence of their eschatological hope were admirable. It was undoubtedly an *eschatological* community. There are religious communities today following a rigorous life of work and prayer, but it is doubtful that their eschatological hope rivals that of the Ephrata Community. Impressive as their life, witness and eschatological expectation may have been, it is unlikely to be a model for church communities now. The sense of the church as an eschatological community is greatly diminished, perhaps almost non-existent, throughout the church. The question is whether it should be so.

The church as the eschatological community

One of the most striking and unforgettable statements made by Bultmann decades ago in his *Theology of the New Testament* is that "the earliest Church regarded itself as the Congregation of the end of days" and that this Congregation is "the vestibule . . . of God's Reign that [was] shortly to appear."[29] Without suggesting that the church and the "kingdom" of God can be equated, Bultmann saw a very important link between them. We tend to understand the church from its beginnings in the ministry—and certainly the resurrection—of Jesus. It is rare to find an understanding of the church from its future. It is *not* the kingdom (reign) of God, but to see it as the kingdom's vestibule, the place in a Roman house which gives entry to the main room, is a significant corrective. In recent decades, work on ecclesiology has moved much more in an eschatological direction. In regard to this, it has struck me increasingly that a small but important part of the eucharistic liturgy should prod us to think *eschatologically* rather than *protologically*: the "Memorial Acclamation."

The most common form of it is the triplet: "Christ has died, Christ is risen, Christ will come again." It came into the Roman Mass in 1969 from some of the Eastern rites. In the current Roman Missal, there are several variations, including "We proclaim your Death, O Lord, and profess your Resurrection, until you come again" and "When we eat this Bread and drink this Cup, we proclaim your Death, O Lord, until you come again." In the Catholic Church, the acclamation is the response to the priest's call: "the mystery of faith," *i.e.* the mystery of salvation through the death, resurrection, and ascension of Jesus Christ. In the Anglican Church of Australia, the basic version, "Christ has died, Christ is risen, Christ will come again,"

29. Bultmann, *Theology of the New Testament*, 37.

was part of the Second Order for Holy Communion in *An Australian Prayer Book* (1978). It was taken up in this version in all five of the Great Thanksgiving Prayers in the Second Order for Holy Communion in *A Prayer Book for Australia* and in a different form—"we eat this bread and drink this cup *to proclaim the death of the Lord. We do this until he returns. Come, Lord Jesus!*"—in the Third Order for Holy Communion.[30] It should at least be noted that the Memorial Acclamation is part of the eucharistic liturgy in some other churches as well.

At the heart of the Christian faith, there is a foundational and central conviction about the economy of salvation: the Incarnation of the *Logos* in Jesus Christ, his salvific death on the cross, and his resurrection from the dead "on the third day." It is indeed a *memorial* acclamation, recalling particular events in human history. The third of these acclamations, however, is not "memorial": it looks to the future, the *eschatological* future. Stephen Pickard once described these three acclamations as the "co-ordinates of the dynamic structure of the economy of salvation."[31] No Christian theology can afford to drift away from this indispensable anchorage. Borrowing from Otto Weber, Jürgen Moltmann remarks that Christianity "has its essence and goal not in itself and not in its own existence, but lives from something and exists for something which reaches far beyond itself."[32] The church is "the community of eschatological salvation" and "the risen Lord is always the Lord expected by the Church." This is incontrovertibly a theological truth but as an empirical statement about the church it seems barely credible. People expert in theology would presumably assent to it but its truth appears scarcely to have permeated the life of the church to any significant extent.

At the beginning of his *Theology of Hope*, which appeared almost sixty years ago, Moltmann makes what has become a programmatic statement: "The eschatological is not one element *of* Christianity, but it is the medium of Christian faith as such, the key in which everything in it is set, the glow that suffuses everything here in the dawn of an expected new day."[33] Believers have been assured that, though now they know only in part, they *will* know fully, even as they have been fully known. (1 Cor 13:12) They live *from* their baptism and *into* their baptism; they live *towards* the end of the age and they live *from* that end. There is always a sense in which they must "keep awake," open to the day when the promised future will have become the present.

30. Sherlock, *Australian Anglicans Worship*, 145.

31. He is an Anglican bishop and an academic, until recently the Director of the Australian Centre for Christianity and Culture. I am not aware that he has published such ideas; I heard this line in personal conversation.

32. Moltmann, *Theology of Hope*, 325.

33. Moltmann, *Theology of Hope*, 16.

Wolfhart Pannenberg, Moltmann's contemporary, equally committed to theology in eschatological perspective, though expressed in a very different way, sees every aspect of Christian doctrine in an eschatological light, not least Christology and the doctrine of salvation, but also the doctrine of the church, "the messianic community," the major topic of volume 3 of his *Systematic Theology*, chapter 13 of his *magnum opus*.[34] The previous chapter is a discussion of the Spirit, "an eschatological gift that aims at the eschatological consummation of salvation, that guarantees this, and that gives assurance of salvation in all the earthly fragility of Christian existence."[35] Salvation is an eschatological gift, but already available in anticipatory but real form in the life of the church through its preaching, its sacraments and its *koinonia*.

This is a statement about salvation as such, not about the subjectivity of the believer. Those who participate in the church's life and worship "receive a full share in the one mystery of salvation that unites Christ with his church as the circle within which the reconciliation he has made has taken effect, and the completed form of which will come with the future of God's kingdom."[36] For Pannenberg, eschatology is not only a central theological category but is also decisive in his ontology. A key concept is that of *anticipation*, which he uses invariably in an ontic rather than a noetic sense: it is about *being*, not about the mind.

Conclusion

To conclude this discussion, a brief contribution from an Eastern Orthodox view of the church may be of interest. In this view, the church is never just the empirical church; it is very much more. John Zizioulas, a Greek Orthodox bishop and theologian, who has spent many years working in Protestant and Catholic circles, writes, "The Church lives in history, but its true identity is to be found in the future . . . The church preserved a strong eschatological sense through its hymns, vestments and the iconography of the saints, all of which served to make it clear that the kingdom is imminently present to us in the liturgy."[37] The church and its worship are the presence

---

34. Pannenberg, *Systematic Theology*, 432. He goes on to assert that the church, even as a social unit, "is ordained to be a sign of God's will to save humanity, a sign of reconciliation with God and of the resultant renewal in intra-human relations, a sign of the future fellowship of humanity in the kingdom of God."

35. Pannenberg, *Systematic Theology*, xiii.

36. Pannenberg, *Systematic Theology*, 352.

37. Zizioulas, *Lectures in Christian Dogmatics*, 127.

of the (eschatological) future. It is "primarily a foretaste of the eschatological assembly of the Lord, made present in the world." Many of the mission-oriented churches of the West will not like hearing the following: ". . . social action or activism cannot define the Church. So though the Church serves the mission for which it has been sent to every corner of the world, mission does not constitute the basis of the identity of the Church."

Worship is indeed not instrumental to mission; it has its independent justification, primarily doxological, though including petitionary and intercessory elements. It will ordinarily motivate people to participate in the church's task of mission, which is a divine imperative. But the church is a great deal more than a society for mission. For Zizioulas, the divine liturgy gathers people to be "an instalment of the final assembly."[38] Putting our feet firmly on the ground again, he laments the lack of clarity about this eschatological view of the church already from ancient times: the future fulfillment was displaced by the idea of an original perfection of the church. But this distortion is not uniquely a problem for the Orthodox churches.

Perhaps the church, with the exception of adventist communities, has for most of its history found it very difficult, nigh impossible, to "keep awake," to *live* its eschatological identity. Except perhaps for times of persecution, internal strife or conquest, the church has settled into a comfortable sleep, as it were. The imagery of falling asleep or keeping awake is blunt, allowing only a sharp antithesis, whereas Christian existence in the world is unavoidably tensive. There are elements in the Judeo-Christian tradition that encourage settlement rather than yearning for the past, e.g. Jeremiah 29:7, or even for the future. The Apostle Paul might, of course, counter this by saying that, since our citizenship is in heaven (Phil 3:20), we are exiles in a quite different context, one in which the eschatological belonging has primacy. But the tension involved in being people of faith in this time and place is never far away. Nevertheless, the church has a great deal to lose by ignoring or rejecting its essential eschatological belonging and a great deal to gain by recovering or discovering it for the first time. Christian faith is inescapably eschatological.

Bibliography

Allison, Dale C. "The Eschatology of Jesus." In *The Encyclopaedia of Apocalypticism, Vol. 1: The Origins of Apocalypticism in Judaism and Christianity*, edited by Collins, John J., 267–3 02. New York: Continuum, 1998.

———. *Jesus of Nazareth: Millenarian Prophet*. Minneapolis: Fortress Press, 1998.

38. Zizioulas, *Lectures in Christian Dogmatics*, 129.

———. "A Plea for Thoroughgoing Eschatology." *Journal of Biblical Literature* 113:4 (1994) 651–68.

Beker, J. Christiaan. *Paul the Apostle: The Triumph of God in Life and Thought.* Philadelphia: Fortress Press, 1980.

Borg, Marcus. *Jesus in Contemporary Scholarship.* Valley Forge, PA: Trinity Press International, 1994.

Borg, Marcus J. *Jesus: A New Vision.* San Francisco: HarperSanFrancisco, 1991.

Boring, M. Eugene. *Revelation.* Louisville: John Knox Press, 1989.

Bultmann, Rudolf. "New Testament and Mythology." In *Kerygma and Myth: A Theological Debate*, edited by Bartsch, Hans Werner, 1–4 4. New York: Harper & Row, 1961.

———. *Theology of the New Testament.* Translated by Grobel, Kendrick. Vol. 1. London: SCM Press, 1965.

Byrne, Brendan. *Paul and the Economy of Salvation: Reading from the Perspective of the Last Judgment.* Grand Rapids: Baker Academic, 2021.

Funk, Robert W. *Honest to Jesus: Jesus for a New Millennium.* Australian and New Zealand ed. Sydney: Hodder & Stoughton, 1996.

Harnack, Adolf von. *What is Christianity?* (reprint of 1901 edition). CT: Eastford: Martino Fine Books. 2011.

Martyn, J. Louis. *Galatians, The Anchor Bible.* New York: Doubleday, 1997.

Moltmann, Jürgen. *Theology of Hope; on the Ground and the Implications of a Christian Eschatology.* Translated by Leitch, J.W. London: SCM Press, 1967.

Pannenberg, Wolfhart. "Can Christianity Do without an Eschatology?" In *The Christian Hope*, edited by Caird, G. B. London: SPCK, 1970.

———. *Systematic Theology.* Translated by Bromiley, G.W. Vol. 3. Grand Rapids: Eerdmans, 1998.

Sanders, E. P. *Jesus and Judaism.* Philadelphia: Fortress Press, 1985.

Schweitzer, Albert. *The Quest for the Historical Jesus: A Critical Study of Its Progress from Reimarus to Wrede.* Translated by Montgomery, W. New York: Macmillan, 1955.

Sherlock, Charles. *Australian Anglicans Worship: Performing Apba.* Melbourne: Broughton Publishing, 2020.

Thiselton, Anthony C. "Hermeneutics." In *Dictionary for Theological Interpretation of the Bible*, edited by Vanhoozer, Kevin J., 283–87. Grand Rapids, Michigan: Baker Academic, 2005.

Van 't Spijker, Willem. *Eschatologie.* Kampen, The Netherlands: Uitgevertij de Groot Goudriaan, 1999.

Weiss, Johannes. *Jesus' Proclamation of the Kingdom of God.* Edited by Keck, Leander. Philadelphia: Fortress Press, 1971.

Wright, Marcus J. Borg & N.T. *The Meaning of Jesus: Two Visions.* London: SPCK, 1999.

Wright, N.T. *Jesus and the Victory of God.* London: SPCK, 1996.

Ziegler, Philip G. *Militant Grace: The Apocalyptic Turn and the Future of Christian Theology.* Grand Rapids, MI: Baker Academic, 2018.

Zizioulas, John D. *Lectures in Christian Dogmatics.* Edited by Knight, Douglas H. London & New York: T & T Clark, 2008.

16.

"This teaching is difficult; who can accept it?"

Theology in Australian Tertiary Institutions

PETER CAMPBELL

Introduction

With the consecration in 1836 of William Broughton as the first Anglican Bishop of Australia, the appointment of clergy became a colonial responsibility, but local ordinations were few. The Society for the Propagation of the Gospel sent more than eighty English and Irish priests over the next decade—Australia was essentially a missionary opportunity—and Broughton's successor as Bishop of Sydney, Frederick Barker, found a further sixteen priests, only one of whom "proved a misfit," though in general he had to "take what he could get, and by and large this meant any English clergyman who had the will and the means to come."[1]

It was the same in Melbourne, where the first bishop, Charles Perry, had arrived in 1848 accompanied by three clergymen and three lay readers who had responded to his appeal for qualified men to join him. Neither Barker nor Perry was keen on the English tradition of men being ordained

---

1. Cable, "Bishop Barker and his Clergy," 17. See also Gladwin, *Anglican Clergy in Australia.*

soon after graduating, often with little or no specific theological training. At "home," high-church interests founded St Augustine's College in Canterbury in 1848, preparing five hundred men for missionary work in the colonies to a standard "equivalent to that of a university degree" before its closure in 1947. Of these, ninety-eight were sent to the Antipodes.[2]

What, then, was the response of the church to the lack of a local clergy? What forms has theological instruction taken, and who has provided it? Ian Breward, Robert McIver, Stuart Piggin and Charles Sherlock, among others, have undertaken valuable historical work, but recent changes mean it is time for this to be reassessed.[3] The place of Divinity as a university discipline in Australia is discussed, and the attitudes toward it examined. The detailed history of the many diocesan training colleges, though intimately connected to this story, is, however, beyond the scope of this chapter.

Theological Training and Australia's Early Universities

The higher education of young men likely to be ordained was a desire in the colonies from the beginning, well before tertiary institutions were in place. Broughton needed a benefactor for the "institution of a College, where youth might be instructed in the liberal arts," and he found one in early settler Thomas Moore, who died in 1840 leaving all his property to the church, but the endowment was too little to begin.[4] When the cornerstone of Moore College was finally laid in 1857, the intention was to "combine the advantages of that theological course which distinguishes the University of Dublin from the English Universities, together with that practical training which no university can supply."[5] Certainly not the new University of Sydney.

During parliamentary debates in 1849, William Wentworth proposed a secular university that would not teach theology, such that it "should be open to all, though influenced by none." His model was London University, created in 1826 as an alternative to Oxford and Cambridge, both of which still administered religious tests for admission. Wentworth was firm that "no religion at all should be taught," but he would allow affiliated

2. Carey, *God's Empire*.

3. See Breward, "Historical Perspectives"; *History of the Australian Churches*; McIver, "Theological Education in Australia"; Piggin, "History of Theological Education in Australia"; C. Sherlock, "Australian Theological Education."

4. See William Broughton, letter to Diocesan Committee, 1 October 1841, "Church of England," *Sydney Herald*, 25 November 1841, 2.

5. "Moore College, Liverpool," *Sydney Morning Herald*, 16 January 1857, 2; Loane, *Centenary History*.

"denominational collegiate institutions" that "might, if they thought fit, establish foundations for degrees of divinity, and share in the advantages of the university by attendance on its lectures."[6]

This position of "abstaining from blending secular and religious teaching" was upheld, and at the university's inauguration in 1852, Vice Provost Sir Charles Nicholson observed that, as the new institution was "limited to no sect and confined to no class, its sphere of action is calculated to embrace men of every creed and of all ranks." The "inculcation of religious truth" would be left to the "spiritual guardians of each denomination of religionists" at affiliated colleges.[7] There was then not enough public money for colleges, but there was no reason why the "secular part of the education of such persons should not be obtained at the University."[8] New South Wales legislated in 1854 to provide for the "partial endowment" of colleges by the government, requiring matching funds from the churches, leading the Anglicans to found St Paul's College, which opened in 1856.

Melbourne University's founding legislation, modelled on that of Sydney, also prohibited the teaching of Divinity, but allowed for the affiliation of colleges, so long as "no such statutes shall affect the religious observances" therein. Charles Perry, the first Bishop of Melbourne, urged the founding of a college from 1853, its objects being to give students a "sound religious education . . . strict moral discipline [and] instruction in those branches of learning and science which are omitted in the University course."[9] At the 1863 Church Assembly, William Stawell argued that: "At present, the university was but the half of a university, and must remain so until colleges were established . . . An institution might be established where a theological training would be afforded, and where any young man passing through the university could be received."[10] Public funding for colleges was rejected entirely in Victoria, but the ideal of university and theological training being combined remained. Eventually, in 1872, the Anglicans opened Trinity College, "of and within" the University of Melbourne, though the appointment of a theological faculty had to wait a further five years.

While the Bishop of Brisbane, William Webber, was overseas at the 1897 Lambeth Conference, it fell to the Reverend Arthur David as Administrator to push through plans for a theological college, the creation of a

6. "Legislative Assembly—Foundation of a University," *Sydney Morning Herald*, 7 September 1849, 2.

7. "Inauguration of Sydney University," *Sydney Morning Herald*, 12 October 1852, 2.

8. "Legislative Assembly—Foundation of a University," *Sydney Morning Herald*, 7 September 1849, 2.

9. "Church of England Grammar School and College," *Argus*, 21 July 1853, 5.

10. "Church of England Assembly—Eighth Day," *Argus*, 16 January 1863, 6.

university still being more than a decade away: that such colleges, David noted, "lack the large life and opportunities for wide culture offered by a university goes without saying, but that they have special merits of their own is equally certain."[11] Webber had observed that as Queensland was "be-hindhand: no university, and no provision for the higher education necessary to the training of men up to the level of scholarliness requisite for the work of a ministry in which the ministers must be intelligent teachers of the people."[12] Investigation of the founding of a university began seriously only in 1891. The head of the commission, Sir Charles Lilley, thought that "no chair of theology should be endowed out of the funds of the State, but if the people of the colony endowed a theological chair, it would undoubtedly be a great advantage to the university," and he "could see no objection to the conference of degrees in theology, if it were so desired."[13] At a later hearing, Bishop Webber said that he "saw no difficulty in establishing a theological school without a chair, irrespective of denomination," as was the case in Germany, and thus theology might be "taught from an outside view without importing any special view," though he acknowledged that a "theological teacher could be obtained to suit all Protestants, but not Roman Catholics at the same time."[14] The University of Queensland did not begin teaching until 1911, and would not teach Divinity. Denominational differences would be a continuing issue for the sector.

In Adelaide, Bishop Augustus Short commandeered four rooms at St Peter's Collegiate School from 1875 for theological students who would be granted a pension of £50 a year to help them in their university education until they reached 23, the minimum age for ordination to the Diaconate.[15] As in Melbourne, this pre-dated his theological college, St Barnabas', founded in 1880, but also the university; Adelaide opened for students only in 1876, again without legislative authority to grant degrees in Divinity.

The Anglicans in Tasmania attempted a different path. Christ's College had been opened there in 1846, despite the founding of a university being still some 45 years away. The experiment did prove premature and the college closed in 1856. In 1877, the second Bishop of Tasmania, Charles Bromby, observed that the "great defect of the temporary arrangement has been the want of systematic classical and theological education."[16] He re-

---

11. "Diocesan Synod," *Brisbane Courier*, 16 December 1897, 5.

12. "Return of Bishop Webber," *Brisbane Courier*, 1 December 1897, 6.

13. "University Commission," *Brisbane Courier*, 12 March 1891, 6.

14. "University Commission," *Telegraph*, 4 April 1891, 3.

15. "Diocesan Synod," *Evening Journal* [Adelaide], 28 April 1875, 3.

16. "Church of England Diocesan Synod," *Mercury*, 21 February 1877, 2.

opened Christ's in 1879 only for it to close again in 1892 upon the opening of the University of Tasmania. Its Act granted the council power to confer such degrees and certificates "as it shall think fit in all branches of knowledge, except Theology or Divinity." At that time, Bishop Henry Montgomery told his synod that the "establishment of a Tasmanian University makes it absolutely incumbent upon us to undertake the work for which Christ's College was really established, namely, to be a college under the direction of the Church of England in connection with an university and besides this, to create a theological section when the time was ripe for it."[17]

In the farthest-flung reaches of the Empire, the second Bishop of Perth, Henry Parry, told his 1877 Synod of plans to re-found a collegiate school as a "first step towards training a native ministry for the Diocese."[18] By 1888, the Perth Diocesan Fund was seeking donations toward projects including completion of the cathedral and erection of a "Church of England college for young men, with special provision for theological students."[19] Several short-lived attempts were made before the University of Western Australia was founded in 1911, and it was not until 1957 that the foundation stone for the John Wollaston Theological College was laid.[20]

The regional dioceses, too, founded their own training colleges, usually with little expectation that their candidates would be graduates, or resigned to the fact that any able students would have to be sent away for many years to study. But those who did attend university were still not to find their theological education within the ivory towers; other avenues for degrees had to be found.

Examining Bodies and Degrees

In 1886, Canon William Chalmers urged General Synod to investigate establishment of an "Australian Theological University, or some other approved method of holding divinity examinations and conferring divinity degrees in Australia" in order to "promote the systematic study of theology among the clergy."[21] The inquiry noted that the "universities of Australia being State institutions for the promotion of secular learning only, it seemed practically impossible that any theological faculty of a satisfactory character

17. "Anglican Synod," *Mercury*, 27 April 1892, 3.

18. "Church of England Synod," *Inquirer* [Perth], 1 August 1877, supplement, 1.

19. "Anglican Church Notes," *Western Mail* [Perth], 21 July 1888, 20.

20. "Theological School Wanted in Perth Diocese," *West Australian*, 29 September 1954, 15; "Synod Starts Fund for New College," *West Australian*, 1 October 1954, 10.

21. "Notes of the Month," *Church of England Messenger*, 8 December 1886, 2–3.

could ever be established in them." Thus, they should either establish their own examining body with power to confer degrees, or enter into agreements with "such universities in England or elsewhere as might be willing to hold examinations for divinity degrees."[22]

They recommended that General Synod establish an Australian College of Theology to "foster and direct the systematic study of divinity" by correspondence, and that it offer the ThA (Associate in Theology), ThL (Licentiate in Theology), ThSchol (Scholar in Theology) and ThSoc (Fellow of the College). The ThL would be open to "all clergymen holding licence . . . who have a certificate of having completed the course of an approved theological college, or are matriculated members of a recognised University." Following an exhaustive inquiry, the ACT was created in 1891, with the first examinations conducted in 1898.[23]

Two other examinations, from overseas authorities, were also endorsed. The first was at the University of Durham, which was requested to agree to examine candidates for the Bachelor of Divinity. Certainly by the late 1890s, this was already a well-established pathway in Melbourne.[24] In November 1897, Durham approved local examinations for the BD in all dioceses of Australia and Tasmania (requiring a completed BA or ThL for admission), and the DD (Doctor of Divinity), for which an MA and submission of a "published theological treatise approved by senate or a special examination" was needed.[25] The other was the University of Trinity College, Toronto. In Melbourne, Bishop Moorhouse had earlier been sent a proposal, which he agreed to in 1886:

> The University of Melbourne, no doubt, gives us a guarantee that such of the clergy of Victoria as are among its Graduates will be well-grounded in the various branches of secular learning, and our own Trinity College is more than sufficient to offer to its alumni such training in theological subjects as will enable them to pass the Bishop's examination for holy orders with credit to themselves and satisfaction to him. But even the most distinguished of our University men can never hope to attain any *Degree* in theology, simply because the power to confer such degrees exists in no college or university throughout Australia . . . If some scheme could be made practicable by which Divinity

22. "General Anglican Synod," *Sydney Morning Herald*, 26 September 1891, 7.

23. For a general discussion, see Treloar, "Three (or Four) Identities."

24. See, for example, examination notice, *Church of England Messenger*, 12 March 1888, 2.

25. "Theological Degrees for Australians—Arrangement with Durham University—Local Examinations to be Held," *Argus*, 12 January 1898, 6.

> Degrees could become a possibility to all the clergy of the diocese
> … it could hardly fail to offer the exact stimulus which is needed
> to secure the attainment of a fairly high standard of theologi-
> cal learning. Under present circumstances there is scarcely any
> inducement to the clergy to continue their theological studies
> after ordination save the love of knowledge for its own sake.[26]

Following several years of successful operation in Melbourne, in 1890, the advertisement of the Toronto examinations once again raised the question of local degrees. The Registrar for Australian candidates, Canon George Vance, DD, agreed it would be "better that our students should be able to gain theological distinctions without having to send for them to Toronto," but none of the local alternatives was found satisfactory.[27] The Master at the Wesleyan Queen's College, the Reverend Edward Sugden, confirmed the "absence in our otherwise well-equipped University of any recognised course of theological study, leading, as in the case of the other professions, to a degree" but saw no reason why a general "unsectarian" course could not be offered there. As this was beyond any hope, he asked:

> is it not possible for the theological halls in connection with the
> colleges to unite in prescribing a course of study which should
> follow upon the arts course in the University, and to have
> granted to them the power of conferring the degrees of Bach-
> elor and Doctor of Divinity on students passing the requisite
> examinations?[28]

The Methodists were "perfectly willing to co-operate in this thing with any or all of the other churches of the colony." With such lecturers as Vance and Robert Potter at Trinity and John Rentoul and Murdoch Macdonald at the Presbyterian training college at Ormond, next door, "we have no lack of teachers and examiners whom the churches and the public could entirely trust to set up and maintain a high and worthy standard." More letters ensued, but with little immediate effect.

In September 1909, the founding of a new training college was proposed in Melbourne, based on the "contention that Victoria offered no means for the evangelical student for the ministry to pursue his studies in his own school of thought."[29] It was hoped that Ridley College could be "brought into close relationship with Trinity College," such that the

---

26. "Theological Degrees," *Church of England Messenger*, 10 May 1886, 2, 4–5.

27. "Toronto Theological Degrees," letter, *Argus*, 6 May 1890, 6.

28. "Toronto Theological Degrees," letter, *Argus*, 8 May 1890, 5.

29. "New Theological College—Evangelical Scheme," *Argus*, 17 September 1909, 8; "Training Anglican Clergy—Proposed Evangelical College," *Age*, 17 September 1909, 5.

"relationship would promote the interests of the Church generally," and it would "contemplate a University course."[30] Co-location on Trinity College's grounds did not eventuate, and at Ridley's 1910 inauguration Bishop Langley of Bendigo acknowledged that Trinity had "done splendid work in training men for every profession" but that only a very few could afford it. Ridley's Secretary, Walter Buntine, observed that the new college would provide all the "advantages of college life, at less cost than was possible at the existing affiliated colleges of the University."[31] (Ridley did later affiliate itself as a residential college of the University of Melbourne from 1965 to 2005.) Once again, training was separated from the universities.

Theology in the University

The founding of Ridley was one aspect of the wider push from various churches for the award of degrees in Theology from some central, accredited institution. In 1905, the Council of the University of Melbourne had determined that the prohibition against theological teaching in the *University Act of 1903* was absolute,[32] but in December 1909, a deputation from the Victorian Council of Churches asked the Minister for Education to introduce legislation allowing examinations for degrees in Divinity at Melbourne.[33] The Victorian Director of Education, Frank Tate, sought the University Council's opinion, but the debate was postponed. Archbishop Clarke, a member of Council, moved that a committee be appointed to look into how other universities had established faculties of Theology, but this was lost, six votes to five.[34] Debate raged across the newspapers as to whether Theology was a worthy university subject. The Catholic Archbishop of Melbourne, Thomas Carr, was against it, hoping that the "unsectarian character of the University would be preserved, and that the jarring sounds of religious strife would never be heard within its walls."[35] The Council of Churches wished to give students "recognition within Australia of the attainments for which they alone in all branches of science are now compelled to go abroad, and by the establishment of the highest standard in the degrees to stimulate their

---

30. Walter Buntine, letter to the Secretary, Trinity Council, 28 August 1909, Trinity College Archives.

31. "Training of the Clergy—New College Opened," *Argus*, 2 March 1910, 15; "New Evangelical College—Opened by Bishop Langley," *Age*, 2 March 1910, 10.

32. Minutes, University of Melbourne Council, 6 November 1905, vol. 14, 124–25.

33. "Divinity at Melbourne University," *Advocate*, 11 December 1909, 27.

34. Minutes, University of Melbourne Council, 20 December 1909, vol. 15, 217–18.

35. "Chair of Divinity," letter, *Argus*, 13 December 1909, 7.

efforts." For now, Theological instruction would remain within the affiliated colleges, where it was currently "carried forward to a high pitch of efficiency," and would not be transferred to the University, at least in Melbourne.[36]

A few months earlier, the annual Methodist Conference had "strongly approved" of the proposal that the University "institute examinations in divinity and confer degrees therein."[37] Sugden was then one of nineteen signatories—others included the five Anglican bishops of Victoria, the Warden of Trinity College (Alexander Leeper) and David Adam, Professor of Theology at Ormond—to a petition to the University.[38] The University Council discussed amending the Act, but Sugden's motion was ultimately abandoned. It would be up to some other body to confer such degrees.[39]

Those expecting this outcome had not been idle, with a parallel process taking place in Parliament. Clarke, Sugden and Adam waited on the Premier, John Murray, in April, explaining that they had no desire to "establish any body that would enter into rivalry with the University," and Murray agreed that "legislation for the establishment of a body empowered to confer degrees in divinity" would be discussed by Cabinet.[40] The Minister for Education then brought forward a Bill for the creation of a Melbourne College of Divinity (MCD), providing for a council of representatives of the Church of England, Presbyterians, Methodists, the Baptist Union and the Congregational Union of Victoria.[41]

This time, Archbishop Carr was supportive of the move, though his church would not join the MCD as it already had access to its own pontifical degrees.[42] There were, however, twenty "leading clergymen" from the Church of England who objected, claiming in the Melbourne Diocesan Synod in September that the degrees would have no recognized standing. The chief objection appeared to be that, "if a State college of divinity were once established, it would make any university scheme impossible."[43] Although he distanced himself from the protest, Leeper was not a supporter

36. "Degrees in Divinity," letter, *Argus*, 14 December 1909, 9.

37. "Methodist Conference—Divinity Degrees at University," *Age*, 5 March 1910, 14.

38. "Divinity Degree—Appeal to University," *Age*, 12 March 1910, 12.

39. Minutes, University of Melbourne Council, 21 March 1910, vol. 14, 260–61; "Faculty of Divinity—University Council Disapproves," *Argus*, 22 March 1910, 5.

40. "Degrees in Divinity—Legislation Promised," *The Argus*, 21 April 1910, 9.

41. "Divinity Degrees—College for Melbourne," *Argus*, 27 August 1910, 18; *Debates*, Legislative Assembly, 5 October 1910, vol. 125, 1525–34; Beirne, "Melbourne College of Divinity"; P. Sherlock, "Foundation of the Melbourne College of Divinity."

42. Beirne, "Melbourne College of Divinity," 125; "Legislative Assembly—Divinity College," *Age*, 6 October 1910, 9.

43. Hart, "Divinity Degrees."

of the new college either, predicting that Anglican clergy would "continue to seek from London, Manchester, and other liberal-minded Universities in Britain or America, the degrees in theology which they are for the present refused by the short-sighted policy of their own Alma Mater."[44] Archdeacon Hindley pointed out that Australia was "the only part of the British Empire of English-speaking people in which a man could not study and gain a degree in divinity." While Archbishop Lowther Clarke thought there was "no harm in joining with the Presbyterians and others to obtain theological degrees," Synod did not support the moves.[45] Nonetheless, in November, the Bill did pass through parliament, with the Anglican Diocese of Melbourne as a founding signatory. Due to a shortage of funds, for its first few years Clarke provided the MCD with rooms for meeting and examinations in the cathedral buildings.[46]

Despite this development, further attempts were still made to introduce Theology degrees in the public universities. In Sydney, Moore College had from 1907 been using the University of Durham examinations leading to the LTh, which "gave the students a distinct University status," but it was felt that "something should be done to bring the college into closer touch with the Sydney University."[47] In 1910, the Principal, Nathaniel Jones, observed that:

> The intellectual conditions of to-day . . . demanded a learned as well as a pious ministry. He was sorry that the Sydney University did not offer the same facilities as Durham. It would be easy to bring the students for the ministry into closer touch with the students for the other learned professions, by giving men with theological diplomas the status of second year students, and by putting Hebrew and Hellenistic Greek among the alternative subjects in the arts course . . . It seemed that the only profession that needed no training was that of a minister . . . The clergy would more and more move among people who had university degrees, therefore, they should have them.[48]

44. "Proposed Divinity College," letter, *Argus*, 4 October 1910, 9.

45. "Anglican Synod—Divinity Degrees," *Argus*, 1 October 1910, 20; "Anglican Synod—College of Divinity," *Age*, 1 October 1910, 14.

46. "Melbourne College of Divinity," *Argus*, 14 May 1912, 5.

47. "Moore Theological College—Arrangement with Durham University," *Sydney Morning Herald*, 1 April 1908, 11.

48. "Moore College—An Historic Institution—Theology and Education," *Sydney Morning Herald*, 16 April 1910, 8.

Following a letter to the editor in 1912 asking why the "Moore College men go to Durham and, apparently, ignore their own university at home," David Davies, Jones's successor as Principal, happily expressed his dissatisfaction with the necessary arrangement:

> The whole system of training of the clergy in Australia is hampered by the lack of that co-ordination between teaching and examining bodies, such as would be assured by the endowment of a theological faculty at the Australian universities. But the Australian churchmen have not yet done this. They have not even endowed theological teaching at their own colleges, as the Presbyterians have done. The solution of the problem raised by your correspondent lies with the Australian laymen.[49]

The Council of the University of Tasmania amended its legislation to allow Divinity degrees in November 1927, resolving unanimously to "get rid of this restriction of its own usefulness." A recommendation that the "Universities of the Commonwealth should be invited to found Faculties in Theology" had been passed by General Synod in 1926, and the Tasmanian Synod had supported this, believing that the experience in Britain proved that "Theology could be established without the slightest risk of sectarian friction and without the slightest infringement of the principle of religious equality."[50] But when the Anglican Bishop of Tasmania, Robert Hay, moved in April 1928 to appoint a committee, he was vigorously opposed by Hobart's Catholic Archbishop, William Barry, on the grounds that the proposal was "purely Anglican in design": such a degree would merely "sanction denominational teaching" and no amendment was passed.[51]

When the question of establishing a Chair of Divinity at the University of Western Australia was raised in 1936, the Vice-Chancellor, Professor Whitfeld, replied:

> Action of the kind was not considered possible in the present state of the University's finance unless money were provided by gift or endowment. For some years there had been talk of the establishment of one or more courses in religion in the Faculty of Arts, and possibly associated with the department of philosophy. It had been suggested that this course or courses should

49. Davies, "Durham University Examinations."

50. "Faculty of Theology—Establishment in Tasmania—Request to University Senate," *Mercury*, 8 September 1927, 7.

51. "Degree of Theology—Bishop Hay's Appeal—Debate at University Council," *Mercury*, 18 April 1928, p. 9; "Proposed Degree of Theology," *Mercury*, 19 April 1928, 8.

deal chiefly with comparative religion. It might also touch upon the philosophy of religion.[52]

The Sub-Warden at the affiliated Anglican St George's College, the Reverend C.E. Storrs, had, however, examined courses in religion in Europe and America and had "already sent to the University syllabuses and other information about courses given in American universities," but no new degrees would eventuate in Perth.

Ecumenical Consortia

Though not within universities, cross-denominational cooperation was beginning elsewhere. The small theological colleges were agreeing to help each other and become "recognised teaching institutions" in consortia preparing students for the examining bodies. Despite not being from universities, the awards were now degrees rather than the old ThL; society was demanding increased recognition for learning in a broader range of professions, including those in the church.

General Synod's Commission on Theological Education reported in 1969, making sixteen recommendations, including the belief that theological colleges should be sited "within easy reach of other colleges, a University, and institutions such as teachers' training colleges." A careful investigation of courses and teaching methods was needed, but it was clear that degrees were the way forward.[53] Both the MCD and ACT began to plan for accreditation of undergraduate degrees in Theology. The possible merger of the ACT and MCD had been discussed for years. By 1967, Robin Sharwood, warden of Trinity College in Melbourne, felt that the "academic advantages" were obvious, for a "consequence of the long-standing rejection of theological studies by our universities has been that other institutions created to provide for them have lacked the prestige necessary to promote the best scholarly endeavour."[54] It was important to maintain the distinction between clergy training and academic study, but that opened:

> possibilities of most beneficial co-operative arrangements between colleges . . . There may be a number of places in which this kind of academic co-operation has already begun. Certainly it is now well-established in Melbourne. Ormond College (Presbyterian), and Queen's (Methodist) run what is virtually a single

52. "Chair of Divinity—No Move at the University," *West Australian*, 14 July 1936, 7.

53. *Theological Education*, 8–10.

54. Sharwood, "Why Not Establish a University School of Theology?"

theological school. Whitley College (Baptist) is joining with them, and my own College too (Trinity, Anglican) is anxious to do so.[55]

What Sharwood was prefiguring was the United Faculty of Theology (UFT), established in July 1969 as Australia's first ecumenical consortium, with joint teaching and centralized administration. The faculties of the Presbyterian Theological Hall at Ormond and the Methodists' Queen's College Theological Hall had been teaching under a formal agreement since 1967, and informally for perhaps ten years before that. Negotiations during 1968 to incorporate Ridley College "came to nothing," as it aligned instead with the Australian College of Theology, feeling that this "gave them more freedom to teach their distinctive Evangelical emphases."[56] The Congregational College of Victoria in Kew was added to the partnership in September 1968, and the Jesuit Theological College, soon to be moved from Sydney to Parkville, joined in September 1972.[57] Recommendation 3 from the 1969 General Synod Report read: "Given the current Melbourne developments in ecumenical co-operation, the Australian College of Theology and the Melbourne College of Divinity should consider a closer relationship," and this was followed up in a resolution moved at the 1969 General Synod.

The Brisbane College of Theology was a very similar ecumenical consortium that operated from 1983 to 2009, comprising the Anglican St Francis' Theological College, the Roman Catholic St Paul's and the Uniting Church's Trinity Theological College. The consortium broke up in 2009 partly due to the prohibitive cost of accreditation under Federal government reforms that had seen many self-accrediting tertiary institutions such as conservatoriums of music, art schools and drama academies absorbed by mainstream universities, often in disruptive and difficult mergers.[58] St Francis transferred its degree programs to Charles Sturt University.

Following the rejection of independent applications to offer degrees in theology by several Sydney-based colleges during the 1970s, and advice from the government that they consider a "rationalisation of resources . . . and the establishment of a degree-supervising authority administered by the institutions," the Sydney College of Divinity was established in 1983.[59] It ended up with a very broad membership including Assemblies of God,

---

55. Sharwood, "Theology and Tertiary Education."

56. Breward, "Holding Fast, Letting Go," 13–14.

57. Breward, "Holding Fast, Letting Go," 13–14.

58. Ormerod, "Theological Colleges on Shaky Ground."

59. Hill, "Foundation of the Sydney College of Divinity"; Nobbs, "From Nowhere to Know-How."

Brethren, Churches of Christ, Greek Orthodox, Methodist, Nazarene, Roman Catholic and Salvation Army colleges from across the country, and gained self-accrediting status in 2016.

Old and New Universities

Despite the earlier prohibition, Sydney was the first Australian university granted power to award degrees in Theology, the first students in a graduate Bachelor of Divinity degree being admitted in 1938 following a legislative change. A Doctor of Divinity degree was introduced at the same time.[60] The "Recognised Teachers for the purposes of the degrees in Divinity" were drawn frequently from the senior staff of the affiliated denominational residential colleges and associated theological halls until well after the war.[61]

A further attempt to introduce an ecumenical theology department to the University of Melbourne was made in 1958, but again without success. The University of Queensland introduced Religious Studies units taught in the Arts Faculty and in the early 1960s upgraded its Diploma of Divinity to a BD in what in time became the School of History, Philosophy, Religion and Classics. In 1965, the Martin Report, the outcome of a Federal government inquiry by its Committee on the Future of Tertiary Education in Australia, devoted a chapter to theological education, recommending that universities should "consider the provision of courses of a non-dogmatic character which are relevant to theological studies" such as comparative religion, classical languages and ancient history.[62]

Two significant consultations arose from this. In 1965, the MCD held a two-day conference to review its award programs. The almost 60 delegates included representatives from its own colleges, with the heads of various bible colleges and of the church-based university colleges invited as guests. They discussed the need for Biblical languages to be included in degrees, and the possibility of introducing a Bachelor of Theology, though there was significant opposition to it on the grounds that the BD would be devalued and seen as equivalent to a BA, despite being a graduate qualification. The proposal was eventually lost in a close vote.[63]

Then, in February 1966, a conference on theological education was convened by the Bishop of Newcastle at St John's College, Morpeth, to "re-examine the basis of theological education with a view to its re-establishment

60. "State Parliament—Education Bill," *Sydney Morning Herald*, 20 May 1936, 10.

61. See, for example, *Calendar*, University of Sydney, 1940, 42.

62. Martin, *Tertiary Education in Australia*, especially Part 2, para 15.

63. C. Sherlock, *Uncovering Theology*, 26–27.

as a field of study alongside other disciplines of learning, as well as its application in the training of the ministry."[64] Newcastle itself had since 1964 been discussing a bachelors degree in Theology taught at the Newcastle University College once it achieved full, independent university status, which it did in 1965.[65] In 1967, Sharwood pushed for a Department of Theology in Melbourne's Arts Faculty that could engage with existing courses in the departments of History, Philosophy and Middle Eastern Studies. There was already a "great concentration of potential staff and students . . . in Parkville, in the various Colleges around the University's boundaries."[66] Despite the well-argued case, there was no likelihood of the proposal being adopted by Melbourne University, though Max Charlesworth did teach a religious studies unit there from 1970.

The slow rise of religious studies (as opposed to theological training) into the public universities had begun, but it would be at the expense of degrees in theology. The first to create a separate religion department was the University of Queensland, in 1975, though it would not appoint a chair in it until the arrival of Francis Anderson in 1981. Queensland's board of studies for theology was dismantled as the new department was formed. Sydney also created a Department of Studies in Religion in the Faculty of Arts teaching toward the BA. The first professor in the department, Eric Sharpe, was appointed in 1977. Religion was also seen in a number of the new universities envisaged by the Martin Report. From 1969, Edward Judge offered Biblical studies units at Macquarie University (founded 1967). Monash (1961) created a Centre for Studies in Religion and Theology in 1992 to promote interdisciplinary teaching and research. A little earlier, LaTrobe (1964) introduced a major in Philosophy and Religious Studies at its Bendigo campus, but this was eliminated in a 2008 review.[67] Macquarie (1964) now offers a minor study in Religion and Society in the BA. Griffith (1971) offered theology courses from 1991 in conjunction with the Brisbane College of Theology, and a major in religious studies can be completed at Deakin (1974), though the current curriculum contains few units with any significant study of Christian thought.[68]

64. Davis, *Morpeth Papers*, [iii].

65. "Newcastle University College: proposal for first degree course in Theology, correspondence and papers, 1964–1967," papers, A8326(vii), Anglican Diocese of Newcastle Archives.

66. Sharwood, "Why Not Establish a University School of Theology?"

67. "Major Bendigo Uni Shock," *Bendigo Advertiser*, 3 Nov. 2008.

68. See, for example, "Philosophies of Religion." The required level 2 unit "Religion, Spirituality and Popular Culture" has been replaced from 2022 by "Mindfulness, Meditation, and Buddhism."

Sydney University's separate School of Divinity was increasingly staffed by lecturers borrowed from History, Classics and Philosophy and by part-time faculty and graduate students, including Dorothy Lee from 1985 following completion of her BD there.[69] A Master of Theology degree had been introduced in 1975, while the Bachelor of Divinity degree was removed in 1994. The board of studies at Sydney ceased in 1991. Thereafter it was possible to complete a combined BA/BTh degree with the theology component—now at undergraduate level—undertaken at (and awarded by) the Sydney College of Divinity.[70]

This type of partnership between university and theological college was also being investigated elsewhere. In Adelaide, St Barnabas' had closed in 1950 but reopened in new premises in 1965. In 1979, along with Baptist, Roman Catholic and Uniting Church colleges, it was a founding member of another ecumenical consortium called the Adelaide College of Divinity, which had its theological degrees accredited through Flinders University (1966).[71] In fact, the ACD had the status of a School in the Flinders University structure, enabling staff accreditation and some sharing of students. St Barnabas' left the ACD in 2009, entering into a new arrangement with the School of Theology at Charles Sturt University. A similar system operated in Perth, where the Perth College of Divinity was created in 1985 to "enable co-operation between Murdoch University and the churches in WA." Under a 1994 agreement, each of the denominations jointly funded an academic appointment at Murdoch, and degree offerings from 1986 included a specialized BA(Religion) and a full suite of graduate awards.

Paul Oslington suggests that such partnerships were in part driven by economics: the small, independent theological colleges were struggling financially, while "Entrepreneurial arts deans looking down the road saw the absorption of a local theological college as a new source of revenue."[72] Later government reforms saw the amalgamation of many professional training colleges, particularly teachers colleges, language schools, fine arts colleges and music conservatoria, into public university where they could get accreditation that was far more difficult for them as small independent schools. This was especially true of the seminaries and theology colleges,

---

69. "School of Divinity," *University of Sydney Calendar*, 1986, 45; Trompf, "Survey of New Approaches," 154.

70. See, for example, "Joint resolutions of the Faculty of Arts and Sydney College of Divinity (BA/BTh)," *Faculty of Arts Undergraduate Handbook* (Sydney: University of Sydney, 1997), 14–15.

71. Biggs, *Ecumenical Adventure*.

72. Oslington, "Australian Universities and Religion."

which were effectively prevented from amalgamating amongst themselves by their sectarian or denominational partisanship.[73]

Federal government reforms of higher education under the Hawke Labor government in the late 1980s led to significant change in the sector. Neil Ormerod predicted that the "formation of ACU [Australian Catholic University] and the offer of theology programs within the university sector would shift theological education away from the private sector and towards the university sector."[74] The first religion-based new university was the University of Notre Dame, established by an Act of the Western Australian Parliament in 1990. This was followed by ACU in 1991, which amalgamated four institutes previously specializing in teacher and nursing training, though the curriculum was expanded significantly after achieving university status. While the denominational training colleges still existed, with some ramping up their research activity and revising curricula with a view to seeking university status themselves, most would either send their student to a public university now offering theological programs—particularly ACU, Flinders, Murdoch, and Newcastle—or enter agreements to teach accredited units within a university curriculum, such as at Charles Sturt. One of the largest religion departments in the country was established within the new University of South Australia on its elevation to university status in 1991. In the School of Education, a systematic theology unit (coded as Philosophy) was taught until 2015 and "Theology and Education" until 2016, both as part of the training of teachers of Religious Education in Catholic schools. A minor (four units) in Catholic Studies is still offered.

In 1995, St Mark's Theological College in Canberra joined with the United Theological College in Sydney (a 1974 consortium of the denominations that would form the Uniting Church in 1977) to create the School of Theology at Charles Sturt University (CSU) so as to provide theological degrees by distance education. The Diocese of Newcastle began using this CSU degree option for its students in 1997, though it continued ordination training at St John's Theological College, Morpeth, until 2006 when the facility was sold. Education then continued at the University of Newcastle, the Chair endowed by the diocese (which also gave over its library), effectively returning diocesan training to the university model hoped for by Ernest Burgmann, the visionary head of St John's from 1918.[75]

---

73. See Treloar, "Introduction," 6; Douglas and Lovat, "Theology in Australian Higher Education," 78.

74. Ormerod, "Theology Under Siege (II)"; "Winds of Change in Theological Studies"; "Theological Colleges."

75. See Douglas and Lovat, "Theology in Australian Higher Education," 82–84.

His plan was not to be realized before his appointment as Bishop of Goulburn in 1934, but Burgmann persisted, creating St Mark's Library in Canberra in 1957 as "an institution which would become like a permeable membrane between the church and the university work done in a secular city."[76] Later, while an Assistant Bishop in Canberra-Goulburn, Bruce Wilson was Director of St Mark's Theological College, established in 1987 through amalgamation of the Library and the Canberra College of Ministry. Wilson wished for a system that allowed lay people to undertake an undergraduate degree in theology, with the "important spin-offs being that people training for full-time ministry will have to 'rub shoulders' with people in the ordinary workforce who are trying to think and work through their faith."[77]

Throughout this time, the Australian College of Theology operated outside the university system. In 1972, it established its own Board of Studies, and its degrees were eventually accredited with the NSW government authorities during the early 1980s. This attracted several non-Anglican colleges to affiliate with the ACT in order to be able to access degrees, but at the same time the ACT lost some of its more liberal-catholic Anglican colleges to the newly formed state colleges of divinity discussed above, leaving it an increasingly evangelical institution. As Treloar notes, the new recruits to the ACT "were deterred from entering the college of Divinity by a lingering sectarianism that would not countenance cooperation with Roman Catholic institutions." Ridley College was the only "full-fledged Anglican college" left in the ACT by 2002.[78]

Other consortia would struggle over the coming years. In 2009, Ormerod reported the "imminent closure" of the Brisbane College of Theology, with its constituent parts realigning with ACU and CSU, while the thirty-year-old Adelaide College of Divinity "essentially defunct," though it managed to survive despite the departure of the Anglicans (St Barnabas' College), which went to CSU and a 2010 restructure under the name of the Adelaide Theological Centre of the dominant Uniting College and the Catholic Theological College.

The Present Theological Landscape

Oslington has identified serious anomalies between Australia's public and private tertiary institutions, including differentiated fee structures and

76. "Brief History," online, St Mark's National Theological Centre website
77. Downie, "Introducing St Mark's Canberra."
78. Treloar, "Three (or Four) Identities."

faculty access to Commonwealth research funding.[79] Doctoral students outside universities are excluded from fee-remission scholarships and stipends.[80] The few religious studies departments that still exist also seem to be in jeopardy. The agreement between Murdoch University and the churches in Western Australia has recently been abandoned. By 2015, only the Anglican Wollaston Theological College and the Uniting Church Theological Hall were active members of the consortium, and the university began to question the ability of the partners to make their agreed commitments to teaching. Admission to the BA(Religion) was wound back, leading to difficulties for undergraduates in completing the subjects required under new Anglican ordination requirements under the National Standards for Theological Education passed by synod in 2016.[81] With the disbanding of the theological department at Murdoch, Wollaston chose instead to affiliate with the University of Divinity from 2022.

Only a few years after accepting the funding for its academic positions from the Diocese of Newcastle's sale of Morpeth, establishing the Bachelor of Theology and then from 2010 partnering with the (Roman Catholic) Broken Bay Institute to offer theology degrees from 2012,[82] the University of Newcastle closed down its Theological faculty entirely at the end of 2014, "resting" the degree from 2015; it is still possible to include a minor sequence in "Studies of Religion" in an Arts degree.[83] Similarly, as of 2021, all the named theology degree programs at Flinders University were placed in teach-out mode, and the agreement with the Adelaide Theological Centre to provide the faculty abandoned, leaving only a few HDR students to complete. Ormerod had predicted the possibility when examining the difficulties faced by the consortia in 2009:

> The movement to the university sector of course restores the ancient place of theology as a discipline within a university. But there are dangers in such a move. Theological colleges should be under no illusion that the interest of most of these universities extends beyond the financial. The colleges bring student

79. Oslington, "Australian Universities and Religion."

80. See "Commonwealth Scholarships Guidelines (Research) 2017," issued under section 238–10 of the *Higher Education Support Act 2003*.

81. John Dunhill, Perth College of Divinity report in *2017 Annual Report of the Synod of the Uniting Church in Western Australia*, F3; "Summons," Third Session of the Forty-ninth Synod of the Anglican Diocese of Perth, 2017, 67.

82. "BBI and Uni of Newcastle Team up to Teach Theology," *CathNews*, 20 February 2012.

83. https://www.newcastle.edu.au/degrees/bachelor-of-arts/what-you-will-study/majors/studies-of-religion-minor.

numbers, and their theologians contribute relatively well to research outputs with minimal investment from the university. Apart from ACU they have no particular interest in theology for its own sake. A decline in student numbers or changes in government funding formulae for research could lead to a colder relationship.[84]

The public universities were faltering in their theological offerings, but others filled the space. The now 100-year-old Melbourne College of Divinity, Australia's sixth oldest degree-awarding body, achieved independent university status in 2012, becoming the University of Divinity. Having been appointed Dean of the Trinity College Theological School in 2010 after teaching with the United Faculty of Theology as a Uniting Church lecturer, Dorothy Lee was one of two Trinity faculty members among only ten inaugural professorial appointments by the University of Divinity in 2012. A 2019 application by the ACT to achieve university status was unsuccessful, but Australia's newest university is the Seventh Day Adventists' Avondale University, approved in July 2021. Among other organizations aspiring to full university status are Moore Theological College, approved as a "university college" in July 2021 and Alphacrucis College, founded in 1948 by the Assemblies of God, which was granted the same status in January 2022.[85]

A more recent article by Oslington calls on Australia's still disparate and splintered theological education sector to consider more consolidation in order to overcome the issues associated with small scale, quality control, research funding, attractiveness to international students and access to government-supported student places. He sees the "duplication of consortia" as unsustainable, but a coming together would require "theological colleges from different traditions being willing to sit around a table for accreditation purposes."[86] A recent realignment has seen two further colleges, the Anglican St Francis's College in Brisbane (previously with ACT) and Uniting College for Leadership and Theology in Adelaide (ACD) become colleges of the University of Divinity from 2023.

The exclusion of religion from Australia's university system dating from the second half of the nineteenth-century means that today we "have

---

84. Ormerod, "Why Universities Welcome Theological Colleges."

85. Alphacrucis was originally the Commonwealth Bible College, changing its name to Southern Cross College in 1993 and then Alphacrucis in 2009. It had previous been at the entry level of "Institute of Higher Education."

86. Oslington, "Speculations on the Future of Australian Theological Education."

a lesser education system than we could."[87] The complexity of our modern landscape is described by Charles Sherlock in these terms:

> The large number of theological colleges, and the diversity of their church, academic and government accountabilities, indicate the need for further collaboration in Australian theological education. This cannot be imposed from outside the sector: further working together needs to be initiated from within, since some of the diversity reflects substantial, long-term theological difference. The patterns of relationships between colleges and churches are correspondingly diverse, including funding: some colleges continue to rely on tuition fees and donations, and few have endowments. Even so, the churches are likely to continue as the "industry partners" of Australian theological education (including university contexts), whether or not a college is church-sponsored.[88]

The disciples' complaint to Jesus that "this teaching is difficult," recorded in the Gospel of John (6:60), appears as valid today as it was two thousand years ago, and the place of theological teaching in our tertiary institutions as still a matter of much change and debate.

Bibliography

Bain, Andrew M. and Ian Hussey, eds. *Theological Education: Foundations, Practices, and Future Directions*, Australian College of Theology Monograph. Wipf and Stock, 2018.

Barnes, Robert. "Religious Studies and Theology: A Short Historical Survey, 1850 to the Present" in Anthony Low (ed.), *Knowing Ourselves and Others: The Humanities in Australia into the 21st Century*, vol. 2, ch. 24. Australian Research Council, 1998.

Beirne, Paul. "The Melbourne College of Divinity: A Selective Historical Overview," *Pacifica*, 23 (2010) 123–36.

Biddington, Ralph. "Rationalism and its Opposition to a Degree in Divinity at the University of Melbourne, 1905–1910," *History of Education Review*, 33.1 (2004) 28–43.

Biggs, C.R. *An Ecumenical Adventure: A History of the Adelaide College of Divinity*. ACD, 2011.

Breward, Ian. "Historical Perspectives on Theological Education in Australasia" in G.R. Treloar (ed.), *The Furtherance of Religious Beliefs: Essays on the History of Theological Education in Australia*. Centre for the Study of Australian Christianity, Macquarie University, 1997, 8–23.

———. *A History of the Australian Churches*, Allen & Unwin, 1993.

87. Oslington, "Australian Universities and Religion."

88. C. Sherlock, *Uncovering Theology*," 13.

———. "Holding Fast, Letting Go: A History of the United Faculty of Theology," Commencement Lecture, United Faculty of Theology, 1999, Queen's College, Melbourne.

Cable, Ken. "Bishop Barker and his Clergy," 1st Moore College Library Lecture, 17 April 1975, 17.

Carey, Hilary. *God's Empire*. Cambridge University Press, 2011.

Davies, David J. "Durham University Examinations," letter, *Sydney Morning Herald*, 15 October 1912, 13.

Davis, Rex (ed.), *The Morpeth Papers: A Collection of Papers Read at the Bishop of Newcastle's Conference on Theological Education held at St John's College, Morpeth, NSW, February 14–17, 1966*. Diocese of Newcastle, 1966.

Douglas, Brian and Terence Lovat. "Theology in Australian Higher Education: the 'Newcastle Model' Brings Theology Home to the Academy, *Higher Education Research & Development*, 29:1 (February 2010) 75–87.

Downie, Graham. "Introducing St Mark's Canberra: A New Institution," *Canberra Times*, 17 December 1986, 26.

Gladwin, Michael. *Anglican Clergy in Australia, 1788–1850: Building a British World*. Boydell & Brewer, 2015.

Hart, J. Stephen. "Divinity Degrees," letter, *The Argus*, 13 September 1910, 9.

Hill, John. "The Foundation of the Sydney College of Divinity—Part I: Form the Origins to 1980," *Journal of Christian Education Papers*, 88 (April 1987), 39–53.

Hilliard, David. "Pluralism and New Alignments in Society and Church: 1967 to the Present," in Bruce Kaye (ed.), *Anglicanism in Australia*. Melbourne University Press, 2002, 124–49.

Loane, Marcus. *A Centenary History of Moore Theological College*. Angus & Robertson, 1955.

Martin, L.H. *Tertiary Education in Australia: Report of the Committee on the Future of Tertiary Education in Australia to the Australian Universities Commission*. Government Printer, 1964–65.

McIver, Robert K. "Theological Education in Australia: Past and Present as Possible Indicators of Future Trends," *Colloquium: The Australian and New Zealand Theological Review*, 50.2 (2018) 43–68.

Nobbs, Raymond. "From Nowhere to Know-How—Sydney College of Divinity: The First Twenty Years," *Pacifica*, 17 (2004) 121–36.

Ormerod, Neil. "Theological Colleges on Shaky Ground," *Eureka Street*, vol. 18:24, 26 November 2008.

———. "Theology Under Siege (II): Enter the (Dawkins) Dragon," *National Outlook*, 126 (1990) 8–12

———. "Why Universities Welcome Theological Colleges," *Eureka Street*, 18 November 2009.

———. "Winds of Change in Theological Studies," *National Outlook*, 16.2 (1994) 4–6.

Oslington, Paul. "Australian Universities and Religion: Tales of Horror and Hope," *The Conversation*, 26 Feb. 2014.

———. "Speculations on the Future of Australian Theological Education," *Eternity*, 15 October 2021.

Piggin, Stuart. "A History of Theological Education in Australia" in G.R. Treloar (ed.), *The Furtherance of Religious Beliefs: Essays on the History of Theological Education in Australia.* Centre for the Study of Australian Christianity, Macquarie University, 1997, 24–43.

Sharwood, Robin. "Theology and Tertiary Education in Australia," in Rex Davis (ed.), *The Morpeth Papers: A Collection of Papers Read at the Bishop of Newcastle's Conference on Theological Education held at St John's College, Morpeth, NSW, February 14–17, 1966.* Diocese of Newcastle, 1966, 10–11.

———. "Why Not Establish a University School of Theology?" *The Age,* 22 September 1967, 4.

Sherlock, Charles. "Australian Theological Education: An Historical and Thematic Overview" in *Handbook of Theological Education in World Christianity* (ed.) Dietrich Werner, et al. Cluster, 2010, 458–65.

———. *Uncovering Theology: The Depth, Reach and Utility of Australian Theological Education,* Australian Learning and Teaching Council. ATF Press, 2009.

Sherlock, Peter. "The Foundation of the Melbourne College of Divinity," *Journal of Religious History,* 40.2 (June 2016) 204–24.

Tandan, Ranuka. "Studies in Religion is Worth Far More than a Financial Surplus," *Honi Soit,* 16 May 2021.

Theological Education: Report of a Committee Appointed by the General Synod of the Church of England in Australia. General Synod, 1969.

Thomis, Malcolm. *A Place of Light & Learning: The University of Queensland's First 75 Years.* University of Queensland Press, 1985.

Treloar, Geoffrey R. "Introduction" in G.R. Treloar (ed.), *The Furtherance of Religious Beliefs: Essays on the History of Theological Education in Australia.* Centre for the Study of Australian Christianity, Macquarie University, 1997, 4–7.

———. "The Three (or Four) Identities of the Australian College of Theology, 1891–2016," in Andrew M. Bain and Ian Hussey (eds.), *Theological Education: Foundations, Practices, and Future Directions.* Australian College of Theology Monograph. Wipf and Stock, 2018.

Trompf, Garry. "The Academic Study of Religion in Australia and Oceania" in Lindsay Jones (ed.), *Encyclopedia of Religion,* 2nd ed. Thomson/Gale, 2005

———. "A Survey of New Approaches to the Study of Religion in Australia and the Pacific," in Peter Antes, Armin W. Geertz and Randi R. Warne (eds), *New Approaches to the Study of Religion,* vol. 1. Walter de Gruyter, 2004, 147–81.

Interdisciplinary Approaches

17.

Why Didn't the Transfiguration Make the Cut?

Exploring the Omission of the Transfiguration in Jesus Films

ROBERT A. DERRENBACKER JR.

Introduction

Without question, Jesus is one of the most filmed characters in the history of cinema—more than Robin Hood, Sherlock Holmes, Dracula, or even James Bond, with at least eighty-four film titles with Jesus as a (if not the main) character.[1] Jesus films often attempt to present a "historical" portrait of Jesus, with their screenplays usually based (at least in part) on one or more of the canonical Gospels, in sometimes entertaining, and occasionally controversial, ways. Included in the canon of Jesus films are somewhat "traditional" (or, one might say "domesticated") portraits of Jesus like *The Greatest Story Ever Told* (George Stevens [1965]) or *Jesus of Nazareth* (Franco Zeffirelli [1977]), controversial films such as *The Last Temptation of Christ* (Martin Scorsese [1989]) or *The Passion of the Christ* (Mel Gibson [2003]), the irreverent *Monty Python's The Life of Brian* (Terry Jones [1979]), or even the thought-provoking *The Gospel according to Saint Matthew* (Pier

---

1. See, for example, the following Wikipedia catalogue: "Portrayal of Jesus in Film."

Paolo Pasolini [1964]) or *Jesus of Montreal* (Denis Arcand [1989]). Jesus films span from (at least) 1905's *The Life and Passion of Jesus Christ* (Ferdinand Zecca and Lucien Nonquet) to the current television series *The Chosen* (Dallas Jenkins [2017–]).

This genre of film is worth paying attention to for a number of reasons, not least of which is the power that film and television have in influencing viewers' perceptions of Jesus. Richard C. Stern, Clayton N. Jefford, and Guerric DeBona note that "media have the potential to influence the basic values of those who watch and listen, with the further potential to influence the direction and shape even of our religious faith and our understanding of the person of Jesus of Nazareth, a person who lived two thousand years *before* moving pictures were even invented."[2]

Likewise, New Testament scholar Adele Reinhartz argues the following about the impact (and shortfalls) of the Jesus film genre:

> It would seem . . . that Jesus films demonstrably fall short both as history and entertainment. Yet people continue both to enjoy these films, and to view them at least to some extent as a source of information about the historical Jesus. Some use them as a vehicle for reflecting upon their own Christian faith. Others watch these films out of habit or tradition, particularly at Christmas and Easter time when many networks will screen one Jesus biopic or another.[3]

She continues: Jesus films "reshape the past in the image of the present, out of conviction that the past, or their versions thereof, continues to be relevant for audiences today."[4]

Just as it is telling what stories from the Gospel of Mark—the main literary source for Matthew and Luke—are included, altered or omitted by later evangelists, it is also telling what Gospel stories about Jesus are included or omitted by Jesus filmmakers. Many, if not most, of the films within the Jesus film genre portray significant events in the life of Jesus between and including his birth and infancy on the one hand, and his suffering, death, and resurrection on the other. Yet there is one story in the life of Jesus that is almost universally ignored by Jesus-filmmakers—the Transfiguration.[5] By one author's count, only three films explicitly portray the story of the

---

2. Stern, Jefford, and DeBona, *Savior on the Silver*, 8 (emphasis original).

3. Reinhartz, *Jesus of Hollywood*, 6.

4. Reinhartz, *Jesus of Hollywood*, 20.

5. See Mark 9:2–10, and its later Synoptic parallels in Matt 17:1–9 and Luke 9:28–36; cf. also 2 Pet 1:16–18.

Transfiguration of Jesus.[6] This is a surprising phenomenon as the story of the Transfiguration is as unique as it is memorable in the Synoptic tradition, as well as narratively and structurally significant for Matthew, Mark and Luke. Besides, it is a major feast day in church calendars, celebrated by eastern Christians and by most western denominations, with its commemoration either 6 August or the last Sunday before the start of Lent in the West. By comparison, the virginal conception and birth of Jesus is mentioned in the New Testament only twice (Matt 1–2 and Luke 1–2), and yet features much more prominently in Jesus films than does the Transfiguration (which is mentioned explicitly in all three Synoptic Gospels plus 2 Peter, along with the possible implicit influence of the story in the Fourth Gospel[7]). Likewise, the Ascension of Jesus provides a similar example. While only occurring in one Gospel (Luke 24:50–5 3; cf. Acts 1:6–11), the Ascension is a scene that a number of filmmakers are not immune from depicting.[8]

Yet this neglect of the Transfiguration is not just limited to Jesus-film-makers. Dorothy Lee, in her book on the Transfiguration, notes a similar (Western) ecclesial disregard:

> Given its dramatic and theological import, it is strange that the transfiguration should be one of the most neglected stories in the New Testament. This neglect is confined largely to the Western tradition. Christians in the East regard the transfiguration as central to the symbolism of the gospel, disclosing as much about themselves as about God. In the West, by contrast, the feast of the transfiguration is a minor event and ignored entirely in some denominational traditions. For the most part, post-Enlightenment biblical scholars have shown little interest in the transfiguration, minimizing its theological status. If anything, biblical studies has tended to "experience the story as alien" and to "rationalize this strangeness."[9]

6. See Chattaway, "Could Moses have a cameo in the next *Bible* episode?" (cited 21 October 2022)

7. See, for example, Lee, *Transfiguration*, 100–111. Lee argues that while the Gospel of John does not include an account of the Transfiguration of Jesus, "John did know something of the transfiguration and chose to use it, not as a single tale, but as a motif—a series of symbols—throughout his Gospel. . . . [I]nstead of re-telling the story with his own editorial changes, John has chosen to weave the threads of the transfiguration into the warp and woof of his tale, so that the main symbols are rehearsed again and again throughout the Johannine narrative. If so, the whole of the Gospel could be viewed as a 'transfiguration' story . . ." (*Transfiguration*, 101).

8. The Ascension of Jesus is found in seven out of eighteen films catalogued by Staley and Walsh (*Jesus, the Gospels, and Cinematic Imagination* 188).

9. Lee, *Transfiguration*, 1–2, quoting Luz, *Matthew 8–20: A*, 403.

This essay will suggest some reasons for the neglect of the Transfiguration scene in Jesus films. This will be prefaced by a description of the features of the story in the Synoptics, a summary of some of the recent scholarship on the Transfiguration in the Synoptic tradition, and conclude with an overview of the Transfiguration portrayal in the very few films that actually include the scene.

The Transfiguration in the Synoptic Tradition (and 2 Peter)

All three Synoptic Gospels include an account of the Transfiguration. The evangelists locate the scene roughly in the middle of each Gospel, strategically and centrally after the Peter's confession in Caesarea Philippi (Mark 8:27–3 0 and par.), the first "Passion Prediction" (Mark 8:31–3 and par.), and Jesus' teaching on the cost of discipleship (Mark 8:34–9:1 and par.). Narratively and structurally then, the Transfiguration functions as a "pivot point" of sorts in Mark's (and Matthew's and Luke's) narrative(s). In the Gospel of Mark, the Transfiguration, along with the preceding Confession of Peter at Caesarea Philippi, mark the conclusion of the first half of the Gospel that is focused on the identity of Jesus. The Transfiguration, in tandem with the three Passion Predictions (Mark 8:31–3 3; 9:30–3; 10:32–4), looks ahead, then, to the suffering, death, and vindication of Jesus that concludes the Gospel narrative.

In the Transfiguration story in all three Synoptics, Peter, John, and James are present with Jesus on an unnamed mountain in Galilee; the appearance of Jesus is then transformed in some way, including his clothing, followed by the presence of, and conversation with, Moses and Elijah; Peter responds by offering to build three booths; a cloud then overshadows them, with a voice coming from the cloud saying "This is my . . . son . . . ; listen to him." At the very least, this is a story that reveals something about Jesus' identity—as a Moses-like figure, as a prophet (like Elijah), as Messiah, and as the Son of God.

Despite these common elements that make up this story shared by all three Synoptic Gospels, there are some differences:

- Both Matthew and Mark locate the story six days after Jesus' sayings on discipleship (Matt 17:1//Mark 9:2), while Luke indicates it was "about eight days" later (Luke 9:28).

- In typical Lukan fashion (see, for example, Luke 3:21), Luke portrays Jesus as praying just before "the appearance of his face changed" (τὸ εἶδος τοῦ προσώπου αὐτοῦ ἕτερον) (Luke 9:29); on the other hand, Matthew and Mark describe Jesus as being "transfigured" (μετεμορφώθη) (Matt 17:2//Mark 9:2).

- In Matthew, the face of Jesus also "shone like the sun" (Matt 17:2).

- Luke adds a summary of the content of Jesus' conversation with Moses and Elijah ("They . . . were speaking of [Jesus'] departure [ἔξοδος], which he was about to accomplish at Jerusalem" [Luke 9:31]), as well as the sleepiness of Peter and the other two disciples (Luke 9:31–33a).

- Both Mark and Luke mention the fearful reaction of the disciples (Mark 9:6//Luke 9:34), with only Luke describing the disciples as entering the cloud (Luke 9:34).

- The voice from heaven describes Jesus as the "beloved" son in both Matthew and Mark (Matt 17:5//Mark 9:7); Matthew adds the phrase "with whom I am well pleased" (Matt 9:5), while Luke adds "my chosen [one]" (Luke 9:35).

- Only Matthew relates an immediate reaction of the disciples and Jesus' response—"When the disciples heard this, they fell to the ground and were overcome by fear. But Jesus came and touched them, saying, 'Get up and do not be afraid'" (Matt 17:6–7).

- In Matthew and Mark, Jesus commands the disciples to keep silent about what they had witnessed (Matt 17:9//Mark 9:9–10), while in Luke, the silence of the disciples is not ordered by Jesus (Luke 9:36).

- And in both Matthew and Mark, the disciples query Jesus about the (eschatological) coming of Elijah (Matt 17:10–13//Mark 9:11–13; cf. Mal 4:5), while there is no parallel in Luke.

In addition to the Synoptic accounts of the Transfiguration, 2 Pet 1:16–18 makes reference to the event, likely either relying directly on one (or more) of the Synoptic Gospels, or an already commonly-known account of this episode in the life of Jesus.[10] The writer of 2 Peter[11] presents himself among "eyewitnesses" (v 16) when Jesus "received honor and glory from God the Father" (λαβὼν γὰρ παρὰ θεοῦ πατρὸς τιμὴν καὶ δόξαν) "while we were with him on the holy mountain" (vv 17–18). In addition, the writer of 2 Peter recalls the words of the divine voice: "This is my Son, my Beloved,

---

10. Lee has a helpful and thorough treatment of the Transfiguration account in 2 Peter—see *Transfiguration*, 88–99.

11. While 2 Peter makes reference to the Transfiguration tradition, and in doing so, implies that the writer of 2 Peter was an eyewitness (1:18), this author follows the consensus of scholarship that 2 Peter is pseudonymous and likely originates in the late first century at the earliest, several decades after the Gospel of Mark was composed.

with whom I am well pleased" (v 17)—most closely following the divine voice from Matthew's account (17:5).

There are elements of the Synoptic Transfiguration accounts that 2 Peter omits, most notably the mention of the change in the appearance of Jesus, the characters of Moses and Elijah, and the overshadowing cloud. Instead, what 2 Peter emphasizes, according to Dorothy Lee, are two important themes. First, the Parousia of Jesus is guaranteed by the Transfiguration, a theme central to the letter. Lee states: "[The Transfiguration's] function as a precursor to and pledge of the Parousia gives it a distinctly saving role within the theological framework of the epistle."[12] Second, the Transfiguration is established by the author of 2 Peter "as a non-negotiable part of the apostolic faith, central to its evangelical message. The transfiguration lies at the core of the apostolic tradition, inspiring hope in the return of Christ and God's final redemption."[13]

What is the Transfiguration and why is it important to the Synoptic Evangelists?

What, then, is the genre and purpose of the Transfiguration of Jesus, especially in the Synoptic tradition? There have been various (and occasionally overlapping) scholarly explanations of the historical and literary origins of the Transfiguration story (see below), with a lack of consensus emerging, one that likely reflects the uniqueness of the scene in the Synoptic tradition and its apparent strangeness to interpreters down through the centuries. What is certain is that Mark's version is the earliest we have, which is then utilized by the other two Synoptic Gospels. What is also certain is that the scene is significant Christologically to the Synoptic Gospels as it reveals and confirms something (or *some things*) about the identity of Jesus— Jesus as a prophet, Jesus as Son of God, and Jesus as Messiah.

In addition, the Transfiguration evokes stories found in the Hebrew Bible. For example, the Transfiguration may echo the wilderness experiences of the Israelites. Peter suggests that he build three "dwellings" (σκηνάς;; Mark 9:5 and par.), perhaps echoing the establishing of the "Feast of the Tabernacles" (Sukkot) in Lev 23:40–43. The Transfiguration is also reminiscent of the experiences of Moses on Mount Sinai in Exo 24:15–18 and 24:29–35.[14] This is particularly seen in Exodus' description of Moses' first

---

12. Lee, *Transfiguration*, 96.

13. Lee, *Transfiguration*, 96–97.

14. Chilton describes it as a *bat qôl*—lit. "daughter of a voice"—an echo of Moses's experiences on Mount Sinai ("Transfiguration," in *Anchor Bible Dictionary*, 6:640–42.)

ascent of the mountain (24:15), which is covered by a cloud (24:15–16) which Moses enters (24:18); this cloud covered the mountain for "six days" (24:16; see Jesus' ascent of the mountain of Transfiguration "six days later" in Mark 9:2 and Matt 17:1). In addition, after Moses' second sojourn up and then down Mount Sinai, Exodus tells the reader that Moses' appearance changed, with "the skin of his face shining" (Exod 34:29–30, 35; cf. Matt 17:2 where Jesus' "face shone like the sun" after being "transfigured"). But apart from drawing parallels between the divine encounters of Moses and Jesus on a mountaintop, there is clearly more to the Transfiguration in the Synoptic Gospels.

As well, the identity of Jesus is established in the voice from the cloud that declares Jesus to be the "Son of God" (Mark 9:7 and par.). In addition, Jesus' identity as Messiah is confirmed in all three Synoptics with the appearance of Elijah on the mountain (Mark 9:4 and par.; see the tradition in Mal 4:5 where Elijah would reappear just before the appearance of the messianic "day of the Lord"). As well, Jesus' messianic (and prophetic) identity is explicitly established by Luke in the voice from heaven: "'This is my Son, *my Chosen* [ὁ ἐκλελεγμένος]; listen to him!'" (Luke 9:35). The first readers of the Synoptics would have recalled a similar story—the baptism of Jesus (Mark 1:9–11 and par.)—which also included a divine voice which served to establish Jesus' identity as the "beloved" "Son of God."

The story of the Transfiguration may also be both looking backwards and looking ahead in the Synoptic tradition. Larry Hurtado has argued that the Transfiguration functioned as a fulfillment of Mark 9:1 (and parallels): "And [Jesus] said to them, 'Truly I tell you, there are some standing here who will not taste death until they see that the kingdom of God has come with power.'"[15] The same disciples who accompany Jesus up the mountain—Peter, James, and John—are the same three disciples who accompany Jesus in Gethsemane according to Matthew and Mark (Matt 26:37//Mark 14:33). In addition, Luke's Transfiguration account looks ahead to the "departure" of Jesus "which he was about to accomplish at Jerusalem" in his summary of the conversation between Jesus, Moses, and Elijah (Luke 9:31; cf. Luke 9:51).

Thus, the Transfiguration is unique in the Synoptic tradition, narratively significant, plays an important role in establishing the identity of Jesus, looks back to the experiences of Moses and the Israelites, exhibits echoes from the story of the Baptism of Jesus, and looks ahead to the suffering, death and ultimate vindication of Jesus in resurrection.

On the surface, the Transfiguration may appear (understandably) to the contemporary reader as a somewhat strange story without a parallel.

15. See, for example, Hurtado, *Mark*, 139–40.

However, it clearly was not perceived with the same sense of "strangeness" by the earliest known inheritors of the Marcan tradition of the Transfiguration—both Matthew and Luke (independently of each other on the Two-Document Hypothesis) decided to include the story in their Gospels and in the Marcan sequence. As Morna Hooker notes:

> Although the story causes problems for the modern reader, it is unlikely that Mark was aware of them. In his God-filled universe, a heavenly confirmation of Jesus' identity would have seemed no more out of place than the acknowledgement of his identity by the unclean spirits. The true nature of Jesus is a hidden mystery which breaks out from time to time, and for Mark these revelations do not require explanations.[16]

Form critically, Rudolf Bultmann classified the Transfiguration as a "legend"[17] that was "originally a resurrection story."[18] Martin Dibelius described the story as a "myth," with the Baptism of Jesus, the Temptation, and the Transfiguration the "only narratives in the Gospels which really describe a mythological event, i.e., a many-sided interaction between mythological but not human persons. . . . "[19] Others have picked up on Bultmann's suggestion and have argued that the Transfiguration is a (misplaced) story of Jesus' resurrection, or perhaps even a story brought forward of his ascension, second coming, or heavenly enthronement.[20]

Most recently, Delbert Burkett has argued against seeing the Transfiguration as a misplaced resurrection story (or epiphany). Instead, in terms of genre, it is more properly to be seen as an "apocalypse," a revelation of Jesus' *apotheosis*.[21] Burkett maintains that the earliest form of Transfiguration scene in Mark's Gospel prefigures some other event—not likely the resurrection or Parousia of Jesus, but more likely the exaltation of Jesus in his ascension, which, according to Burkett, is his *apotheosis* or deification,

16. Hooker, *Gospel according to Saint Mark*, 214.

17. Bultmann defines "legends" as "those parts of the tradition which are not miracle stories in the proper sense, but instead of being historical in character are religious and edifying. For the most part they include something miraculous but not necessarily so . . ." (*History of the Synoptic Tradition*, 244–45).

18. Bultmann, *History of the Synoptic Tradition*, 259. See also Stein, "Is the Transfiguration (Mark 9:2–8) a Misplaced Resurrection Account?" 79–96.

19. Dibelius, *From Tradition to Gospel*, 271.

20. See, for example, Boobyer, *St Mark and the Transfiguration Story*; Riesenfeld, *Jésus Transfiguré*; and F. R. McCurley, "'And after six days' (Mark 9.2), a Semitic literary device,": 67–81.

21. See Burkett, "Transfiguration of Jesus (Mark 9:2–8): Epiphany or Apotheosis?" *JBL* 138 (2019) 413–32.

a future time when Jesus is transformed from a human figure to a divine figure, a time when a human ascends "into heaven to be transformed into a divine or heavenly being."[22] Burkett writes:

> [T]he transfiguration narrative gives a preview of Jesus' apotheosis. It puts him in the same category as other mortals who ascended to heaven at the end of their lives and were transformed into heavenly beings. It thus identifies Mark's Jesus not as an innately divine being but as a moral who would become divine or immortal being at the end of his life.[23]

Thus, in the Transfiguration narrative (at least in Mark's Gospel),

> Jesus undergoes [a] temporary transformation [at the Transfiguration] so that the disciples can witness the heavenly nature that he would have later, after his ascension. In the future, no one would ascend with Jesus into heaven to bear witness. Consequently Mark's Jesus arranges a preview for his disciples so that they can attest to it.[24]

One wonders, however, if seeing the Transfiguration as a misplaced story that is something else (resurrection, ascension, enthronement, or Parousia) is to miss its point in terms of what it reveals about Jesus. Burkett does not ignore this feature, but argues that as an apocalypse, the Transfiguration, especially through the divine voice, reveals Jesus as "messianic son of God" and a "prophet like Moses."[25] Dorothy Lee concurs in her work on the Transfiguration. "Jesus' identity as the divine Son," Lee stresses, "is the keystone" of the pericope in Mark.[26] Thus, the Transfiguration scene is key to a more complete understanding of each of the Synoptic Gospels' Christology and their understandings of just who Jesus is.

In addition, the Transfiguration is essential to understanding the narrative movement of the story of Jesus in at least the earliest Synoptic Gospel (Mark). M. Eugene Boring notes: "The major thematic transition that occurs in [Mark 8:22–10:52] is the transition from veiled, parabolic speech and actions to clear and explicitly revelation from God/Jesus regarding the identity of Jesus and his function in the divine plan of salvation," with "the Christological meaning of Jesus' identity [coming] more clearly into focus."[27]

22. Burkett, "Transfiguration of Jesus," 424.

23. Burkett, "Transfiguration of Jesus," 425.

24. Burkett, "Transfiguration of Jesus," 431.

25. Burkett, "Transfiguration of Jesus," 428, 432.

26. Lee, *Transfiguration*, 9.

27. Boring, *Mark*, 232.

So Why Didn't the Transfiguration Make the Cut?

So why does the Transfiguration get cut from—or at least, not get included—in virtually all Jesus films? It is difficult to answer this question with any certainty, for we largely lack the resources that would describe the filmmakers' thoughts and motives along these lines. So, one is left to speculate and make educated guesses.

To begin, it is worth pondering the uniqueness, ambiguity, and potential strangeness of Synoptic account of the Transfiguration, an account that lacks many of the details of this supernatural event. As a result, how would a director and cinematography communicate the content of the Transfiguration visually? How does a filmmaker present a "transfiguration" (or, literally a "metamorphosis") where the face of Jesus "shines like the sun" (Matthew) or "changes appearance" (Luke)? How does one film an event that Matthew calls a "vision" (ὅραμα [17:9]—but a "vision" that is observed not just by Jesus, but also by Peter, James, and John)? Perhaps, then, the overly mystical and strange character of the scene is a primary reason why filmmakers have avoided the Transfiguration in their films.[28]

Yet there is likely more than this answer to this question. Whatever the Transfiguration is in terms of its genre, it is a story that reveals something important about the identity of Jesus and is crucial for understanding the Christology of the Synoptics. "This is my Son, the Beloved" (Matthew and Mark), or "This is my Son, my Chosen" (Luke), ". . . listen to him!" reveals much as it echoes the royal Psalm 2 (especially v 7: "I will tell of the decree of the Lord: He said to me 'You are my son; today I have begotten you.'") and reveals much about the identity of Jesus—king, messiah, divine. As noted above, the pericope that has the most in common with the Transfiguration is the Baptism of Jesus (Mark 1:9–11 and par.; cf. John 1:31–34), where a divine, heavenly voice also declares Jesus' sonship.

Yet it seems that filmmakers often struggle with heavenly affirmations of Jesus' identity, especially an identity that can connote divinity. As Adele Reinhartz notes, most Jesus films have difficulty with "superhuman witnesses" to Jesus' identity as Son of God.[29] Instead, when Jesus films are revealing something of Jesus' identity they cope more easily with human characters or "objects and elements associated with the divine" bearing witness to this aspect of Jesus' identity as opposed to witness borne by a supernatural

28. In private communication (22 February 2016) with this author, Peter Chattaway—film critic and blogger on faith and film—noted the following: "I suspect [the Transfiguration is] too miraculous/mystical for some filmmakers, who would rather focus on the healing of the sick and things like that."

29. Reinhartz, *Jesus of Hollywood*, 102.

revelation or annunciation.[30] Reinhartz's point is supported to a certain extent when one observes how the story of Jesus' baptism is portrayed, a narrative in all three Synoptics which culminates with a divine voice from heaven (implicitly God the Father) declaring Jesus to his son.[31] Interestingly, in the eighteen films that Staley and Walsh survey in their handbook on Jesus films, eleven include a scene of Jesus' baptism, and yet only four of which include an explicit depiction of a divine voice from heaven declaring Jesus' sonship.[32]

As noted above, we have very few opportunities to get a sense of the thinking of filmmakers and the decisions they have made in terms of what to include in their stories about Jesus and how to present that content. It does seem, however, that filmmakers generally have struggled with presenting the supernatural and the epiphanic, and especially the miraculous. As Reinhartz rightly remarks, Jesus' ability to perform miracles in the Gospels provide "the most graphic evidence that [he] is divine."[33] However, as she also notes, Jesus films have approached the miraculous in a variety of different ways—some films have interpreted (and portrayed) the miracles of Jesus literally; other films might "take them literally but only talk about them rather than portray them visually";[34] still others interpret the miracles of Jesus metaphorically, or even omit any explicit portrayals of Jesus performing miracles all together.[35]

Franco Zeffirelli is a filmmaker who did not shy away from portraying the miracles of Jesus in his film *Jesus of Nazareth* (1977).[36] Yet he writes about the limitations of the film genre and the production of his film, especially as it pertains to portrayal of the supernatural. Zeffirelli describes

30. See Reinhartz, *Jesus of Hollywood,* 98–102.

31. In all three Synoptic Gospels, the Holy Spirit descends "like a dove" and the voice from heaven declares, either publicly (Matthew) or privately (Mark and Luke), that Jesus is "my Son, the beloved, with you [or 'whom'] I am well pleased" (Mark 1:11 and par.).

32. Again, see Staley and Walsh, *Jesus, the Gospels, and Cinematic Imagination,* 177. These four films include *Gospel According to Saint Matthew* (Pasolini), *Jesus of Nazareth* (Zeffirelli), *Jesus* (Young), and *Miracle Maker: Story of Jesus* (Hayes). *Jesus Film* (Sykes/ Krisch), which includes an account of the Transfiguration (see below), has the narrator recall what the voice from heaven communicated to Jesus at this baptism ("You are my son . . .").

33. Reinhartz, *Jesus of Hollywood,* 103.

34. Reinhartz, *Jesus of Hollywood,* 104.

35. Reinhartz, *Jesus of Hollywood,* 104–9.

36. Even with an epic runtime of 382 minutes, there are just a few representative (?) miracles in Zeffirelli's *Jesus of Nazareth*— a miraculous catch of fish (cf. Luke 5:1–11), two different accounts of a healing of a paralyzed man (cf. Mark 2:1–12 and par.), the multiplication of loaves and fishes (cf. Mark 6:35–44 and par.; Mark 8:1–10 and par.; John 6:1–15), and the raising of Lazarus (cf. John 11).

events in the life of Jesus that should be classified as "pure mystery" which are "beyond portrayal, especially in an art form so tenuous and limited such as cinematography."[37] Zeffirelli mentions the Temptation of Jesus as an example of the limitations of film in portraying "mystery." While included as a scene in *Jesus of Nazareth,* the Temptation, Zeffirelli states, "was one of those instances in which the medium of film manifested its limitations. The effects were splendid [in the filmed scene of the Temptation], yes, but they seem contrived, ersatz, false."[38] He continues, comparing what can be communicated effectively in film versus theatre:

> Today we employ a very sophisticated medium [film] that, because it is mechanical, and because of its perfection (or imperfection in certain instances), doesn't help at all in communicating the incommunicable that say, the Delphic oracle, uttering disjointed and muted words through a mask [on a theatrical stage], was able to transmit to a predisposed and rapt viewer.[39]

Finally, it may be that a rather linear and unfolding approach to (some) Jesus film narratives might be a reason for the Transfiguration's omission. In their cinematic stories of the life of Jesus, filmmakers seem to present a rather "flat" understanding of their Jesus narratives, with their "straightforward" and linear stories occasionally (but only) looking ahead and finding their climax in the suffering, death, and resurrection of Jesus. However, to do so misses the rather sophisticated, somewhat non-linear approach to narrative that the Evangelists might have taken. Boring makes an important point about both the elusive genre of the Transfiguration and how the Marcan (and therefore Synoptic) narrative of the life of Jesus is constructed: "While the transfiguration is not a story of a specific resurrection retrojected into the pre-Easter life of Jesus, the Marcan narrative as a whole is indeed seen from the perspective of the risen Lord of the church's faith, so that there is a sense in which much of his narrative is a retrojection of post-Easter faith onto a pre-Easter screen."[40] As well, if a purpose of the Transfiguration is tied to its central location in the Synoptic Gospels, causing the reader to look both backwards and forwards in the narrative, it becomes less relevant to a flat, forward-moving, and unfolding cinematic narrative.

37. Zeffirelli, *Franco Zeffirelli's Jesus,* 80.

38. Zeffirelli, *Jesus,* 80.

39. Zeffirelli, *Jesus,* 81.

40. Boring, *Mark,* 261.

Conclusion

This essay has described the important role that the Transfiguration, despite its apparent strangeness and uniqueness, plays in the narratives of the Synoptic Gospels. Clearly, the Transfiguration is a central and essential element to these narratives in a variety of different ways, especially as it reveals important elements of the identity of Jesus and contributes to the Christology of each of the Synoptics. This essay has also suggested several reasons for why filmmakers almost exclusively have omitted this scene from their cinematic portrayals of a life of Jesus. Therefore, by omitting this scene, one can argue that these films, especially those films based on one or more of the Synoptic Gospels, present a picture of Jesus that is flat, incomplete, and often uninteresting. As such, one could make the cast that Jesus films have never—and will never—present portraits of Jesus that can be substitutes for those presented in the New Testament Gospels.

In her book on the Transfiguration, Dorothy Lee notes that while the trend in the (especially Western) church has been to ignore or downplay the significance of the story of the Transfiguration of Jesus, the times are changing for good.[41] For the Transfiguration, "with all its symbolic wealth, is a vitally important story in the New Testament, standing at the heart of Christian faith. Its pervasive presence in the Gospels and elsewhere, as well as its theological significance, gives it a central place in the faith and worship of the Church."[42]

As a result, Dorothy Lee reminds her readers (and reminds us, and perhaps filmmakers in the future) of the following (and it is appropriate to give her the last word):

> To recover the story, we need to recognize that the transfiguration is not an other-worldly narrative, disconnected from the body and ordinary human experience. On the contrary, it is precisely Jesus' transfigured body that discloses the face of God and the hope of God's future, addressing the concrete reality of a fearful, uncomprehending group of disciples and a tragic, unbelieving world. In the end, it is as much about their transfiguration, the luminous glory shining in the ordinariness of their flesh, as it is about Jesus' transformation. The transfiguration on the mountain is the meeting-place between human beings and God, between the temporal and the eternal, between past, present and future, between everyday human life—with all its hopes and fears—and the mystery of God. The attachment between them, at every point,

41. Lee, *Transfiguration*, 2.
42. Lee, *Transfiguration*, 137.

is Jesus himself. The transfiguration presents him dressed in the garments of divine light yet clothed also in the garb of creation. He is the point of intersection, the bridge between heaven and earth, the source of hope, bringing to birth—through incarnation' death, and resurrection—God's eschatological future.[43]

Appendix: Summaries of Transfiguration scenes in three Jesus films

The Life and Passion of Jesus Christ (1905)

Directed by Ferdinand Zecca and Lucien Nonquet, *The Life and Passion of Jesus Christ* is one of the earliest, if not the earliest, Jesus films. A silent film running some forty-four minutes in length, this film harmonizes different stories from the Synoptics and the Fourth Gospel, from the birth of Jesus through to his death and resurrection. As one might expect from silent films that portray the life of Jesus, there is very little from Jesus as a teacher and much more on Jesus as a miracle worker, with the Transfiguration concluding a series of miracle scenes in the film.

Located between the raising of Lazarus (John 11:1–44) and the Triumphal Entry into Jerusalem (Mark 11:1–10 par.), a title card introduces the Transfiguration, which is a scene that lasts no more than a minute (23m38s-24m33s), with stationary cinematography, typical of early silent films. Jesus is accompanied by three disciples (presumably Peter, James, and John) in a wilderness setting (the scene is filmed outdoors). Jesus climbs on top of a small rock pile, the three disciples then kneel. Jesus is then "transfigured"— his colored robes turn white, a (color-tinted) golden halo encircles his upper body, and Elijah appears on his right, and Moses on his left, achieved through the special effect of superimposing another exposure of these two characters over the characters of Jesus and the three disciples. Jesus acknowledges both Moses and Elijah, while the disciples are somewhat agitated and surprised by what they witness. After some dialogue between Jesus and the disciples, the disciples resume a posture of worship by kneeling, and Moses and Elijah disappear, and Jesus' pre-Transfiguration appearance reappears.

The Jesus Film (1979)

Relying on the Gospel of Luke, *The Jesus Film* (1979) was directed by Peter Sykes and John Krisch. Produced as an evangelistic resource for the

43. Lee, *Transfiguration*, 2.

evangelical organization Campus Crusade for Christ, the film's "cultural context," as Staley and Walsh put it, "is American Protestant evangelicalism," with the producers intending "the film to fulfill the Great Commission (Matt 28:16–20)."[44] With the film's screenplay relying almost exclusively on the Gospel of Luke, and with an omnipresent voice of a narrator who often paraphrases the Gospel, the film takes on a sort of "documentary" feel to it.[45]

Sandwiched between Jesus' first (but only) passion prediction (Luke 9:21–22) and teaching on the cost of discipleship (Luke 9:23–27) on the one hand, and the healing of the demoniac boy (Luke 9:37–43a) on the other, Sykes and Krisch portray the Transfiguration of Jesus. About ninety seconds in length (47m38s-49m17s), the scene begins with a long shot of four individuals (Jesus, Peter, James, and John) ascending a hillside. At the hilltop, the three disciples lie down to rest (in the middle of the day beneath a clear blue sky; but see Luke 9:32, which states that the disciples were "weighed down with sleep"). Jesus wanders away from them, but still stays within the same camera frame. Jesus looks back at the disciples, puts on his shawl in prayer, and turns his head (still in closeup) away from them. The narrator tells us that Jesus' "face changed in appearance" (following Luke 9:29), with an edited shot that has Jesus now dressed in a bright white shawl over his head and a white light shining on him.

In the next shot, the camera has pulled back, with Jesus (all in white), flanked by Moses on his right and Elijah on his left, both appearing somewhat out of focus, but brightly dressed, with the blue sky as background. One of them says to Jesus: "You will fulfill God's purpose"; the other says, "You will die in Jerusalem." (It is worth recalling that while the Synoptic Gospels all portray Jesus talking with Moses and Elijah [see Mark 9:4 par.], only Luke summarizes the content of that discussion.[46]) After both Elijah and Moses speak, the disciples awaken from their naps and witness the two of them fade into oblivion. Then in a still long shot, the three disciples flank Jesus, again with a blue sky as a background. A cloud envelops all four of them (and the entire frame of the shot), as the voice (of God) from heaven is heard (through the narrator): "This is my Son, the Chosen One. Listen to him" (Luke 9:35).[47]

---

44. Staley and Walsh, *Jesus, the Gospels, and Cinematic Imagination*, 95.

45. According to Staley and Walsh, some DVD versions of the film explicitly identify themselves as a "documentary" (Staley and Walsh, *Jesus, the Gospels, and Cinematic Imagination*, 96).

46. Luke 9:31: "[Moses and Elijah] appeared in glory and were speaking of his departure (ἔξοδος), which he was about to accomplish at Jerusalem."

47. Staley and Walsh describe the Transfiguration scene in *Jesus Film* as follows: "Sykes and Krisch confirm Jesus' first prophecy of his death and resurrection with the

The Visual Bible: Matthew (1993)

Running 265 minutes in length and directed by South African Regart van den Bergh, *The Visual Bible: Matthew* precedes *The Visual Bible: John* (2003), in what was intended to be part of a larger series of four Jesus films that were to be based completely, word-for-word, on each of the four New Testament Gospels (to date, only *John* and *Matthew* have been produced).[48] Thus, the "screenplay" for *The Visual Bible: Matthew* is essentially the New International Version (NIV), with much of the film being the Gospel writer's narration (read offscreen by actor Richard Kiley). As such, the Transfiguration scene is verbally faithful to the NIV at Matt 17:1–8, clocking in at about ninety seconds in length.

The scene begins with the three disciples clambering over some large rocks on their way up a hillside. On the top of the hill, they see the sole figure of Jesus (already transfigured), dressed in a bright white robe. Jesus' face is oriented upwards towards the sky, with his eyes closed and a big smile on his face. After a quick shot of the disciples below, the viewer sees a longshot (with the camera oriented upwards) of Jesus again, this time flanked by two hooded, white-robed figures (Moses and Elijah), followed by a close-up of the face of Peter, who offers to build three shelters. Then turning back to Jesus, Moses, and Elijah on the hilltop, the three figures embrace, and the mist of a cloud begins to envelope them. Then returning to the disciples, the voice from heaven is narrated by Richard Kiley, with the disciples hearing the voice as well, as they fall face-down towards the ground in fear (cf. Matt 17:6). And then, faithful to the NIV text of Matthew, Jesus comes back down the hill to the three disciples (Elijah and Moses have disappeared off-camera) and tells them to get up and not to be afraid.

---

transfiguration (9:28–36), a relatively rare scene in Jesus films. In extremely soft focus, Moses and Elijah stand beside Jesus, now in blindingly white clothing, and tell him that 'he will fulfill God's purpose and die in Jerusalem.' As a heavenly cloud descends, the narrator, again standing in for God, intones God's heavenly words of affirmation." (Staley and Walsh, *Jesus, the Gospels, and Cinematic Imagination*, 91–92).

48. Staley and Walsh noted the following in 2007: "The Visual Bible project (part of Visual Bible International, which is solely distributed by Thomas Nelson, one of the largest retailers of Bibles in the world) is now in bankruptcy; nevertheless, it managed to produce three Bible films before folding: *Gospel of Matthew* (1997) [*sic.*], *Book of Acts* (1994), and now, most recently, *the Gospel of John* [2003]. *Gospel of Mark* was in production when it was cancelled for financial reasons. It is highly unlikely that any more Visual Bible films will be produced" (*Jesus, the Gospels, and Cinematic Imagination*, 149).

Bibliography

Boobyer, G. H. *St Mark and the Transfiguration Story.* Edinburgh: T & T Clark, 1942.

Boring, M. Eugene. *Mark: A Commentary.* New Testament Library. Louisville: Westminster John Knox, 2006.

Bultmann, Rudolf. *History of the Synoptic Tradition.* Rev. ed. Peabody, MA: Hendrickson, 1963.

Burkett, Delbert. "The Transfiguration of Jesus (Mark 9:2–8): Epiphany or Apotheosis?" *JBL* 138 (2019) 413–32.

Chattaway, Peter T. "Could Moses have a cameo in the next *Bible* episode?" *Filmchat with Peter T. Chattaway.* March 23, 2013. https://www.patheos.com/blogs/filmchat/2013/03/could-moses-have-a-cameo-in-the-next-bible-episode.html.

Chilton, Bruce D. "Transfiguration." *The Anchor Bible Dictionary.* Edited by David Noel Freedman. New York: Doubleday, 1992. 6:640–42.

Dibelius, Martin. *From Tradition to Gospel.* Cambridge/London: James Clarke & Co. Ltd., 1971.

Hooker, Morna D. *The Gospel according to Saint Mark.* Black's New Testament Commentaries. Peabody, MA: Hendrickson, 1991.

Hurtado, Larry W. *Mark.* Peabody, MA: Hendrickson, 1989.

Lee, Dorothy. *Transfiguration.* New Century Theology. London/New York: Continuum, 2004.

Luz, Ulrich. *Matthew 8–20: A Commentary.* Hermeneia. Minneapolis: Fortress Press, 2001.

McCurley, F. R. "'And after six days' (Mark 9.2), a Semitic literary device." *JBL* 63 (1974) 67–81.

Reinhartz, Adele. *Jesus of Hollywood.* Oxford: Oxford University Press, 2007.

Riesenfeld, H. *Jésus Transfiguré.* Copenhagen: Munksgaard, 1947.

Staley, Jeffrey L., and Richard Walsh. *Jesus, the Gospels, and Cinematic Imagination: A Handbook to Jesus on DVD.* Louisville: Westminster John Knox, 2007.

Stein, Robert H. "Is the Transfiguration (Mark 9:2–8) a Misplaced Resurrection Account?" *JBL* 95 (1976) 79–96.

Stern, Richard C., Clayton N. Jefford, and Guerric DeBona. *Savior on the Silver Screen.* New York/Mahwah, NJ: Paulist Press, 1999.

Wikipedia. "Portrayal of Jesus in Film." https://en.wikipedia.org/wiki/Category:Portrayals_of_Jesus_in_film. (accessed 26-9-22).

Zeffirelli, Franco. *Franco Zeffirelli's Jesus: A Spiritual Diary.* San Francisco: Harper & Row, 1984.

18.

Ecce Homo
Jesus and the call to authenticity

CHRISTY CAPPER

Why Authenticity?

Authenticity is an idea that is popular within our culture, regularly promulgated by our media. However, while authenticity is often the subject of papers and chapters within Biblical studies and archaeology, this is not the type of authenticity discussed here; rather, this chapter will focus on the authenticity of the self. Authentic selfhood is not a binary concept, but a person normally grows and changes over the course of their life, so what may have been an authentic expression at one point may no longer be at another. Unlike an object or test, the authenticity of self is intrinsically subjective. While a piece of art may be verified as authentic or inauthentic and remains in that state, a person continues to grow and change throughout their life. Thus, their authentic expression will also change and develop, and that individual must continually explore the question of authenticity.

The 2010 research *Shaping Australia's Spirituality* completed by the Christian Research Association identified that "[o]ne of the greatest 'sins' identified by the younger generations is inauthenticity."[1] That inauthenticity can be identified as "sin" indicates that the concept of authenticity

---

1. Hughes, Reid, and Pickering, *Shaping Australia's Spirituality*, 77.

is highly regarded among younger Australians as a cultural value. More broadly, the number of texts published encouraging the pursuit of authenticity keeps growing.[2]

However, it is not only within modern Australia that authenticity is recognized as important. Indeed, Charles Taylor entitles the chapter on the present in *A Secular Age* as "The Age of Authenticity."[3] While Taylor explores the value of authenticity as expressed in ideas such as fashion and self-expression, attention is not paid to any theological understanding of the concept. Although Taylor's omission of a theological understanding of authenticity may be due to his background and philosophical focus, the decision of theologians to omit or ignore the concept of authenticity cannot be so easily bypassed.

While the concept of authentic selfhood tends to be simply ignored by many theologians, some do mention it but then dismiss it.[4] A common argument by critics of authenticity is that it is simply an excuse to do whatever one wants without the interference of other people.[5] Within popular Christian writing, arguments that the word "authenticity" fails to appear within the Scriptures are explored to explain why this is a dangerous concept and should not be taken seriously.[6] In the reception history of Scripture and Christian theology, theologians have attempted to interact and interpret the culture around them. This assumes even greater significance in our secular culture, as the church must be able to comprehend and relate to the community surrounding it to facilitate dialogue.[7] Understanding authenticity from a theological perspective is imperative to these discussions. Taylor points out that while there has been much debate around authenticity, it should

2. See for example Braman, *Meaning and Authenticity*; Burrowes, *Little Book of Authenticity*; Guignon, *On Being Authentic*; Inam, *Wired for Authenticity*; Joseph, *Authenticity*; Lindholm, *Culture and Authenticity*; Steinvorth, *Pride and Authenticity*; Thacker, *Art of Authenticity*.

3. Taylor, *Secular Age*, 473.

4. Wright, *Early Christian Letters for Everyone: James, Peter, John, and Judah, 8*. Note also the work of Rosner whose book *Known by God* (24–64) focuses on the Biblical theology of identity, the dismissal of authenticity as a topic worthy of conversation is problematic, not least because of the importance of theological discussion of ideas of high value within the surrounding culture. To dismiss the values of the culture around us is to fail to engage in a meaningful way missiologically and a failure to recognize the value of Incarnation within Christian theology and practice.

5. Taylor, *Ethics of Authenticity*, 21.

6. See, for example, De Young, "Christian Virtue in the Age of Authenticity"; Dorinai, "'Broken', 'Authentic', 'Surrender': The problem of Christian jargon"; McCracken, "Has Authenticity Trumped Holiness"; Josh Reibock, "Fighting for Authenticity"; Scrivener, "Problem with Authenticity"; Wax, "Discipleship in an Age of Authenticity," .

7. See Bosch, *Transforming Mission*, 483.

not focus on whether scholars support or reject the idea of authenticity but rather on its definition.[8] This statement is understandable. It is difficult to engage in lively discussion an idea without defining its scope.[9] Authentic selfhood is challenging, and many authors choose not to define it. Marina Oshana states, "The term 'authenticity' has been used with such frequency and such confidence in discussing the autonomy of persons that few have stopped to enquire exactly what is meant by them."[10] Trilling goes so far as to say that the term "may well resist such efforts of definition."[11] Before defining the concept of authentic selfhood, it is essential to lay out some foundation from a theological point of view.

Human Becoming

We have already noted that authenticity concerning a human person cannot be defined in a static fashion, rather, people normally continue to change and develop throughout their life. While this development is most noticeable during childhood, identity and self-expression are not unchangeable once a person reaches adulthood. John Macquarrie argues that the human being should instead be called a "human becoming," stating that "'[b]ecoming' suggests a process, transition, incompleteness, movement from non-existence into existence (or the reverse)."[12] Macquarrie argues that we become more fully human and more fully ourselves as we discover and actualize what that humanity is. However, is it not only that we grow, change, and discover our identity through the process of "becoming." For Macquarrie, the act of "becoming" is where the human person joins God in a creative role.[13] Macquarrie argues that

> [h]umanity is not a finished product. The human race is coming to be, living in history, seeking a goal which would be a fuller being, both for individuals and the whole race. At least within limits, this goal can be chosen, and humanity can determine what it is to become.[14]

8. Taylor, *Ethics of Authenticity*, 72–73

9. See Capper, *Theological Imperative to Authenticity*, for a more extensive analysis of these ideas.

10. Oshana, "Autonomy and the Question of Authenticity" *Social Theory and Practice* 33, 3: 413.

11. Trilling, *Sincerity and Authenticity*, 10–11.

12. Macquarrie, *In Search of Humanity*, 2.

13. Macquarrie, *In Search of Humanity*, 13–14.

14. Macquarrie, *In Search of Humanity*, 15.

The continuation of human growth and changing of self-understanding is a crucial aspect of human "becoming." It is both an individual and a communal activity, and it is as we shape ourselves that we also work to shape the world around us.[15] Thus for Macquarrie, this freedom to create and join God in the creation of ourselves and our world is where the image of God is most clearly revealed within humanity.

The Image of God

Across Christian history, the *Imago Dei* has been the focus of significant theological dispute; however, much of the debate has been over what the image of God *is* within the human person. The understanding that the human person, and humanity as a whole, is created in the image of God is generally accepted—Genesis 1:26–27 gives little room to reject the idea that human persons, and humanity as a whole, are created in the image of God.

When considering the concept of authentic selfhood, Taylor points to the need for the recognition of "horizons of significance"[16] and the ultimate horizon of significance is found in God and the understanding of the human person as created in the image of God. Thus, for the human person, authenticity must correlate with the character of God. Rather than being an excuse for moral relativism, authenticity becomes an expression of one's uniqueness within the context of one's creation in the image of God.

Here, Jesus Christ as the "image of the invisible God" takes precedence. Athanasius describes the importance of Jesus Christ to the human understanding of the image. He writes: "You know what happens when a portrait that has been painted on panel biomes is obliterated through external stains. The artist does not throw away the panel, but the subject of the portrait has to come and sit for it again, and then the likeness is re-drawn on the same material."[17]

Athanasius points to the consequences of sin, preventing the ability to clearly see the image of God and understand what it should look like in our lives. For Athanasius, this is a crucial reason for the Incarnation. Jesus Christ—the image of the invisible God—comes to re-sit for the portrait. By this, humanity understands what the image of God should look like in human persons.[18] When reading the Gospels and looking at the character of

15. Macquarrie, *In Search of Humanity*, 15.

16. Taylor, *Ethics of Authenticity*, 66.

17. Athanasius, *On the Incarnation*, 2.14.

18. By this, I mean to draw attention to the character of Jesus rather than the particularity of his embodied form.

Jesus Christ, we come to understand the God in whose image we are created and gain a better understanding of what it means to be human. It can be understood as both currently present in the human person and as the *telos* of humans, individually and corporately, to be the people God calls us to be. This is the overarching framework for human identity and authenticity.

Identity and the True Self

Authentic selfhood is, in some measure, being true to oneself, as Trilling says:

> Who would not wish to be true to his own self? True, which is to say loyal, never wavering in constancy. True, which is to say honest: there are to be no subterfuges in dealing with him. True, which is to say, as carpenters and bricklayers use the word, precisely aligned with him.[19]

Thus, for Trilling, authenticity is about honesty, loyalty to oneself and whom one perceives oneself to be. However, this understanding of being true to oneself has also prompted discussion around expressing one's "true self." One of the critiques of the concept of authenticity is that it seems to require an understanding of one's true self and that this understanding is difficult to achieve.[20] Additionally, the concept of the "true" self is problematic. As Anthony Rudd explains, we "needn't assume that there is only one way that I could be authentically myself—there may be several ways of life that I could adopt in which I could be true to who I most deeply am. But the range is not unlimited."[21] The focus on the concept of the "true" self suggests that each person has only one way of truly being themselves. However, Rudd's argument that a range of authentic expressions of oneself shows that one might better express this concept as that of the "true" *selves*. Our decisions regarding our self-expression and identity are exhibited in the multiple paths a person may take in their "becoming." There is more than one way to be oneself, there is not a singular "true" self, and yet there is a range of possibilities that is not endless.

19. Trilling, *Sincerity and Authenticity*, 4.
20. Rosner, *Known by God*, 24.
21. Rudd, *Self, Value and Narrative*, 30.

Identity and Narrative

Narrative identity formation helps with an understanding of who we are and what range of self-expression and self-understanding is possible, for as human persons, we live in a narrative context. As Gottschall writes, "story is for a human as water is for a fish—all-encompassing and not quite palpable."[22] In terms of identity, as Ricoeur explains, asking who a person is "is to tell the story of a life."[23] To explain one's identity is to tell the story of who we are and what has made us this way: to understand a continuity of identity in our life. For example, we might look back through photos of our childhood and find that the person depicted is "me" despite the physical, emotional, and developmental differences between the person we are now and the person we once were. We understand this as narrative intelligibility, recognizing a unity to life, and existing through the continuity of one's character. Without continuity, the character in our narrative becomes unintelligible.[24] MacIntyre explains:

> We should be puzzled, for example, by someone of whom we knew three things: first that he wanted to keep healthy, second that he had sincerely asserted *both* that to get cold and wet could be bad for his health *and* that the only way to keep warm and dry in winter was to wear his overcoat, and thirdly that he habitually went without his overcoat. For his action appears to express a belief inconsistent with his other expressed beliefs. Were anyone systematically inconsistent in this way, he or she would soon become unintelligible to those around them. We should not know how to respond to them, for we could no longer hope to identify either what they were doing or what they meant by what they said or both.[25]

Here we see the problem of understanding a person when their actions differ from their expressed beliefs, the credibility of the person must be questioned due to the break between claimed belief and action. So too, narrative understandings of identity formation are vital to authentic selfhood, for when a person's actions are not consistent with their expressed values, we may question that person's authenticity.

As humans who participate in our own "becoming," we are not only the subject of our narrative but also its narrator. As we tell the story of who

---

22. Gottschall, *Storytelling Animal*, xiv.

23. Ricoeur, *Time and Narrative*, 3:246.

24. Capper, *Theological Imperative to Authenticity*, 86.

25. MacIntyre, *After Virtue*, 161.

we are to ourselves and others, we interpret the events within our lives. Gottschall explains that "[a] life story is a carefully shaped narrative that is replete with strategic forgetting and skilfully spun meanings."[26] Telling and retelling stories, to ourselves and to others, utilizes current perspective to reinterpret past and current events, shaping them to fit our current self-understanding.

As human persons immersed in stories, we are formed not only by the stories that we tell ourselves but by the stories that we hear within our context and culture. The stories we tell in our socio-cultural context teach us the language and how to understand "what is right and wrong, good and bad, better and best."[27] Through the telling of fairy tales, Bible stories, and family legends, we understand how we function within the world and our place within it.

For all that we like to believe that we can do whatever we want to do with our lives, these stories shape us and can provide limitations for one's story. For women and people of color, for different socioeconomic groups, stories are often the voice of the powerful, showing people their proper place. The stories we read as children tell us what a hero looks like and what is possible for our particular group. Conversely, when we learn our role and place in society through narratives that show a limited representation of "people like us," the roles in which we can picture ourselves are limited. This is because our story does not begin with us.

The Social Human

Those who come before us and are involved in telling family and cultural narratives also show us that identity is socially driven. We come to understand who we are by comparing our narratives to those whose narratives are both similar and different to our own. In the contemporary West, one's identity is not simply given but discovered and built—achieved rather than ascribed.[28] Thus, there is the need for the person to participate in their identity formation, understand who they are and how they stand in relation to the world around them, and participate in their own "becoming." Taylor explains the importance of dialogue within identity formation, saying:

> My discovering my identity doesn't mean that I work it out in
> isolation but that I negotiate it through dialogue, partly overt,

26. Gottschall, *Storytelling Animal*, 161.

27. Capper, *Theological Imperative to Authenticity*, 92.

28. Lindholm, "Rise of Expressive Authenticity," 389.

partly internalised, with others. That is why the development of an ideal of inwardly generated identity gives a new and crucial importance to recognition. My own identity crucially depends on my dialogical relations with others.[29]

Taylor's instance that identity must be worked out in dialogue rather than in isolation is critical to understanding identity. McFadyen takes this further and points to the importance of engaging with God as a dialogue partner.

> Dialogue here means that, on God's side at least, there is respect for freedom and independence and an absence of overdetermination. In the mystery of God's grace, human beings are addressed as God's dialogue-partners. They are therefore free to make what response they will, and all they do and make of themselves is in fact a response to God.[30]

The willingness of God to engage in dialogue with human persons and respond in the formation of human identity is crucial to a Christian theology of identity formation. Indeed, we recognize that humanity is created in the image of a God who is Trinity, a God who exists in relationship. As Macquarrie explains, "[e]xistence is fundamentally communal in character, and without the others I cannot exist."[31] This is true not only in terms of human reproduction but also in terms of the formation of personhood and identity. Humanity requires community. As Marianne Hicks states, "In the perspective of Christian theology, to be human always means to be in relationship."[32]

However, being a person in relationship with others also has complexities. While we often share cultural and social values, each human is not the same as another. Each human person is also unique, even in physical existence. As Macquarrie says, "even their bodies bear a stamp of uniqueness—the human face, which seems to come in an infinite variety of forms and by which each human being can be recognised and named."[33] Here we see that while the uniqueness of the human person as a physical characteristic is an important aspect of human identification and understanding of different people's identities, human uniqueness does not stop with the physical. Each person has a unique potential, actualized through the process

29. Taylor, *Ethics of Authenticity*, 47–48.
30. McFadyen, *Call to Personhood*, 19.
31. Macquarrie, *Existentialism*, 75.
32. Hicks, *Our Search for Identity*, 2.
33. Macquarrie, *In Search of Humanity*, 84.

of "becoming." Each person is also unique in that their identity is formed through a combination of relationships, experiences, and other factors that are unique.

Without uniqueness there would be no desire for authenticity, for authenticity would not be questioned if all human persons were identical in body and character. There would be no discernible difference between persons, no discernible other, and no need to be involved in one's own "becoming."[34]

Definition of Authenticity

As a result, should we define authenticity? If the concept requires a definition prior to an argument regarding its usefulness, what should that definition be? My research into the theological imperative to authentic selfhood has resulted in the following definition: "Authenticity is to bring the fullness of one's unique, God-inspired self to life."[35]

This focus on the unique, God-inspired self emphasizes the importance of uniqueness which remains and has at its foundation the creation in the image of God. As such, each person is "a unique irreplaceable centre of freedom and creativity, engaged in his or her task of fashioning a unique human life-story."[36] The experiences of each person and their journey of "becoming" through their life extend their uniqueness throughout their lives.

Of course, the authenticity of a God-inspired self is grounded in the image of God, for those expressions that are not in God's character must be questioned. We bring the fullness of our unique, God-inspired self to God, who is the source of life and brings this self to flourishing, to fulfillment. It means continuing to "become" and to do so in recognition that we are in the company of God.

Christ and the Call to Life Abundant

When we consider a call to live authentically as a call to live fully—to bring the fullness of one's unique, God-inspired self to life—we can learn from Jesus regarding the fullness of life and life abundant. In John 10:10, Jesus states, "The thief comes only to steal and kill and destroy. I have come that

34. This is one of the reasons that authenticity is such a popular idea within the Western world where the understanding of the individual within the context is different to more communitarian cultures where this is not an issue.

35. Capper, *Theological Imperative to Authenticity*, 129.

36. Macquarrie, *In Search of Humanity*, 85.

they may have life, and have it abundantly." In *The Gospels Speak*, Lee explains the concept of life in the Gospel of John, stating: "In John's Gospel, everything is about the disclosure of life, eternal life. This life fills and makes meaningful the present moment, yet lasts for eternity. . .True life, for John, donates a rich and abundant sense of meaning to human life."[37] This understanding of life relates closely to the sense of "becoming" in the work of Macquarrie; coming from God, just as the potentialities within each person are given in creation. The process and work of "becoming" is a work with a *telos* extending into eternity, and yet it is this process and our participation within it that brings meaning and fullness to life in the present. As Jesus offers abundant life in John 10, he offers, as Lee explains, "authentic and copious life."[38] For Jesus Christ himself is the one in whom life exists, the life that is a light to all people (John 1:4). As Athanasius illustrates, by seeing the life and light of Jesus, we begin to understand what authentic life might look like, the life we were intended to live from the beginning, but which has been smudged or forgotten.

Jesus Christ as the one who demonstrates to us what being created in the image of God and being God is like, is central to the definition of authentic selfhood above. Life abundant is a life that contains both the highs and lows of being human, and yet, it is a life that God calls us to live. A life of both being and becoming the image of God, and by this, becoming more fully our unique selves is an essential aspect of life abundant. As we know and come to trust this God, revealed in the person of Jesus, so too can we bring the fullness of our God-inspired selves to this God, this Jesus, who is life and has life abundant to gift. The invitation of Christ to life abundant is an invitation to rediscover that which was lost. As Lee explains regarding the prologue of John's Gospel, "[h]uman beings are so separated from their Creator that they fail to recognise him, indicating a tragic disjunction not only from their Maker but also from their true, creaturely identity as children of God, made in the divine image."[39] Humanity has so forgotten both God and their divine image that they do not recognize Jesus as the exact image of this God. The invitation to life abundant is an invitation to live an authentic life as those unique persons, living in relationship with one another and with God.

To understand Jesus Christ as the image of God and what this might look like for humans to imitate, we must consider Jesus' relationship with others. As we have seen, human persons are social and relational, so an

37. Lee, *Gospels Speak*, 72.
38. Lee, *Gospels Speak*, 73.
39. Lee, *Creation, Matter and the Image of God*, 8.

understanding of how Jesus treated others and an examination of his relationships can tell us what it might look like for us to live a "God-inspired" life. It is also vital to consider that continuity is essential to understanding authenticity, as we have seen above in the illustration of the man who does not wear an overcoat despite his belief that he needs it. While there is no space within this essay to consider all of the relational dynamics within the Gospels, Lee states that "Jesus's own words and actions are obvious examples of ethical being and ethical behavior in self-donating, sacrificial love, which, as the footwashing demonstrates, consists in Jesus loving 'his own', even to 'the end.'"[40]

More so, we see the relationships that Jesus built with those neglected by society and his treatment of those cast out or dismissed by others. From choosing fishermen as disciples to dining with tax collectors, from speaking to the Samaritan woman at the well to first appearing to women after the resurrection, Jesus offered life and enlivened the life of others. He healed the blind and the lepers, he washed the feet of the disciples. Jesus preached of a kingdom where all are included and where liberation was a reality for all people.[41]

The offer of life abundant that Jesus made is authentic and genuine life. It is an offer to bring the fullness of our unique, God-inspired self to the God that is life, who enlivens and inspires us to live into the fullness of life and be the people God has created us to be.

Authenticity and the Need for Liberation

Although Jesus called many kinds of people to follow him and spoke to groups that were ignored or cast aside by society, it seems to be a human tendency to differentiate groups between "us" and "them." Life is more straightforward when hierarchy and uniformity exist, and we follow the rules and discourage diversity.

However, uniqueness is central to authenticity, and living authentically requires the freedom to have space to create identity and to create oneself through the narratives in our socio-cultural space and the stories of our community. However, this is also problematic, as Macquarrie discusses humanity's social and relational aspects and what it means to be a "being-with-others."

---

40. Lee, *Creation, Matter and the Image of God*, 39.

41. Schüssler Fiorenza, *Jesus: Miriam's Child, Sophia's Prophet*, 100.

> Authentic-being-with-others is precisely that mode of relation to the other that promotes existence in the full sense; that is to say, it lets the human stand out as human, in freedom and responsibility. On the other hand, inauthentic being-with-others supresses the genuinely human and personal. Whatever kind of relation to the others depersonalises and dehumanises is an inauthentic one. Thus, there is a paradox involved here. A purely individual existence is not possible and could not properly be called an 'existence'; yet existence with the others is to be judged to the degree that it lets individuals be free to become the unique persons that they are. True community allows for true diversity. Inauthentic being-with-others is the kind that imposes uniformity, perhaps in the name of a mistaken egalitarianism. Any kind of excellence is supressed.[42]

In our world, and even in our churches, inauthentic being-with-others—the kind of relationships that do not allow for true diversity or do not allow freedom—still exist and even abound. Thus, while a kind of egalitarianism is needed for authenticity to exist, it cannot be the kind that requires uniformity of people, whether this is uniformity of belief within religious systems, uniformity of dress, or uniformity of passion. Authentic being-with-others must value diversity. These kinds of communities will attract people, those where they have the freedom to be their unique selves rather than finding that uniformity is expected.[43]

For many of Australia's First People, the call of Christ was accompanied by a demand for Westernization. Aunty Rev. Denise Champion tells the story of the involvement of her people, the Adnyamathanha, and their return to celebrate the 80th year of the Nepabunna mission in 2012:

> I went back as one of the descendants of the Adnyamathanha peoples. That was where our faith journey too, of the Western understanding of Christianity, began. It was the United Aboriginal Mission that took care of the spiritual development of the Adnyamathanha people. Sadly, though, the missionaries said, 'You can come into the church but you must leave your culture at the door.' The mothers obeyed because they knew if they didn't do that, the children wouldn't get fed because the missionaries controlled the rations. But the fathers still went out to find work. Because my great grandfather Fred McKenzie, who was the head of ceremonial law, could see the dilemma of living

42. Macquarrie, *Existentialism*, 91.

43. McSkimming, *Leaving Christian Fundamentalism and the Reconstruction of Identity*, 229.

in two worlds, Adnyamathanha made the decision to bury the
law and after that our cultural ceremonial life ceased.[44]

The experience of the Adnyamathanha people is not unique, the church has given many non-Western people groups similar messages. They have been told that they must conform to a particular way of being to be Christians to be part of this being-with-others. The demand of Westernization resulted in the loss of identity for many indigenous groups, like the Adnyamathanha, who decided to bury their cultural life to stop the tension of living in two worlds. In this, the world and the church have lost some of the authentic being-with-others that might have been possible. They have forced out uniqueness and the possibility of authenticity for conformity from a fear of the unknown.

Macquarrie also points to the need for freedom in the development of identity and the recognition of uniqueness. If a person does not have some choices in their path forward, they will be limited in their "becoming." Often this limitation exists because of the expectations of our socio-cultural context. Marya Schechtman explores this, using the following illustration:

> Imagine a woman in a traditional American town in the 1950's who is wholeheartedly committed to fulfilling her duties as a wife and mother as understood by her social context. She is, however, frequently troubled by desires to take classes at the local college, spend time with friends, apply for part-time jobs, or get involved in political causes. As powerful and persistent as these desires are, this woman does her best to resist them. She views them as selfish and unfeminine, and struggles hard to keep them at bay.[45]

Here, society's expectations at this time are so ingrained within this woman that she struggles with her expressions of desire. She understands her role as a woman, as a wife and mother, to look a certain way, and she wants to be happy and satisfied with that. The boundaries of society and her expectations prevent her from fulfilling her desires and potentiality. While this woman may find peace with her decision to put these desires aside, it may also be that her "becoming" is inhibited by the lack of possibilities open to her role within this cultural context. She lacks the freedom to follow what seem to be perfectly reasonable desires because of the rigidity of gender roles within her cultural context. Schechtman suggests that coping with these desires may lead to depression and anxiety. Alternatively, she may

44. Champion, *Yarta Wandatha*, 17.
45. Schechtman, "Self-Expression and Self-Control," 417–418.

begin to follow her desires to study or work but find conflict with herself at her decision, feeling "out of control, at the mercy or irresistible forces."[46] For this woman, an expression of authenticity may involve the need to question her underlying assumptions and the cultural context in which she exists. Yet this may result in the breakdown of relationships with those she cares for as she struggles against feeling trapped or forced into a role in which she feels that she does not fit.

It is crucial to consider the cultural assumptions in the narratives that shape our lives. The woman in Schechtman's illustration is bound by the cultural narrative that tells her that her proper place is at home as a wife and mother. The stories she hears shape her in this understanding of herself and her role. Martin and Sugarman explain that the relationships and stories that we learn help us to understand what possibilities are open to us, that the way that human persons "talk and relate to one another" and the language that is used act to constrain our understanding of the opportunities that are open to us based in ethical and moral terms.[47] The use of language also tells us who is included and excluded. There are references to "man" in several quotes from sources within this essay. I have left them true to their original authors. However, this language is important. As Chittister explains, "Language is not a trivial issue. Language is the ultimate delete."[48]

The ability to act as authentic human persons also requires agency to see oneself in a new role and have the freedom and opportunity to move towards it. As Xiao explains, "[s]elves can become—and be—autonomous selves, genuine moral *agents*, only to the degree that their autonomy is recognized by others."[49] This ability to be a "genuine moral *agent*" is limited by society's views and by the understanding of the individual themselves. When one does not have the freedom to make decisions and engage their deep passions and desires, their own "becoming" is limited. In the definition of authenticity above, the ethical and moral aspects of authenticity are limited by understanding the human person as both being and becoming the "*God-inspired* self," yet other limitations exist. Making one decision about a path in life can often mean foregoing another; however, this does not necessarily stop the full expression of authenticity, instead it allows some possibilities to have space to grow to their full potential.

46. Schechtman, "Self-Expression and Self-Control," 418.

47. Martin and Sugarman, "Bridging Social Constructionism and Cognitive Constructionism," 299.

48. Chittister, *Awakenings*, 47.

49. Xiao, "Feminist Concept of Self and Modernity," 120.

How then can we decide which possibilities to actualize and which to forego? In discussing the question of actualizing different possibilities, John Macquarrie states the following:

> [C]an we say that Christ's fullness or perfection is attributed to him because he gave up all other possibilities for the sake of the most distinctively human possibility of all, and that one that has most claim upon all men, namely, self-giving love? And can we also say that because this love is the most creative thing in human life (for it brings men freedom and personhood), then Christ manifests the "glory of man" by becoming transparent to the ultimate creative self-giving source of all, to God.[50]

Here Macquarrie echoes the call within the Scriptures and the tradition to a self-giving love, a kenotic love that gives itself. However, self-giving love has often been understood to encourage the forgoing of selfhood, the laying down oneself. However, to have a self to lay down, we must first have a fully developed identity and self-understanding. Christ's call to "love one another as you love yourself" assumes a love of self. The call for self-giving love has impacted women and minorities by keeping them subservient and focused on helping the dominant members of society fulfill themself and aid their own "becoming" at the cost of one's own. Here, the call to self-giving love is a call to understand and "become" oneself so that within a community, one may contribute and love others through the pouring out and giving of one's gifts, skills, and personality, rather than the call to a less developed "unique, God-inspired self."

Rather than using the call to self-giving love as a limitation to specific groups of people, it must be used as a call to live life in orientation to others. McFadyen argues, "personal existence means living beyond one's borders in an orientation to others, to be in the other and to understand oneself from the perspective of the other."[51] Understanding self-giving love as living in this kind of self-giving community, where there is mutual understanding and empathy, is necessary for authentic selfhood to flourish. When only one group of people benefit from the self-giving love of others without a commitment to "be in the other and understand oneself from the perspective of the other," individuals are more likely to be marginalized and unable to fully develop their sense of self.

Freedom is never complete; we are always bound by the world we live in. MacIntyre explains: "[W]e are never more (and sometimes much less)

---

50. Macquarrie, *Three Issues in Ethics*, 88.

51. McFadyen, *Call to Personhood*, 29.

than co-authors of our narratives. Only in fantasy do we live as we please."[52] However, this does not mean all people have the same levels of agency within our society to engage in co-authoring their narratives.

It is difficult to see people of color and women in leadership positions in Western nations, even within the Christian church, whether this is through glass ceilings or public doctrinal statements. As Lee explains,

> much of it is due to an implicit racism within white communities and the difficulties indigenous women and women of colour find in attempting to break through racial and cultural barriers. The issue of women's ministry challenges not only male dominance but equally white dominance. Racism and misogyny are potent coworkers in this equation and make the marginalization more extreme and painful for women of colour than for white women.[53]

The link between racism and sexism within the church is not myth—it exists. However, that these barriers impact all women and people of color is significant, and for those who themselves are in the intersection of these groups the barriers faced are multiplied. Thus, any advocacy of justice-making that aims for the liberation of these groups to pursue authentic becoming must be intersectional. We cannot deal with complex justice issues without complex and intersectional approaches, and without challenging and breaking through these barriers to inclusion in leadership, the representation of whole Kingdom of God through the church will never be full or authentic.

Chittister explains that inclusion is crucial because "the Christian community will never be whole, and its discipleship will never be authentic."[54] Without representation from these groups at all levels, without valuing their potentiality and diversity and unique gifts being shared, we can never consider a community to be encouraging authenticity.

The orientation of Christ toward those who were marginalized and lacked opportunities and freedom within society shows that we, too, as followers of Jesus, must act in an orientation towards others. It must be the church's work to break down barriers and enable authentic being-with-others, which liberates people and creates space for human flourishing through the work of "becoming." For it is only when all people can bring the fullness of our unique, God-inspired selves to life that the Christian community,

52. MacIntyre, *After Virtue*, 199.

53. Lee, *Ministry of Women in the New Testament*, 3.

54. Chittister, *Awakenings*, 33.

and society, can begin to truly see the diverse and beautiful community that images our creative and loving God.

Bibliography

Athanasius, *On the Incarnation*. Translated by John Behr. Yonkers, N.Y.: St Vladimir's Seminary Press, 2011.

Bosch, David. *Transforming Mission: Paradigm Shifts in Theology of Mission*. Maryknoll, New York: Orbis Books, 1991.

Braman, Brian J. *Meaning and Authenticity: Bernard Lonergan and Charles Taylor on the drama of authentic human existence*. Toronto: University of Toronto Press, 2008.

Burrowes, Nina. *The little book on authenticity*. London: NB Research Ltd., 2014.

Capper, Christy. *The Theological Imperative to Authenticity*. New York: Routledge, 2023.

Champion, Denise with Rosemary Dewerse. *Yarta Wandatha*. Salisbury, South Australia: Denise Champion, 2014.

Chittister, Joan. *Awakenings: Prophetic Reflections*. Mulgrave, Victoria: Garratt, 2022.

De Young, Kevin. "Christian Virtue in the Age of Authenticity." *The Gospel Coalition*, September 9th, 2015. https://www.thegospelcoalition.org/blogs/kevin-deyoung/christian-virtue-in-the-age-of-authenticity/

Dorinai, Dan. "'Broken', 'Authentic', 'Surrender': The problem of Christian jargon." *The Gospel Coalition*, November 12th, 2018. https://www.thegospelcoalition.org/article/broken-authentic-surrender-problem-christian-jargon/

Gottschall, Jonathan. *The Storytelling Animal: How Stories Make Us Human*. New York, USA: First Mariner Books, 2012.

Guignon, Charles B. *On Being Authentic*. London, UK: Routledge, 2004.

Hicks, Marianne H. *Our Search for Identity: Humanity in the image of God*. Philadelphia: Fortress Press, 1982.

Hughes, Philip; Stephen Reid and Claire Pickering. *Shaping Australia's Spirituality: A review of Christian ministry in the Australian context*. Preston, Victoria: Mosaic Press, 2010.

Inam, Henna. *Wired for Authenticity: seven practices to inspire, adapt & lead*. Bloomington, Indiana: iuniverse, 2015.

Joseph, Stephen. *Authenticity: How to be yourself and why it matters*. London: Piakus, 2016.

Lee, Dorothy A. *The Gospels Speak: Addressing Life's Questions*. New York, Paulist Press, 2017.

———. *Creation, Matter and the Image of God: Essays on John*. Adelaide: ATF, 2020.

———. *The Ministry of Women in the New Testament: Reclaiming the Biblical Vision for Church Leadership*. Grand Rapids, Michigan: Baker Academic, 2021.

Lindholm, Charles. *Culture and Authenticity*. Oxford: Blackwell, 2008.

Lindholm, Charles. "The Rise of Expressive Authenticity" *Anthropology Quarterly* 86, no 2 (2013) 361–396.

McCracken, Brett. "Has Authenticity Trumped Holiness." *The Gospel Coalition*, January 26th, 2014. https://www.thegospelcoalition.org/article/has-authenticity-trumped-holiness-2/

McFadyen, Alistair. *The Call to Personhood: A Christian Theory of the Individual in Social Relationships*. Cambridge, UK: Cambridge University Press, 1990.

McSkimming, Josie. *Leaving Christian Fundamentalism and the Reconstruction of Identity*. New York: Routledge, 2017.

MacIntyre, Alasdair C. *After Virtue: a study in moral theory*. Notre Dame, Indiana: University of Notre Dame Press, 2007.

Macquarrie, John. *Existentialism*. New York, N.Y.: Penguin Books, 1973.

———. *In Search of Humanity*. London: S.C.M. Press, 1993.

———. *Three Issues in Ethics*. London: S.C.M Press, 1967.

Martin, Jack and Sugarman, Jeff. "Bridging Social Constructionism and Cognitive Constructionism: A Psychology of Human Possibility and Constraint" in *The Journal of Mind and Behaviour*, 17:4 (Autumn 1996) 291–319.

Oshana, Marina. "Autonomy and the Question of Authenticity" in *Social Theory and Practice* 33:3 (2007) 411–429.

Reibock, Josh. "Fighting for Authenticity." *Relevant,* October 1st, 2007. https://relevantmagazine.com/god/deeper-walk/features/1292-fighting-for-authenticity

Ricoeur, Paul. *Time and Narrative vol.3*. Translated by Kathleen Blamey and David Pellauer. Chicago: University of Chicago Press, 1988.

Rosner, Brian S. *Known by God: A Biblical Theology of Personal Identity*. Grand Rapids, Michigan: Zondervan, 2017.

Rudd, Anthony. *Self, Value, and Narrative: a Kierkegaardian Approach*. Oxford: Oxford University Press, 2012.

Schechtman, Marya. "Self-Expression and Self-Control" *Ratio* 17:4 (2004) 410–427.

Schüssler Fiorenza, Elisabeth. *Jesus: Miriam's Child, Sophia's Prophet: Critical Issues in Feminist Christology*. Second Edition. London: Bloomsbury, 2015.

Scrivener, Emma "The Problem with Authenticity." *The Gospel Coalition*, September 7th, 2017. https://www.thegospelcoalition.org/article/the-problem-with-authenticity/

Steinvorth, Ulrich. *Pride and Authenticity*. Cham: Springer International Publishing House, 2016.

Taylor, Charles. *The Ethics of Authenticity*. Cambridge, Mass: Harvard University Press, 1992.

Taylor, Charles. *A Secular Age*. Cambridge, Mass: Belknap Press, 2007.

Thacker, Karissa. *The Art of Authenticity: tools to become an authentic leader and your best self*. Hoboken, New Jersey: Wiley, 2016.

Trilling, Lionel. *Sincerity and Authenticity*. Cambridge, Mass: Harvard University Press: 1972.

Walker, Esther. "Good Night Stories for Rebel Girls—a revolution at bedtime," *The Times,* November 26th, 2017. https://www.thetimes.co.uk/article/good-night-stories-for-rebel-girls-a-revolution-at-bedtime-k8clzwlmv

Wax, Trevin, "Discipleship in an Age of Authenticity," *The Gospel Coalition*, November 10th, 2014. https://www.thegospelcoalition.org/blogs/trevin-wax/discipleship-in-the-age-of-authenticity/

Wright, N.T. *The Early Christian Letters for Everyone: James, Peter, John and Judah*. London: SPCK, 2011.

Xiao Wei. "The Feminist Concept of Self and Modernity." *Diogenes* 56:1 (2009) 117–27.

19.

"It is accomplished!"

Perfection and Accomplishment in J. S. Bach's John Passion

KATHERINE FIRTH AND ANDREAS LOEWE

Introduction

The *John Passion* (BWV 245, 1724) by Johann Sebastian Bach (1685–1750) sets to music chapters 18–19 of the Gospel according to St John, complementing the Gospel text with reflective hymns and contemporary devotional poetry. The movement that marks the turn to the final part of Bach's *John Passion, Es ist vollbracht* (movement 30), explores the Johannine paradox of the completion and perfection of Christ's work being achieved through his brokenness on the cross.[1] This chapter provides a reading of the music and text of the movement, in the context of the oft-repeated descriptions of Bach's music in terms of completeness, accomplishment, or perfection.[2] The same words can also be used to translate Christ's final word from the cross in the Gospel of John, "τετέλεσται" (*tetélestai*): "it is finished/accomplished," "es ist vollbracht" (John 19:30). In this chapter, we relate the idea of completion as played out in Bach's musical interpretation of Christ's journey

---

1. For other close readings of this aria, see Wolff, *Bach's Musical Universe*, 207–47; Loewe, *Theological Commentary*, 267–73.

2. For example, Wolff, *The Learned Musician*; Wolff *Bach's Musical Universe*.

to the cross by entering into conversation with Dorothy Lee's studies *Flesh and Glory* (2002) and *Transfiguration* (2004).

As we have demonstrated extensively elsewhere, Bach's theological understanding significantly influenced the textual choices he made in collaboration with an unknown librettist-editor, as well as the music he composed; thereby setting orthodox Lutheran theology as "sermons in sound."[3] Likewise, Bach's audience would have had some degree of theological erudition. The churchgoers attending St. Thomas's and St. Nikolai Leipzig were educated by their own participation as listeners of Bach's weekly *Musique*, the cantata he composed and performed to provide a musico-theological reflection on the set Scripture readings for that Sunday. Bach provided printed libretto booklets of these cantatas to subscribers.[4] In addition, as part of their worship, the congregation would also have had access to Luther's Bible translation, as well as to the explication of the Bible in Lutherans hymns and sermons. At home, they may well have owned, like Bach himself, personal collections of religious commentaries and poetry collections.[5]

Eric Chafe, in his *J. S. Bach's Johannine Theology: The St. John Passion and the Cantatas for Spring 1725*, affirms that in the *John Passion*, Bach explores a Christus Victor approach to the atonement, as a "drama of stark oppositions: light versus darkness, good versus evil."[6] German theologians of Bach's time regularly used contrasting tropes of high and low to understand the paradox of the crucifixion; what Martin Luther called the "glory" and "majesty" versus the "humility" and "ignominy" of the cross.[7]

---

3. Loewe, "Sermons in Sound," 1–11; Loewe, "God's Capellmeister," 141–71; and Loewe, *Theological Commentary*, 100–34. All translations of Bach's libretto are taken from Firth, "Study Translation," 100–34; Loewe, "Christology of Bach's St John Passion," 79–90. See also Firth and Loewe, "Johannine Glory in Bach's St John Passion," in Derrenbacker, Lee and Porter, *Enduring Impact of the Gospel of John, 144–160.*

4. Loewe, *Theological Commentary*, 16.

5. Loewe, *Theological Commentary*, 66. For more on Luther's approach to church music, see Loewe and Firth, "Mighty Fortress," 124–7; Loewe and Firth, *Luther and the Arts*, chapter 2.

6. Chafe, *Bach's Johannine Theology*, 113, draws on Gustaf Aulén's classification of atonement theory of the same name, *Christus Victor*. See further Chafe, *Analyzing Bach Cantatas*, 23–41; Pelikan, "Christus Victor in the Saint John Passion," 106.

7. The word ἐκένωσεν (*ekénōsen* is a form only used in Philippians 2:7. Cognate versions in Romans 4:14; 1 Corinthians 1:17, 9:15; and 2 Corinthians 9:3 are about making a power or promise "empty" or "void," while the classical Greek form suggests something more like "purging" or "waning." The Lutheran theologian Johann Jakob Rambach, whose *Betrachtungen* Bach owned, interpreted Philippians 2:7 in terms of Christ "exchang[ing] greatest glory for deepest lowliness, / utmost bliss for greatest sorrow / and highest pleasure for utmost pain" (*die höchste Ehre mit der tieffsten Schmach / die höchste Freude mit der grösten Traurigkeit / die höchste Vergnügung mit den äussersten*

The inspiration for the aria text that forms the basis for this movement is a poem attributed to the Leipzig and Hamburg librettist Christian Heinrich Postel.[8] However, the text used in the *Passion* substantially changes the poem: not much remains of Postel's otherwise generic poetic reflection on the death of Christ apart from the overall theme, the rhyme scheme and meter, and the final line. The *Passion's* librettist-editor was making intentional theological and artistic choices which, in turn, are matched by Bach's intentional theological and artistic compositional choices. In this chapter, we make use of our own 2014 scholarly translation and commentary, *Johann Sebastian Bach's St. John Passion: A Theological Commentary*, to elucidate further the paradox, in John's Gospel and Bach's *Passion*, of perfection in brokenness.

Christ's Perfection and Accomplishment

The concluding word of our aria, *vollbracht*, "τετέλεσται" (*tetélestai*), is itself the bearer of this paradox. The full range of its double meaning is intended by John and by Luther and is exploited by Bach's setting. Jesus is "done": his life is "over." His work is also "complete": the prophecies are "fulfilled," and he has "successfully carried out" his mission. In explaining why it is that the soldiers are gambling for Jesus's clothing in John 19:23–24b, John points to the fulfillment of the Old Testament prophecies by quoting Psalm 20:19. As he asks for a drink, Jesus does so in the knowledge that he was doing so "to fulfill Scripture." Τελειωθῇ (*teleiōthē*) here may be read as "completed," (v. 28b), whereas "now all things had been accomplished," τετέλεσται (*tetélestai*), has the meaning of "it has been made," "the preparations have led to the thing being built," "it has been wrought" (v. 28b).[9] As he breathes his last, Jesus dies with the word τετέλεσται (*tetélestai*) on his lips (v. 30b).

This is the word that, in John 19:28b and 30b, Luther translates into German as "*vollbracht*."[10] The German word has component root parts that suggest a sense of being "brought to fullness:" to be completed, to be accomplished, to be perfected. While some modern English translations of

---

Schmertzen/ zu verwechseln, 98). For Rambach's work in Bach's theological library, see Leaver, *Bachs theologische Bibliothek*, 121, 150.

8. Postel's poem was used in two earlier Passion oratorios, Johann Mattheson's *Das Lied des Lammes* and the *St John Passion* by Hamburg composer Christian Ritter (c. 1645–1725).

9. Lee, *Flesh and Glory*, 46: "Jesus' knowledge that all things have been 'accomplished' (*tetélestai*), including that of Scripture (*teleiōthē*)19:28), and . . . Jesus' last utterance in this Gospel: 'It is accomplished.'"

10. Also, πληρωθῇ (*plērōthē*) which translates as "fulfilled," (v. 24), Luther uses *erfüllet*.

John 19:30 also render τετέλεσται (*tetélestai*) as "completed,"[11] the majority use "finished."[12] According to the *Oxford English Dictionary* "finished" gives us two contradictory senses:

> To complete the destruction of; to dispatch, kill. Also in a weaker sense: To complete the discomfiture or defeat of; to reduce to complete exhaustion or helplessness; or To perfect finally or in detail; to put the final and completing touches to. . . To complete or perfect the education of.[13]

Thus, to be "finished" can mean to be summarily dispatched, or to be polished to a high gleam. While the etymology of our English words "completion" and "accomplishment" and "finish" are aligned to this biblical meaning, in our everyday language, they do not have quite the right weight.[14] One "completes" or "finishes" tasks on a to-do list; "accomplishments" imply the ability to play the piano or fold napkins. The *telos*, however, is the ultimate goal or aim, one does not tick a *telos* off a list, or applaud a *telos*. Rather, to achieve a *telos* is almost beyond human power; in fact, Aristotle considers a *telos* to be beyond the grasp of any single organism, more like an eternal striving by a species.[15] In *On the Soul* (II, 415b. ll. 10–16), Aristotle claims that "ἔτι τοῦ δυνάμει ὄντος λόγος ἡ ἐντελέχεια" (*éti toū dunámei óntos lógos hē entelécheia*—clearly the soul is also the cause [*lógos*] in the final [*télos*] sense); while in John's Gospel, in the beginning, is the *logos* (John 1:1), and in the end is the *telos* (John 19:30b). For this reason, in this chapter, we have translated *vollbracht* and "τετέλεσται" sometimes as "brought to fullness" and sometimes simply as "perfection."

11. Notably, Mounce Interlinear and the New English Translation.

12. Among them, NIV, ESV, RSV, and Geneva.

13. "finish, v.," *OED Online*, senses 1–3 (end something) and sense 4 (perfect something).

14. "Finished," from the Latin *finis* (end); "accomplish" and "complete" from the Latin *complēre* (to fill up, finish, fulfill). "complish, v.," *OED Online*; "complete, adj.," *OED Online*.

15. Aristotle, *Physics*, II. III.1 95a, lines 24–26: "τὰ δ' ὡς τὸ τέλος καὶ τἀγαθὸν τῶν ἄλλων· τὸ γὰρ οὗ ἕνεκα βέλτιστον καὶ τέλος τῶν ἄλλων ἐθέλει εἶναι" (*ta d' hōs to telos kai tagathon tōn allōn to gar hou heneka beltiston kai telos tōn allōn ethelei einai*—And finally, there is the goal or *end* in view, which animates all the other determinant factors as the best they can attain to; for the attainment of that "for the sake of which" anything exists or is done is its final and best possible achievement); *Physics*, II. VIII. 199b, lines 15–16: "φύσει γάρ, ὅσα ἀπό τινος ἐν αὑτοῖς ἀρχῆς συνεχῶς κινούμενα ἀφικνεῖται εἴς τι τέλος" (*physei gár, hosa apó tinos en autois arches sunechōs kinoumena aphikneitai eis ti telos*—For natural things are exactly those which do move continuously, in virtue of a principle inherent in themselves, toward a determined goal).

Yet in the sense of *vollbracht* and "τετέλεσται" is always the Johannine paradox of brokenness alongside completion, at the point of the crucifixion, as Dorothy Lee clarifies in *Transfiguration*:

> In John's understanding, the cross is not the low point of Jesus' ministry . . ., but the high point, a lifting up, a moment of glory and radiance (3:13–15; 12:32; 13:31–2).[16]

In Lee's reflection on the crucifixion in *Flesh and Glory*, she points out that the language of *télos* echoes the language used by the evangelist in the story of the Samaritan woman, where Jesus assures the woman: "my food is to do the will of the one who sent me to accomplish his work" (*teileiōsō*) John 4:34).[17]

In Lee's reflection on Jesus' death, she focuses on Jesus' word from the cross, "I thirst" (John 19:28b), as he is given some *oxous*, or verjuice, on a hyssop reed.[18] Both in his meeting with the Samaritan woman at the beginning of John's Gospel, and his discussion with his disciples while the woman is away in the city collecting her friends, Jesus points out to his interlocutors that they do not know of the food or drink he is talking about. Jesus contrasts physical food and drink with the much superior heavenly water and meals. Real water is fine, but if you drink it, you will soon be thirsty again (John 4:13–14); real food is fine, but it is better to be filled by carrying out your calling (John 4:32–34).

According to the synoptic gospels, on the day before the crucifixion, Jesus had fully explained that his own body was the food and drink of eternal life (Matt 26:17–29; Mark 14:12–25; Luke 22:7–38). In John's Gospel, in contrast, this truth is made known in Christ's "farewell discourses" in John 13–17. It is, therefore, only at the final moment of revelation on the cross, that Christ merges his physical thirst with the symbolic, Lee argues. At the point of the crucifixion, all is revealed, all is being made known (2 Cor 4:1–6), including the true meaning of food and drink.

> The Son glorifies the Father by revealing the radical nature of God's love . . . revealing the glory which is the meaning of his life and death.[19]

---

16. Lee, *Transfiguration*, 109.

17. Lee, *Flesh and Glory*, 46.

18. In the *Passion*, this moment is only set in the recitative. The continuo resolves, for a moment on F-sharp major, and Loewe, *Theological Commentary*, 267, suggests that the upward movement of the hyssop reed is sketched in the music with the rising minor sixth on *dar* (*up to*).

19. Lee, *Transfiguration*, 109.

Here Jesus is not only metaphorically thirsty and hungry for eternal life and God's will, but also physically thirsty.[20] And yet even in his thirst, he chooses to ensure that absolutely everything was accomplished to fulfill the Scriptures by echoing Psalm 22:15: "my mouth is dried up like a potsherd, and my tongue sticks to my jaws"; as well as king David's plea, "purge me with hyssop and I shall be clean" (Ps 51:7). As Jesus had earlier set out in the Beatitudes, "Blessed are those who hunger and thirst for righteousness, for they will be filled" (χορτασθήσονται, *chortasthēsontai*). The "completion" of the task of salvation is thus accomplished by offering the one acceptable sacrifice (Ps 51:18–19) so that "posterity will serve him; future generations will be told about the Lord, and proclaim his deliverance to a people yet unborn, saying that he has done it" (Ps 22:30–1).

"Paradoxically, the crucified body of Christ becomes an icon of life and glory," as Lee reminds us.[21] Icons give physicality to faith, whether made of paint or any other media, which "makes present" the perfection of Christ that otherwise is beyond human knowledge (Rom 1:20, Heb 11:1).[22] The εἰκών/icon has been described as "theology in color" by Orthodox theologians.[23] Another icon that demonstrates this perfection, by attempting in some way to match—however incompletely—Christ's own accomplishment on the cross by exploring this very paradox, is Bach's "sermon in sound," the *St. John Passion*.

Perfection and Accomplishment of, and in, the John Passion

The canonical status of the music of Johann Sebastian Bach as the epitome of baroque music, and one of the greats of western classical music, hardly needs rehearsing.[24] Yet, if we are to speak of perfection and accomplishment, we must do so here. Bach was fully aware of his own talent and

20. As Lee, *Flesh and Glory*, 46, puts it, "thirst is symbolic not just of the Samaritan woman's need for 'living water' (John 4:10) but also of Jesus' mission and of that unity of love and purpose binding together Father and Son."

21. Lee, *Transfiguration*, 110.

22. Ouspensky, *Theology of the Icon*, 199: "The image, as we know, expresses the same thing as the word . . . by using forms, lines and colors, a language of artistic symbols, and their evidence is just as truthful," see further Ouspensky, Lossky, *Meaning of Icons*, 26

23. Trubetskoi, *Icons: Theology in Color*, 28: "Our religious art expresses this joy not in words but in marvelous colorful visions." Liddell, Scott, and Jones, *Greek-English Lexicon*, 485; and Sophocles, *Greek Lexicon*, 423, define εἰκών/*eikon* as "image," "likeness," "representation," and "depiction" respectively.

24. For example, see Buelow, *History of Baroque Music*, 503–59; Wolff and Emery, "Bach, Johann Sebastian," *Grove Music Online*.

achievements. Bach once characterized cantatas "of my own composition" as "incomparably harder and more intricate" than those of his contemporary composers, "conveying," as Wolff puts it, "that his works were 'harder' to perform and 'more intricate' in their construction."[25] Already during his lifetime, and since at least 1738, Bach has been credited with "musical perfection."[26] Bach's contemporaries, notably Johann Abraham Birnbaum and Johann Friedrich Agricola, were in awe of his abilities, in

> composing music in which practice and theory coalesce, in which original thought, technical exactitude, and aesthetic beauty become congruent, all with the ultimate purpose—as the *Clavier-Übung* dedications put it—of the 'renewal of the soul.'[27]

What is more, Bach's abilities ranged across musical styles, "from simple dance to strict canon, from two-part to multiple-voice counterpoint, from instrumental and vocal to mixed scores."[28]

Commentators such as Wolff consider this achievement "natural, uncontrived, and truly effortless," while others (ourselves included) have tended to see the achievement as the outcome of deep study and refined technique.[29] Bach's extensive understanding of church and secular music, performance capacity, and Lutheran theology enabled him to mobilize these aspects to produce complex works that reward careful analysis. As Wolff explains, "it was Bach's highly personal and unorthodox approach to composition that resulted in music so exemplary, superlative and transcendent."[30] It may, therefore, be noted that Bach's own music can be described as achieving a status of being "brought to fullness" or perhaps simply as "brought to perfection" (*vollbracht*/τετέλεσται/*tetélestai*).

In Bach's *John Passion, Es ist vollbracht* (movement 30), is sandwiched in the middle of the verse in John's telling of the crucifixion of the crucial moment of Christ's death, *Es ist vollbracht! und neigte das Haupt und verschied*—"it is accomplished! [brought to fullness or completion] and bowed his head and expired [breathed his last]" (John 19:30a and 30b). In the aria, the librettist-editor comments on the cross event, Christ accomplished the victory over death and sin, enabling all people to enter into eternal life with God: *Der Held aus Juda siegt mit Macht / und schließt den Kampf / Es ist*

---

25. Wolff, *Bach's Musical Universe*, 336.

26. Wolff, *Bach's Musical Universe*, 338; Wolff, *Learned Musician*, 470; and Wolff, *New Bach Reader*, 347.

27. Wolff, *Bach's Musical Universe*, 338.

28. Wolff, *Bach's Musical Universe*, 338; Wolff, *New Bach Reader*, 347–8, 358.

29. Wolff, *Bach's Musical Universe*, 338.

30. Wolff, *Bach's Musical Universe*, 341.

vollbracht—"the hero of Judah triumphs with power / And concludes the conflict. / It is accomplished!" (movement 30).[31]

The composer and librettist-editor continually bring together this paradox in the section of the Passion story focusing on the cross (movements 19–31), starting from the moment Jesus was crowned with thorns and striped with lashes in the *Herzstück* (central point) of Bach's *John Passion* (movements 19 and 20). The "heaven-key-flowers blossom" from Jesus's forehead bruised by thorns (movement 19); the bloody stripes on Jesus' back are the rainbow "sign of God's mercy" (movement 20); Jesus's imprisoning "dungeon" is also "the throne of mercy" (movement 22). This paradox should influence the actions of the faithful: troubled souls should fly on "wings of faith" to Golgotha where alone their "welfare blossoms" (movement 24); the name and cross of Jesus, the contemplation that he has "bled to death," allows the chorus to be "cheerful" in their consolation (movement 26); and contemplating that, even as he hung on the cross, Jesus set a "guardian" for his mother is a reason for others also to "act with righteousness . . . and do not grieve!" (28). Movement 31 is a call and response bass aria and chorus that weaves all of these threads together, repeating the realization that "it is accomplished" means we have been "set free from dying," and that the Jesus who was dead will rise again. The movements of free poetry in the final section of the *Passion* (32–40), by contrast, are less interested in this paradox, moving instead through modes of lament and lullaby depicting Jesus's death and burial.

The movement of accomplishment *Es ist vollbracht* (30) is sung by an alto soloist and accompanied by a reduced number of the musicians, drawing on strings and continuo instruments. The A section is a quiet, moderately slow instrumental introduction by viola de gamba and violone continuo (measures 1–19a). The work shifts radically from an opening and closing of restrained sorrow to the aria's B section depicting triumphant victory, the musical setting mirroring the contrast inherent in John's Gospel: brokenness and completion, suffering and victory, humiliation and glory (measures 19b–40a).

The words of movement 30 similarly demonstrate this radical contrast. The opening and closing lines echo the preceding recitative (movement 29, measures 13–14), in which Jesus exclaims, *Es ist vollbracht* ("It is completed"), with movement 31 providing the evangelist's recitative response, *Und neigte das Haupt und verschied* ("and bowed his head and died"). Bach's setting of the Luther Bible translation of chapters 18–19 of John's Gospel makes

31. For a theological reading of this aria, see Loewe, *Theological Commentary*, 267–74; Breyfogle, "Redemption and Human Freedom in the Bach 'Passions,'" 340; and Chafe, *Tonal Allegory*, 284.

use of a sparse recitative style, with the evangelist or other soloists chanting the story, and instruments providing simple continuo accompaniment. Mirroring the recitative proclaiming Christ's death, the first four lines of the poem also are sung in relatively unadorned style by the alto soloist; some repetitions and melismata are the only adornments. Melismata are rarely used in Bach's *John Passion*, and nowhere as frequently as in this movement. A melisma is a musical ornament emphasizing "brokenness," singing a single syllable of text to more than one note.[32] As always in the sense of *vollbracht* and τετέλεσται (*tetélestai*) is this paradox of brokenness alongside completion. Thus, this brokenness might be the cracking open of the "night of mourning" or the "last hour" of the conflict fought on the cross, to allow the light of dawn to break through. In other places, human brokenness and Christ's brokenness on the cross are brought together to emphasize Christ's work of bringing salvation through brokenness, as with the broken ornaments on *vollbracht* and *Trost* (for instance, in measures 5–6).

Lines 5 and 6 of the aria mark a radical shift in musical style and tone, indicated by Bach's tempo marking of *vivace* (lively). The text affirms that *Der Held aus Juda siegt mit Macht / Und schließt den Kampf* (the hero of Judah triumphs with power / and concludes the conflict). Full continuo instrumentation with organ and contrabassoon joins the upper strings, rounding out with full height and depth of the instrumentation the previously sparse setting of alto voice and strings. The pace of the aria speeds up, and the ornamentation moves from the plangent 2-note neuma melismata to long coloratura strings, extending *Kampf* (conflict) and *Macht* (might) as, demonstrating jubilant triumph, the battle is won and closed. While 2-note neuma melismata emphasize "brokenness," long "coloratura" melismata are considered as elaborate, virtuosic, and highly ornamented. The music ornament itself, therefore, carries both the meaning of brokenness and accomplishment. The music then returns to its stripped-back, restrained spareness to repeat the first line again.[33]

The poetry plays with ideas of perfection as well. The aria is seven lines long, a number of perfection and completion. The poem begins and ends with the repeated line *Es ist vollbracht*, both a completed return and a perfect rhyme.[34] Almost-perfection is emphasized within the poem, as

---

32. Loewe, *Theological Commentary*, 170, 271; this is particularly so when the melismata take the form of a 2-note neuma melisma, as in measure 5 of the movement on the word *Trost* ("comfort").

33. The Lion of Judah context is fascinating, but beyond the scope of this chapter. See Loewe, *Theological Commentary*, 268–71 for a more extended discussion.

34. In English we call identical rhymes "perfect rhymes." In German, identical rhymes are called *rührender Reim*—stirring/touching rhymes.

-*nacht* and *Macht* end lines 3 and 5, the rhymes created by the minimal pair only slightly varied in its initial nasal consonant. In lines 2 and 4, *Seelen* and *zählen* are pronounced almost identically (ˈzeːlən and ˈtseːlən). Internally, *Seelen* (souls) half-rhymes with *siegt* (triumphs) and *schließt* (concludes), emphasizing by their repetition these key concepts. In the central fourth line, the repetition of almost identical sounds, *Läßt* (lɛst) *nun die letzte* (ˈlɛtstə), emphasizes the importance of the *letzte Stunde*, the "final," "complete," "last hour." It is triumphant. It is powerful. It is complete. It is perfect.

Except the poem is not perfect. Line 6, *Und schließt den Kampf* (and concludes the conflict), has a final word that does not rhyme with anything. The rhyme scheme is ABABACA. Nothing in the poem rhymes with *Kampf*, not even internal or half rhymes. The "conflict" is isolated, alone, it does not connect to anything. Christ *schließt*—"concludes" or, as the word might also be translated, "locks," or "shuts down"—the *Kampf*—"conflict," "war" or "struggle." Rhymes connect, they carry sounds forward, they create meaning through repetition. Thus, denying a significant end-word a rhyme, especially in a poem that uses it so intensively, denies it connection or a way forward. There is no future for conflict; it is completed, it is shut down. What an accomplishment.

Conclusion

In this chapter, we have shown how the aria *Es ist vollbracht* (movement 30 of Bach's *John Passion*, BWV 245) provides an evocative commentary in music and devotional poetry on the events of the cross. We demonstrate how the composer's theological formation influenced the musical choices he made in order to give voice to the paradox at the heart of John's Passion: that it is by dying on a cross that Christ defeated death, and forever closed the conflict. The movement enacts, in both the words and the music, the revelation of Christ's true nature on the cross as a triumphant hero who will bring an end to suffering through his own suffering. The *Passion*'s artistic accomplishment seeks to portray the perfect work of Christ, combining both plangent mourning at the death of Christ and triumphant rejoicing at his victory. The aria demonstrates why contemporary musicians and later commentators claimed that Bach's music possesses inherent completeness, accomplishment, or perfection.

Dorothy Lee's *Transfiguration* and *Flesh and Glory* take as their focus the completeness, accomplishment, and perfection of the work of Jesus, but also that, "paradoxically, the crucified body of Christ becomes an icon of life and glory."[35] Reading this paradoxical icon, this "theology in color," through Lee's vivid and compelling studies adds color and depth to our reading of the music and text of Bach's "sermon in sound," *Es ist vollbracht*.[36] Our tracing of the connections in the artistic interpretation of John's story by Johann Sebastian Bach is filled in by being brought into conversation with Lee's work to illuminate the symbolism in John's Gospel. These masterful works of theology recognize the greater work of Jesus on the cross and attempt to explain how it was accomplished. In this chapter, we hope we have, in our turn, recognized these masterful works of theology, and attempted to show their achievement, how they have "brought to completion" their aims, their accomplishment, in their attempts to portray something of the perfect work of Christ.

Bibliography

Aristotle, *Physics*. Translated by P. H. Wicksteed and F. M. Cornford. Loeb Classical Library 228. Cambridge, MA: Harvard University Press, 1957.

Aulén, Gustaf. *Christus Victor*. Translated by A. G. Herbert. New York: Macmillan, 1969.

Bach, Johann Sebastian. *Johannes-Passion BWV 245*. Edited by Arthur Mendel. Neue Bach-Ausgabe Serie II: Messen, Passionen, oratorische Werke IV. Kassel: Bärenreiter, 1973.

Breyfogle, Todd. "Redemption and Human Freedom in the Bach 'Passions.'" *New Blackfriars* 84:989/990 (2003) 335–45.

Buelow, George J. *A History of Baroque Music*. Bloomington, IN: Indiana University Press, 2004.

Chafe, Eric T. *Analyzing Bach Cantatas*. Oxford: Oxford University Press, 2003.

———. *J. S. Bach's Johannine Theology: The St. John Passion and the Cantatas for Spring 1725*. New York: Oxford University Press, 2014.

———. *Tonal Allegory in the Vocal Music of Johann Sebastian Bach*. Berkeley, CA: University of California Press, 1991.

"complete, adj." *OED Online*. June 2022. Oxford University Press. https://www.oed.com/view/Entry/37656?rskey=tJPxBP&result=1.

"complish, v." *OED Online*. June 2022. Oxford University Press. https://www.oed.com/view/Entry/37730?redirectedFrom=complish%E2%80%8E&.

Derrenbacker, Robert, Lee, Dorothy, Porter, Muriel (eds) *The Enduring Impact of the Gospel of John*. Eugene OR: Wipf and Stock, 2022.

Dürr, Alfred. *Johann Sebastian Bach's St John Passion: Genesis, Transmission and Meaning*. Oxford: Oxford University Press, 2000.

"finish, v." *OED Online*. June 2022. Oxford University Press. https://www.oed.com/view/Entry/70447?rskey=6D5Vbr&result=2.

Firth, Katherine. "Study Translation." In *Johann Sebastian Bach's St John Passion (BWV 245): A Theological Commentary with a New Study Translation by Katherine Firth*

---

35. Lee, *Transfiguration*, 110.

36. Trubetskoi, *Icons: Theology in Color*, 57; Ouspensky; Gythiel; Meyendorff, *Theology of the Icon*, 191–93.

and a Foreword by N. T. Wright, 100–134. Studies in the History of Christian Traditions 168. Leiden: Brill, 2014.

Leaver, Robin A. *Bachs theologische Bibliothek: eine kritische Bibliographie.* Neuhausen-Stuttgart: Hänssler-Verlag, 1983.

Lee, Dorothy A. *Flesh and Glory: Symbolism, Gender and Theology in The Gospel of John.* Chestnut Ridge NY: Crossroad, 2002.

———. *Transfiguration.* Sheffield: Continuum, 2005.

Liddell, Henry George, Robert Scott, and Henry Stuart Jones. *A Greek-English Lexicon.* 9th ed. Oxford: Clarendon, 1996.

Loewe, Andreas. "Sermons in Sound: The Theology of Johann Sebastian Bach's Passions." University of Divinity Repository (2010) 1–11. https://repository.divinity.edu.au/841/

———. "'God's Capellmeister': The Proclamation of Scripture in the Music of J. S. Bach." *Pacifica* 24:2 (2011) 141–71.

———. *Johann Sebastian Bach's St John Passion (BWV 245): A Theological Commentary: With a New Study Translation by Katherine Firth and a Preface by N. T. Wright.* Studies in the History of Christian Traditions 168. Leiden: Brill, 2014.

———. "'Zeig uns durch deine Passion': The Christology of Bach's St John Passion." *Paradosis* 3 (2016) 79–90.

Loewe, Andreas, and Katherine Firth. "Luther's 'Mighty Fortress.'" *Lutheran Quarterly* 32:2 (2018) 125–45.

———. *Martin Luther and the Arts: Music, Images and Drama to Promote the Reformation.* Studies in Medieval and Reformation Thought 236. Leiden: Brill, 2023.

Luther, Martin. *D. Martin Luthers Werke: Kritische Gesamtausgabe.* Edited by Joachim Karl Friedrich Knaake et al. Weimar: Hermann Böhlau, 1883–1985.

Marissen, Michael. *Bach & God.* New York: Oxford University Press, 2016.

Ouspensky, Léonide, Anthony P. Gythiel, and Elizabeth Meyendorff. *Theology of the Icon.* Crestwood, NY: St. Vladimir's Seminary Press, 1992.

Ouspensky, Léonide and Lossky, Vladimir, *The Meaning of Icons.* Crestwood, NY: St. Vladimir's Seminary Press, 1982.

Pelikan, Jaroslav. *Bach among the Theologians.* Philadelphia, PA: Fortress, 1986.

———. "Christus Victor in the Saint John Passion." In *Bach among the Theologians*, 102–29. Philadelphia, PA: Fortress, 1986.

Rambach, Johann Jakob. *Betrachtungen über die Sieben letzten Worte des gecreutzigten Jesu.* Halle: Waisenhaus, 1732.

Sophocles, Evangelinus Apostolides. *Greek Lexicon of The Roman and Byzantine Periods.* New York: Olms, 2005.

Trubetskoi, Evgeny N. *Icons: Theology in Colour.* Crestwood, NY: St. Vladimir's Seminary Press, 1973.

Wolff, Christoph. *Bach: The Learned Musician.* New York: W. W. Norton & Co., 2013.

———. *Bach's Musical Universe: The Composer and His Work.* New York: W. W. Norton & Co., 2020.

———, ed. *The New Bach Reader: A Life of Johann Sebastian Bach in Letters and Documents.* New York: W. W. Norton & Co., 1998.

Wolff, Christoph, and Walter Emery. "Bach, Johann Sebastian." *Grove Music Online.* 2001. https://www.oxfordmusiconline.com/grovemusic/view/10.1093/gmo/9781561592630.001.0001/omo-9781561592630-e-6002278195.

20.

Dürer's Apocalypse Woodcuts as a New Form of (Visual) Commentary

ROBYN J. WHITAKER

Introduction

The visual force of the Book of Revelation is apparent to readers of the Bible and observers of Western culture alike.[1] Images and symbols from the biblical text appear in a range of visual media from Michaelangelo's famous ceiling in the Sistine Chapel to graphic novels, political satire, and modern movies. Just weeks before the 2022 Australian federal election, for example, a cartoon by Cathy Wilcox appeared in one of Australia's major newspapers satirizing sitting members' views on climate change and depicting four of

---

1. It is an honor to be included in this Festschrift for Professor Dorothy Lee. I chose to write on the Book of Revelation because I first studied Revelation as a coursework student with Dorothy as my teacher. Later on, when I returned to do a Master's thesis on the images of evil in Revelation, Dorothy was my supervisor. She encouraged me to pursue my questions and helped convince me that I was capable of doing research in New Testament. Both her writing and her abilities as a teacher have been enormously influential upon my own sense of vocation as a teacher and academic. I hope that this essay is a way of bringing together many of Dorothy's loves—the Bible, art, the church, and theology (with apologies for failing to include dogs and cats too).

them as the four horsemen of the Apocalypse.[2] Viewers of the cartoon may or may not have recognized that the motif of four horsemen comes from the Book of Revelation, but the image works regardless. Four horsemen have entered our culture's cognitive storehouse as a group that signal doom, horror, and pending catastrophe even when radically removed from their biblical context.

Such use of Revelation's images has a long history. While the apocalyptic genre—with its vivid images and strange creatures—lends itself to visualization, the subject matter is also particularly poignant at moments of great change and uncertainty. Cathy Wilcox's cartoon stands in a long tradition of leveraging Revelation's images in ways that move far beyond traditional exegesis or interpretation that is attentive to the first-century CE setting of the text. Central to this shift that separates image and text are, I will argue, the fifteenth-century *Apocalypse* woodcuts of Albrecht Dürer.

In 1498, Dürer self-published his *Apocalypse* series, taking advantage of the cutting-edge technology of the printing press. In so doing, he was free from the constraints of ecclesial authority or patronage. His unprecedented arrangement differed from the conventional manuscripts of both medieval and early printed editions of the Bible in which an illustrator supplied the requisite images to accompany the text. Instead, Dürer arranged his fifteen woodcuts as a visual story separated from the biblical text. As such, the images are not simply an accompaniment to the text but, arguably, a replacement for the text.

This essay explores the reception of the Book of Revelation in the *Apocalypse* woodcuts of Albrecht Dürer, proposing that Dürer's work represents a pivotal moment in the reception history of Revelation. We will focus on Dürer's depiction of the Son of Man (Rev 1:9–20) and the Four Horsemen (Rev 6:1–8) as examples. Some have argued that Dürer is a proto-reformer; others describe his woodcuts as a paratext.[3] Whatever label one uses, it is clear that Dürer is not only an innovative and talented artist but also an innovator when it came to interpretation of the biblical text. Dürer's woodcuts are, I suggest, not simply commentary or even paratext but a form of visual exegesis that captures the *Sacheselbst*, the substance, of Revelation. If I am correct, Dürer's woodcuts are distinctive in the reception history of Revelation as they push the boundaries of both visual exegesis and scriptural authority, challenging traditional understandings of each.

2. Wilcox, *Four Horsemen of the Climate Apocalypse*, published in the *Sydney Morning Herald*, 24 March 2022.

3. Low, "Then I Saw," 345.

Reception history

The approach I am using here is that of reception history of the Bible. Reception history attempts to capture the dynamic interplay between texts, interpreters, and their readers over time. As Ulrich Luz famously asserted, an interpreter "does not yet understand what the subject matter of the text *means* if one only understands what it *has meant*" (italics his).[4] Reception history recognizes a dynamic relationship between texts and readers and shifts the focus from an author focused historical-critical approach that seeks a historically located (or originally intended) meaning, to one that recognizes the interpretive potential of a passage for different communities in different contexts. Ian Boxall writes:

> attention to reception history [is] "an integral and inescapable part" of the question of understanding New Testament texts, offering an account of the meaning(s) of a text that is truly more diachronic than historical critical attempts to get "behind the text" in order to establish original meaning.[5]

Reception history, framed in such a way, might include the examination of anything from Sunday school notes, to art, music, films, sermons, commentaries, devotional material, and so on. Such an approach is less focused on the "history of interpretation," which typically looks at scholarly works and key figures to trace theological and ecclesial shifts in interpretation. While history of interpretation is important, it is a subset of the wider enterprise of the reception history of the Bible. Reception history, more broadly conceived, focuses on the interpreters and how they receive the biblical text(s), even when their voices might be marginal or removed from ecclesial tradition.[6] It looks at the effects or effective history (*Wirkungsgeschichte*) of interpretation. In the case of Dürer's *Apocalypse* woodcuts, the effects were both immediate and long lasting. In the words of Peter Klein, "Dürer's woodcut Apocalypse represents the exact borderline between medieval and modern illustration of the Apocalypse."[7] His visual interpretation of the text would dominate Western art of Revelation, particularly in the nineteenth-century,

---

4. Luz, *Matthew 1–7.*, 98. Luz did, however, place denominational or confessional boundaries around hermeneutics that some contemporary work in reception history does not. See Mark W. Elliott, "Effective-History and the Hermeneutics of Ulrich Luz," 161–73.

5. Boxhall, *Patmos in the Reception History*, 3.

6. See Boxall, *Patmos in the Reception History*, 6, for a discussion on the distinction between *Auslegungsgeschichte* and *Wirkungsgeschichte*.

7. Klein, "Introduction: The Apocalypse in Medieval Art," 199.

and arguably forged the way for contemporary, popular depictions of the Book of Revelation.[8]

Dürer's Apocalypse Woodcuts

Albrecht Dürer was the child of a goldsmith and trained in engraving early in life. He did his apprenticeship in painting under Michael Wolgemut in Nuremberg where he was introduced to woodcuts as a medium. Wolgemut was well- known for his "blockbooks," which had appeared as early as 1455. As an apprentice in Wolgemut's studio, Dürer would have witnessed the entire process of design, cut, and print of a blockbook illustration, each role traditionally undertaken by different specialists.

Dürer's training under Wolgemut and location in Nuremberg placed him at the very heart of the burgeoning print revolution.[9] Additionally, Dürer's godfather, Anton Koberger, ran one of the pre-eminent print houses in all of Germany, if not Europe. His studio produced the "Nuremberg Chronicles" (1475) and the Koberger Bible (1473–8), both of which show an emerging awareness of the importance of images in accompanying text. Koberger, like Wolgemut, employed artists to design and draw the images, but the actual woodcutting was usually done by a specialist and handed over to the printer for copy. A process that usually involved several different specialists is one that Dürer would take on for himself in the *Apocalypse* series; designing, drawing, cutting, and overseeing the printing and layout by himself.

The fifteenth-century was a time of heightened apocalyptic expectation and the Book of Revelation was extremely popular. The previous few centuries had brought forth a vast and creative amount of exegetical material on Revelation, the majority of which took the form of commentaries, but illuminated manuscripts and monumental art such as commissioned church windows or altars were also common.[10] Dürer capitalized on both the popularity of Revelation and the technological opportunity afforded by the printing press to produce an affordable illustrated version of Revelation.

8. Klein, "Introduction: The Apocalypse in Medieval Art," 198.

9. His geographic location in Nuremberg is important because Nuremberg lay in the heart of the Holy Roman Empire and at the nexus of several trade routes. It hosted several games and festivals each year and thus boasted a large tourist trade. The city, unusually, had two paper mills so the cost of production was minimized through access to local resources and an easy means of dispersing the text.

10. McGinn, "Introduction: John's Apocalypse and the Apocalyptic Mentality," 4.

Published in 1498, Dürer's *Apocalypse* was a book of fifteen woodcut pictures and the text of Revelation. There were two editions that came out in the same year; the pictures in each were the same but one included the text in Latin (the Vulgate) and the other printed Koberger's German translation. Several things make Dürer's *Apocalypse* series unusual. The obvious is that the technical skill involved was unprecedented. Art historian, Jane Hutchison, calls Dürer's woodcuts "the most complex and impressive ever to appear in European art."[11] The subtleties of his lines give his images both a naturalistic depth of perspective as well as a level of complexity not previously seen. It is not, however, his artistic brilliance that is of interest here, but rather the visual exegesis he employs and the impact and effect of his woodcuts on the reception history of Revelation.

Part of Dürer's innovation was the physical layout of his *Apocalypse*. He deviated from the dominant Anglo-Norman manuscript tradition in producing only fifteen images instead of ninety or more smaller images.[12] One of the fifteen is not a scene from Revelation but rather a portrayal of the author, John, depicted as a martyr being boiled alive in oil. While there are a handful of examples of similar reductions,[13] Dürer's woodcuts are striking for the significant reduction of the standard ninety or so images to a mere fourteen. As a result, Dürer has made editorial and exegetical decisions about which scenes to illustrate and what to highlight, conflating some scenes and omitting others.

The size of the images in the *Apocalypse* woodcuts was also unprecedented. Each image took up a whole sheet, measuring 39.4 by 28 cms (in the 1487 German edition).[14] Again there was no precedent for this. Even richly illustrated printed Bibles, such as the Koberger Bible, had images that occupied, at most, a third of the page or perhaps included a full-page front

11. Hutchinson, *Albrecht Dürer*.

12. Camille, "Visionary Perception and Images," 280. The Anglo-Norman Manuscript tradition emerged in the mid-thirteenth century. These manuscripts generally included ninety to one hundred images of the Apocalypse illustrating each section or pericope. These ninety or so images were copied relatively consistently for about 200 years making them as "standard" as anything can be prior to a printing press. According to Camille, these Anglo-Norman standardized images would become models for the Angers Tapestries in 1373 and possibly influenced the illustrations in the Book of Hours. See Camille, 280–281.

13. There were some Flemish manuscripts of Revelation that reduced the number of images to twenty-three. One dating to 1400 CE devotes a full-page illustration (19 x 25.8cm) to each chapter of Revelation. The text is cramped on the opposite side accompanied by the Berendaudus gloss. Klein says the tendency to reduce the number of images increased in the fifteenth century. See Klein, "Introduction: The Apocalypse in Medieval Art," 196–98.

14. O'Hear, *Contrasting Images*, 154.

image followed by the complete text. The size of Dürer's woodcuts allowed for a density of images in the compilated scenes as well as increasing the visual effect upon the viewer.

Most notable is Dürer's arrangement of the text and image. The images occupied the *recto* (right) side of the page with text opposite in two columns. This placed the visual interpretation of the text on an equal scale to the words as they occupied equal space. What effect might this have had on the reader-viewer? On a practical level, given the binding on books of this period, the right side of the page lay flat and was able to be viewed more easily. One could turn the pages of Dürer's *Apocalypse* and "read" the images independently of the text (a bit like a modern graphic novel but without any words). The biblical text ran on the left side but did not necessarily correspond with the images.[15]

"The impression given to the 'reader' is therefore of a dual Book of Revelation, one visual and one textual, coexisting with one another," writes O'Hear.[16] I would go a step further, however, in suggesting that the "dual book" created by Dürer has the effect of separating word and image. Panofsky hints in this direction when he writes that that Dürer must not have wanted the reader to compare text and image "but to absorb the whole text and the whole sequence of pictures as two self-contained and continuous versions of the same narrative."[17] No longer are images a supplement to the text. In Dürer's *Apocalypse,* the images are able to stand alone, thus changing the relationship between image and text.[18] The fact that the images were later sold separately further confirms this separation of word and image.[19]

The size as well as the arrangement of the images on the *recto* suggests that Dürer is actually giving priority to his images, something O'Hear acknowledges.[20] When we consider the norms at the time, such large imagery actually has the effect of dominating or superseding the text. The absence of written commentary or glossa, standard in thirteenth-century manuscripts, additionally hints that Dürer presents his woodcuts as a kind of visual commentary. We will explore these aspects of Dürer's work further below.

15. Price points out that while the text does not correspond with the images there are references within the text to the relevant image. See Price, *Albrecht Dürer's Renaissance,* 38.

16. O'Hear, *Contrasting Images,* 137.

17. Panofsky, *Life and Art of Albrecht Dürer,* 52.

18. Camille, "Visionary Perception," 277.

19. O'Hear, *Contrasting Images,* 154, 165.

20. O'Hear, *Contrasting Images,* 168. About the relationship between text and image she writes that they "serve to elucidate each other, the images perhaps ultimately even overpowering the text."

In summary, the technical skill, arrangement, and layout of Dürer's self-published *Apocalypse* was infused with innovation. Yet one other feature makes Dürer's *Apocalypse* remarkable and that is its autonomy. The marvel of the print arts was that the artist could take the initiative and turn out, very affordably, images from his or her imagination. This "democratization" of the Bible meant it was "[n]o longer the domain of wealthy and powerful patrons who commissioned expensive hand copies."[21] Free from the constraint that accompanied ecclesial commissions, Dürer had autonomy and creative control over the entire production without having to limit himself to accepted religious iconography.[22] This autonomy is evident in the lack of glossa or traditional commentary in Dürer's *Apocalypse,* the effect of which is to give further weight to his visual depictions as an interpretation of and commentary on the text. It is to this aspect of Dürer, as exegete and interpreter, that we now turn.

Dürer as Exegete

Albrecht Dürer *The Vision of the Seven Candlesticks,* c. 1496/1498

21. Beal, *Book of Revelation*, 119.

22. Such autonomy was rare for an artist at this time given the majority of work came through commissions. See O'Hear, *Contrasting Images*, 143–44.

We shall look at two woodcuts as examples of Dürer's exegetical and theological contributions, beginning with the first woodcut of Revelation which depicts Christ among the lampstands (Revelation 1:9–20).[23] This is the second image in Dürer's *Apocalypse* and the first illustrating a scene from Revelation. In the text, this scene is an epiphany of "one like a Son of Man" who is clothed in priestly garments and appears among the lampstands holding seven stars in his right hand with a sharp sword coming out of his mouth. John writes,

> . . .in the middle of the lampstands was one like a son of man, clothed with a long robe and a golden sash wrapped around his chest. His head and his hair were white, like white wool, like snow; his eyes were like a flame of fire, his feet were like burnished bronze, refined as in a furnace, and his voice was like the sound of many waters. He had in his right hand seven stars, and from his mouth came a sharp, two-edged sword, and his face was like the sun shining in its full strength. (Rev 1:13–16, my translation)

Dürer has captured some elements of the textual epiphany quite literally, including the seven stars, the seven candlesticks, the sharp double-edged sword, long robes and a golden sash, white hair, and a face shining like the sun. Dürer's illustration indicates he is a careful reader of the text and has understood the biblical echoes in Revelation 1:9–20. He has, however, also made some unusual interpretive decisions.

Theologically, Dürer's visual commentary asserts that this Son of Man is the Lamb of God and is also God. He has conflated three different scenes describing the divine to make one divine being. It is an iconography not found in previous images of Revelation 1 in the tradition. The face of the "one like a son of man" in Dürer's image has ram-lamb like qualities. You can see small horns protruding from his forehead and curly, wool-like hair. In adding these lamb features, which are not described in Revelation 1, Dürer has read ahead and conflated this Christological figure with the Lamb that appears in Revelation 5. He has further combined these two Christological figures with the ancient, enthroned one who is central to the vision in Revelation 4 and usually interpreted as God.[24] Like the enthroned deity in Revelation 4:2–3, Dürer's Son of Man is seated on a throne and holds a book (*biblion*) in his hand.

Michael Camille notes three striking aspects of representation of Revelation in the late medieval period: a changing relationship between image

23. Durer, *Vision of the Seven Candlesticks*
24. Koester, *Revelation*, 367–69.

and text, more naturalistic modes of representation, and a pictorial focus on John as "subject."[25] We have already noted the changing relationship between word and image embodied by the physical layout and arrangement of Dürer's *Apocalypse*. We will return to the naturalistic modes below. Here, however, we look at the shift away from John as subject.

In a new move, Dürer has inserted himself into the story of Revelation. His woodcut of Revelation 1 includes a figure kneeling before the enthroned Son of Man. In Revelation, this figure is John, who falls as though dead as a result of the theophany (Rev 1:17).[26] Here, the Seer is larger than typical, almost rivalling the size of the divine.[27] He is in a posture of worship, hands clasped in prayer, kneeling before the divine but not prostrate.

In the Anglo-Norman manuscripts, John is typically portrayed looking in or up as a viewer of the scene, often just out of the main frame. This emphasizes his role as mediator of the vision and perhaps attempts to imbue the images with a realism that John is seeing or experiencing these as visions. It reminds the viewer that what is unveiled in Revelation is mediated through John. Dürer radically omits John from many of his scenes, but when he does include "John" as the biblical text does, he places him in the scene as an active participant, reflecting the times in the text when John has an active role. John, however, is depicted with striking similarities to that of Dürer's self-portrait, including long curly hair and a narrow, pointed nose. Dürer has arguably positioned himself in a posture of reverence as devotee and receiver of divine visions from the enthroned one.

Dürer repeats this pattern in the third woodcut which depicts the heavenly throne room (Rev 4). While standard depictions of this scene depict the enthroned deity as the most prominent, Dürer has made John (or himself) the largest figure in the scene, bringing him front and center and creating perspective through curved lines and shading. In a move that parallels the increasing importance of the authorial voice in the medieval period, Dürer has amplified the visual presence of the artist.[28]

The effect of Dürer's change to tradition in amplifying the Seer is twofold. Firstly, it has the effect of inviting the viewer-reader into the experience and to imagine themselves kneeling before the divine. I have written elsewhere about the ekphrastic nature of Revelation.[29] That is, that the vivid

25. Camille, "Visionary Perception and Images of the Apocalypse," 277.

26. Cranach, whose illustrations in the Luther *Septembertestament* rely heavily on Dürer's *Apocalypse*, changes this scene to have John prostrate as though dead to reflect the text more literally.

27. Camille, "Visionary Perception," 285.

28. Camille, "Visionary Perception," 287.

29. Whitaker, *Ekphrasis, Vision, and Persuasion in the Book of Revelation*.

descriptions invite the reader to "see" with John and experience the visions and their emotional impact. Dürer, through image, has captured precisely this textual form and ekphrastic function in minimizing the gap between reader-viewer and text. We, as viewers, are called and invited to join Dürer in worshipping God. But we are called to do so precisely through seeing Dürer's woodcuts, not reading the text.[30] He has created a space where the viewer has unfettered access to the divine through his images of John's words. As O'Hear writes, "the hermeneutical implications of Dürer's self-understanding as an *alter Johannis* are serious. If the Book of Revelation is to be viewed as a series of words which engender pictures, a definitive visualization of the text, produced by an *alter Johannis*, may render the text redundant."[31]

The second effect of Dürer's change to the tradition is that he has presented himself in the place of the Seer, or as Seer. The visions we see are now his, mediated by him. Three other pieces of information are vital to recall here: that while it was common to include commentary, or quotes from authoritative commentators throughout an illuminated manuscript, Dürer includes only the biblical text and his images; that Dürer's woodcuts were printed and circulated separately from the text making them the first mass-produced, purely visual Apocalypse; and that the quality of the images was far superior to the quality of the printed text.[32] In a move that would foreshadow many of the reformers, Dürer removes ecclesial tradition and authority as the interpretive lens through which the text must be viewed.

While not usually applied to images, the category of rewritten Bible could be applicable here. Molly Zahn writes that "the faithful transmitter of the ancient and sacred textual tradition could, at the same time, be an innovator, whose own faithfulness to that textual tradition demanded the reshaping of it."[33] In this dynamic, the authority of the new creation is dependent on the authority of what is being reproduced. Dürer's *Apocalypse* woodcuts may not have been so popular had they not depicted a text already considered canonical, authoritative, and sacred. Dürer utilizes biblical authority to support, paradoxically, and give weight to his rather innovative visual interpretation of the text. In replicating the substance of

30. Dürer's woodcuts circulated separately and became affordable devotional images for private homes, things previously only available to the wealthy. In doing so, the need for the text itself is diminished.

31. O'Hear, *Contrasting Images*, 165.

32. It is likely Dürer reused existing lettering as the text is very similar to the Koberger Bible text. If he has made the letters himself then he has not given the same attention to detail to the text as to the images. See O'Hear, *Contrasting Images*, 157.

33. Zahn, *Rethinking Rewritten Scripture*, 242.

Revelation—both in terms of content and rhetorical form—Dürer reshapes it for his own time, locating the visions in the fifteenth-century German landscape and context.

Albrecht, Dürer. *The Four Horsemen,* 1498

We turn now to a second example from the woodcuts, the four horsemen, where we can see Dürer's contextualization and naturalistic style at work.[34] In Revelation 6:1–8, the first four of seven seals are opened by the Lamb, each unleashing judgment from the heavenly realm in the form of a horse rider. From a literary point of view, they are not a group in Revelation, but rather a series of figures each with their own symbolism and purpose: one conquers, one takes peace from the earth, one creates economy inequity, and one is personified as Death itself and permitted to kill a quarter of the earth.

34. Dürer, *Four Horsemen.*

Likely influenced by the Koberger Bible's illustrations of Revelation 6, Dürer depicts the four horsemen as a group or a singular event.[35] Earlier manuscripts typically depicted each of the horsemen separately but the Koberger Bible, unusually, groups them together in the one scene. In that scene though, they each face a slightly different direction with the first three horsemen depicted in fifteenth-century garb and the fourth as a skeletal death figure. Dürer builds on the Koberger tradition, keeping the fourth rider (Death) slightly separate but presenting the other three lined up with military precision, riding out to battle. An angel hovers overhead, pointing the way. His visual rendering increases the coherence of the group and presents them as sharing a clear mission and purpose.

As an exegete, Dürer has captured the original sense of Revelation 6 and its judgment upon the world's violence and injustice but transposed it into his own context. The first person to be destroyed by the horsemen is the Emperor, who is depicted as fallen and trampled under the feet of the Death rider.[36] In the following scene, depicting the fifth and sixth seals, the Emperor is joined by the Pope, bishops, and other leaders as the destruction wrought by the opened seals is unleashed upon the world. Taking John's claim that "the kings of the earth and the magnates and the generals and the rich and the powerful, and everyone, slave and free" are affected by God's judgment (Rev 6:16), Dürer grounds it in his own context, using late fifteenth-century Germany as his setting for the earthly realm. He tends to present elites as primary victims of judgment and ordinary folk as being on God's side. His naturalistic style renders the images believable, powerful, and relevant to the time. The effect of this is to evoke emotion and imitate the ekphrastic effect of the text of Revelation.[37]

While Dürer's images are not as pointedly political as those of Cranach in the *Septembertestament,* he paves the way for such (re)contextualization and politicization.[38] Cranach's simplified and more literal images are clearly based on Dürer's woodcuts. Where Dürer had demonstrated the "the potential for producing richly complex and expressive artwork in the new medium of the print book," Cranach's images in the *Septembertestament* would further increase the polemical and visual force of Revelation giving it a "disturbing supernatural vitality, popularizing it among hundreds of thousands

35. Price, *Albrecht Dürer's Renaissance,* 47.

36. Price, *Albrecht Dürer's Renaissance,* 44–45.

37. O'Hear, *Contrasting Images,* 161.

38. It is widely recognized that Cranach was strongly influenced by Dürer as the images in Luther's *Septembertestament* are close copies of Dürer's, albeit with less technical skill but heightened political polemic. See Klein, "Introduction: The Apocalypse in Medieval Art," 198.

of new readers."[39] The four horsemen, along with other images from Revelation, were popularized and politicized as agents of doom. Removed from the text and context of Revelation the four horsemen took on a life of their own from the time of Dürer onwards.[40] In doing so, they morphed from heavenly agents doing God's will to symbols of violence and doom more generally, as we saw in Cathy Wilcox's political cartoon.

Conclusion: Dürer's Legacy

Christopher Rowland writes that it "is no exaggeration that the Book of Revelation both explains the nature of Christianity and epitomises its problems."[41] The interpretation and application of Revelation tends to be among the most problematic of all biblical interpretation particular for the way symbols and images from the text have taken on a life of their own, far removed from their context in the text of Revelation. Think, for example, of the appeal to the "mark of the beast" in conspiracy theories, graphic popular images of heaven and hell, or the politicizing of four horsemen or the number of the beast (666) which are so often used to denounce and infer that one's opponents are evil. So many of these symbols have taken on a life of their own in Western culture and imagination.

Whether or not Dürer intended to advance such a strong separation of word and image, it has been one of the lasting legacies of his work. By choosing to begin his independent print career with the *Apocalypse* woodcuts, Dürer ensured not only his own place in art history but also the place of the book of Revelation in popular religious imagination. His images spawned numerous copy-cats, including those who would intensify the political dimensions of the text by continuing to update and contextualize the figures therein. The affordability of his woodcuts, the separation of text and image, the autonomy he had as an artist-print maker, and the placement of himself as viewing subject effectively democratized biblical interpretation. To view Dürer's *Apocalypse* is to be invited into a spiritual, visual encounter with the divine. It is an invitation to kneel before the throne with him and witness the unveiling of God's judgment and justice.

39. Beal, *Book of Revelation*, 125, 137.

40. O'Hear and O'Hear. *Picturing the Apocalypse*, 75. See their discussion on pp. 79–91 which charts the influence of Dürer's *Apocalypse* woodcut 4 (Four Horsemen) on art throughout the next few centuries.

41. Rowland, *By An Immediate Revelation*, 570.

Bibliography

Allen, Garrick V., Ian Paul, and Simon P. Woodman, eds. *The Book of Revelation: Currents in British Research on the Apocalypse*. Tübingen: Mohr Siebeck, 2015.

Beal, Timothy. *The Book of Revelation: A Biography*. Princeton: Princeton University Press, 2018.

Boxhall, Ian. *Patmos in the Reception History of the Apocalypse*. Oxford Theology and Religion Monographs. Oxford: Oxford University Press, 2013.

Camille, Michael. "Visionary Perception and Images of the Apocalypse in the Later Middle Ages." In *The Apocalypse in the Middle Ages*, 276–89. Ithaca: Cornell University Press, 1992.

Dürer, Albrecht., *The Four Horsemen*, 1498. Public Domain. NGA 2008.109.5.

———. *The Vision of the Seven Candlesticks*, c.1496/1498. Public Domain. NGA 1941.3.6.

Elliott, Mark W. "Effective-History and the Hermeneutics of Ulrich Luz." *Journal for the Study of the New Testament* 33:2 (2010) 161–73.

Emmerson, Richard K, and Bernard McGinn, eds. *The Apocalypse in the Middle Ages*. Ithaca: Cornell University Press, 1992.

Hutchinson, Jane Campbell. *Albrecht Dürer: A Biography*. Princeton: Princeton University Press, 1992.

Klein, Peter K. "Introduction: The Apocalypse in Medieval Art." In *The Apocalypse in the Middle Ages*, 159–99. Ithaca: Cornell University Press, 1992.

Koester, Craig R. *Revelation: A New Translation with Introduction and Commentary*. Anchor Bible. New Haven: Yale University Press, 2014.

Kovacs, Judith, and Christopher Rowland. *Revelation: The Apocalypse of Jesus*. Blackwell Bible Commentaries. Oxford: Blackwell, 2004.

Lieb, Michael, Emma Mason, and Jonathan Roberts, eds. *The Oxford Handbook of the Reception History of the Bible*. Oxford: Oxford University Press, 2011.

Low, U-Wen. "Then I Saw: The Influence of Albrecht Dürer's Apocalypse as Paratext." *Religion and the Arts* 23 (2019) 341–59.

Luz, Ulrich. *Matthew 1–7*. Translated by Wilhelm C. Linss. Minneapolis: Augsburg Fortress Press, 1989.

McGinn, Bernard. "Introduction: John's Apocalypse and the Apocalyptic Mentality." In *The Apocalypse in the Middle Ages*, 3–19. Ithaca: Cornell University Press, 1992.

O'Hear, Natasha F. H. *Contrasting Images of the Book of Revelation in Late Medieval and Early Modern Art*. Oxford: Oxford University Press, 2011.

O'Hear, Natasha F. H., and Anthony O'Hear. *Picturing the Apocalypse: The Book of Revelation in the Arts Over Two Millennia*. Oxford: Oxford University Press, 2015.

O'Kane, Martin. "Wirkungsgeschichte and Visual Exegesis: The Contribution of Hans-Georg Gadamer." *Journal for the Study of the New Testament* 33:2 (2010) 1459.

Panofsky, Erwin. *The Life and Art of Albrecht Dürer*. Princeton, N.J: Princeton University Press, 2005.

Price, David Hotchkins. *Albrecht Dürer's Renaissance: Humanism, Reformation, and the Art of Faith*. Ann Arbor: The University of Michigan Press, 2006.

Rowland, Christopher. *By An Immediate Revelation: Studies in Apocalypticism, Its Origins and Effects*. Tübingen: Mohr Siebeck, 2022.

———. "Revelation." In *The Oxford Handbook of The Reception History of the Bible*, 161–74. Oxford: Oxford University Press, 2011.

Strand, Kenneth. *Woodcuts to the Apocalypse in Dürer's Time: Albrecht Dürer's Woodcuts Plus Five Other Sets from the 15th and 16th Centuries.* Ann Arbor: Ann Arbor Publishers, 1968.

Weissenrieder, Annette, Friedrike Wendt, and Petra von Gemünden, eds. *Picturing the New Testament Studies in Ancient Visual Images.* Tübingen: M. Siebeck, 2005.

Whitaker, Robyn J. "The Poetics of Ekphrasis: Vivid Description and Rhetoric in the Apocalypse." In *Poetik Und Intertextualität in Der Apokalypse,* 227–40. Wissenschaftliche Untersuchungen Zum Neuen Testament. Tübingen: Mohr Siebeck, 2015.

Zahn, Molly M. *Rethinking Rewritten Scripture: Composition and Exegesis in the 4QReworked Pentateuch Manuscripts.* Vol. 95. Studies on the Texts of the Desert of Judah. Leiden; Boston: Brill, 2011.

21.

On Entry into Paradise

SCOTT KIRKLAND

"To become immortal . . . and then die."

We were expelled from paradise, Kafka reminds us, not because we sinned, but lest we eat of the fruit of the tree of life.[1] The force of that expulsion, then, is the force of expulsion from life. Cut off from the exogenous source of our life we find ourselves in the very midst of life wandering with Dante in deep dark woods, trying to find our way back.[2] Yet the further we go, the stronger the force of expulsion seems to become. That storm blowing from paradise drives us further and further back. "What we call history is this storm."[3]

Thinkers since the Second World War have theorized in different ways what Francis Fukuyama most famously identified as the end of history.[4] The end that Fukuyama invoked came at the end of the Cold War with the emergent hegemony of liberal capitalist democracies. With the final opponent to the domination of the globe by the forces of liberal international order, Soviet Communism, overcome, we were entering a period in which things

1. Kafka, *Aphorisms*, 65.
2. Dante, *Inferno*, in *Divine Comedy*, I:1–3.
3. Benjamin, "On the Concept of History," 389–400.
4. Fukuyama, *End of History and the Last Man*.

would certainly happen, but nothing would change. History was entering a phase echoing the catch cry of the Italian ruling class in *The Leopard*, "everything must change so that everything can remain the same."[5] That is to say, while all manner of events might take place, time extending on indefinitely, no world shaping change could take place now that humanity had reached its, frankly, rather disappointing *telos*.

This prophecy had been offered earlier in the century by the French-Russian emigre philosopher-cum-bureaucrat Alexandre Kojève. Kojève had, with the withdrawal of his famous historian of science uncle, Alexandre Koyré, offered a series of lectures ostensibly on Hegel's *Phenomenology of Spirit* at the *Ecole des Hautes Etudes* between 1933–1939. These lectures were famously well attended by many of the leading lights of French philosophy, literature, and psychoanalysis at the time. From Raymonds, Queneau and Aron to Jean Paul Sartre, Maurice Merleau Ponty, and Jacques Lacan, anyone who was anyone was in the seminar room to hear from the oracle. What we have are the transcribed notes of Raymond Queneau, the only material proceeding from Kojève's pen being the footnotes.[6] In one particularly curious note, Kojève comically announces the end of history on three different occasions. First, at the French Revolution, second at the onset of Stalinism, and finally, with an orientalist gesture, Japanese "snobbery." He writes in the first edition,

> The disappearance of Man at the end of History, therefore, is not a cosmic catastrophe: the natural World remains what it has been from all eternity. And therefore, it is not a biological catastrophe either: Man remains alive as an animal in *harmony* with Nature or given Being. What disappears is Man properly so-called—that is, Action negating the given, and Error, or in general, the Subject opposed to the Object. . . . Practically this means the disappearance of wars and bloody revolutions. And also the disappearance of *Philosophy*; for since Man himself no longer changes essentially, there's no longer any reason to change the (true) principles which are the basis of his understanding of the World and of himself. But all the rest can be preserved indefinitely; art, love, play, etc. etc.,; in short, everything that makes man happy.[7]

5. Di Lampedusa, *Leopard*.

6. Kojève. *Introduction á la Lecture de Hegel*. This was redacted by Allan Bloom and translated into English in redacted form as Kojève, *Introduction to the Reading of Hegel*. More recently, the fourth and fifth lectures were published in English as Kojève, "Interpretation of the General Introduction to Chapter VII [The Religion Chapter of Hegel's *Phenomenology of Spirit*]."

7. Kojève, *Introduction to the Reading of Hegel*, 153.

This first rendition of Kojève's end of history is the end of human action. By this he means the attempt of the human to construct a world through activity that *negates* something and so produces a new object. This negating activity is, for Kojève, the ground of the antagonism between the masters, the antagonism driving history as a history of desires and desired desires. For Kojève, what characterizes humanity is a desire in excess of a "natural" or animal appetite. Where the animal simply satisfies its bodily need, the human maintains a desire for recognition from other humans. This desire for recognition is marked by the relationship between masters, as each attempts to capture the desire of the other. However, at the point at which the other's desire is captured, they become a slave, and so are unable to offer the recognition the master craves. History is interminable, then, for mastery becomes an "existential impasse."[8]

The moment of the disappearance of the human at the end of history is the moment of the disappearance of this competition between masters and the return of humanity to its animality. So it is that we return to art, love, and play; a kind of secularization of paradisiacal re-entry. This is, however, simultaneously, the end of a certain vision of work. The struggle between masters had always been the struggle for a kind of immortality attained through accomplishment. One can find this impulse elsewhere in mid-twentieth-century European leftist and liberal thought. In Jean-Luc Goddard's *Breathless* (1960), Parvulessco the writer responds to Patricia Francini's question, "What is your ambition in life?" with, "To become immortal . . . and then die." The immortality attained here is a kind of recognition by history itself, memorialization. Hannah Arendt in *The Human Condition* identifies a similar impulse in classical political life. The goal of the human as *homo faber* is to make something that exceeds one's death: to become immortal in spite of death.[9] Work is given value in excess of mere *labor,* the use of one's body,[10] the sweat of one's brow, through its recognition in the construction of the *polis.* Kojève's figure of the human at the end of history is the figure of a humanity that has finished with this attempt "to become immortal . . . and then die" and has given itself to art, play, and love.

As Kojève returns to this note later on, however, he realizes there is something inconsistent in its logic. That is, after the end of history there is no art, play, or love that remains as "human," for the human has returned to its animality, and so the arts, play, and love of the human must become "natural" again. This means that "after the end of history men would construct

8. Kojève, *Introduction to the Reading of Hegel,* 19.

9. Hannah Arendt, *Human Condition,* 17–21.

10. For Aristotle, the slave is the one who has "the use of the body." *Politics,* 1254b, 18.

their edifices and works of art as birds build their nests and spiders spin their webs, would perform musical concerts after the fashion of frogs and cicadas, would play like young animals, and would indulge in love like adult beasts."[11] This would be, then, the dissolution of art, play, and love in something like a form of life unreflexively produced. We would make music as the frog does, not because we want to, but because that is what we do. The starkest instance of this reduction to animality at the end of history comes in the human's relation to language, *Logos:* "'The *definitive annihilation* of man *properly so called*' also means the definitive disappearance of human Discourse (*Logos*) in the strict sense. Animals of the species *Homo Sapiens* would react by conditioned reflexes to vocal signals or sign 'language,' and thus their so-called 'discourses' would be like what is supposed to be the 'language' of bees."[12] Language must come to an end at the end of history, for language implies a *gap* between subjects that sustains the possibility of a misrecognition. It mediates a relation between subjects while being irreducible to subjects. So it is that at the end of history we return from language to the mere voice.

We might ponder why this problem of language and the problem of work are here bound together. Why must both end at the end of history? Well, for Kojève, the answer is quite simply that there is no work left for us to do, we become animals grazing upon the earth. After all, in this supremely alienated moment in the history of the West, we are so removed from the labor necessary for the production of what is necessary for our life that we shop in the supermarket in the way a cow might graze in a field. The layers of mediation here relay at the linguistic level through the erasure of forms of misrecognition in digital technologies. The art, play, and love that Kojève initially imagines becomes impossible as we are returned to our animality, it can only ever be the art of the cicada, not the art in which my very being is at stake. The rings of Dante's *Paradiso* are, in Kojève's vision, transfigured into the rings of an Ikea, the beatific vision reduced to the perfectly alienated and expropriated life. A life in which no-thing is at stake.

Specters and Cities

One of the various cities Italo Calvino's Marco Polo conjures in conversation with Emperor Kublai Khan in *Invisible Cities* is named Leonia. The city "refashions itself every day: every morning people wake between fresh sheets, wash with just unwrapped cakes of soap, wear brand-new clothing,

11. Kojève, *Introduction to the Reading of Hegel,* 154.
12. Kojève, *Introduction to the Reading of Hegel,* 154.

take from the latest model refrigerator still unopened tins, listening to the last-minute jingles from the most up-to-date radio." Each day, "street cleaners are welcomed like angels" who come to remove "the residue of yesterday's existence," and so are welcomed "by a respectful silence." Nobody in Leonia worries where this excrement goes, and Marco Polo muses whether the city in fact enjoys this act of "expelling, discarding, cleansing itself of recent impurity"[13] rather than the consumption of the new. Repetition in service of preserving the present comes at the cost of monstrous piles of rubbish mounting outside the city, encroaching upon the rest of the earth. The preservation of a pure presentness, the act of discarding history being a daily routine, creates the form of the city itself. The present can only be maintained as the new through a perpetual disavowal of the past. Leonia is the post-historical city.

In the 2013 German interview, Giorgio Agamben notes that the museumification of the past has begun in European cities "that are transformed into historical zones, and in which the inhabitants are forced to feel themselves tourists in their own life world [*Lebenswelt*]."[14] Agamben himself was living in Venice, the UNESCO World Heritage Site into which 55,000 tourists pour each day. Venice has also suffered greatly with the lagoon surrounding the city being poisoned by tourism and industry, the great cruise ships' emissions creating hazardous air. Yet, paradoxically, the industry poisoning the waterways of the city has become blood/capital coursing through the economic veins/canals of the city. In many ways, Venice resembles Marco Polo's Leonia, a city preserving its past as the presentness of its commodification. The inhabitants now not so much the locals, who are now outnumbered by the tourists beginning each day with fresh towels and soap in their AirBnBs.

We might think of the ways in which this kind of vicious deadening of the life of a city plays out, and, indeed, the complex ways life escapes and survives this deadening force. Venice is preserved as a site for tourists to gaze upon the past, and yet it, of course, remains a city with real inhabitants. A historical site in which History can no longer take place, Venice is, Agamben argues, a "spectre." In "On the Uses and Disadvantages of Living Among Spectres," Agamben begins by evoking the image of Venice as "cadaver" used by the Italian Marxist architect Manfredo Tafuri in 1993.[15] However, more than two decades later, in 2009, Agamben suggests, Venice

13. Calvino, *Invisible Cities*, 114–116.

14. Agamben, "Die endlose Krise ist ein machtinstrument."

15. Agamben, *Nudities*, 37. This address was offered at the University Institute of Architecture in Venice.

"has managed to move beyond the state that follows death and the consequent decomposition of the corpse. This new state is that of the specter, of the dead who appears without warning, preferably in the middle of the night, creaking and sending signals, sometimes even speaking, though in a way that is not always intelligible." Venice's whispers, "are an unbearable sound to the modern ear."[16]

He goes on to speak of the ways Venice appears before its inhabitants, perhaps "during a nocturnal stroll when, crossing a bridge, one's gaze turns a corner alongside a canal immersed in shadows, as a glimmer of orange light is switched on in a distant window, and an observing passerby on another bridge holds out a fogged up mirror." This poetic description might feel almost nostalgic, a kind of romance for a time without foreigners. However, he points to the very origins of the city, "this spectre appears at the very origins of this city, which was not born, like almost every other city in Italy, as a result of the encounter between late antiquity in its decline and new barbarian forces, but rather as a result of exhausted refugees who, abandoning their riches behind them in Rome, carried its phantasm in their minds, to then dissolve it into the city's waters, streaks, and colors."[17] Venetians were always in exile, then. This specter appears already as a signature of a phantom, a city constituted in loss and memory, now standing as a monument to that memory. Precisely as such the city lives in excess of itself, bearing what Agamben calls signatures, that is "signs, ciphers, or monograms that are etched into things by time."[18] The specter, as signature, witnesses to time's passage, to a certain loss, but also to redemption. As Walter Benjamin writes in *On the Concept of History*, "The past carries with it a secret index by which it is referred to redemption."[19] It is this index that Agamben identifies with the signature. Benjamin will identify this signature with the *jeztzeit*, the now-time or *kairos*, of recognizability, as he writes in *The Arcades Project*,

> For the historical index of the images not only says that they
> belong to a particular time; it says, above all, that they attain
> to a legibility only at a particular time . . . Every present day
> is determined by the images that are synchronic with it: each
> "now" [*jetzt*] is the now of a particular recognizability . . . it is
> not that what is past casts its light on what is present, or what
> is present its light on what is past; rather image is that wherein

16. Agamben, *Nudities*, 37–38.

17. Agamben, *Nudities*, 38.

18. Agamben, *Nudities*, 39.

19. Benjamin, "On the Concept of History," 400.

what has been comes together in a flash with the now to form a constellation. In other words, image is dialectics at a standstill.[20]

This stalled dialectic might be thought in and through Agamben's Venice. Venice has, he says, ended. An echo perhaps of Guy Debord, another influence on Agamben, who states in his 1978 film *In Girum Imus Nocte et Consumimur Igni* [We spin around in the night and are consumed by fire], that his native Paris "no longer exists." Agamben compares living in Venice to trying to speak Latin. We might try to learn, we might navigate all the byways of the declensions, but it is impossible to "assume the position of the subject in such a language, of the one who says "I.""[21] In this sense, dwelling in Venice is to dwell in a city that has lost its condition of possibility. Yet, again, this closure cannot serve as a moment for melancholic refusal, but rather, we might suggest that it is when a language dies that "for the first time, this language speaks" as a language the "philosopher refers to . . . by saying that *it* speaks—not we."[22] Deprived of the world in which it might change, develop—deprived of the subject—this language is closed, is rendered *inoperative*.

What might it mean for some-thing/one to survive their/our final cause? Agamben suggests the Swiss writer Robert Walser might help us here. Surviving the end of history might mean surviving as the irreparable. "The irrepairable is the monogram that Walser's writing engraves into things. Irreparable means that these things are consigned without remedy to their being-thus, that they are precisely and only their *thus* . . . but irreparable also means that for them there is literally no shelter possible, that in their being thus they are absolutely exposed, absolutely abandoned." Here, after the final judgement, the world is "necessarily contingent, and contingently necessary."[23] Life might find a way to escape, as Kafka's figures in various and convoluted ways so often do, the machinery, and return to what Guy Debord calls the "clandestine." Yet, this might also be the possibility of love. As Agamben notes via Kierkegaard, the work of love in recollecting the one who is dead "is the most disinterested, free and faithful love."[24] For it is a love which owes no debt but that of memory, we do all we can to sustain the living precisely as the bond of love. The necessity of contingency, then, is the condition of love precisely as the beloved eludes our grasp. Mastery over the other becomes impossible.

20. Benjamin, *Arcades Project*, 462.
21. Agamben, *Nudities*, 40.
22. Agamben, *Nudities*, 40.
23. Agamben, *Coming Community*, 39–41.
24. Kierkegaard, *Works of Love*, 358., cited in *Agamben*, Nudities, 39.

Limbo

In *The Coming Community,* Agamben begins the first chapter with a description of "whatever being" as the figure of the "coming being." He follows the scholastic formula—*quodlibet ens est unum, verum, bonum seu perfectum*—in order to figure "whatever" as the adjective "remaining unthought" in each of the transcendentals, and so a marker not of a generic universality, being *qua* being, rather being as singularity irreducible either to the generic and universal or to the predicative function of the particular. The generic and the particular both, then, pass over being such that it is, singularity. Following Gersonides' formula, this singularity is "singularity insofar as it is whatever singularity."[25]

Playing with the Latin *quodlibet*'s relation to the will (*libet*), Agamben renders its sense in Italian as *qual-si-volia,* whatever as what-you-like, admitting of a relation of desire constituting whatever singularity. This desire is disclosed through love, in which the beloved is irreducible to any predicate, but the lover wants the beloved "*with all of its predicates,* its being such as it is."[26] Love desires that in which each remains in their singularity unrepresentable, *whatever.* This "coming" being, *venie,* is not to be thought of as a future, but as the coming itself, the taking place which Agamben thinks as the universality of singularity in the gaze of the lover.

Anticipating the objection in his third chapter, Agamben moves to show us how singularity is not reducible to a void of non-representation, and yet is precisely not representable. This singularity is to be thought in and through the example, in which the generic and the particular collide in the irreducibility of the resemblance. This forms the logic of the paradigm (*para-deigma*) in which "what is shown is alongside."[27]

In the second chapter, Agamben inserts a paradigm of the paradigm, finding it in the medieval notion of limbo. Thomas Aquinas, and subsequently Dante, locates limbo at the threshold of hell. It is the zone in which the "Fathers," the righteous who preceded Christ, remained in the bosom of Abraham until the coming of Christ. After this event, limbo remains as a place in which there is no torment, but the guilt of original sin remains. As Thomas puts it, "the state of the saints before Christ's coming may be considered both as regards the rest it afforded, and thus it is called Abraham's bosom, and as regards its lack of rest, and thus it is called the limbo

25. Agamben, *Coming Community,* 1.
26. Agamben, *Coming Community,* 2.
27. Agamben, *Coming Community,* 9; 9–13.

of hell."[28] Before Christ, then, limbo and Abraham's bosom were the same place, whereas after they are separated.

On his journey through limbo, Dante has a master (maestro) explain the condition, ""For these defects, and for no other evil / we now are lost and punished with just this / we have no hope and yet we live in longing.""[29] The punishment meted out on these figures in limbo is the absence which produces this hopeless longing. Agamben turns this "into a natural joy: Irremediably lost, they persist without pain in divine abandon."[30] This procedure thinks what he will later call profanation, the rendering inoperative of a theological apparatus. What makes this paradigmatic is the procedure which refuses to offer a teleology in which these subjects recover themselves in incorruption. Their being thus is a liberation from the "world of guilt and justice" on the other side of the *novissima dies* of judgement."[31] Limbo, therefore, is the paradigm of the rendering inoperative of the theological apparatus in which representation captures life in teleology, a liberation to live on the other side of judgement. The other side of judgement, at the realization of the necessity of contingency, discloses itself as the site of love in wait.

Saving Potentiality

To survive judgment, to survive history's end, on this score is not to move toward a teleology but is to abandon teleology in favor of the grace that is already nature. In her *Paradiso* Gillian Rose cites Simone Weil's *Gravity and Grace*, "The tree is really rooted in the sky."[32] Weil's aphorism points to the way grace is the "light falling continuously from heaven," that which is universally available without discrimination, "which alone gives a tree the energy to send powerful roots deep into the soil."[33] Which is to say, it is grace that gives us to nature, it is that which comes to us as gift which is most properly ours. Yet, it can only be ours insofar as it is improper, for the "tree is really rooted in the sky." We might illustrate this through two visions of angels. The first from Walter Benjamin's *On the Concept of History*, Thesis XI, where he takes Paul Klee's *Angelus Novus*, and looks at the angel, wings spread, eyes and mouth wide open, as if screaming.

28. Aquinas, *Summa Theologica*, IIIae.69.4.

29. Dante, *Inferno*, in *Divine Comedy*, IV:1–63.

30. Agamben, *Coming Community*, 6.

31. Agamben, *Coming Community*, 6.

32. Rose, *Paradiso*, 68.

33. Weil, *Gravity and Grace*, cited in Rose, Paradiso, 68.

> [The angel's] face is turned toward the past. Where a chain of events appears before *us, he* sees one single catastrophe, which keeps piling wreckage upon wreckage and hurls it at his feet. The angel would like to stay, awaken the dead, and make whole what has been smashed. But a storm is blowing from Paradise and has got caught in his wings; so strong the angel can no longer close them. The storm blows him irresistibly into the future, to which his back is turned, while the pile of debris before him grows toward the sky. What we call progress is *this* storm.[34]

Benjamin's image pictures the past as an immense pile of rubble, a ruinscape piling up at the feet of the helpless angel. The storm blowing from Paradise, that powerful force of divine expulsion from the garden, drives history itself. History [*Geschichte*] becomes a site of pure catastrophe, and yet only visible as such from the point of view of the angel looking backward. For, as Benjamin continues, what we call *progress* is this storm. As he will state in thesis XIII, progress imagines history as "homogenous, empty time."[35] Time as a kind of tunnel through which we move, formless other than in its pure duration as progress [*Fortschritt*]. Yet this progress, viewed backward from the point of view of the angel, retroactively, is nothing but rubble piled upon rubble, expired attempts at immortality.

In his essay "Creation and Salvation," Agamben rehearses his own version of Benjamin's thesis IX, but instead of *Angelus Novus,* we are presented with Iblis, a fallen angel from Islamic tradition. Agamben writes,

> After all, there is nothing in creation that is not ultimately destined to be lost: not only the part of each and every moment that must be lost and forgotten—the daily squandering of tiny gestures, of minute sensations, of that which passes through the mind in a flash, of trite and wasted words, all of which exceed by great measure the mercy of memory and the archive of redemption—but also the works of art and ingenuity, the fruits of long and patient labour that, sooner or later, are condemned to disappear.
>
> It is over this immemorial mass, over the unformed and immense chaos of what must be lost that, according to islamic tradition, Iblis, the angel that has eyes only for the work of creation, cries incessantly. He cries because he does not know that what one loses actually belongs to God, that when all the

---

34. Benjamin, "On the Concept of History," 399.
35. Benjamin, "On the Concept of History," 401.

work of creation has been forgotten, when all signs and words have become illegible, only the work of salvation will remain indelible.[36]

In the first place, Agamben is conceptualizing the loss that fills each moment. Precisely as each moment of life is so very full, there is no way of scooping it all up into the nets of memory. What is lost is lost, passing even before it can arrive in speech and memory. So it is that Iblis looks upon this great loss and weeps. Iblis, in Islamic tradition, refuses to prostrate himself before Adam. For his arrogance he is condemned, and yet here Agamben figures his condemnation as his not knowing that all that is "belongs to God." Benjamin's rendering of the angel of history has the angel impotent before the storm blowing from Paradise, the power of expulsion from the garden. Both angels are similarly impotent, and yet in the case of Agamben, the force of the storm from Paradise is figured as a kind of superabundance of the moment that can never remain.

What then is salvation here? Agamben writes, "What is a 'saved' potentiality, this power to do (and to not do) that does not simply pass into actuality, so as to exhaust itself in it, but rather conserves itself and dwells (it is "saved") as such within the work? The work of salvation coincides here point for point with the work of creation: the former undoes and decreases the latter at the very same moment it carries and accompanies it into being."[37] Each moment is lost, irredeemably, it is complete, it has ended. Yet, what remains is *potentiality* itself, the power to do and not do that does not undergo the passage to the act. Here Agamben invokes the language of Simone Weil, decreation. Weil writes,

> Creation is an act of love and it is perpetual. At each moment our existence is God's love for us. But God can only love himself. His love for us is his love for himself through us. Thus he who gives us our being loves us in the acceptance of not being. Our existence is made up only of his waiting for our acceptance not to exist. He is perpetually begging from us that existence which he gives. He gives it to us in order to beg it from us.[38]

Agamben's rendering of Weil's concept here binds the perpetuity of the act of love to the passing away of the present. That which never finally arrives, that passes in its coming, is the fullness of this perpetual love. Yet, that love is not available to be possessed. Such are the tears of Iblis, unable

36. Agamben, *Nudities*, 8.
37. Agamben, *Nudities*, 9.
38. Weil, *Gravity and Grace*, 56.

to preserve that which constitutively passes. What remains, then, is that which does not come to be, potentiality, and impotentiality. For Weil, in this perpetual act of love the non-being of the creature comes to coincide with this inappropriable superabundance. Benjamin's notion of the messianic coincides here in Agamben's use of Weil, with this moment of passing. The passing of time is that which "saves" that which never came to be, potentiality itself.

The Tree of Life

Dorothy Lee's contribution to theological and biblical scholarship, particularly in the land we now call Australia, is immense. Having had the privilege of being her colleague for the past five years, I have learned a lot about biblical texts, particularly the Gospel of John, but, more importantly, about a scholarly life led in the profound awareness that what is being held forth for students is not immortality but resurrection.

To become immortal is to seek to survive history; it is to seek to insure oneself against the future by creating something that retains its forceful hold over others. Resurrection does not work this way. Resurrection is profoundly aware of the vanity of things, of their contingency, of our waiting. Our waiting, however, is that movement whereby God gives us his life in order to beg for it back from us.

For Dorothy, I know everything begins and ends in incarnation and resurrection, and therefore in sacrament. What else is the visible sign of the necessity of our contingency than the very tree of life given to us in the blood poured out by a Galilean messiah carrying his cross. As Weil writes, again, "Adam and Eve sought for divinity in vital energy—a tree, fruit. But it is prepared for us on dead wood, geometrically squared, where a corpse is hanging. We must look for the secret of our kinship with God in our mortality . . . I have to be like God . . . Like God almighty in so far as he is bound by necessity."[39]

Bibliography

Agamben, Giorgio., *Nudities* trans., David Kishik and Stefan Pedatella. Stanford, CA: Stanford University Press, 2010.
———. "Die endlose Krise ist ein machtinstrument" https://www.faz.net/aktuell/feuilleton/bilder-und-zeiten/giorgio-agamben-im-gespraech-die-endlose-krise-ist-ein-machtinstrument-12193816 (Accessed 18 Jan, 2021)

39. Weil, *Gravity and Grace*, 97.

———. *The Coming Community,* trans., Michael Hardt, Minneapolis, MN: University of Minnesota Press, 1993.

Aristotle, *The Complete Works of Aristotle: The Revised Oxford Translation,* ed. Jonathan Barnes, 2 vols. Princeton, NJ: Princeton University Press, 1984.

Arendt, Hannah., *The Human Condition.* Chicago, IL: Chicago University Press, 1998 [1958].

Benjamin, Walter., trans., Harry Zohn, "On the Concept of History" in *Selected Writings IV: 1938-40.* Cambridge, MA: Belknap Harvard, 2003, p. 389–400.— *The Arcades Project,* trans., Howard Eiland and Kevin McLaughlin. Cambridge, MA: Belknap, 1999.

Breathless, directed by Jean-Luc Goddard, Les Filmes Imperiá, 1960.

Calvino, Italo., trans., William Weaver, *Invisible Cities.* Boston: Houghton Mifflin Harcourt, 1974.

Dante Aligheri, trans., Robin Kirkpatrick, *The Divine Comedy: Inferno, Purgatorio, Paradiso.* London: Penguin, 2012.

In Girum Immus Nocte et Sonsummimur Igni, directed by Guy Debord, independent, 1978.

Di Lampedusa, Giuseppe Tomasi., trans., Archibald Colquhoun. New York, NY: Vintage, 2007.

Fukuyama, Francis. *The End of History and the Last Man.* New York, NY: Free Press, 1992.

Kafka, Franz., trans., Willa and Edwin Murir and Michael Hoffman. New York: Schoeken Books, 2015.

Kierkegaard, Søren, trans., H. V. Hong, *Works of Love.* Princeton, NJ: Princeton University Press, 1995.

Kojève, Alexandre. *Introduction á la Lecture de Hegel.* Paris: Gallimard, 1947.

———.*Introduction to the Reading of Hegel: Lectures on the* Phenomenology of Spirit, Assembled by Raymond Queneau, Ed., Allan Bloom, Trans., James H. Nichols Jr. Ithaca: Cornell University Press, 1980.

———. "Interpretation of the General Introduction to Chapter VII [The Religion Chapter of Hegel's *Phenomenologyof Spirit*], trans., Ian Alexander Moore in *Parrhesia: A Journal of Critical Philosophy,* 20 (2014), 15–39.

Rose, Gillian. *Paradiso.* Bristol: Menard Press, 1999.

Thomas Aquinas, *The Summa Theologica of St. Thomas Aquinas,* 2nd rev. ed., trans. Fathers of the English Dominican Province (1920). Online edition, 2008: http://www.newadvent.org/summa.

Weil, Simone, trans., Emma Crawford, *Gravity and Grace.* London: Routledge, 2002.

Contributors

THE REVD DR MICHAEL F. BIRD is Academic Dean, Postgraduate Coordinator, and Lecturer in Theology at Ridley College, Melbourne (Australian College of Theology)

THE REVD PROFESSOR BRENDAN BYRNE SJ is Professor of New Testament at Jesuit College of Spirituality

DR PETER CAMPBELL is the Registrar, Trinity College Theological School, University of Divinity, and Honorary Research Fellow, Melbourne Conservatorium of Music, University of Melbourne.

THE REVD DR CHRISTY CAPPER is Deputy Warden and Lecturer in Systematic Theology at Wollaston Theological College, University of Divinity.

THE REVD DR JOHN MARK CAPPER is Assistant Academic Dean and Senior Lecturer in Theology with the Australian College of Ministries.

PROFESSOR MARY L COLOE is Professor of New Testament Yarra Theological Union, University of Divinity

THE REVD CANON DR ROBERT ("BOB") DERRENBACKER JR is Dean of the Theological School at Trinity College, University of Divinity, where he also serves as the Frank Woods Associate Professor in New Testament.

DR KATHERINE FIRTH is the Head of Lisa Bellear House, the University of Melbourne, Lecturer in Research Education and Development at La Trobe University and a professional librettist and translator.

Assoc Prof Rachelle Gilmour is the Bromby Senior Lecturer in Old Testament at Trinity College Theological School, University of Divinity

The Revd Dr Fergus J. King is the Farnham Maynard Lecturer in Ministry Education, Director of the Ministry Education Centre at Trinity College Theological School, University of Divinity, and Professor of New Testament Mission (Sociocultural Interpretation) at the Missional University.

The Revd Dr Scott A. Kirkland is the John and Jeanne Stockdale Lecturer in Practical Theology and Ethics at Trinity College Theological School University of Divinity.

The Revd Professor Mark R. Lindsay FRHistS is the Joan E.W. Munro Professor of Historical Theology at Trinity College Theological School, University of Divinity.

The Very Revd Dr Andreas Loewe FRHistS is Dean of St Paul's Anglican Cathedral Melbourne, a Fellow and Lecturer in Music History at the Melbourne Conservatorium of Music, Faculty of Fine Arts, the University of Melbourne, and an Adjunct Member of Faculty of Trinity College Theological School, University of Divinity

The Revd Professor Francis J. Moloney SDB, AM, FAHA is a Senior Professorial Fellow at Catholic Theological College, University of Divinity

The Revd Professor Emeritus Christiaan Mostert is Emeritus Professor of the University of Divinity

The Revd Dr Colleen O'Reilly AM recently retired as the Chaplain to Trinity College, Melbourne

The Right Reverend Professor Stephen Pickard was assistant bishop in the Anglican Diocese of Canberra and Goulburn and recently retired as Executive Director of the Australian Centre for Christianity and Culture, Canberra.

The Revd Dr Christopher A. Porter is Postdoctoral Research Fellow at Trinity College Theological School, University of Divinity

DR MURIEL PORTER OAM is a Melbourne journalist, author and historian, an Honorary Research Fellow of the University of Divinity, and an adjunct member of faculty, Trinity College Theological School

THE RIGHT REVEREND RICHARD TRELOAR is Bishop of the Anglican Diocese of Gippsland, and honorary associate of the University of Divinity.

THE REVD ASSOCIATE PROFESSOR ROBYN WHITAKER is Coordinator of Studies—New Testament at Pilgrim Theological College at Pilgrim Theological College, University of Divinity.

THE REVD ASSOCIATE PROFESSOR SEAN WINTER is the Head of Pilgrim College, and Associate Professor at Pilgrim Theological College, University of Divinity.

9 781666 799804